The Carrying Capacity of a Nation

The Carrying Capacity of a Nation

Growth and the Quality of Life

Peter W. House
University of California

Edward R. Williams
Department of Commerce

Lexington Books
D.C. Heath and Company
Lexington, Massachusetts
Toronto London

Library of Congress Cataloging in Publication Data

House, Peter William, 1937-
The carrying capacity of a nation.

Bibliography: p.
Includes index.
1. Economic forecasting—United States—Mathematical models.
2. United States—Economic conditions—1971—Mathematical models. I. Williams, Edward R., 1935- joint author. II. Title.
HC106.7.H68 330.9'73 75-16623
ISBN 0-669-00056-6

Published simultaneously in Canada

Printed in the United States of America

International Standard Book Number: 0-669-00056-6

Library of Congress Catalog Card Number: 75-16623

Contents

	List of Figures	ix
	List of Tables	xi
	Preface	xiii
Chapter 1	**Introduction**	1
	Problem Background	1
	The Real World Dictates	2
	Models of Reality	3
	Forecasting Techniques	5
	Problems with Predicting Everything	6
	Assumptions and Forecasts	7
	Summary	18
Chapter 2	**Scenario Analysis**	21
	A Model for National Carrying Capacity	22
	Alternative Futures of the Nation: Circa 2000	28
	Using Models	35
Chapter 3	**Carrying Capacity: A Perspective for Environmental Management**	41
	Carrying Capacity: Interaction of Natural and Human Environment	41
	Ecological Systems and Carrying Capacity	45
	The Links between the Human System and the Ecosystem	53
Chapter 4	**Resources of the Human Ecosystem**	57
	Resource Definitions	58
	Grouping Resources for the Model	59
	Resource Functions	67
Chapter 5	**Model Overview**	69
	Purpose and Applications	69
	Structure	70

	Assumptions and Simplifications	71
	Alternate Systemic Descriptions and Adjustment Loops	74
	Summary	78
Chapter 6	**Model Formulation**	81
	General	81
	Cycle Calculations and Adjustments	81
	System Inputs	84
	System Outputs	90
	System Adjustments	91
Chapter 7	**The Basic Model (SOS-2)**	103
	Model Characteristics	103
	Model Structure	105
	The Descriptive Module of a Cycle	106
	The Systemic Module of a Cycle	126
	Cycle Bookkeeping	144
Chapter 8	**Data Requirements**	149
	Population Totals Data	149
	Age-Year Data	150
	Population Partitions	150
	Resource Status	152
	Component Production Data	158
	Resource Utilization Data	160
	Demand Measures Data	161
Chapter 9	**Model Output**	167
	Input Data Verification	167
	Annual System Status	167
	Yearly Output	167
	Total System Expenditure	170
	Summary Scenario Data	170
	Other Scenario Input Options	171
Appendix A	**Source FORTRAN Listings for SOS-2 Including Example Case Data**	173
Appendix B	**Base Case Scenario**	231

Appendix C **Program Flowcharts** 343

Notes 353

Bibliography 355

About the Authors 357

List of Figures

1-1	Basic Carrying Capacity Procedures	8
1-2	Historical Growth Rates	9
1-3	Technological Fix	11
1-4	Population Control	12
1-5	ZPG and Technology Fix	14
1-6	Cultural Adaptation	16
1-7	Anomic Society	18
2-1	Conceptual Form of the Model	28
2-2	State of the System—Base Case	30
2-3	State of the System—ZPG	32
2-4	State of the System—ZEG	34
2-5	State of the System—ZPG and ZEG	36
2-6	State of the System—Stabilized Employment	37
3-1	Population Growth	46
3-2	A Carrying Capacity Model	55
3-3	Flow Diagram of Carrying Capacity in Operation	56
5-1	Conceptual Form of the State of the System Model	72
5-2	Model Procedural Flow	75
6-1	Elements of the Model	82
6-2	One Cycle of the Model	83
6-3	System Adjustment Procedure	100
6-4	Resource Base Adjustment Process	101
7-1	Example Model System Flow Chart	106
7-2	Step 1 Flowchart	108
7-3	Step 2 General Flowchart	113
7-4	Step 3 Flowchart	122
7-5	Time Change Interpolation Function	127
7-6	Step 4 Flowchart	128
7-7	Step 5 General Flowchart	132

7-8	Step 6 General Flowchart	137
7-9	Step 7 General flowchart	142
7-10	Step 8 General Flowchart	145
C-1	Flowchart for the SOS-2 Executive Program, Main	343
C-2	Flowchart for Step 1: Describe the Population	344
C-3	Flowchart for Step 2: Describe the Production Components	345
C-4	Flowchart for Step 3: Describe the State of the System	346
C-5	Flowchart for Step 4: Adjust Resource Reserves and Utilization Factors	347
C-6	Flowchart for Step 5: Perform Short Term Output Adjustments	348
C-7	Flowchart for Step 6: Perform Long Term Component Output Adjustments	349
C-8	Flowchart for Step 7: Adjust Long Term Population Demands	350
C-9	Flowchart for Step 8: Reset Data Base for Next Cycle	351

List of Tables

7-1	Step 1 Parameters	109
7-2	Step 2 Parameters	114
7-3	Step 3 Parameters	123
7-4	Step 4 Parameters	129
7-5	Step 5 Parameters	133
7-6	Step 6 Parameters	138
7-7	Step 7 Parameters	143
8-1	Population Totals Data	150
8-2	Age-Year Population Data	151
8-3	Example Age-Year Data	151
8-4	Partition Coefficient Data	152
8-5	Example Partition Coefficients	153
8-6	Resource Status Data	154
8-7	Example Resource Parameters	155
8-8	Resource Usage Adjustment Data	157
8-9	Example Resource Depletion Warnings	157
8-10	Example Substitution Formulas	158
8-11	Component Funds Data	159
8-12	Example Component Funds Data	160
8-13	Example Durable Goods Expenditure Data	160
8-14	Resource Utilization Data	161
8-15	Production Formulas	162
8-16	Demand Measure Data	163
8-17	Demand Functions	164

Preface

In an earlier draft of this effort an attempt was made to document a methodology which would wed the ecological precepts of carrying capacity to present policy interests as part of the research work on limits both to our national growth and to the existence of man's life on the planet Earth. Unfortunately, many of the past efforts on limits analysis have turned out to be a mixture of pet theories, poorly tied partial conceptualizations and overly gross approximations of the total system.

Incremental additions to our scientific knowledge are laudatory and fit well with a general agreement as to how research should proceed. On the other hand, if it is suddenly perceived that there is a policy need for specific information, the mere desire for knowledge does not make its appearance occur. The recent recognition on the part of many policy makers that our system may have limits that should be addressed when considering future options has brought forth numerous studies and methodologies which purport to be able to handle such broad based issues. Many of these "global" methodologies seem to lead to results that portend doom for our society. The forms of doom are legion—including that we shall either suffer the fate of a wastrel of one or more of our resources or we shall perish in our own waste.

Scare analyses such as these belie historical experience. Societies have run out of resources before (wood in western Europe at the end of the nineteenth century, for example) and have polluted their rivers, oceans, and air to noxious, or even toxic, levels. In each case they adjusted or overcame the problem. Consequently, any long term analysis that purports to represent the actual workings of our world should at least allow for a way out.

The analysis and the methodology which follows does just that. There was a conscious effort not to swing to a Pollyanna-like attitude to compensate for the dismal school prognostications but merely to allow man to respond to crisis as any other species does. There is, among living things, a heavy bias towards survival, even if survival means a lower quality of life. On the other hand, if a sufficient number of the possible adjustments to the system to not come about in time, the possibility of collapse exists. The issue then shifts from one of survival versus extinction to one of adjustment—while leaving the possibility of too-little-too-late.

The actual system chosen for analysis was the United States from the years 1970 to 2000. Although it is difficult to argue that the resulting reference case is a "prediction" in the sense of a prognosis, its result is reasonable, and our checks against the growth in economic activity and population appear quite good. Rather than claim perfection, however let us be satisfied with a reasonableness test and proceed to apply the system. In fact, we do this in two fashions. First, we take a couple of goal statements that have been put forth both by the research community, the press, or the policy makers. These goals are attempted to be reached using the methods of this book and note will be made of the "critical choices" necessary for their attainment. Second, using this model, a test is made of a half-dozen of the conceptual theories of human growth and development. By exercising only certain portions of the model based on the conceptual theories it was possible to demonstrate that the end result of each of these were prejudiced by the analyst's predilections.

Although the studies carried out in this report are all at the national level, the model was designed to be used also at any regional level where it is possible to define closure. It is hoped that the model will be used to test comprehensive plans to see whether it will be possible for local governments actually to achieve stated goals.

The following model represents years of work. Earlier efforts go back as much as a decade and owe their nurturing to Allen Feldt and Dan Sisler at Cornell University. The present form derives from a response to an order by the Assistant Administrator for Research and Development of the Environmental Protection Agency (EPA), Stanley Greenfield, for development of a forecasting model to be used to analyze the environmental problems with which we all were concerned. For many reasons, we chose not to evolve the present theory of this book further to the detail that would be required for Agency policy analyses. It was developed concurrently with a model called SEAS, the Strategic Environmental Assessment System, a more standard input-output approach which has gone into widespread policy use by EPA and other government units. However, several of our colleagues who read the earlier version of this model encouraged us to go on to its present form. Russ Peterson, Chairman of the Council of Environmental Quality (who helped pick the "goal statements" listed in chapter 2), and Sandy Archibald of the Commission on Critical Choices are two of these.

It should be noted that the responsibility for this model lays with us. Although the model was developed by us as EPA employees, this book was written by the two of us in our private capacity. No official support or endorsement by the Environmental Protection Agency or any other agency of the Federal Government is intended or should be inferred. The final writing of the manuscript was completed when each of us was no longer present at the EPA; Ted Williams now works at the Department of Commerce, and Peter House is on temporary assignment in Berkeley, California at the Institute for Transportation Studies (ITS). In this latter instance we would like to thank Professor William Garrison and his ITS staff for the time and assistance to finish the manuscript.

The model in the background of this analysis, State Of the System, is a relatively new modeling form, a hybrid of several model forms available in the life and social science literature. Models such as these will have to continue to be developed and be used by various professions. This early exposure and subsequent multiple use will begin to allow us to improve our planning process in estimating our future states of being.

The Carrying Capacity of a Nation

1 Introduction

Problem Background

The "generation gap," so evident in the sixties as the youth culture gained recognition, grew to such proportions that many elders shifted from tolerance to counterrebellion. Without arguing the pervasiveness of the youth subculture, it is useful to recognize the underpinnings of the phenomena. The counterculture was apparently the inverse of an existing culture and, at least in its early days, rejected much of the contemporary American ethos as illegitimate and useless. This extreme posture attracted sufficient public attention so that issues were examined across the resulting polarity. Those portions of both extreme positions which appear most useful to society are slowly being melded into a new ethos.

Similar turnabouts can be found throughout sociological literature as research, action, and reaction flow from one period to the next. One example is of particular interest for this work. For years, both public and private planners have practiced their art assuming a fruitful earth. Problems were usually couched in terms of improving societal efficiency. For example, a comprehensive or master plan was normally prepared for a community to answer questions concerning its ultimate size and the most efficient way to distribute spatially the people and their activities. A few of the better plans have included social amenities or other qualitative goals. Few of the plans questioned the probability of achieving the goals that were established in these plans.

On the other hand, an increasing reaction against the "growth at any cost" school has come from a number of environmentalists and others. Some have even seriously suggested that all growth be stopped immediately in some regions of the nation. These conflicting perspectives, like those in the youth versus establishment conflict, cannot result in viable goal statements without compromise of the polar positions. The purpose of this book is to describe a model that will analyze the possible ranges of social and economic growth under conditions of limited available resources and minimal environmental damage. Thus our model parallels the procedure of compromise and melding noted above.

With the objective above in mind, let us reflect on the goals of local and regional communities, which are to provide the better things of life for their citizens. In the past few decades, the unfettered development of our cities and suburbs, responding primarily to economic stimuli, has not achieved its purpose of maximum benefit to the majority of the society. Recognition of this failure became institutionalized with the widespread appearance of the planning profession. The nation soon saw the appearance of the "master" plan and more recently, the comprehensive plan. The latter plan was envisioned as the guide to how a community could (and should) structure its total growth including population, labor, urban form, transportation, tax laws, and easement and land rights.

At present, many planning efforts to control the development of an urban area are based on the thesis that growth and the preservation of the environment must be complementary, not conflicting, goals. This perspective on environmental quality challenges the unlimited growth assumptions of the early planners, invalidating a great number of the early plans. This occurs because these early plans were seldom subjected to any credibility test other than to see if the current political community and the citizenry wanted to aim at the plan's goal. Also, the reality of the plans was seldom tested in terms of the communities' actual ability to achieve the prescribed goals within the expected time frames. This lack of testing is not surprising, since the planners and their communities both subscribed to the beliefs that this was the nation of inexhaustible resources and that technological ingenuity could solve any problem. Today, many are beginning to question the possiblity of unlimited growth. Thus the comprehensive plans of localities need to be tested for realism under situations of limited resources and established environmental quality requirements.

The Real World Dictates

Adjusted for the mandates of the pragmatic world, the wedding of diverse goals—say, growth and environmental preservation—will only be accomplished through intensive environmental management. Unfortunately, having named the required cure, we are not further along in development of a procedure to implement it.

First steps toward environment management are along the worn path of the attempt to reduce all of the alternatives to a least common denominator so that they can be objectively traded off against each other. Some cost benefit analyses of this variety have been attempted. On the assumption that no benefit can be gained without a corresponding cost, such a methodology attempts to correlate the costs and benefits. Unfortunately, the environment is nothing if it is not comprehensive; it is related to everyone and every action and they are related to it. The environmental relationships are difficult to define in general and almost impossible to define in detail. The delineation of environment-societal relationships is often subjective, and the perception of the linkages are correspondingly vague. Hence, this approach has met with limited success.

This book will deal with a second approach. The ecologist's rhetoric speaks of a "holistic" representation of the man-environment relationships. This analysis approach attempts to reduce the set of possible components to a dominant group which can be handled conceptually from the vantage point of the whole system. According to its proponents, this perspective best assures that all of the various subsectors of the system will be taken into account and that the chance for occurrence of totally unexpected events will be mitigated. Additionally, the holistic school argues that the overview has to be continued over a period of time, since present-day actions not only affect all portions of the system, but continue to do so for long periods of time, with decisive effects often occurring after significant delay.

In short, a planning system sèt up to develop holistic guidance would display to the decision maker the widest set of options possible for his decisions. Its dangers include the fact that the system would also offer him the greatest potential for confusion due to information overload.

Operationally, such holistic planning systems must require a change from the planning assumptions of the past. The extrapolation or trend continuance paradigm must be altered. Planning cannot assume that the future is merely more of the past and that the public role is to provide those goods and services necessary to assure a foundation for the laissez faire growth of the private sector. Peterson[1] suggests that there is a rapidly developing counter view that:

Today's problems are a result of successes as they were defined in yesterday's terms,

An extension of the past is not generally the right prescription for the future,

The primary planning goals for this nation should be altered to high quality life styles as the major long term objective with economic development shaped to complement this overriding determinant,

Science and technology, if oriented toward harmony with nature, can, within limits, assist in reaching the highest attainable quality goals, and

Through social and political action it is possible to design, modify, or block growth and development trends based on their compatibility with long-range planning goals that are supported by a popular consensus.

Models of Reality

There are several ways of helping today's manager as he begins to make decisions in this new milieu. One of these methods is application of modelling. The model described in this report is in an early stage of development; it needs significantly more design before it can be used for policy use. This model likely never would have had an audience in the public sector if it had not been for the current interest in many regions of the United States in preserving and restoring an aesthetically healthy and pleasing environment coupled with growing uneasiness about the acceptability of unlimited growth assumptions.

A brief statement should be made concerning the utility of mathematical computer based models. To begin, it is useful to remember that all decisions are based on models of one sort or another. Almost no problem is simple enough to be defined in absolute terms; for decision purposes, it must be abstracted to the level of its most dominant components. A mathematical model merely makes this process explicit. Further, these explicit statements of assumptions within the model, coupled with the inherent nature of the computer, allows us to try to capture a far larger set of variables than is usually attempted in day-to-day intuitive decision making. Of course, the validity and utility of any model is a function of the accuracy with which the model designers reduce the problem area to pertinent model variables and relationships; however, the same characteristic is true of all problem solving techniques.

The eventual users of the model described here will be well advised to take these caveats into consideration. The developers of this model can not state with absolute certainty the confidence factor to be attached to the output of such models. However, like most policy information, the direction of the predicted effect and the order of magnitude of the change appear correct. Thus, this model, the State of the System model, should afford new insight into real world situations.

The needs or desires for a model that focuses on carrying capacity is referred to favorably in a recent report of the Public Works Committee of the U.S. House of Representatives.[2]

Carrying capacity is a basic concept well suited for a national growth policy.

A national policy for growth and development that would provide guidance for activites at the regional and community levels needs to be couched in terms that relate directly to problems experienced at those levels. With overtones of keeping within limits, stability, and balance, "Carrying Capacity" echoes the concerns of growing number of citizens and public officials as they contemplate the future population and economic growth with which their communities, state, and country will have to contend.

Although the term has inherent ambiguities, they can serve a constructive purpose within the context of public policy. By requiring specificity in its application, "Carrying Capacity" forces attention to be focused on existing social values and priorities. Noncommensurate benefits and costs are necessarily involved in determining the threshold at which further growth and development would destroy community values or damage its environment to an unacceptable degree. While debate among partisan groups about the merits of various tradeoffs involved in a community's further growth does not assure agreement, it is prerequisite for consensus.

A national growth policy focusing on the concept of carrying capacity would increase empirical information about the "limits to growth" for cities, regions, states, and the country.

If staying within carrying capacity were made a condition of future public programs to promote growth, it would stimulate applied research to determine just where those limits were for each community. As present ignorance about the real consequences of future development is reduced, so too will be the risk of public works triggering unforeseen, damaging results.

Before we begin to discuss the use of a system such as this model to compare alternative scenarios of our national goal statements, it is necessary for us to set the stage for the use of such a system for forecasting. This will be the purpose of the next section. During this analysis we shall present a brief overview of the model.

Forecasting Techniques

Our ability to "foresee" is still not improved a great deal from the days when our ancestors turned to soothsayers and wizards for a similar service. Our primitive forecastors had little known formal techniques and knowledge to rely upon and so, had to turn to magic and visions to ply their trade. There are numerous differences, as well as similarities, between the spells and incantations of the days of yore and the methodologies put forth to carry out a similar art today.

Recently, a study for the Environmental Protection Agency listed a number of the current techniques used over the past decade or so by various groups or scientists engaged in a series of studies, all included under the rubric "futureology." There were at least two earlier studies on technology forecasting readily available to us. The first is the well known text by Joseph Martino entitled, "Technological Forecasting for Decision Making;"[3] and the second, a comprehensive study done by the International Research and Technology Corporation on the same subject.[4] Since both of these studies as well as others, covered the topic of what kinds of processes were used, ranging from the Delphi technique through formal modeling, the EPA study was to review the techniques as well as to review how they were actually applied in the field.

It is not the intent of this book to analyze any of the techniques noted above. On the other hand, the EPA study serves to show that the method of forecasting by mathematical models discussed in this book is not unique and that the obvious weaknesses associated with the technique are being, or have been, investigated and mitigated more or less systematically by others. It is likely as the forecasting techniques evolve and are increasingly used on real world problems that they will actually be developed to use less formal partitions than would be assumed by the above descriptions. Consequently, the resulting applied methods for specific problems would be combinations of the "pure" methodologies. One of these methodologies that is often chosen to be a part of these technique combinations is computer based mathematical modeling.

It is the purpose of this book to look, in some depth, at the potential for modeling routes from the present into the future. We shall not be concerned with all of the various modeling tricks and techniques practiced today (although reference to a sampling of these will inevitably come up on the course of the discussion) but will be concerned with what we can learn about the future by using such models. Further, because such a topic could lead us off in numerous different directions, we shall deliberately confine our discussion to an analysis that is "global" in scope. We use this term not to suggest that the subject matter will be another addition to the ever growing literature of world models [5] (although the discussion will be applicable to this group as well), but more to suggest the completeness of the range of topics addressed by the procedure. Such global models might include regional variables like population, raw materials, pollution loads, the quality of life, the private and public sectors of the economy, and so forth. It is the attempt to deal with this wide scope that presents us with our first set of problems.

Problems with Predicting Everything

The age-old description, "jack of all trades, master of none," is often ascribed to models which attempt to be comprehensive versus those which are more specialized in scope. This statement is hypothesized from the assumption that because time, funds, and knowledge are always more or less constrained in any endeavor, it seems logical to assume that more information about fewer things will give greater forecasting accuracy. Personally, we are not convinced that this seemingly reasonable hypothesis has much validity in the present state of the art due to inadequacies in our knowledge base at all grains—coarse and fine. However, to placate those who would raise a fuss in this regard, let us seek refuge in the assertion that accuracy is likely to be improved by adding both depth and scope to all analysis techniques as our science allows us. Our specific contribution to the day when all information required will be available will lie in the area of improving the algorithms to handle the scope of available data. What is lacking in terms of definitive hard information will be assumed to be compensated for in part by the way in which we construct and apply our forecasts. The lack of science is therefore to be overcome, not by illusion as practiced in the past, but by techniques somewhat akin to art: innovative application techniques. It is these application methods to which we shall now turn.

Assumptions and Forecasts

Long familiarity (or common sense) leads one to the eventual realization that the results of many modeling forecasts were built in to the structure by the designer of the model. To demonstrate this we shall in this chapter take the same model with the same basic data set[a] and progressively move it through six stages, ranging from a pessimistic outcome, to one with disaster mitigated first by technology and then by adding on varying population growth measures, and finally, to a forecast that utilizes a constantly changing cultural base to forestall cataclysm. In the end we will attempt to synthesize these assumptions into a technique that will be of use to present day decision makers.

The Doomsday Paradigm

Mathematically, it is trivial to note that the iteration of two interrelated variables through time, the larger constant and the smaller growing at a nondecreasing rate, regardless how slow that growth is, will eventually result in the reversal of the size of the variables. It does little to this basic postulate either to vary the rates at which the variables grow, or to add more variables. Eventually, the most rapidly growing variable will become dominant. In physical terms, this suggests that Nature, which abhors a vacuum, is also intolerant of rigid stability.

This logic is the basis of forecasts from Malthus[6] to many made today which predict an exhaustion of one or more of our resources. Although there are various ways such a model could be constructed, we can hypothesize that one might take the following form (Figure 1-1).

Let us assume that we have an initial population of 200 million people begin born at the rate of 0.0182 per capita and dying at a rate of 0.0094. Taking migration also into account, the natural rate of increase is 2.2 million people per year. For purposes of this scenario, the populace is divided into several age categories (each with its own birth, death, and

[a] The model actually used is a version of SOS that is slightly different from the one documented later in this book; for example, the resource set allows for a more discrete look at certain natural resources.

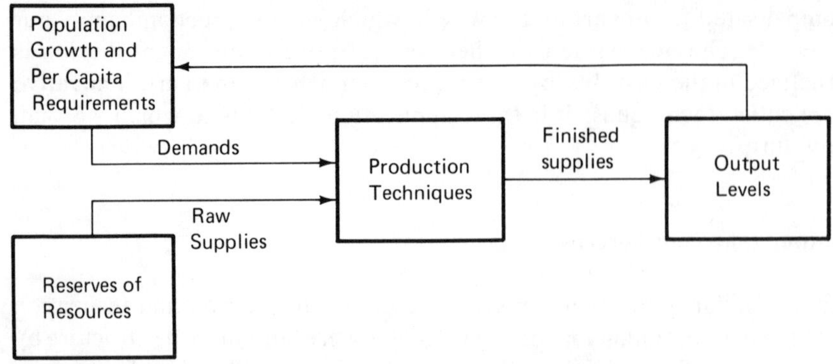

Figure 1-1. Basic Carrying Capacity Procedures.

migration rates) and also partitioned by its needs and resource contributions. For example, in the first year of our forecast, 59 million people require education, 20 million are on welfare, 80 million are available for the labor force, and so forth.

There are a total of about twenty raw materials included in our model. Among these are iron, water, lumber, chemicals, services, labor, the externalities of pollution, and so forth. These items are segregated on the basis of being either replenished each year (the number of workers or food stocks, for examples) or exhaustible (coal or oil). The latter category has the possibility of being expanded through more expensive extraction methods, but there is assumed to be some finite limit to the resource reserves.

The productive methodologies are represented by some twelve production functions—or components—which take the expressed needs of the populace and provide goods for their demands by seven private components, including heavy and light industry, commercial, agricultural, and residential; and five public components, including transportation, education, welfare, health, and safety. These outputs are assumed to be similar to those of the past. It is the rate of provision of these goods and services that will determine when our demand satisfaction procedures will be adequate; if we assume that each year we shall want more and more of everything, the crash will be sooner—but in any case, the rate chosen will not greatly influence the outcome since resources will be used at ever increasing rates.

Analysis of Run 1: Historical Growth Rates. For illustrative purposes, we have taken the historical growth rates of funds availability and have projected the rate of growth on a basis constant for this and every run.

Figure 1-2 provides the forty-year summary graph of this first case,

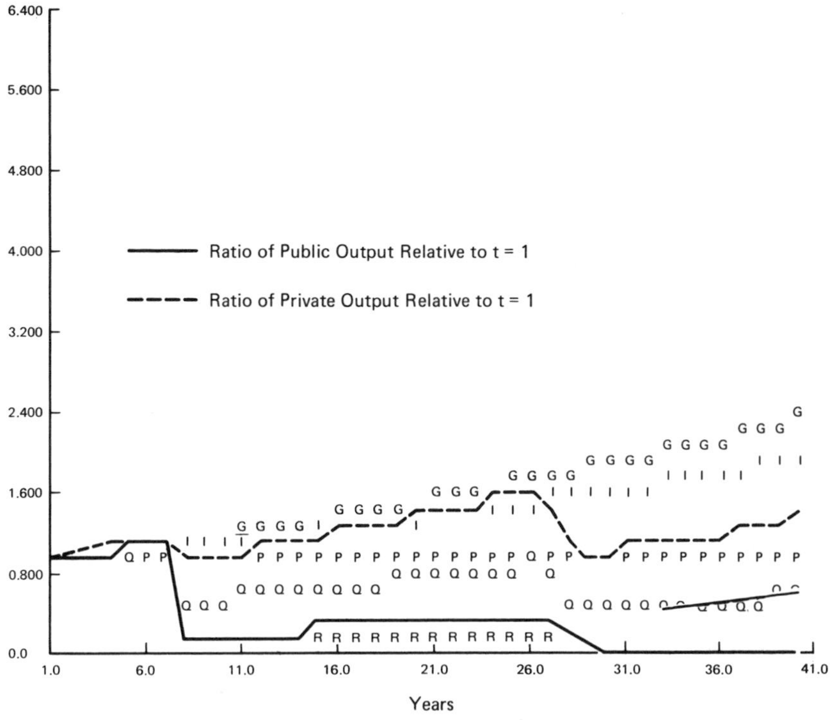

Figure 1-2. Historical Growth Rates.

supplying a set of statistics as ratios to the initial year values. The statistics used here are:

G is public sector funds
+ is public sector output
I is private sector funds
* is private sector output
Q is the composite measure of demand satisfaction, made up by weighted averaging of 11 individual demand measures
P is population size
R is rate of resource usage

The results of this first run reflect straightforwardly the basic assumptions. The funding patterns have no mechanism to cause change and therefore they yield smooth graphs of growth until resource reserves are critical. The output of the private sectors (*) collapse because of exhaustion of a resource as predicted by the static resource assumptions, the raw material being mercury, in Year 7. Since four of the five sectors require this material for production, private output immediately collapses to about 20% of the original private output. In Year 27, oil is also depleted, causing all private sector outputs to become negligible.

The public sector requires mercury in only one of its five sector production functions, that being a relatively slow growing sector. Thus, the Year 7 mercury depletion causes only a 15-percent output collapse. The Year 27 oil depletion has a greater effect on the public output, depressing output 40% and affecting three output sectors.

The composite demand satisfaction measure after Year 7 recovers about 75% of its original value. Analysis of the more detailed measures affords the obvious insight that demands are not met in a balanced form, hence the true demand satisfaction is much lower.

Thus, we see that the rigid, nonadjusting assumptions produce an answer close to the static analysis. Early depletion of a necessary resource caused a general collapse of goods output and a lesser depression of service output. No method of adjustment was available to move from this early, inevitable fate.

The Technological Fix Scenario

We shall next discuss a scenario that has variously been suggested as one which would mitigate against the blind enigma of resource depletion. The logic behind this philosophy is that the usage of the resource base is not really static but through greater use of increasingly advanced technology and increased economic incentives, more resources can be found or exploited, plus substitutes can be developed for many resources where natural limits are noncontrovertable. Certainly, there is much to be said for such arguments, particularly in western society, where the example of the Industrial Revolution shows when mechanization apparently broke the man/land ratios that were originally determined on the basis of an agrarian society, where size is largely determined on the basis of the food supply.

To simulate the technological fix scenario we added the features of substitution of raw materials to the model and allowed the system also to substitute alternate component production functions that are more economically suitable under the given resource constraints. Again, it is the timing and choice of these substitutions and alternate production functions that largely determine when meeting the society demands will result in a societal crash rather than meeting the society goals. In this scenario, if we are willing to engage in great optimism or science fiction, there could be no foreseen limit of mankind's existence. Although a comforting thought, an ever-fructful technology is not apt to be the answer for all time. For our

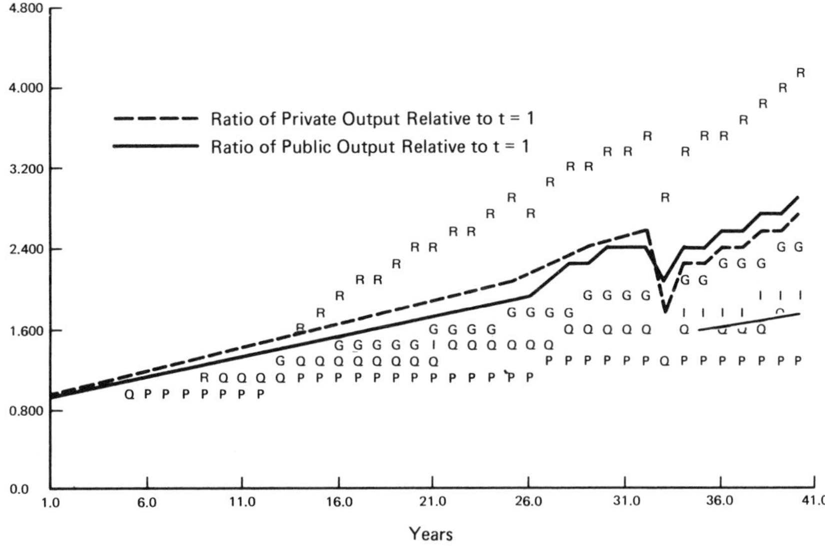

Figure 1-3. Technological Fix.

purposes, we have chosen a limited number of substitutions and production functions and only permitted inclusion of changes that are believed to be possible in the next decade or two. Admittedly, a conservative tack but one that is sufficient for illustrative purposes.

Analysis of Run 2: Technological Fixes. In contrast to the previous graph, the production system collapse does not appear and modest growth with some perturbations is produced throughout the forty-year period (see Figure 1-3). The model made some early adjustment to overcome the mercury and other scarce material depletions and maintains a smooth growth pattern until Year 31. The cost of these fixes is essentially in greater use of other resources and fuels as reflected in the rapid increase of resources usage statistics. The problem is not fully gone, however: in Year 33, a production dip occurs due to oil becoming scarce.

In comparison to the first graph, note that the demand satisfaction measure rises steadily until Year 30 and then its growth is somewhat moderated. Also, the population statistic shows steady increases, unlike that of the first run where outmigration matched the birth rate increases.

The pattern shown here is typical of technology-fix outputs of a finite fix set. The output can extend the period of growth; the sawtooth drops in levels will occur to flag a need for a fix; many fixes may be possible, but finally the set of adjustments that are viable are exhausted and the output drops to below original output levels.

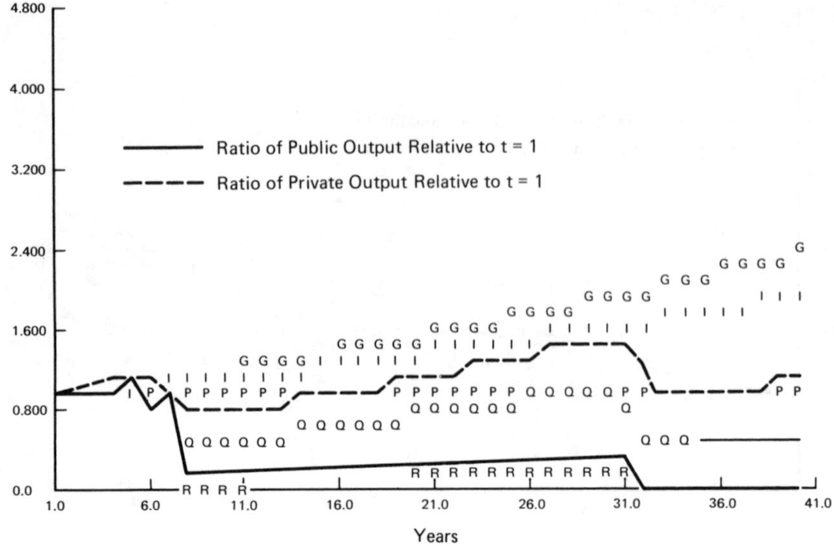

Figure 1-4. Population Control.

Population Control Policy

Population policy has been historically Nature's own means of adjustment to limited resources. When a species outstrips its resource base, the anticipated reaction is for the numbers to decrease, through decreased births, exmigration, and ultimately increased deaths. Many man-created programs have encouraged the former two policies with the hope that a reduction in the number of people would allow the society to begin to establish sufficient needs surpluses to "take off" into greater industrialization. This stratagem is therefore an extension of the previous one—increasing the resource base through technology.

On the other hand, there is much to be said for keeping a population that is in equilibrium with its environment through mechanisms such as zero population growth. By definition, an equilibrium position is the maximum size for survival of a populace in a particular locale, given certain living standards. Regardless of the rationale, for demonstration purposes we shall illustrate the impact of our limited growth scenario by adjusting the population to fit within the bounds determined by the resource base.

Analysis of Run 3: Population Control. Figure 1-4 utilizes the same data base as the first graph except the native birth rate is set equal to the death rate and immigration is set to zero. The results—much the same as for the first case.

On reflection this is not surprising since a ZPG adjustment system, which may have utility in long term adjustments, is not a useful short term measure by itself—and this effect is graphically illustrated here; the collapse due to mercury depletion still occurs in Year 7; the impact still reduces the goods production to unacceptable levels. The slowed population growth policy does have some effect after a generation; the secondary collapse in the public sector now occurs in Year 32 rather than Year 27. Thus, although the same patterns must finally occur where the only system adjustment is population demand levels, we do see a longer performance time if the major collapse of Run 1 is a generation or more away.

This effect can now be combined with the effect given in the technology-fix scenario, where the first major perturbation occured with a production drop at Year 30.

Combining Population Policy and Technology

This fourth situation is reminiscent of that found in several present day Western societies, including the United States. We have a combination of a declining or stable population and a technology that has changed the natural resource usage of the society, allowing a significantly greater man/land ratio than that of a simple agrarian society.

As with the technological-fix scenario above, the assumptions made will truly determine the societal future. With a stable population (able and willing to adjust demands downward to maintain a constant standard of living) and a set of very liberal assumptions concerning technological discovery and substitution, such a society could have a very long run. Again, we shall assume a more conservative technological future for our analysis purposes.

Analysis of Run 4: ZPG and Technology Fixes. This fourth case, combining the adjustments of technology (Run 2) and reduced population growth (Run 3) does in fact moderate the effect noted in the later years of the run. The problem still exists: note that the output trends of both the public and private sector outputs are slowing as well as becoming more ragged. However, the single-year drop of 30 percent is no longer produced (see Figure 1-5).

A penalty was paid for this smoothing, however, and was paid early. Note the output reduction that occurred in Year 5 for both public and private sectors. The lessening of immigration due to the ZPG assumptions reduced the labor force, causing a rise in salaries above the salaries in the pure technology-fix scenario. The drop and the output growth trends from Year 5 to Year 35 cause the level of outputs to be 10-15 percent below the pure technology-fix case (Run 2). Therefore, while smoother growth oc-

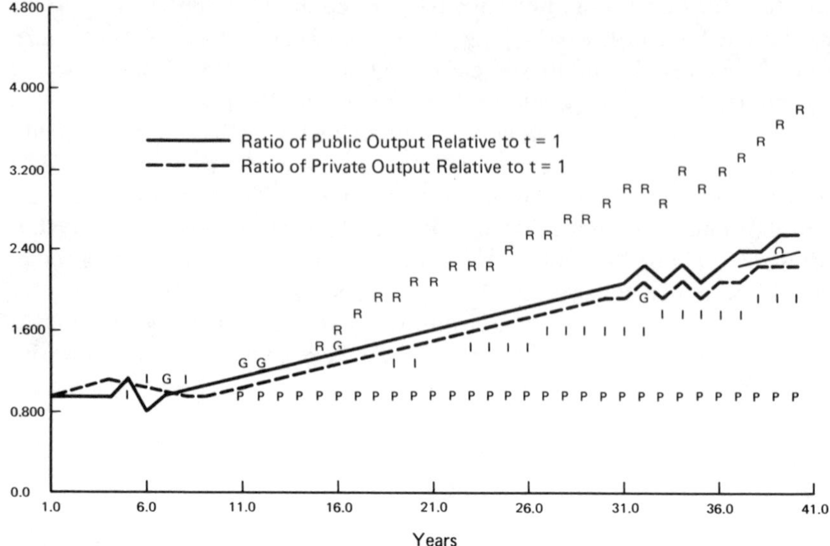

Figure 1-5. ZPG and Technology Fix.

curs, it occurs at a lower output level, and when the two rates are approximately the same, the ZPG case shows at least as much raggedness as the non-ZPG case.

Resource consumption in the later years is much the same; hence the merit of ZPG versus other adjustment techniques over this period of simulation suggests that population growth has an effect but certainly not a dominant effect on the system becoming more viable.

Cultural Expectations

It is the contention of this analysis that possibly the greatest weakness of most of the adjustments analyzed above is that they assume the maintenance of a constant standard of living. This assumption means that resources will be absorbed at specified rates and societal decline is synonymous with being unable to sustain such a standard.

Such an assumption is an oversimplification and cannot help but lead to conclusions that are erroneous. A more complete analysis would contend that a single person or groups of people are much more adaptable than the assumptions made above would suggest.

When things are going well and there appear to be surpluses, there is a tendency to increase the demands of the group, either across the board or selectively. Further, this increase in demands comes about in a ratchet-like manner, meaning that each new level of demand for satisfaction is associated with production having met the demands of an earlier level.

On the other hand, Aesop, in one of his many tales, relates the human characteristic of "sour grapes." This trait allows us to rationalize our required behavior to act as if the behavior were desired all along. For example, it suggests that if wood is scarce, cultural substitutes will not only be found (in the technological sense) but that the society will change in demand patterns so that the lack of wood will be overcome by preferring the use of other materials in building and the like.

This cultural feature can be surrogated by using a measure of demand satisfaction. Recent studies[7] have suggested that an overall measure is very difficult to quantify and there is still considerable disagreement as to how (or if) such a measure should be constructed. A recent study of the Standford Research Institute[8] defined the measure as a dissatisfaction statistic; i.e., as the relative distance the society is from a set of standards or thresholds it sets up for itself. To discover these thresholds, we can use the culture of the United States as defined by various laws and customs to quantify the measure and will allow for changes in these thresholds (both increasing and lessening) with the growth of the system and the associated levels of demand satisfaction through time. Unfortunately, it will likely be some time before the validity of these concepts will be proved, even conceptually. It will be even longer before adequate data will be available. For our purposes we shall use surrogates based on percapita expenditures.

With this point of view added to the last analyses related above, it is very difficult indeed to picture a society that can get into terminal decay; for whatever is not handled by population adjustment is overcome by technology. If the decay is not mitigated by either of these adjustments, then it is redefined by the culture so that the "crisis" disappears as long as subsistance living conditions are met.

Analysis of Run 5: Cultural Adaptation. As our fifth case then, a new set of adjustment procedures in addition to technology adjustments is allowed. These include funds transfers between production sectors plus changing of levels of output demands when the system demonstrates its inadequacy to meet the specific demand at the present expectation level.

Our graph (Figure 1-6) in this case shows similar patterns to the technology-fix case through Year 26—that set of adjustments were sufficient to provide all needed system adjustments. During the last fifteen years of the run, other, nontechnology adjustments were effected.

Due to the greater set of adjustments available, the system in Year 28, three years prior to the technology-only case, begins to show adjustments. A short term depressant on output is observed that puts into effect a shifting

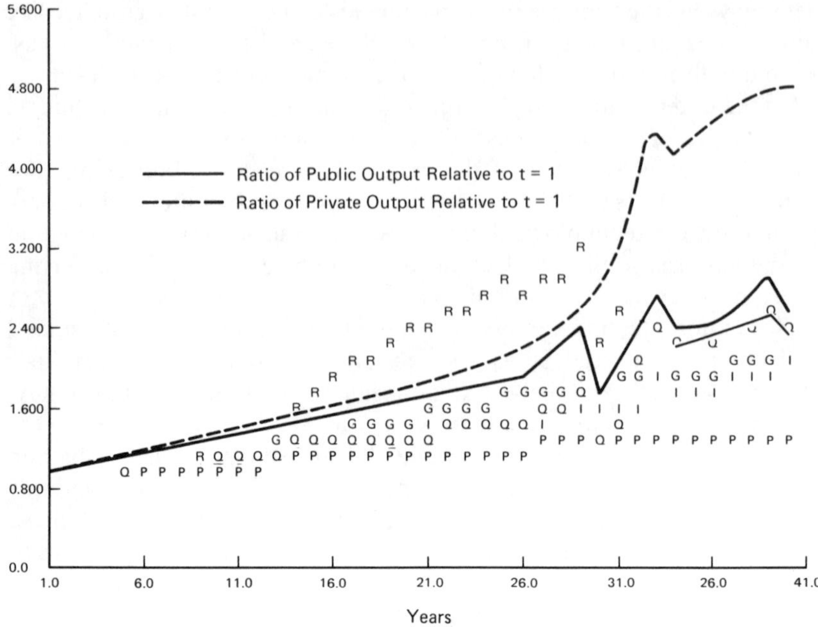

Figure 1-6. Cultural Adaptation.

of funds from public sector areas to private sector areas. At the same time changes are made in the production process for some public components allowing for an overall increase in public sector output at reduced funding levels.

The shifting of funds toward the private sector allowed a rapid recovery to the output growth trend accomplished prior to Year 26 and this trend is maintained.

The demand measure at the end of the simulation is running 50% higher for this case as compared to the technology-only case. All of the measure components are being met adequately and the cultural expectations are shifting to expect future growth to be more services oriented.

The penalty for having this new set of adjustment measures is increased raggedness in individual outputs. Since the system is shifting funds and modifying its cultural expectations, more short run perturbations are produced about the long term trend. The model algorithms now allow not only for adjustments but also for overcompensations.

Generally, however, these true world additions to the system offer greater hope for a successful long term healthy society, even with the small number of adjustments given in our simple model.

Whither Crisis?

Since we hold that the above scenario is conceptually the most reasonable picture of how the long run future of a society is determined, how then do we explain crisis and societal collapse in a technological society? It is clear that the logical flaw in the above lies in the implicit assumption that adjustments will take place smoothly. In the majority of cases such an assumption is justified in a long run model, as the dislocations caused by system adjustments are not likely to be important in the long run. On the other hand, it is these very adjustments that can be looked upon as crises. The shift of a culture from two houses to one, from large cars to small cars, from public entertainment to television, and so forth is not apt to come about overnight. Most of the adjustments required are benign and, given the fact that the society is reasonably healthy, not apt to be overly troublesome. Bottlenecks and short term distributional problems are therefore put forth as explanations for the possibility of crises, even in a highly flexible society.

Nevertheless, there is the possibility that these intermittent adjustment crises can be highly damaging and even fatal to a culture. A recent work suggested a possibility of cultural dullness on the part of a society that was experiencing repeated actions to adjust its cultural basis.[9] Continued perturbations in this manner might bring about a situation of anomie or normlessness with concomittant sluggishness in the adjustment mechanisms. Thus, the society may not be prepared to adjust when a true distributional crisis arises. Added to this could be a situation where a continuingly upward climbing ratchet in terms of major elements of the societal demands caused successive strains in the technological and substitutional ability of the system in too rapid a pattern for adjustment.

As with the previous scenarios, this situation is possible to simulate only in a pedagogical fashion because the variety of situations really attainable is very large. Consequently, in the scenario below we shall take the picture of the United States as presented in Run 5 and adjust it in such a fashion that its total resilience to required cultural change is low and cultural and technological adjustment ability to react is slow.

Analysis of Run 6: Anomic Society. This graph (Figure 1-7) depicts the effects of sluggishness, considered here as an unwillingness to lower specific and cultural learned needs.

Note that once again the run results through Year 26 are similar to the last graph and similar to the second, the technology-fix graph. Also as in the last graph, a set of fixes are put in motion that make required adjustments to provide additional funding and production adjustments to output sectors in trouble.

In Run 5, however, these adjustments included compensations by low-

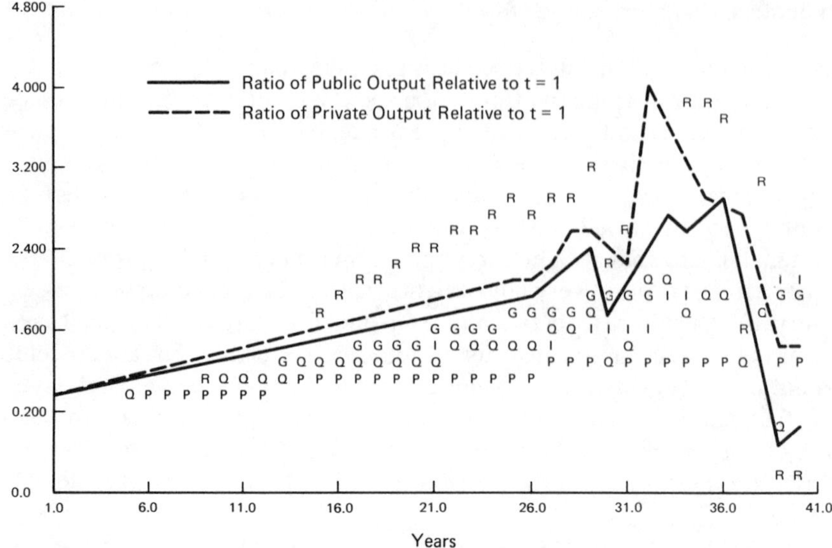

Figure 1-7. Anomic Society.

ering expectations in areas that are not as critical. For this case those expectations are not allowed to be lowered. The results of the "guns and butter" syndrome is a rapid depletion of the critical resources, causing all expectations to be met well for three years, then all expectations to be slightly missed for about six years and finally, a collapse of the outputs in the final two years of proportions similar to that which occurred in the first graph when no adjustments were allowed.

Summary

Thus, we complete our survey of six sets of assumptions by returning to a rigid resource use system due to an unwillingness of the demands of specific area to be reduced. This rigidity of demand for output returns us to a prediction of collapse—not at seven years as the static data suggests but rather after many adjustments to meet the continuing demands—to a system that has exhausted other resources and hence collapses at Year 39.

Thus, our series of six runs suggests that a long term solution requires not only technology and funds transfers but also a requirement to change cultural expectations not only in terms of moderating rising wants but also in terms of mitigating demands responsively when necessary to moderate critical resource usage.

The six scenarios presented here are variously familiar to the reader depending upon his personal predilections or technical interests and training. It was not our intention to present these as a mere intellectual exercise but to relate each as a predictive scenario based upon existing real world data. As presented, the scenarios differed only in terms of their assumptions; the set of outputs was produced by the use of a single model, progressively modified to take into consideration the various assumptions.

The finding we have demonstrated could be simplistically reduced to a statement asserting that care would have to be exercised in stating the assumptions behind a model's use—undeniably true but not worth the length of this exposition.

More useful is the lesson to be learned from the seeming pendulum swing of potential results obtainable from a set of assumptions based on a long run versus a short run purview. The earlier scenarios, although claiming to be long run in perspective, are logically faulty. One has only to study history and to observe the variety of cultural manifestations around the globe to be convinced of human adaptiveness. Equally decisive is the ability of man to change his technology (regardless of whether the rate of change will be slower or faster than it has been in the past). Possibly western society will move away from an almost totally materialistic society and, because it has the potential for satisfying some equitable set of basic wants for all inhabitants, become more interested in service or philosophical pursuits. Such a society would not require ever growing productivity rates as in the past to adjust to its trends. Herein lies one of the lessons. On the other hand, if this society is measured in terms of an idealized or present demand pattern, it might fall far short of its specified goals and would, in an empirical sense, be said to be headed for collapse. In truth, since it has changed its cultural norms it has ceased to exist in terms of its former measure; however, this cannot be termed a "collapse" except by those who would not want a change from some traditional growth or state. In short, this type of "collapse" is equated to societal change and as such is an example of intellectual panic or subjective bias.

Equally instructive, however, has been the discussion of the last scenario, which points out one of the pitfalls of long range forecasting. Although true that the rules followed by those who would construct such predicions are different in many ways from those interested in day-to-day analyses (or the futurist who is more interested in trends and cycles), it is possible to overlook potential short run adjustment situations that could have serious repercussions for the society. These are not overcome in the long run, but would normally be assumed away by the forecast assumptions. Consequently, the allegation that today's situation requires only that a long range viewpoint be added to standard policy analyses can be faulty. Some problems require not only long range and short range analyses, but also trend analysis so that the long range view be cognizant of short run phenomena—taking them into account selectively as they maintain an impact on the long term trend. There will be much resistance to such efforts, as data and theory are weak. It is much more comfortable to draw profound conclusions from elegant models and take refuge in statements which proffer that the only error likely from this simplifying practice will be of magnitude. As we have illustrated here, such errors can also be ones of direction. It is suggested here we should take the more accurate general long run model of the United States to be one of optimism and adaptability. However, because of the short run distributional or bottleneck-type dangers cited above, research will have to be carried out to discover ways to monitor these adjustments for unfavorable short and long run synergistic effects. The more sophisticated we become and the more we ask for our citizens, the more careful we shall have to be of our policy choices. Assuming that the recurring crises of the past three years or so have been real, such monitoring cannot begin too soon. As with all devices, structural problems in our society have a better chance of being corrected if they are diagnosed in time.

2 Scenario Analysis

Each biological, institutional, or physical entity or system appears to be subject to the idea of a limit. Examples abound so that the notion that one is able to put only a given amount of an item into a specific place or time period is so obvious as to appear trivial. Nonetheless, this nagging, but basic, postulate has been the discussion of philosophers, scientists, and other thinkers for centuries. For example, both Aquinas in his *The City of God* and Plato in his *Republic* concerned themselves with the man/land ratio of their utopian treatises. Although we can find discussion of this ratio of population to the land area or food supply and can trace cyclical activities affecting the size of early and primitive societies using this ratio (controlling for pestilence and weather) there appears not to have been any previous substantial attempt to address this constraint in a policy sense. Mankind appears to have been willing to be affected by the same laws of nature as other creatures, letting disease, starvation, and war keep his numbers in bounds.

Even as recently as a couple of hundred years ago, during a period when western civilization was at an apparent high point, with urbanization and industrialization on the rise, the famous treatise by Malthus[1] on the subject of the man/land ratio appeared. His postulate of the inevitable doom of mankind was reinforced by others such as Richardo and Say, who saw in the emerging economic institutions equally dire certainties for the working man and eventually for all people.

And yet, once again, mankind as a species did not succomb to the prophesied ends. The unsurmountable problems suggested by the above pessimists turned out to be solved by technology advances that exceeded expectations. The man/land ratio was reformulated by those advances so that the "inevitable" end was at least postponed.

More than twenty years ago *Fortune Magazine* did a series entitled "The New Goals." One of the authors in their series was John von Neumann. His topic: "Can We Survive Technology?" Let us quote from this article:[2]

> In the first half of this century the accelerating industrial revolution encountered an absolute limitation—not on technological progress as such but on an essential safety factor. This safety factor, which had permitted the industrial revolution to roll on from the mid-eighteenth to the early twentieth century, was essentially a matter of geographical and political Lebensraum: an even broader geographical

scope for technological activities, combined with an ever broader political integration of the world. Within this expanding framework it was possible to accommodate the major tensions created by technological progress.

Now this safety mechanism is being sharply inhibited; literally and figuratively, we are running out of room. At long last, we begin to feel the effects of the finite, actual size of the earth in a critical way.

Thus the crisis does not arise from accidental events or human errors. It is inherent in technology's relation to geography on the one hand and to political organization on the other. The crisis was developing visibly in the 1940's, and some phases can be traced back to 1914. In the years between now and 1980 the crisis will probably develop far beyond all earlier patterns. When or how it will end—or to what state of affairs it will yield—nobody can say.

So we arrive at the present, suspecting that technology also has feet of clay and that again our world has very real life-support limits. This suspicion of today's society is being discussed and cast aside as our political and industrial leaders promise utopian futures and our people have begun to assert as their right an ever increasing quality of life.

It will be the purpose of this chapter to investigate a handful of these desired goal statements against the backdrop of a rising (or at least, not declining) quality of life (QOL) and a defined carrying capacity. The methodology we have chosen to pursue this investigation is a model designed around the idea of carrying capacity of a large region and uses a data base that more or less represents that of the United States in the year 1970. We will look at the impact of striving for these goals over a thirty-year period ending with the year 2000. Of course, it is not our intention to suggest that these scenarios are a forecast or prediction of the future, but merely that they are reference points for discussion of possible happenings. The goals we shall discuss: (1) the Basic Data Case, (2) Stabilized Employment, (3) ZPG, and (4) ZEG. The technique chosen for analysis will be that of noting the deviations from what might have been expected without the proposed goal, while discussing the choices that society would likely have to make to maintain its present QOL and to achieve its goal.[a]

A Model of National Carrying Capacity

The state-of-the-system (SOS) model is a conceptual attempt to meld the growth desires of population with the limitations of the locale. The model has been designed to test various assumptions about the desired growth of an area for a set of side conditions (boundaries, constraints, or thresholds). Feasibility of the growth pattern is demonstrated if the desired growth can be achieved without violating the side conditions.

[a] Although in no way associated with the Rockefeller Commission on Critical Choices, this technique owes its genesis to members of that staff. Several discussions with Ms. Sandy Archibald were notable in this regard.

As examples of the side conditions, the model would translate higher level laws (federal and state laws and regulations, for example, if the model is of a local government), health thresholds, natural resource levels, and the local desires into quantitative side conditions. Specifically, one could set values such as a minimum level of subsistence per family, a maximum unemployment rate, the various environmental standards, housing and other industrial-commercial codes, density levels, and minimum education levels.

Such a model could be used to perform at least three functions: (1) to test the ability of the present growth trends to achieve the goals of the locale, (2) to test the probable life of a system and discover the most viable and critical linkages and constraints, (3) to analyze the effect of different policy alternatives as starting points.

Structure

Although we have already used the model in the previous chapter and will discuss its components in some detail in chapters to come, it is useful to describe the system briefly here before the analysis of the scenarios is presented. The state-of-the-system model includes three major elements.

Sectors of growth. This consists of three components: the population measured in terms of physical needs—i.e., as consumers; as the private production sector; and as the public services sector. The two latter components are measured in terms of level of expenditures for capital maintenance and output production per year. Redistribution of funds for production can occur. However, while the individual component growth rates can change, the total endogenous and exogenous funds to the regional production system cannot. This level of regional funds sets an upper constraint on inputs to the production components for the current cycle. The process of funds allocation to production components is done subject to the condition that the funds of the components are equal to the total regional funds. The allocation process has two major steps. First, an expected allocation of funds is determined so that the relative growth rates set for each component in the past cycle are followed. Additional increases or reductions of growth rates are introduced as functions of net funds available and the population preference for goods or services.

The production sectors. The sectors of regional growth, other than region population, are the products and services components of the private sector and the public sector. The dimension of growth for both sectors, and hence their input to the system, is the level of funds used annually to procure and transform resources into capital and for ecosystem maintenance and sector production outputs.

For the private sector, the components established are heavy-polluting industry, light-polluting industry, commercial goods and services, mining, agriculture, and household-related industries. In the public sector, components include safety, defense, and administrative services, health, and transportation/communication. In the model, each of these components has related to it a yearly rate of growth of available funds.

The population sector. Population growth as such is not seen as significant in the sense of regional limits until it is related to territory—the larger the physical space in which the population is housed, the less pressure is exerted on the group in the sense of food and living space demands[3]. The population is grouped into ages and activity partitions to represent system characteristics such as labor resources and expected consumption rates of the population in each partition. Included in this partitioning process are a number of factors that can be correlated to the regional production outputs to represent the present socioeconomic level of the society. Typical population partition characteristics include:

Length of immaturity/education time
Rates of short term and long term infirmity
Ratio for education units to work achieved in each age grouping
Death rates by age grouping
Size of worker force, further partitioned as:
—Employed, paid workers
—Unemployed, paid workers
—Workers not in paid status (housewives, volunteers)

The population characteristics are assumed to change due to the production and services levels of the private and public sectors, e.g., shifting population elements from unemployed to employed.

System Outputs

The major measures to be used for system output are the expenditures of the various production components to maintain the system facilities and to produce the output. Expenditures for maintenance include capital depreciation, the costs of effluent treatment,[4] and the annual rate of capital investment required. The maintenance components are obviously not constant over time.

Resources in the Model

A key element in the proposed system is the treatment of resources. The model attempts to anticipate adaptive changes through substitution of resources of similar types, and to account for the discovery and (delayed) development of new resources as a function of resource prices.

The idea of ecological accessibility as a limitor has meaning in resource constraints also. The availability of resources at any particular time is the result of the interactions among the nature and size of man's requirements, the physical occurrence of the resource, and the means of developing it. Estimates of the future availability of resources, therefore, require the assessment of economic and technological conditions, the level of production that would take place under different economic or technological conditions, and the nature and quantity of the total physical stock of both "renewable" and "nonrenewable" resources.

The model follows the traditional definitions of resources used in manufacturing and services, and considers eight resource groups: energy sources, natural resources (durable ores), land, agricultural resources (food and fibers), workers, capital, air, and water. These eight groups can be divided into the categories of nonrenewable resources (natural ore resources and energy sources) and renewable resources.

A key feature of the model's consideration of resources is that the "available" reserve level is the amount that can be extracted (or otherwise obtained) at a relatively fixed unit cost.[5] Thus, resource levels can be increased by improved processing techniques or by accepting a higher unit cost.

Energy. At any time, the total energy stock available to a region is the sum of the amount of the various energy sources.

Natural Resources. Natural resources, like energy, are normally viewed as a nonrenewable category. There are, however, two important hedges in considering the actual stock reserve at any one time. First, for many of the ores a high level of substitution of other resources in the production process is possible. A second hedge available is the possibility of recycling debris from processed, consumed, and scraped goods to regain natural ore in the form of salvage and prompt scrap. This procedure sets a resource reserve that is once again variable by cost, i.e., the recycling costs that will determine the level of ore to be salvaged from the system debris.

Land. Methods for expanding reserves of a land-use category are similar to other resources. From these data, a resource reserve conversion procedure, as used in nonrenewable resources, is possible. In this procedure land-use succession is activated for a given land use type as the unused reserve reaches a stock depletion warning level. At that time additional reserves for that land use are generated by a minimum cost algorithm. The major difference in this category from ores is that generation of new reserves in one land use category requires its removal from others.

Agricultural Resources (Foods and Fibers). Based on resources availability, the agricultural portion of the production output controls resource growth levels for food and fibers.

Capital. Capital is also a renewable resource that can be used to constrain levels of output to satisfy final consumption.

Labor. Labor as a resource is measured in work units. The population partition of paid workers determines at any time the instantaneous maximum labor supply level. The labor cost is a function of the rate at which this level is utilized. Additional labor units can be generated as a function of this rate by transferring, in later time periods, people from the population partitions of in-training or in-unpaid-work categories.

Air and Water. The model is not concerned with the "level" of air or water pollution, but with return of their ambient state to a satisfactory quality level.

Level and Quality of Life

Major elements of the state of the system are measured in terms of societal perceptions—a set of judgments dealing with various components of level and quality of life. Our particular judgments of society must be area-specific and must represent the planning system responsible for the adjustment of growth and output to achieve an acceptable state. Hence, only a general formulation of measures can be presented here.

In the planning systems responsible for the achievement of the goals, the comprehensive plan procedure is reasonably straightforward. Each goal by itself has a specific threshold to be realized. The relative importance assigned the goals in the plan yields a set of weighting coefficients to determine priority in establishing tradeoffs, given that total achievement of all goals cannot be accomplished. Thus the only requirement in setting of goals is to restate the goals in terms of parameters developed in the model operations.

Another alternative is a planning system that requires achievement of certain minimum values to achieve an acceptable state. It involves supplementary measures relating to the resilience of the system in remaining above the minima. Each of the collection of measures has a dissatisfaction threshold and a resilience characteristic which is measured in terms of the relative level above the threshold. Unlike the first system where the measures are generated directly from the comprehensive goals, a set of measures are to be selected in terms of the area-specific needs and desires of the society in the region. A minimum acceptable value for each, rather than a goal of achievement, is set. Of greater difficulty is the setting of relative weights to combine the measures. Instead, an iterative process can be carried out which measures the state of the system and then adjusts fund levels among the production components until all thresholds are met.

System Adjustments

If a given state of the system is found unacceptable, a set of adjustments needs to be effected to improve the situation. The adjustments are performed in the following order.

Short term adjustments:

(a) Short term deferral of capital maintenance and/or

(b) Expenditure of net export balances to achieve additional production output funds for the purchase of additional resources or the importation of goods

Long term adjustments:

(a) Changing input/output production functions to achieve the minimum cost mix for components contributing to unacceptable value

(b) Reallocating the total projected funds level within a sector to better balance projected growth rates and needed outputs of deficient components

(c) Scheduling on a permanent basis the annual transfer of funds from one sector to the other (public to private or the reverse) and then repeating procedure (b)

(d) Adjusting the rates and direction of net migration to reduce per capita consumption needs if significant unemployment exists in the region

If none of the long term adjustments produces a satisfactory correction of the projected state of the system, the system goals are modified to lower levels. This will allow a possibility of maintaining the regional growth projections at the cost of a less acceptable level and quality of life.

The system reaching its carrying capacity may merely suggest a short run imbalance of the demand and supply of a specific resource. This

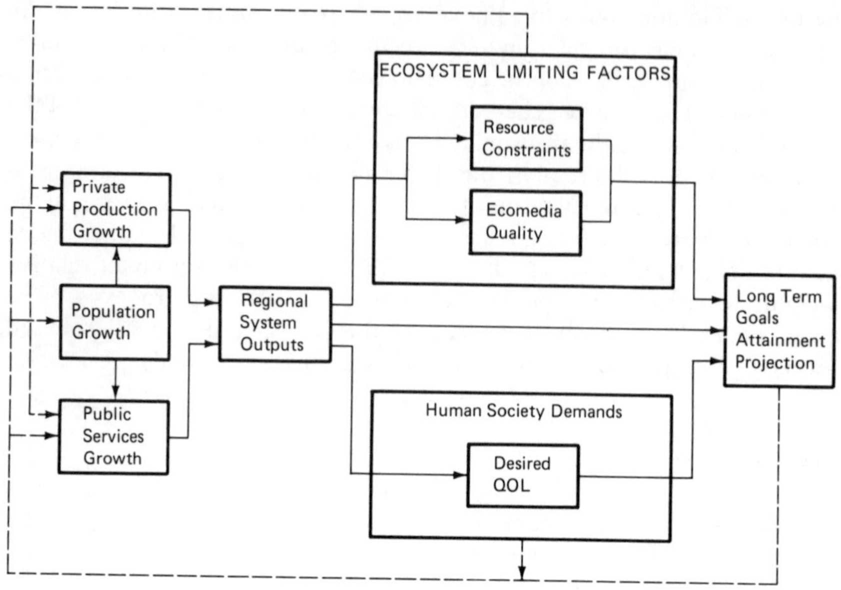

Figure 2-1. Conceptual Form of the Model.

imbalance can be corrected by changing the rate of extraction and distribution of the resource in question. If, on the other hand, the reaching of a depletion symptom at a particular point in time heralds the beginning of a serious shortage of a particular resource, there are numerous possible responses, such as:

Increase the rate of extraction, despite increasing costs.

Receive supply from other regional systems at higher costs.

Change the population's demand function.

Change the growth rate of specific sectors in system.

From this brief description of the model and its structure, summarized in Figure 2-1, we shall proceed to demonstrate the thesis of this chapter: namely, that the results of many of our present modeling efforts may or may not be accurate reflections of reality, but surely are governed by the assumptions made in the analysis.

Alternative Futures of the Nation: Circa 2000

The analysis carried out in chapter 1 was one designed to show that extreme care has to be taken by those who would use the results of models that purport to forecast to the distant future. The data used in the exercise was test data which was not changed for the described runs; i.e., the results were a function of the assumptions, not of a special data base. The specific findings are reported in that chapter, but, in general, it was found that a model that attempted to reflect the resiliency of the human portion of the total system would not be so prone to disastrous crashes but would be more likely to stress adjustment and change within a familiar existing world and to be one that would take into consideration the exigencies of the moment. Consequently, the brief analyses that follow will not stress disaster but adjustment.

Base Case

First, let us examine the base case. The data and assumptions for this case were all taken from fairly readily available secondary source materials such as the *Statistical Abstract*, U.S. Dept. of Commerce, *Survey of Current Business*, the *Minerals Yearbook*, several Congressional or commission reports on natural resources, and so forth. The production function and substitution data was derived from the INFORUM and SEAS models and were based on constant coefficients. In short, a serious attempt was made to redesign the model (from SOS-1) so that it would be possible to load it readily from such sources.

By the year 2000, our base case predicts a fairly healthy world (Figure 2-2). Ignoring a few short run adjustments (which might as easily be model adjustments as system adjustments), the nation appears to be able to grow at a fairly steady pace and, where adjustments are necessary, they appear in a timely fashion. Population is seen to grow by about a third, the public sector by more than a factor of four, the private sector by a factor of 2.7, and resources and employment by a factor of two. All of the growth, however, is not necessarily reflection of a "good life." Since, as noted elsewhere in this book, it is not really possible to measure the term quality of life (QOL) in a truly empirically verifiable fashion, it has been connected here to a measure of the change in the nation's culture. That is, the original values of the parameters are those per capita values existing in the first year. The assumption made is that an attempt will be made on the part of the nation to resist any movement away from the status quo. The QOL is seen to grow, but not as fast as any of the other indices, nor as smoothly. The inference that might be drawn is that although more is better, the cost of getting more is greater than the payoff received.

Looking at the sectors in more detail, in outputs not reproduced here, only the nondurable goods sector does not show an almost uninterrupted growth rate to the year 2000, reacting as it does to a need for greater

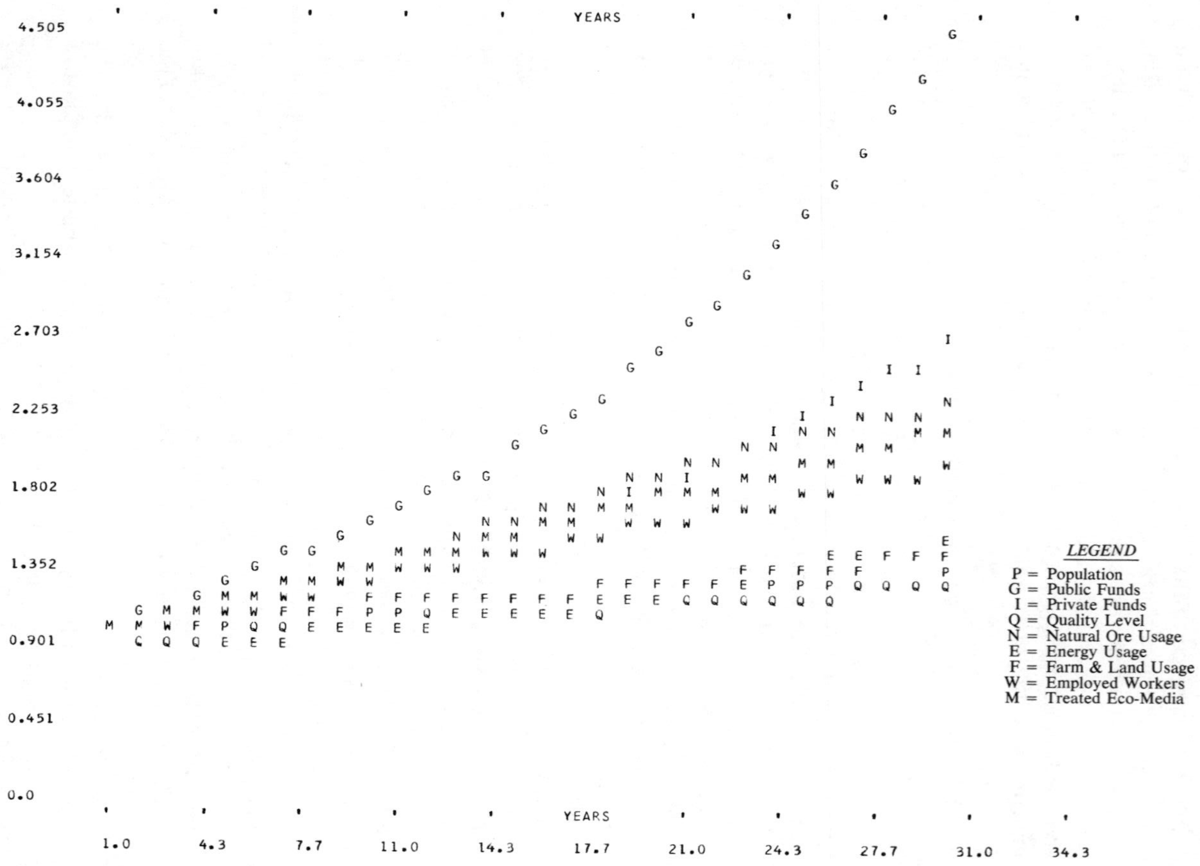

YEARS

4.505
4.055
3.604
3.154
2.703
2.253
1.802
1.352
0.901
0.451
0.0

1.0 4.3 7.7 11.0 14.3 17.7 21.0 24.3 27.7 31.0 34.3

YEARS

LEGEND

P = Population
G = Public Funds
I = Private Funds
Q = Quality Level
N = Natural Ore Usage
E = Energy Usage
F = Farm & Land Usage
W = Employed Workers
M = Treated Eco-Media

Figure 2-2. State of the System—Base Case.

emphasis (out of the limited private funds) on the durable goods sector to sustain the total growth of the nation.

The detailed resource data shows a slowdown in the availability and use of renewable resources for about a decade and then sustained growth. On the nonrenewable side, copper availability and use falls off sharply during the first decade, recovers and then becomes less utilized again toward the end of the century. The assumptions built into the model were as optimistic as possible in the energy case and significant switching was seen from oil to coal and other energy resources. Even with the switching, however, the demand climbs rapidly again in less than twenty years.

The conclusion drawn from the base case assumptions and data appears to fly in the face of many other forecasts. Consequently, the reader is invited to carry out the analysis in more detail as the full output, data base, and model are presented in the remainder of this book. It is admitted, once again, that all of the portions of the economy are not presented nor are all the resources, production functions, or substitutions. Furthermore, the very grossness of the model may hide a real danger that could become apparent at a finer level of detail. On the other hand, it is difficult to find systems available today, forecasting gloom or not, that have such richness included. Consequently, for purposes of this analysis, we will move away from claiming great validity for specific forecasts, and concentrate instead on the relative results one obtains by using the techniques of the SOS model with a given data base. To this end, let us now turn to the other scenarios.

Zero Population Growth (ZPG)

In chapter 1 we used a scenario similar to ZPG to illustrate the philosophy of those who would prolong our existence on the Earth by the expedient of reducing the numbers of people that are around to use up the resources. We shall investigate these assumptions again here (for they are ever popular regardless of the model) but shall not restrain the model in any other fashion. The birth and death rates are set equal. Of certainty, the control possible in a computer model exceeds that of reality.

As would be expected, the growth rates of the national projection associated with ZPG are slower; however, they take decades to have any really telling effects on say, resource use. The world of the base case and ZPG are really quite similar until approximately 1990 where resource usage begins to fall and employment and QOL to level off. As would be expected, those sectors that are almost completely people-based drop off faster, and one, education, which depends upon youth, faster yet. Other activities in the private sectors also begin to show declines in later years; communication and transportation, durable goods, wholesale and retail, services, and mining all fall or level off (Figure 2-3).

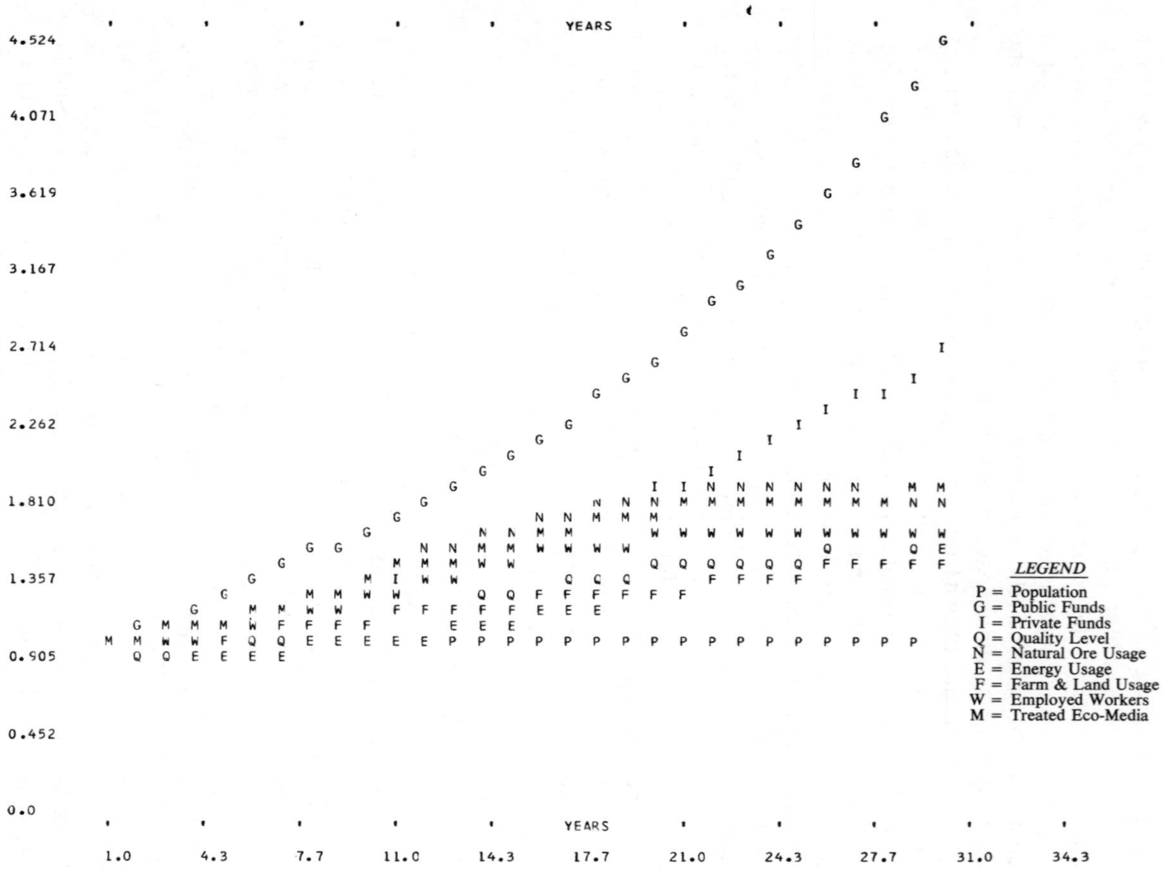

YEARS

4.524
4.071
3.619
3.167
2.714
2.262
1.810
1.357
0.905
0.452
0.0

YEARS

1.0 4.3 7.7 11.0 14.3 17.7 21.0 24.3 27.7 31.0 34.3

LEGEND

P = Population
G = Public Funds
I = Private Funds
Q = Quality Level
N = Natural Ore Usage
E = Energy Usage
F = Farm & Land Usage
W = Employed Workers
M = Treated Eco-Media

Figure 2-3. State of the System—ZPG.

The forecast system expenditures of the base case ($2,685,481 million) and the ZPG Case ($2,646,016 million) are quite close but the mix is quite different, both within the categories of food, raw materials, labor, and capital and in terms of usage by the sectors themselves when the detailed data are reviewed.

There are approximately 37 million less people requiring educational services and a forecasted 76 million fewer people in toto. Given the fact that this change in the absolute number of people came about in a materialistically growing nation through a change in the shape of the age pyramid, the repercussions throughout the system in terms of demands for goods and services and the number of workers able to supply these are as might be expected.

In general though, the habit patterns of the nation are not seen to change all that rapidly, meaning that the same system reactions required to produce desired amounts of goods and services usually still appear, although somewhat later. Further, the QOL measure predicts a populace that is generally satisfied toward the end of the century, so that although things don't get better, they don't get worse.

Zero Economic Growth (ZEG)

Another much talked about policy that many would desire is to stabilize the economy to where it is at any one point in time. Although it is completely unclear exactly how one could actually do such a thing, we have simulated the phenomenon to see what might happen.

In a word, the system flattens out. The model is set so that the growth for all the public and private sectors is begun at zero. By 1974 the need for more durable goods causes the system to adjust (at the expense of the nondurables) and to face an increased growth rate. By 1980, all the demand thresholds are lower than the base case, as is the GNP. By 1990, population growth continues; now both durables and nondurables are forced to expand (although more slowly for durables) and the other sectors still are able to absorb the growth. The population demand threshold levels have reached plateaus and the QOL has begun to deteriorate. In the year 2000, the total population is the same but the GNP in the ZEG Case is only 38% of the base case, meaning that the per capita GNP figure of $9688 in the base case is reduced to $3724 in the ZEG case (Figure 2-4).

On the other hand, if the conservation of resources is a prime goal, only about 60 percent of the resources used in the base case were necessary to provide sustenance in the ZEG case. On the cost side, the unemployment rate is consistently higher, between 6 and 7 percent as compared to about 4 percent for the base case. And finally, although it is stable, the QOL is definitely lower.

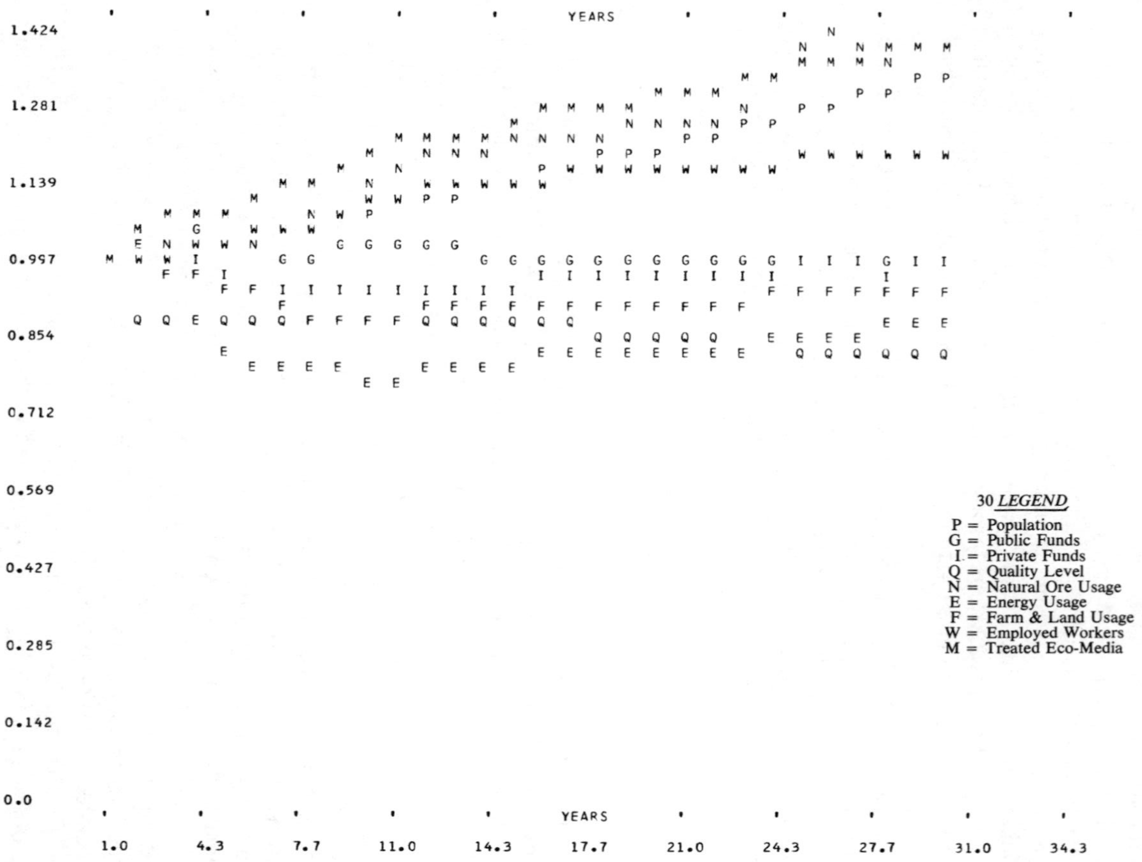

YEARS

1.424
1.281
1.139
0.997
0.854
0.712
0.569
0.427
0.285
0.142
0.0

YEARS

1.0 4.3 7.7 11.0 14.3 17.7 21.0 24.3 27.7 31.0 34.3

30 *LEGEND*

P = Population
G = Public Funds
I = Private Funds
Q = Quality Level
N = Natural Ore Usage
E = Energy Usage
F = Farm & Land Usage
W = Employed Workers
M = Treated Eco-Media

Figure 2-4. State of the System—ZEG

It is not legitimate to say whether this case is better or worse than the base case because the response is so heavily dependent on the results desired. The populace obviously survived. Although not achieving the QOL possible under a continuation of the present growth pattern, it is nonetheless able to be held stable. Less resources are used and the only noticeable cost is a higher unemployment rate.

ZEG and ZPG

Although it is fair to say that both of the previous cases are only hypothetical possibilities in any population over any significant period of time, the weaknesses of each of them are overcome by the other. For example, the fact that the driving growth of the system under ZPG assumptions required increasing output, the number of workers available and the size of consumer demand sectors were the factors that eventually slowed it down. In the ZEG case, the population growth remained stable but the output levels fell (Figure 2-5).

By leveling off the birth rate plus stopping sector growth, QOL does better, although not as well as sustained growth. Resource usage moves up above sixty percent of the base case and the unemployment rate drops.

Stabilized Employment Rate

When these scenarios were first discussed, the unemployment level appeared to be climbing slightly. Even though the base case scenario projected a fairly stable employment level, we reset the model to have the public sector intervene to provide one that was even more stable. This turned out to result in a dampening of the unemployment cycle (i.e., not only were the higher rates lowered, the low rates were increased some). On the whole, because these changes were so very marginal it is difficult to really see any results from the policies. However, the QOL was somewhat higher and the total system seemed not to have to react as sharply to situations. Resource usage was also slightly less. In short, it appears that although the system will adjust to most situations, a positive policy of intervention is to be preferred, provided that the actions taken are those required to carry out the desired end (Figure 2-6).

Using Models

After having briefly presented the results from a few runs, what can we say about the use of models for prediction and particularly about SOS-2? In the

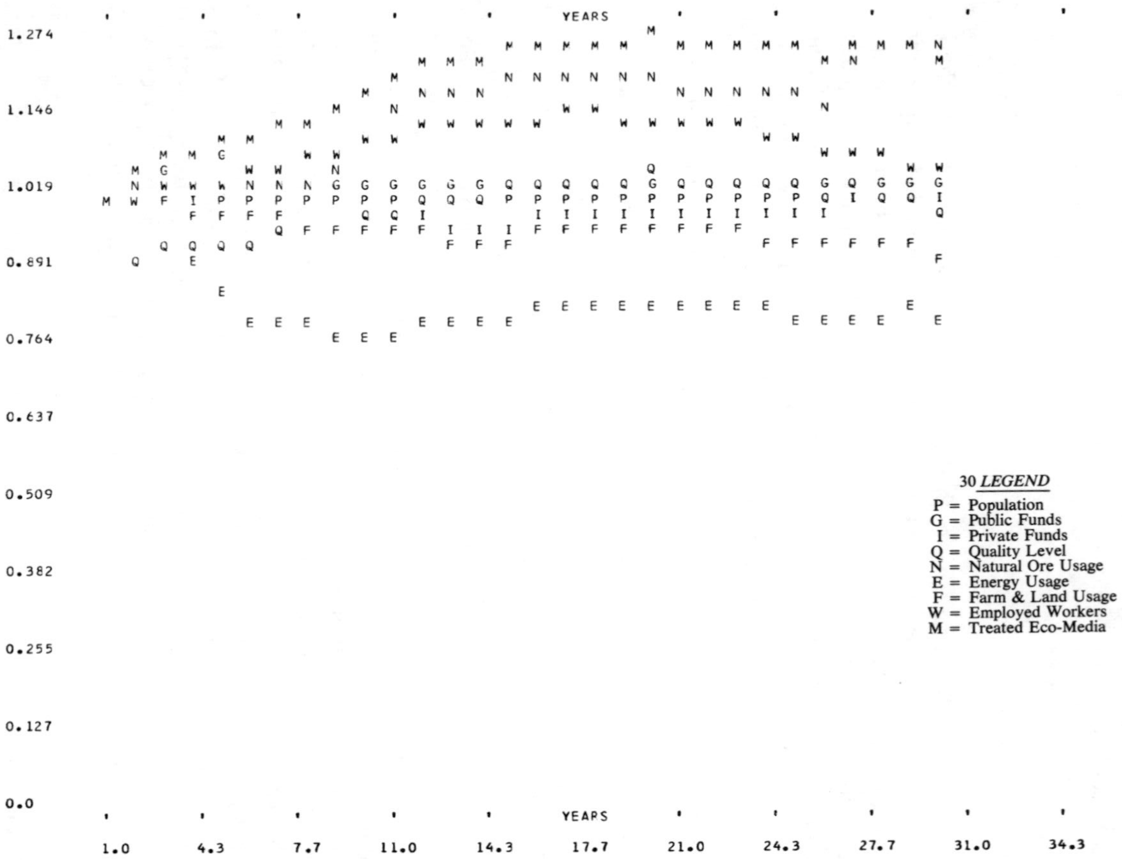

Figure 2-5. State of the System—ZPG and ZEG.

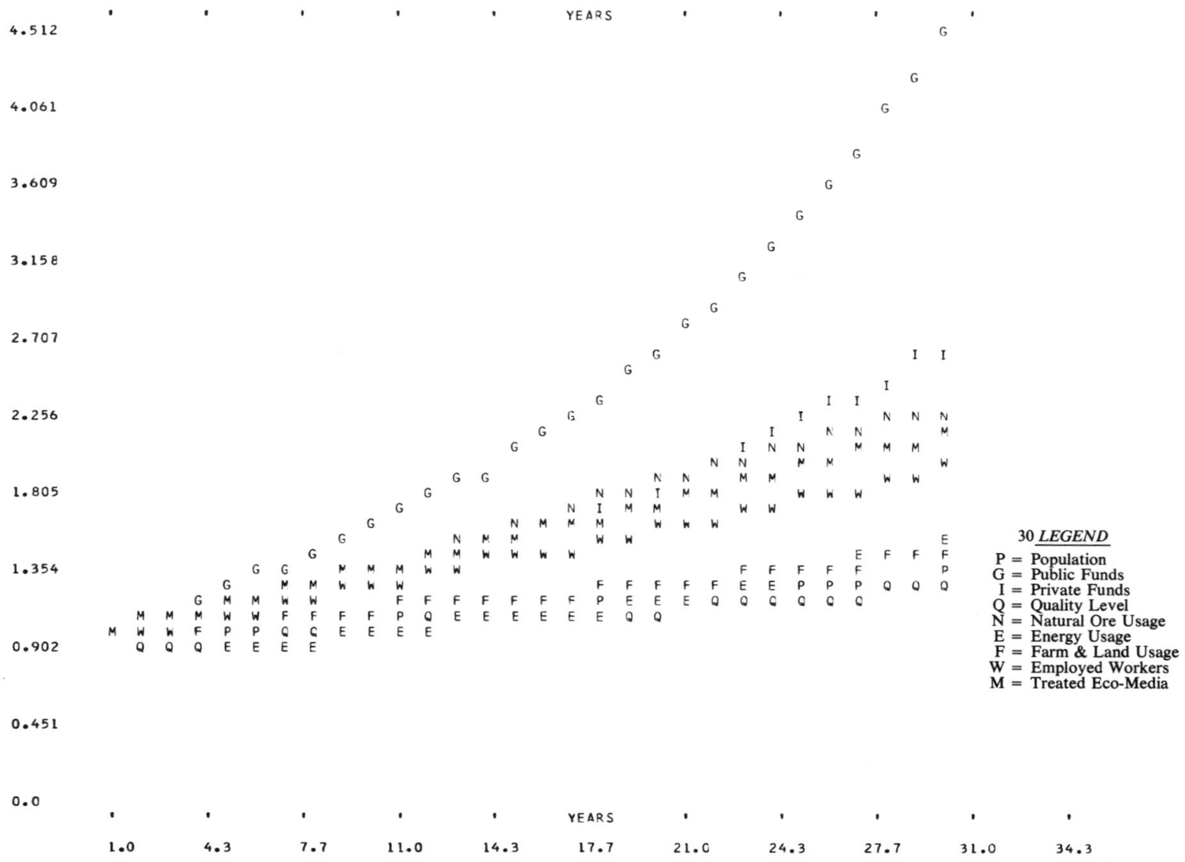

YEARS

4.512
4.061
3.609
3.158
2.707
2.256
1.805
1.354
0.902
0.451
0.0

YEARS

1.0 4.3 7.7 11.0 14.3 17.7 21.0 24.3 27.7 31.0 34.3

30 *LEGEND*

P = Population
G = Public Funds
I = Private Funds
Q = Quality Level
N = Natural Ore Usage
E = Energy Usage
F = Farm & Land Usage
W = Employed Workers
M = Treated Eco-Media

Figure 2-6. State of the System—Stabilized Unemployment.

first place, none of these scenarios, including the base case, is "predictive" in the sense that it is a prognosis of what *will* happen. On the other hand, if the data is correct and the algorithms accurate then they are examples of what *can* happen. The alternative scenarios run off of this base case are even more chancy because they assume that the only perturbations that will occur to the system are those loaded and that the system responses will be those of the past. In no case can this system (or any system) predict the exogenous shocks that would cause it to take significant deviations from the expected. For example, those who would claim that their model would have predicted a world war before it happened, or even OPEC, are in the category of charlatans, liars, or fools.

What then does a model do? More specifically, what does a forecasting model do? The kind of question posed to a forecasting model is of the following sort. If I assume that the model I have available is a time simulation of the system under study, then I can postulate what the future will be if it continues as it has in the past. If I have specialized knowledge about certain portions of the system as to how they will change in the future then I can adjust the model to deviate from the past in a prescribed fashion. Such changes could account for technological advances or higher education levels, for example. These changes are, of course, assumptions and their introduction as to sector and time (and feedbacks) are different from the rest of the model as they are not based upon observations. Finally, when one is convinced that the model he is using is a simulation of the future, then he is able to introduce other changes which he has no reason to expect but in whose impact he is interested. Changes of this type are used in most forms of policy analysis. A discussion of the outputs of such runs are really only legitimate when compared to the base case and are to be used with great caution.

As to SOS-2, what has been presented is a beginning of a modeling form that will have to be perfected as many of us look to improving the modeling art. Recent interest in the environment and energy has pushed us to search for ways to guess the world of the future (ERDA is seriously discussing the world in the year 2000). Present methodologies place too much emphasis on simple minded extrapolations of the past with no correction of obvious troubles that such policies would foster. It is clear that blind reaction to shortages and other crises has been our past experience. There is no reason to believe that we shall suddenly change. On the other hand, the present model is only the first step in attempting to forecast the reaction to endogenous crises. Although the model was built to be utilized for problems significantly more sophisticated and complex than those presented here, we have only presented a few polar extreme cases and have kept the analysis brief so that much would not be made of the results.

The model is fully documented in the next several chapters so that our interested colleagues can review and improve on it. We feel that the existing theory is sound and the system's structure correct. It has been designed to accept data readily and without extensive programming. With the hope that others will join us in using the model for pedagogical purposes and will expand it for research ones, the following chapters are presented.

3 Carrying Capacity: A Perspective For Environmental Management

Carrying Capacity: Interaction of Natural and Human Environments

A significant concern in today's society is whether the environment can accommodate or absorb change without experiencing conditions of instability and degradation.[a] Indeed, in specific areas, the ability of the environment to sustain particular levels of activity without specialized treatment and controls has already been exceeded, and in others similar limits are rapidly being reached.

Recognizing that the regenerative capacity of a region is limited, as well as its resource base, a strong motivation exists for the use of a carrying capacity philosophy as the basis for regional planning. These relatively scarce resources must be managed in the context of competing demands, and the environment must be considered as man changes his social, technical, or economic activities.

The Human Environment

In general, the human environment is a result of man structuring his goals within growth terms, as they relate to the rest of the system. Individual expectations and institutional structures assume and often require this philosophy while expecting an increase in material and energy flow rates. This places ever increasing demands on production and assimilation of resources in the natural environment. Specific examples of stress from this practice are ample. Man has, for example achieved very high productivity in rural-agricultural systems. However, the efficiency of production results in a tremendous energy requirement in order to stabilize the system.

In the urban industrial area, man has built monuments to his ambitions. Limitations of nature have been dramatically overcome by the infusion of

[a] The citations in this chapter have been reduced but are available in Bishop, A.B., et al., "Carrying Capacity in Regional Environment Management." Washington Environmental Research Center, Office of Research and Development, U.S. Environmental Protection Agency, Washington, D.C. Government Printing Office #EPA-600/5-74-021, February 1974 or in Williams, E., & House, P., *The State of the System (SOS) Model*, EPA, ORD, EPA-600/5-73-013. The chapter itself is developed largely from these sources, however, the authors take responsibility for its present focus to the extent that it differs from its original intent.

technology. New technologies, however, have usually resulted in demands on the natural environment to absorb waste from the processes. In some areas, the absorptive capacity has already been exceeded.

The Natural Environment

Therefore, the natural environment can be seen as a constraint on the human sector. This constraint is a function of the rates which it can provide resources and assimilate residuals and wastes. The rates and capacities of the natural environment are often fixed by evolutionary processes. In some places they are more closely aligned to past environmental situations and not to rapidly increasing human demands.

A certain rigidity of the natural environment is implied by the term "constraint." The natural environment has the capability of producing a given output flow of products and assimilating a given input flow of waste products and constraints. This balance defines the stress limits within which the system can compensate and still return to its original condition. The degree to which man can relax these constraints in an ecosystem by technological means is still an open question. A basic problem is in recognizing and quantifying the magnitude of the ecological resource and identifying what proportion of the potential is committed to the base line demands imposed within the natural environment itself. It is important to specify these capacities so that the human sector activities can be reoriented to operate within the constraints of the "natural" sector. If capacities are not defined, then further and possibly undesirable evolution of the natural system will occur.

Growth and Carrying Capacity

Virtually every system in the nation today, natural and man-made, is faced with problems of accommodating some degree of future growth and development. One way of looking at this required adjustment is to specify the situation in dichotomous terms—the environmental versus the economic systems. The evolution of our current demographic structure in the United States is the result of a variety of powerful economic and resource factors. Factors influencing development were ready supplies of raw materials, water and cheap power, and cheap transportation (coastal areas, large rivers, or the Great Lakes). The economic structure benefited greatly from the environmental largesse. The relationship has not always been beneficial in the opposite direction, however. Economists have aptly described the problems arising out of conflict in the progression of natural and human systems. The manifestations of this conflict appear in widely varying aspects, many of which have been labeled "pollution". The problem of pollution arises out of two related aspects of economic activity-congestion and residuals.

If pollution can be simply described as having too much of a substance at a particular time in a particular place, it becomes obvious how congestion would increase the likelihood of such a condition. The failure to consider the finite assimilative capacity of the environment leads to excessive use or congestion of the natural systems. Disposition of residuals (or wastes from production and consumption activities) is the second major aspect of the pollution problem in environmental management. Production and consumption activities of human populations generate residuals and wastes which are discharged to the environmental resource base. The activities of man, therefore, both in terms of waste generation (and resource use) and conglomeration, are potentially dangerous for the environment. Obviously, these practices cannot be continued without regard for the natural sector. On the other hand, it is unlikely that the activities will cease voluntarily either. What is needed is a formalized method for forming symbiotic relationships. Carrying capacity appears to give some hope in this direction.

While economic efficiency has been one of the determinants of the regional growth in the past, this consideration now must be balanced by considering natural systems. Environmental constraints imposed by the ecological characteristics of any given region should be equally influential in determining the spatial configuration. In managing the environment for quality regional growth, questions related to the carrying capacity of environmental resources lie at the heart of the problem of finding socially acceptable systems which are also economically viable. These involve decisions related to types of product outputs, pricing policies relating to residuals discharge, spatial location of economic activities, desired levels of environmental quality, and methods for handling residuals.

Ecosystem Properties

There are four essential properties of ecosystems. These properties form the framework for actions and interactions of the components and processes of the ecosystem. Ecosystems all share:

- *Historical continuity*—The ecosystem responds to past and present events (past events through the succession of previous stages).
- *Spatial accessibility*—The ecosystem responds to specific events at several different points in space. Each component is not an independent unit in itself, it is related to and affected by other components. The level of the interaction is usually associated with the proximity of the components.

- *System control*—The ecosystem encompasses many different component activities governed by complex feedbacks and interactions.
- *Structural inertia*—Ecosystems and subelements exhibit characteristics that are defined in terms of time lags and minimum and maximum constraint levels. Thus change and symptoms of interactions do not appear instantaneously, nor are all changes smooth and evolutionary.

The systems and structural properties require more discussion since two important characteristics of ecosystems, stability and resilience are defined within their context.

Ecological systems are not in a state of delicate balance. They have demonstrated in many instances the capability to either "bounce back" or to "adjust" after severe shock. Nor did man invent severe shocks to ecosystems; long before man emerged as a dominant factor of regional ecosystems, systems were subjected to trauma by climatic changes and other geological processes. The surviving ecosystem forms were those that were able to adapt or to absorb the effects of the trauma. The capability of a system to absorb trauma and recover is its characteristic of stability. The capability of a system to successfully change to a modified form characterizes its resilience. Evolving successional ecosystems are characterized by a high level of resilience, while mature systems usually include high stability.

While major regional ecosystems have demonstrated considerable resilience, we know that their levels of resilience are not infinite. Examples of forests turning into deserts, or lakes into the aquatic equivalent of deserts, exist. Thus, a key feature of ecosystems is that, as resilience is lowered by an incremental series of adaptations or a massive shock, the level of ecosystem resilience may be exceeded and the system may show unexpected and dramatic levels of change. This comes about when the structural thresholds—or the demands on the system—cannot be met.

Thus, an ecosystem may react in several levels to pertubations:

- A minor change may be noted within the thresholds of the structure; the system will eventually return to its previous equilibrium point and meet all processing demands.
- A major change may be noted that exceeds some of the structural thresholds; the system may eventually successfully adapt by finding a new equilibrium point near the original one with a new set of structural thresholds for this equilibrium point.
- A major change may cause damage to a degree that successful adaptation does not occur; the system reaches equilibrium at much lower levels of component support and will include a vastly different set of structural thresholds.

Because an ecosystem is constantly changing, so will its equilibrium point. Even when a climax ecosystem has been reached, it is still dynamic, still changing. Ecosystems that have survived through time are the ones that have been able to keep their demand thresholds broad enough to absorb unanticipated shocks and the accumulated consequences of change over time.

Ecological Systems and Carrying Capacity

The concept of carrying capacity developed historically in connection with the study and description of the growth and dynamics of natural populations. Because of this origin, the term is generally understood to mean the population limit of a species in a given ecosystem or regional habitat.

The earliest popular description of this term as related to human populations was by Malthus and may be expressed in exponential form,

$$N(t) = N_0 e^{kt}$$

where N is population size at any time t, N_0 is the initial population, k is the growth rate per time period, and t is time in appropriate units. This growth model approached no upper bound or population limit, but continues to grow at accelerating rates until catastrophe occurs.

Population Carrying Capacity

According to Bishop,[1] the earliest equation for population growth that recognized limits of growth due to the carrying capacity of the environment was proposed by Verhulst in the eighteenth century.[2] The growth curve was a logistics function,

$$N(t) = \frac{k}{(\lambda - ce^{-kt})}$$

where: N is the population size, k is population growth rate, λ is a density dependent population coefficient, and c is a constant of integration. The solution eventually approaches the asympotote $N = k/\lambda$, with an initial close to exponential increase. Later, the carrying capacity concept was refined as a set of logistic equations developed by Lotka and Volterra.[3] The Lotka-Volterra equations are a set of coupled differential equations,

$$\frac{dN_i}{dt} = \frac{r_i N_i}{K_i}\left[K_i - N_i - \sum_{j=1}^{m} \alpha_j N_j N_i\right]$$

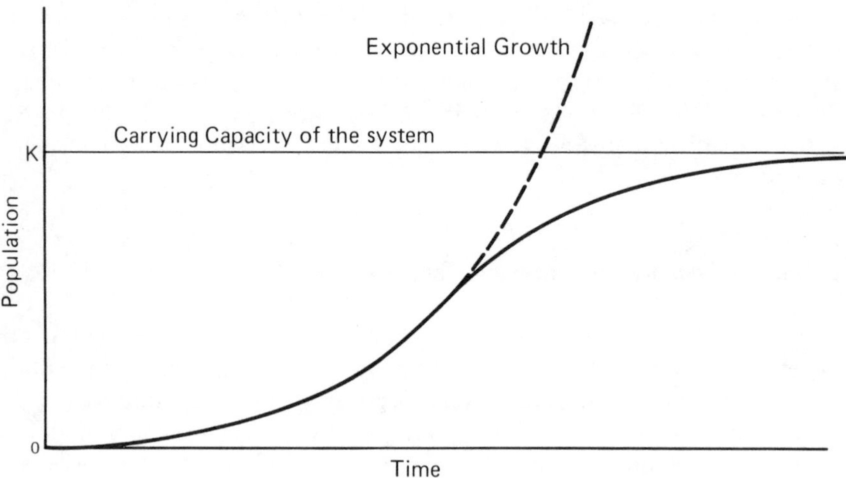

Figure 3-1. Population Growth

where r_i is the growth rate of the ith population, N_i is the size of the ith population, K_i is an upper limit on, or the carrying capacity of, the ith population, and j is a coefficient which represents the effect of such things as predation or competition of the jth population on the ith population (see Figure 3-1).

These equations were designed to describe the change in the size of natural populations which were both in contact with one another and had an upper bound or limit on population density. This upper bound on population density was called the population carrying capacity (K) and was brought to be the result of density dependent negative feedback, resulting from such things as resource shortages, disease, or predation triggered by high population density.

Ecosystem Properties

If the concept of carrying capacity is to be useful it must enable the environmental manager to assess and evaluate the impacts of various proposed certainties on regional environmental quality. This requires insight and understanding of the behavior and interaction of ecological and human systems, the ways in which the "health" of regional support systems can be measured, and the time-dependent changes monitored. If carrying capacity is framed primarily in terms of the ecosystem, then rendering it operational as a basis for environmental management will require corresponding processes applicable to the human environment.

As a first step, it is necessary to specify the limiting factors in an environment to human growth or expression.

The limiting factor is the requirement that is present to the minimum extent proportion to the needs of a collection of ecosystem components. Factors in an ecosystem that can be limiting include:

Food
Climate
Ecosystem space (land)
Cover and protection
Extent of the niche of species
Amount and distribution of water
Species decimating factors predation and disease
Rate of species change or succession

An important factor to note in determining a carrying capacity for a population within an ecosystem is that the species is part of, and subject to, changes in the ecosystem. The contained species react to changes in the ecosystem and make adjustments in order to survive; they do not change the ecosystem to meet their needs. Ultimately, this is the control property with which we must deal when we look at "environmental carrying capacity" for man within a system.

Two other specific problems which arise with an attempt to operationalize this control. Dimensions and boundaries of the special and temporal domains in the human environments do not neatly map onto or correspond with the dimensions in the natural environments. This gives rise to numerous problems in making social and environmental trade-offs.

Simple one-dimensional point estimates of carrying capacity are neither realistic nor practical. It would be completely accidental if the functional boundaries of an urban area of governmental, economic, and social activities were to map onto the natural boundaries of air sheds or river basins. Yet the assimilative capacity of an area is defined by the natural, not human, boundaries. It is difficult for these individual functional subsectors to act independently in ways that are environmentally responsible due to all sorts of other survival pressures. Definition of the "environmental problem" is very much involved with this discrepancy.

Carrying capacity must also be considered in a dynamic or temporal context. Expectations concerning time required for system response or achievement of goals is a fundamental difference between the natural and human environments. The natural environment works on an evolutionary time scale. Those of the human environment which are usually oriented toward present generations are likely to be problematical if their short term nature does not mesh with the longer term design.

Effects of Man on the Ecosystems

The evolution of man has introduced a species into many ecosystems that clearly and increasingly dominates other species. The characteristics of man that promote him as a dominant species are:

- Culture. Man can develop culture and apply it; the application of culture by man plays a major role in evolving and reshaping the relation of man and his physical world (ecosystems).
- Mobility. Through mobility, man can apply culture for specialized functions in best production areas. Transport of products can modify local systems that do not include the production function. Hence, a local area may not be a closed ecosystem. It may supply and be affected by factors and events not developed locally but in distant areas of Earth.
- Social. Man has overlaid the natural, symbiotic relations of organisms with social constraints and judgments, causing local patterns of adjustment to depend on both social and ecological processes.

Thus, the inclusion of man in regional ecosystems provides a dominant species that:

- Through culture, modifies natural levels and cycles of energy and mineral utilization and return to resource pools
- Through mobility, augments or withdraws from the resource pools of a local ecosystem
- Through social regulation, utilizes resource pools and changes populations of other species in patterns not compatible with natural evolutionary and environmental processes

But man can only modify cycles and pools of non-closed ecosystems; he is still subject to the ecosystem carrying capacities and the mobility of resources that act as limiting factors. If his modifications and demands are sufficient to drive the ecosystem past a limiting factor threshold, he will cause a reduction in the carrying capacity by exceeding the threshold of an ecosystem limiting factor.

Thus, the species man, like other species, is subject to the ecosystem relations of:

- Physical. Man's body is subject to the natural laws that apply to all abiotic and biotic substances.
- Natural. Man is affected by ecosystem factors such as climate, food, disease and media quality.

He, like all organisms, consumes energy and is part of the food chain, and through discharge of wastes and death, provides decomposable matter for renewing the nutrient pool. However, as a species employing culture and social judgment, man interacts with his environment in a manner of greater complexity than that of a physical mass and an organism.

It is in the context of the ecosystem and its constraints on man's needs and wants that the concept of environmental carrying capacity for man will be defined. However, man's social and technological abilities to modify ecosystem constraints need to be specified within this context. They are both powerful shapers of man's environment—in degrading it and in finding nondestructive ecosystem modifications.

Man Acts, The Ecosystem Reacts

Through the medium of culture, man has proceeded through a series of technological levels to manipulate his environment over the short run. This mechanism has allowed him to expand his ecosystem niche, to regulate the quantities and locations of all other species in his communities, to modify rate of production of natural products, and to convert system components to specialized products that are not normally part of natural ecosystems. However, application of culture has also fostered new growth rates in species population and consumption of non-food specialized functions. The specialized product growth levels have caused consumption rates of limiting factors in major regional ecosystems that are far beyond the levels that are being naturally recycled back into the resource pools. Even the use of mobility to augment these localized resource needs is insufficient since world supplies of some limiting factors are being exhausted.

Thus, it appears useful to trace rapidly the evolution of man and his application of culture, and by this means identify patterns of specialized man/environmental relationships that need to be included in analyses that expect to predict the likely outcome of man's impacts on regional ecosystems. Since the aim here is to model interaction of human population growth and its demands on environmental carrying capacity, the levels of impact and primary changes of these demands will be noted.

The Niches of Man

Man, by application of accumulated culture, has proceeded through four major niches or stages within his ecosystems and appears now to be entering a fifth niche. The four stages have been within ecosystems that, in most regions, would be defined as mature, climax ecosystems possessing great stability. Yet, to pass from each of the first three stages, man, through application of technology, instituted a new set of limiting factor thresholds on the ecosystems. Thus man superimposed within the natural ecosystem constraints, a dramatic expansion of his niche, his population size, and his quality of life. Expansion of any of these caused an increase in demands placed upon the resources of the ecosystem in which he had influence. The increased demands, even in the earliest stages, caused damage in the locale of his habitation. Fortunately, in early stages the ecological accessibility and the population density of man was sufficiently low to provide spatial limitation of the damage. The niche provided man in the fourth stage included parallel and rapid worldwide expansion of population, quality demands, and ecological accessibility. These forced the present situation in which man cannot simply migrate locally or apply technology to effectively modify resource utilization. He must also recognize the ecosystem limitations for large regions and recognize that he must adjust his demands when his cultural adaptations do not sufficiently protect the ecosystem components. If he does not adjust to the ecosystem requirements, he faces the very real possibility that the carrying capacity of ecosystem Earth may catastrophically limit population and/or quality of life.

Against this background, we will trace species man as he developed new sets of relationships with his encompassing ecosystems.

Man, the Natural Species. In man's first ecological stage, his impact on the ecosystem mechanics appears at a level consistent with the other species of his communities. Prior to development of cultural techniques that would allow him to systematically locate and increase control over food production, he occupied a natural ecological niche. He gathered existent plant supplies, employed rudimentary tools to kill animals, and extended his range of habitation to a minor degree by elemental protection devices. As a natural species augmented by minor tools he was a dominant species in local ecosystems, but his influence on environmental carrying capacities were similar to the effects of other species. His demands were elementary and primarily within the food cycle; functional specialization was minimal; there were no artificial demands on use of ecosystem elements. Population was controlled by natural processes; dense population centers were nonexistent. If environmental damage occurred in a locality, man's inability to modify the damage in the short term caused him to reduce his effect by immigrating, thus allowing natural repair to occur.

Man, the Farmer. The development of crop-culture and animal-culture by man allowed a dramatic change in his relationships within his ecosystem communities. Selective development of artificially-maintained species plus improved control over the ecological niches of competing animal species allowed man to dominate his communities. Ecosystem disruption was caused by cultivation, using artificial plant patterns that increased the utilization of local nutrient pools and caused erosion. Introduction of planned food production—whether crops or domesticated animals—led to increased localized population densities and allowed the support of a larger human population within a locale than had been possible. Rudimentary specialization appeared—huntsmen, farmers, tanners, clan chiefs—allowing improved utilization of labor resources and technological information.

His ecological niche was significantly enlarged. In his communities, man became dominant among competing species and, through technological adaptation, he extended his habitat significantly. Population, although still limited by many natural elements, depended less on occurrence of food since man could both produce and store foodstuffs. His capability to damage an ecosystem was expanded but, due to his low mobility and the limited extent of his artificial controls, damage in large land areas was minimized. A major new factor, however, was growth-causing increased area population and increased demands per capita. The increases in demand also involved increased demand of the products of specialized functions, such as pottery. This represented a dramatic innovation from demand for food and protection. This new element, in particular, blossomed in the next stage because the rise of per capita agricultural productivity, released portions of the population from subsistence employment. Man's unique ability to retain culture allowed development of, and demand for, "artificial" products and services not required as part of his natural functions.

Man, the Specialist. The ability to produce and store food surpluses increased stresses for man as well as the environment. As he acquired, stored, and consumed larger amounts of possessions, questions of shelter, trade and defense became more important. Permanent settlements began to appear, partially because of the realization that many of his production functions could best be undertaken collectively or by specialists in the community.

The growth of settlement from centers for the appropriation and distribution of food surpluses into more complex cities was hastened by a growth in social awareness. Permanent settlements provided an attractive medium for the free exchange of ideas. In an atmosphere conducive to innovation of products and division of labor, collaborative efforts extended the zones of settled life into areas beyond initial centers of agriculture. As newer farming techniques involving irrigation, plowing, and rotation came into being, previously "marginal" areas for habitation become more desirable.

Man, in pursuit of a new set of needs, improved his capability to control the natural conditions of his localities. He introduced higher productivity capabilities and introduced new processes well outside the natural food-chain processes. The new specialized functions often improved his natural defenses against predators and natural cyclical disasters.

While study shows damage to limiting factors of local ecosystems increasing over previous stages, the development of mobility and social mechanisms for goods redistribution expanded the reaches of applicable ecosystems. Hence, these initial social and economic practices continued tc develop under the assumption that the ecosystem had practically unlimited resources—system carrying capacity was of no practical concern. It is interesting to note that this period also gave orders-of-magnitude increase to artifacts of manufacture that were not naturally recycled.

Man, the Technologist. The development of energy converters together with the blossoming cultural innovations that initiated the industrial revolution drove man, as a manipulator of his environment, to a significantly different niche within continental ecosystems. The social and economic patterns became increasingly specialized; urban forms became more dense and more numerous. Productivity per capita in the highly developed countries drove goods consumption well above subsistence needs and toward desires for more and more specialized products. The entrepreneurial spirit and rapidly expanding capital and technological bases allowed a multiplicative increase in goods availability and distribution. It also produced the development of a social structure that would consume the ever-increasing diversity and levels of nonessential goods. Growth became the keyword to measure the goodness of man's social and economic systems—growth of population, growth of industrial output, and growth of material consumption.

Unfortunately, growth also occurred in other areas of human ecosystems. These include intensified population densities in local areas and in the total system, rapid use of densities in local areas and in the total system, rapid use of resources in processes that do not include appropriate decomposers, and increased byproduct effluents deposited into the environmental media. Man has achieved such dominance by his technology that he can modify nearly any ecological process for short-term gain.

The general laws of ecosystems remain inviolate, however, and the widespread occurrence of dense populations has forced reconsideration of the fact that the ecosystem resources and media are not unlimited. Many of the limiting factors of the regional ecosystems appear to have been reached in large localities. Some of these limiting factors can be adjusted by redistribution, but many (such as environmental media, elemental energy processes and land) cannot be relocated. The widespread signals of ecosystem damage under the imposed social value structure of highly developed nations leads us to reconsider the value of growth. Man the technologist has driven man the social organism to high demand levels and has provided biological protection that permits rapid population growth. But he has not devised a mechanism for guaranteeing continuation of his regional ecosystems as resilient, stable entities in which growing human populations can maintain a stable, dominant niche while increasing their resource usage demands.

Man, the Ecologist. As the ecosystems send out their first powerful signals of imminent damage to the environment's carrying capacity, the social structures of man are attempting to determine the levels of societal redesign that are needed to balance man's habits and demands within the regional ecosystem's processes and resources. A major element for redirection is the redefinition of acceptable growth patterns under the assumption that the species size and demands are approaching the ecosystem's renewal limits. Many new concepts, antithetical to the concepts of the industrial revolution period, are proposed—zero population growth, stewardship of goods and resources, alternative lifestyles, return to simpler forms of society.

But the new awareness and willingness to modify society's goals are not sufficient; there is a need for development of mechanisms for evaluating the costs and benefits to the ecosystems caused by alternate proposed solutions. A major question for any region is: What new social and economic technologies are necessary to maintain acceptable qualities of growth within stable ecosystem carrying capacities? A major corollary to that question is: For a given pattern of growth, what are appropriate quality of life demands to maintain man as a dominant, stabilizing element of regional and national ecosystems?

The Links between the Human System and the Ecosystem

The attributes of the natural ecosystems have been discussed in detail, including the concepts of carrying capacity, resilience, and stability. An essential ingredient in the vitality of the system is that the limiting factors to growth within the ecosystem are not overused. If overutilization occurs, the system suffers stress and undergoes change.

Readjustment of the ecosystem can be accomplished in several ways. In the simplest case, the stress is only temporary and a short period of adjustment will return all of the system characteristics to the previous equilibrium. A more severe trauma may cause some redesign of the system characteristics, resulting in a new state of equilibrium with some adjustment to the carrying capacity likely. The trauma can be, and in historical cases has been, enough to severely damage the system, causing a sudden degeneration to a very different ecosystem equilibrium that has much lower levels of carrying capacity—equivalent to the creation of a media-desert.

Man's present relationships to the natural ecosystems include the capability to completely dominate large regional systems. In doing this, he determines, at least for a short term, the level of consumption or utilization of the regional limiting factors. If man demands too high a use of any of these factors for too long a period, he may produce damage to the encompassing ecosystem—pollution of media, lower plant growth due to resource shortages, starvation, too many domesticated non-food animals. In each case, man and the other species of the regional community have passed the natural and technological capabilities to provide increased quantities of limiting factors of the human and natural ecosystems of the region.

The limiting factors for human ecosystems are akin to the resources that technology and agriculture transform into man's products. They are not limited, however, to the more classical definitions of resources applied in manufacture, but include all limiting factors of an ecosystem that can be affected by man. Thus, we must include as generalized resources the media of the ecosystem: air, water and land, labor, and capital, as well as crops, ores, and fuels.

In summary, the carrying capacity theme becomes much more complex when applied to the evolution of human activities. It seems clear that rather than defining carrying capacity as a certain level of population or some other point criterion, it must be defined in terms of a rather complicated function or set of functions, which would include a number of regional characteristics and economic parameters and would make explicit the possible trade-offs that are implicit in the definition. This requires a representation of the set of social trade-offs between the citizen's concept of environmental quality and the degree to which that society desires or needs to utilize the production and assimilation capabilities of the natural environment. In examining the critical interrelationships between human and economic activity, we must be concerned with a number of resource limits and environmental factors that may act as constraints or dampening forces in the dynamic interaction of population growth, related socioeconomic activity, resource base, and environment as an assimilator of waste. This simplified paradigm of carrying capacity is diagrammed in Figure 3-2.

If Figure 3-2 were a closed system, carrying capacity would be seen as the ability of a system to produce desired outputs (goods and services) from a given resource base while, at the same time, maintaining desired quality levels. For an open system, the definition would further have to allow for import of both resources and goods and services, and the export of output and residuals. The diagram yields four relationships that are relevant to the overall measurement of carrying capacity.

1. Resource-production functions: the capacity of available resources to sustain rates of resource use in producing the system output.
2. Resource-residuals functions: the capacity of the environmental media

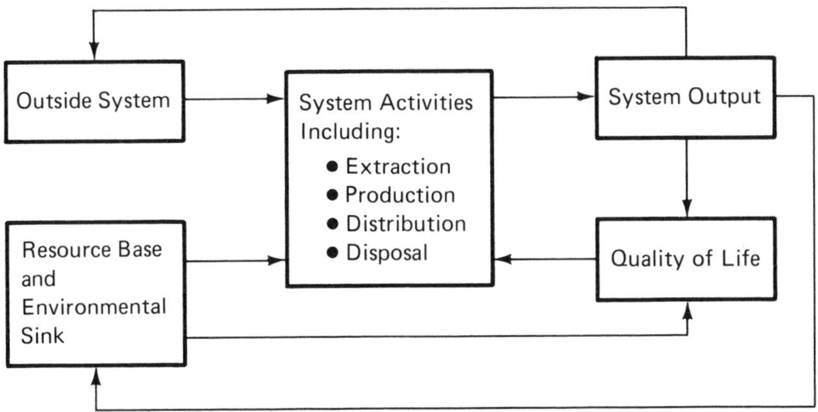

Figure 3-2. A Carrying Capacity Model.

to assimilate wastes and residuals from production and consumption certainties at acceptable quality levels.

3. Infrastructure-congestion functions: the capacity of infrastructure, the distribution and delivery systems, to handle the flow of goods and services and resources.
4. Production-societal functions: the capacity of both resources and production outputs to provide acceptable quality of life levels.

Working from these four relationships, then, human carrying capacity is defined as the level of human activity that a region can sustain at acceptable "quality of life" levels.

The high degree of interrelation among resources, environmental media, and desired quantity and quality states for human and associated socioeconomic activity underscores the fact that trade-offs must inevitably be made among desired production-consumption levels, resource uses, and a clean, healthy, and pleasant environment. From this perspective, carrying capacity must be interpreted as a variable socially determined within our understanding of economic, social, and environmental values and their relative contribution in maintaining quality of life levels. This dual perspective, required to give an operational meaning to the definition of carrying capacity, is presented in the flow diagram of Figure 3-3. The diagram illustrates that the working use of the carrying capacity definition requires a series of adjustments to reconcile the capacity limits related to quality levels of the natural environment and desired levels of consumption of goods and services by society. Each set of decisions is tested for the availability of resources as well as against the natural and social thresholds of an area. If they pass, the plans proceed to implementation. If not, new

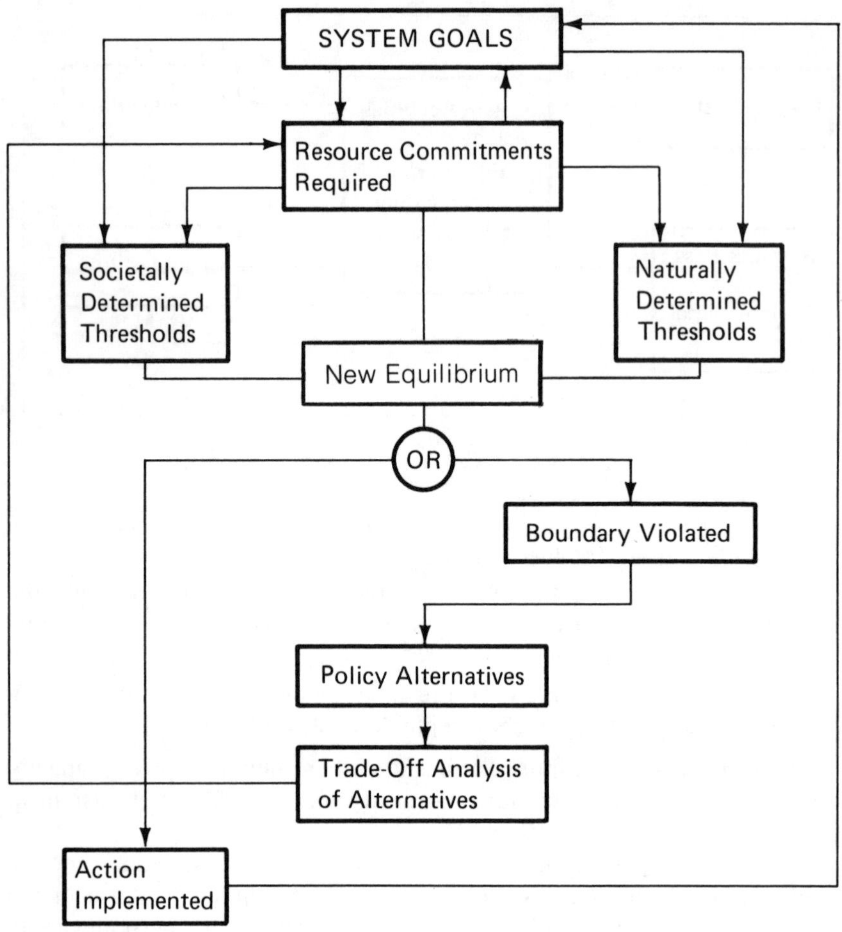

Figure 3-3. Flow Diagram of Carrying Capacity in Operation.

policies must be promulgated and tested. If passed, these policies may actually adjust the overall goals of the system.

Against this backdrop of general ecological theory as it relates to the concept of carrying capacity and maps onto the human component of the system, let us now turn to a discussion of the various nonenvironment relationships conceptualized in the SOS model.

4 Resources of the Human Ecosystem

The carrying capacity of an ecosystem is greatly influenced by the availability of resources and the manner in which they are utilized. Thus a key element in the State of the System (SOS) model is the treatment of resource availability or utilization. This section presents the concepts upon which the model's simulation of resource consumption is based.

To illustrate the danger of prophesizing with certainty, review this outlandishly bad guess of the past:[1]

> It will soon be sixty years since Gifford Pinchot published *The Fight for Conservation*, as informative and succinct a guide to the Conservation Movement's views and judgments as one can hope to find. With regard to resource adequacy, it presents a generally somber picture, supported by careful projections based on the idea that the volume of economic resources in the United States is defined by their identified physical occurrence. The lesson that only careful husbanding can stretch the supply is the logical sequel. Governor Pinchot summarizes the findings of approaching resource exhaustion as follows: The five indispensably essential materials in our civilization are wood, water, coal, iron, and agricultural products . . . We have timber for less than thirty years at the present rate of cutting. We have anthracite coal for but fifty years, and bituminous coal for less than 200. Our supplies of iron ore, mineral oil, and natural gas are being rapidly depleted, and many of the great fields are already exhausted.

Still one more prognosis, from a well-known analyst about a resource that is in the headlines today will underline the problems of forecasting. John von Neumann[2] in the article entitled, "Can We Survive Technology?" said:

> It is likely that we shall gradually develop procedures more naturally and effectively adjusted to the new source of energy, abandoning the conventional kinks and detours inherited from chemical-fuel processes. Consequently, a few decades hence energy may be free—just like the unmetered air—with coal and oil used mainly as raw materials for organic chemical synthesis, to which, as experience has shown, their properties are best suited.

Optimistic resource projections normally include a fair measure of improving technology expectations, a good world-trade picture, and an adaptive organizational structure. Even the optimistic writers admit the likelihood of short term dislocations and that some of these short term problems will cause overreaction by those affected. Two of the characteristics of the SOS model are the attempt to develop changes in availability through substitution of resources using combinations of similar resource types, and the consideration of the discovery and development of new areas of resource reserves based on the existent resource extraction prices. A third, less positive contribution is the model capability to overreact, in some cases driving the system to greater crises in other resources.

In summary, the availability of resources at any particular time is the result of the interactions among the physical occurrence of the resource and the size of man's requirements, and the economic means of extracting or producing it. Estimates of future availability of resources, therefore, require the assessment of:

The particular combination of economic and technological conditions that determine present production,

The level of production that would take place under different economic conditions where the resource unit price is increased by scarcity,

The level of production that could take place under different technological conditions, and

The nature and quantity of the total physically existent stock of resources.

Resource Definitions

Because the relationships between these physical, human, and economic variables are complex and vary with time and place, views concerning future supply need to be carefully expressed and set in a context such as the threefold availability hierarchy of *total stock, resource*, and producible *reserves*. These concepts are summarized below, taken from the work of Lovejoy and Homan,[3] substituting the term *total stock* for their use of *resource base*.

Total stock is the sum of all components of the environment that would be resources if they could be fully extracted from it. Assessment of the total stock is largely the concern of earth and life scientists, and the state of knowledge concerning it depends on the adequacy of prevailing theory, the state of exploration and survey technology and the extent of its application. Applied to resources that are conventionally referred to as nonrenewable resources, the total stock is finite and thus eventually exhaustible. Applied to renewable resources, the total stock consists of highly complex systems in a state of dynamic, delicately balanced, and only partially understood, equilibrium.

Resources comprise that proportion of the total stock that man can make available under technological and economic conditions different from those that prevail. The assumed state of technology will set the limits within which different economic and social variables [will] determine what proportion of the total stock can become available. Assessment of a resource [level] involves not only physical and biological scientists but applied and social scientists as well. They must make judgments: about the directions and rate of change of technological developments (e.g., gradual increase of efficiency of extraction of a mineral deposit or yield of a crop as against dramatic, order-of-magnitude, break-through changes); about the impact of changed economic conditions and new alignments in international relations; and about public attitudes on such varied matters as birth and population control, transportation preferences, and clean air. In essence the question is one of judging man's potential for creating resources out of the total stock; of selecting the chief agent of change from among technological, economic, or other societal forces; and of determining the relevant time and space dimensions.

Reserve refers to that proportion of a resource that is known with reasonable certainty to be available under prevailing technological, economic, and other societal conditions. This term embraces current extraction rates, yield, management practices, legal frameworks, and social attitudes. It is, therefore, the least speculative, shortest term, most place-specific, and smallest of the three types of estimates.

These three concepts form a framework in which each of the many estimates of resource availability may be seen in perspective. By supplying a rationale that accommodates what often appear to be starkly conflicting professional opinions, these concepts reduce the grounds for misunderstanding, overoptimism, or undue pessimism. Furthermore, they incorporate the notion of resources moving from one threshold of availability to another in response to changing values of variables under human control, allow estimates to be made based on physical or economic assumptions, and yet they permit retention of the essentially "physical world" character of the materials involved.

Grouping Resources for the Model

The State of the System model essentially follows the traditional definitions of resources used in manufacturing and services. Along with the traditional list of six resource groups, the model includes two resource-like groups to permit consideration of the level of damage caused to the environmental media of air and water. Thus, the model treats the eight resource groups:

Energy resources
Natural resources (durable ores)
Agricultural resources (food and fibers)
Land
Workers
Capital
Air
Water

The eight groups can be divided into the categories of nonrenewable resources—natural resources and energy sources—and renewable resources—agricultural goods, land, workers, capital, air and water quality. These two general categories and each of the eight resource groups are discussed separately below.

Nonrenewable Resources

The two groups whose primary reserves are usually ores represent a resource category that, when viewed in the long run and under pessimistic technological projections, can easily suggest a dismal future for the human ecosystem as these ores are exhausted. However, even if they are nonrenewable—which for neither minerals nor energy sources is totally true—several hedges exist for prolonging the resource and for reducing its role as a critical production resource—or as an ecosystem limiting factor.

Nonrenewable resources are treated in the SOS model using the following viewpoints:

- All resources are measured in terms of the total stock as defined above. Hence the maximum ore limit is not a function of economics, but is a much larger physical value inherent in the ecosystem.
- The total amount of world resources economically available at any time (the reserve) is finite and less than the total stock. The amount is a function of processed stock-on-hand supplies plus time delays for extracting, recycling, and distributing the ores that economically qualify as reserves under present processing costs.
- The total amount of resources available to a region has an upper limit based on considerations similar to those above plus the maximum import potential as reflected in existing ownership and trade arrangements.
- If a resource mixture that can substitute for a critical resource exists, or if a technological improvement in production reduces the requirement for a resource, the production sectors undergo significant time lag and capital expenditures as part of retooling. Because of the inertia in the processing changeover, these changes will be made only when a resource depletion warning is reached. This warning system of possible resource shortages acts as an alert to all production components simultaneously.

Energy. Since energy cannot be stockpiled in its processed form, the amount of energy produced for a given time is a function of demand. The selection of the specific sources of the energy that will be consumed are based on minimization of cost to produce an energy unit and the system propensity to maintain status quo of sources and processes. Therefore, the mix of energy sources used to meet the demand will remain relatively fixed unless a shortage in one or more fuels or conversion methods is imminent. Although signals for imminent shortages could be based on stock levels, it is considered that the better signalling device in energy (and in the other resources) is the current cost per processed unit. Note that most of the present energy crisis discussions in the United States have not been centered on the total stock level but on facility construction times and increasing costs to extract and distribute the fuel resources by methods that are acceptable to the population. Both of these factors are largely short run problems and only a portion of the picture.

When shortages are signalled, the SOS model will attempt to adapt by substituting one or more competing energy sources for the problem one(s). The new mix of energy sources must satisfy the constraint of lower mean unit cost—the equivalent of improved fuel reserve availability levels—to be an acceptable substitute. Additionally, the model will check to determine if the present sales price for the critical resource ore is sufficient to expand the amount of stock that can now be classified as reserve.

Substitute energy sources can take the form of substitution among currently used resources in new utilization mixes or of the use of a relatively new source that now becomes an economically feasible alternative. For example, two of the more popular new sources in today's discussions are solar and fusion energy. Both are currently under intensive study and the results, from the experimental and prototype uses, run the gamut from very hopeful to hopeless. In the technological areas, changes to the energy supply picture could come about by more efficient application of today's technology; from new sources and better extractive methods; and finally, from new types of applications.

The concepts developed here for increased reserve availability of a particular resource due to changes in the economics of extraction and of substitution of other resources are unique and, until further analysis, should be reviewed with some skepticism. For example, most of the better-known estimates of energy ore availability are highly price-related. This consideration results in different estimates of reserves based on assumptions of changing demand for goods and services coupled with further assumptions of institutional and technological change. The result of this perspective has been a consistent underreporting in absolute amount of resources available as reserves, and the concommitant crisis figures are often reported from a mapping of price-related reserves against historical population growth trends.

Similar anomalies are present in the consideration of substitution among energy sources. It is obvious that price alone will not determine substitution but that habit, legal constraints, media pressures, and the like might influence the time of change to occur either long before or after the time of substitution as dictated by economic indicators. Consequently, a model of the substitution processes will be quite complex in the final analysis. Of course, surrogates of energy usage in production processes are available from analysis of fuel changes in industrial, commercial, and residential uses as extrapolations over time, but such regressions should be viewed only as stopgap expedients fragile in terms of meaningful long run analysis. Due to the present set of crises for several fuel types, it is quite likely that significant departures from historical mixes of fuel sources will occur.

This outcome becomes even more likely when the side effects of energy ore mining and energy consumption on the environmental media are noted. There is a positive correlation between energy/capita utilization and the level of industrialization; thus, sincere trepidation concerning the likely effects of energy needs and of energy consumption rightfully exists. The SOS model considers all affected resources and uses a set of adjustment procedures similar to those being effected by the U.S. planning community.

Natural Resources. Natural resources, like energy, are normally viewed as a nonrenewable reserve category. As was the case for energy, there are several practical hedges in setting or expanding the actual stock reserve at any one time. For many resources, as the unit costs for extraction and distribution of ores increase significantly, new levels of stocks can be converted from the resource category to the reserve category—the economically feasible stockpile. Second, for many of the ores there is a high level of substitution of other resources in specific production processes. These substitutions can be caused by technological improvements or simply by a tradeoff of one ore for another similar material.

Another conservation device available for natural resources that was not available to any great degree for the current primary energy sources is the process of recycling ore from debris from processed and consumed industrial goods; a procedure similar to natural ecosystem decomposition procedures. This procedure, tempered by the mobility of the various component products in passing from ore to goods to debris, sets a natural ore reserve with a size that is once again variable by cost, here the relative cost of recycling to extraction. The comparative recycling costs to extractive costs will be assumed to determine the level of ore salvage from the human ecosystem debris at any time.

Summary: Nonrenewable Resources. In the discussion of energy and of natural ores several caveats must be applied to the definition of nonrenewable. For both energy and natural resources there exist mechanisms to extend the level of usable reserve beyond the static reserve levels of the resource. This does not imply that the production process allows total recapture of the resource ores after a time delay, but it does suggest that through mechanisms such as technological improvement in energy conversion and improved ore recycling procedures as extraction costs increase, the present resource horizons for nonrenewable resources may be unduly pessimistic. The SOS model includes three resource adjustments for ores: substitution among resources, expansion of economically available stocks, and resource recycling.

Renewable Resources

The remaining resource categories have their reserves limited at any time but are considered renewable because procedures to renew the resource presently exist and have been demonstrated. A major problem for many renewable resources is the necessity to expand the instantaneous reserve level consistent with the expansion of demand. Even where expansion is possible, system inertia often causes a several year delay in reserve expansion—e.g., creation of timber stocks.

Land. Within a given region the total amount of land does not significantly change. While it is possible to create some new acreage from surface water areas and to lose land due to erosion, the relative change in total land form is judged insignificant for consideration from the total stock perspective. However, these special land generation sources, when the new land's specific utilization or worth characteristics are viewed, may require consideration due to their high intrinsic value to the population in a highly developed locale.

The land resource can be subdivided by its set of expected usages. Six land usage categories might be considered:

Residential
Commercial
Industrial
Agricultural (including pastures and nonrecreational forests)
Recreational
Other (i.e. not falling into any of the above categories)

The distribution of the total resource reserve among the land categories can change based on the magnitude and priority of the demands in the various categories. Additionally, land utilization can be intensified by use of other resources in the production process (e.g. urbanization or greenhouse densities).

In terms of U.S. land use for developed areas (as opposed to agriculture, recreation, or other) the land resource is presently seen as limited only in ecological distance. Over the whole of the United States, about three percent of the total land area is devoted to developed uses; the percentage has not been increasing rapidly even in the face of historical major increases of population densities in and around our urban areas during the past thirty years. Additionally, the amount of land used for crop culture has remained relatively constant for many years. The problem of ecological distance (or accessibility) is handled in the model by considering the relative utility of the land reservoir around urban areas in terms of combination of aesthetic, topographical, and transformation costs. By this procedure, a capability to increase land availability in any use category exists and is constrained by two factors:

The present unit costs to transform and maintain land as compared to the present accepted land use earnings.

The total reserve of all land categories.

Thus the concept of substitution of similar resources for scarce materials exists for land—subject to payment of the costs of transformation and to reduction of the amount of reserves in the land use category from which the substitution is drawn.

Agricultural Resources. If we are to be concerned with the issues identified by others who have researched in the field of resource availability a great emphasis should be placed on the agricultural portion of the resource base—food and fibers. Because a nation must first meet the subsistence requirements of the population, the prime resource of major concern for a region is the availability of adequate food and shelter.

In America we have land in abundance but it is not of consistent quality. Differences in soil quality, climatology, topography, etc., affect the soil's natural capacity to yield food. These problems have not been critical since, added to the abundance of arable land in the United States, there is a huge technological superstructure that has produced startling agricultural productivity increases on marginally arable land while decreasing inputs of land and labor. However, it is by no means sure that this fortunate circumstance will continue as worldwide demands continue to grow and other land-use and environmental conservation constraints are met.

Production of food can be increased in the United States and many other areas by five principal methods:

New agricultural land

Enhanced productivity of presently cultivated land

Prevention of loss to pests

Technological innovation

Change in the economic base

Some projections suggest that the need both for additional acreage and for additional farm output per acre will occur in the next few decades, as the per capita food consumption rates continue to increase or stabilize and as the population grows. Furthermore, the amount of the limiting total stock base (the land) available for this use will be a function of relative prices among competing land uses. In fact, some of the most fertile land is presently under concrete.

There is a growing need for forest products, but conservation actions of the early twentieth century to assure the supply of timber has made this demand less critical in the short term. In essence, the future needs and production of food and fiber can probably be regulated through the price mechanism. However, the rapid escalation of today's market place food prices suggest that some painful supply dislocations in this area exist even now due to structural inertia in changing production levels.

The possibility of food from the sea is mentioned often as a major "crop-cultural" source in the future. The limit appears to be much lower than is popularly assumed. Large tonnages of fish catches or sea-cultured plants and animals do not appear to be available quickly or inexpensively. Further, it is not clear what heavy fishing will do to the carrying capacity of world's fish supply. This very important source of protein is under study in many nations where dependence on foods from the sea is greater than it is in the United States. Although the sea is certain to continue to play an important role in the world's protein supply, it is clear that, for the reasonable future, the harvest rates of sea-culture will not increase significantly.

Hence, the likely procedures for increasing resources now primarily obtained by agriculture are:

Expansion of cultivated arable land

Intensified yields/acre by increased use of other resources (use of chemicals with increased toxic runoff or large-scale greenhouse production of plants)

Substitution of manufactured materials and fibers for cellular materials and animal fibers

Thus a new set of mechanisms for increase of the annual production of the reserves of foods and fibers exist that are different than those noted for ores and energy. In the last two of the three procedures above the available resource stockpile expands not by increasing the existant extraction procedures or by general substitution of one similar resource for another, but instead by demanding a change in basic agricultural input/output procedures. To obtain this needed model capability one of the private industrial components that includes growth must be agriculture so that production changes can be explicitly made.

Labor. The fifth form of resource used in component production is labor, measured in work units. This resource is directly related to specific population age groups and partitions within the age groups. Like the resources of natural ores, energy, land, and agricultural output, the labor supply is considered to be a function of unit cost, in this case average salaries. Unlike the other four categories the supply does not simply increase proportionately with unit cost increases. Rather, it has an upper limit determined by population size; the proportion of this maximum stock that becomes the labor supply is assumed directly affected by the labor cost in production (salaries). While a time lag for increase of the reserve exists, the total stock (the adult population) can be reallocated more rapidly than most resources in a reserve status. However, after this reallocation is made it is assumed that little additional work unit reserve growth is possible except by immigration. However, immigration regulates work unit increases in approximate direct proportion to the total population and total goods demands growth; hence, work unit shortages in periods of high demand can become a systemic characteristic, requiring a significant capital resource requirement.

Capital. Man-made capital is another resource available to this culture as an intermediate step between raw materials and final consumption. As such it is a vital link in the transfer process and it responds to the same sort of pressures as the other renewable resources. Capital at any time has a definable reserve level, its increase has inertial drag to regulate its rate of expansion. As its value relative to other system resources increases, funds are expended and the rate of capital expansion produces a gain in the existent usable and renewable supply.

Air and Water Quality. As has been evidenced in some areas, urbanization and industrialization have caused massive increases in waste product density in the human ecosystem. A balanced natural ecosystem will produce no persistent waste; wastes will be, through natural processes, converted to the resources of other system processes. The technologies and densities of human-culture processes can result in unbalancing the system through overemphasis on certain processes with high generation of non-economic by-products or through the development of a set of products that cannot be naturally absorbed and converted to natural resources. When these imbalances are created, the production processes must be augmented by treatment facilities to reduce the by-products to useful resources of the ecosystem. If this is not done any of the several forms of pollution will occur. This pollution of air, water, or land may be sufficiently large as to reduce the carrying capacity of the ecosystem—thus affecting the ability of the system to accept growth, and perhaps resulting in permanent damage to the natural environment and the human carrying capacity.

Although the ecosystem media of air, surface water, and ground water (and to a more limited extent, land) are not, in the usual sense, resources absorbed in production processes and goods; they represent life-support resources that can act as ecosystem limiting factors. Our treatment of them will be similar to that of a capital maintenance function—the model requires restoration of that part of the media that is not cleansed by natural ecosystem processes and that is not of a quality that is demanded by the species of the natural and human ecosystems. These funds are allocated prior to use of operating funds for goods output.

Resource Functions

The following general rules can be associated with the SOS model simulation of all resources. (1) The available resources at any point in time can be associated with a unit procurement cost. This cost can be used in a number of model procedures concerned with the detection and the resolution of perceived resource crises. (2) At any period in time, the stockpile of a given resource in absolute terms is unknown. However, the quantities available as resource reserves for a given unit procurement cost are known and act as limitors on the regional goods production systems. (3) For any resource, the indication of a perceived resource crisis is associated with preset stock depletion warning signals. These signals are set when the present resource stocks no longer can produce a unit of the resource within the current unit procurement cost range. (4) The resources of ores, foods, fibers, energy, and land have resource strata within the general resource category. Within any strata the mix of associated resources used to make up a single unit of that resource strata is maintained without change unless a stock depletion signal occurs for a resource in that strata. (5) If a stock depletion signal for a resource or a strata occurs, a check of allowable substitutions is made to determine if another acceptable resource mix (generally called a substitution) can be made in production processes that generates a lower unit procurement cost. If this condition is met, the substitution process is initiated. (6) For any substitution process, increase in economic stockpiles, or change in input/output processes, the full change may require several time periods. The level of attainment achieved for each subsequent time period (cycle of model operation) is calculated and the appropriate level of mixed strategy is used in production processes for that period. (7) In addition to the expansion of a critical resource base by substitution, the availability of resource total stocks is checked to determine if the current unit procurement cost will cause a greater stockpile of the resource to be transferred to the reserve status. Such increments are carried out using a time delay function for activating the new reserve sources. (8) Expansion of the resources of land and labor are subject to additional constraints in that: (a) labor must maintain its total population partition structure and, (b) the total amount of land is constant; hence, expansion of one land or labor strata implies decreases in other strata. (9) The natural resources and subcategories of other resources can include expansion by recycling available ores. The rate of recycling is based on maintaining a minimum unit cost from the complementary sources of extraction and recycling. (10) In its present form, the original source of transportable resources (ores, energy, foods, and fibers) is not considered. The selection of stockpile levels and increments as a function of the price requires calibration to reflect the availability from sources both internal and external to the region.

5 Model Overview

Purpose and Applications

The State of the System (SOS) model is developed as a technique to analyze alternate approaches for melding the growth desires of a population with the limitations of the locale in which the populace exists. To treat this problem, the ecologist's concept of a regional carrying capacity has been used as the basis in building a mathematical model which will constrain growth demand desires to remain within the bounds of the locale's resources. To handle this growth versus limitations paradigm, the model has been designed to test various assumptions about the desired growth of an area under a set of side conditions (boundaries, constraints, or thresholds) that define the status of the region's limiting factors. Feasibility of designed growth is demonstrated if the growth can be achieved without violating these side conditions.

As examples of candidate side conditions, the model would translate higher level laws and regulations (federal and state, for example, if the model is of a local government), health thresholds, natural media limits, and the local desires into quantitative side conditions. For example an analysis could include values for a minimum level of subsistence per family, a maximum regional unemployment rate, the various environmental quality standards, housing and industrial-commercial codes, density levels, and minimum education levels. From these boundaries and the resources of the region that can act as limiting factors, analysis of feasible growth levels could be made.

Implementation of this model would result in the ability to test both the present growth trend and apparently desirable variations. Alternatively the relative impact rates of less desirable variants could be analyzed.

Such a model could be used to analyze at least three types of questions. First, it would be able to test the ability of proposed growth trends to produce the goods of the locale over time as defined by a comprehensive plan. As a tool within a second analysis form, it could allow the user to test the probable life of a system operating within the constraints on growth and to discover the most viable and critical linkages and constraints, given the resources of the locale and the constraints as set in the initial conditions. Finally, analyses similar to the two above could be run that use several different policy alternatives as starting points or adjustment mechanisms. Such analyses would determine the relative utility of each alternative.

Structure

The State of the System model includes four major structural elements.

Sectors of Growth

These consist of three components: the population, measured in terms of physical needs—i.e., consumer demand levels; the private production sector; and the public services sector. The form of population demands has two elements, population size and changing per capita demand levels. The two latter components are each measured in terms of annual change in level of expenditures for maintenance and production funds. The private production sector and the public services sector, each can be subdivided into component categories (e.g., heavy industry production or educational services), with each category being an independent growth component of the region, while the population is divided into age cohorts and then is partitioned into special demand and resource groupings in response to the levels of output being produced by the components of the private and public sectors.

Production Component Output

This system element refers to the outputs by regional economic and government production systems during the period of goods and services that are available for regional consumption. Import and export levels are also accounted for within these outputs as caused by the regional demands for component outputs.

System Limiting Factors

These are of two major forms: the input limitors made up of resource availability and of ecosystem support-media treatment requirements to maintain quality, and the societal constraints representing present demand levels placed upon private and public sector output to maintain an acceptable (or desired) level and quality of life for the present population size.

Long Term Goals of the Society

These comprise, at a minimum, the lowest values of level and quality of life measures that the society will accept as steady-state demand levels. From this minimal statement of society goals, increased planning mechanisms and more specific demands of the society can be introduced into the model by having the demand constraints become increasingly defined and restrictive up to and including exact and comprehensive regional production plans (the long term equivalent of a planned-economy multi-year production plan).

The interaction of these four model elements is illustrated in Figure 5-1: the state of the system at any point in time includes the results of the growth projections and the estimate of output of the regional production components. After this description is established, an analysis of limiting factors on the production output is made, determining apparent shortages in resource availability or deficient quality of ecosystem media. The model also determines short run failures of the system output in meeting level and quality of life demands of the system population.

The failures and shortages of the system put into operation a set of regional subsystem adjustments to achieve short term and long term adjustments within the system. These adjustments are then compared to the long term societal goals to determine if those production and resource availability adjustments appear sufficient to allow attainment of long term goals or, alternatively, to determine the extent to which the regional population must relax its demand levels. The forms of adjustments are discussed later in this section.

For those conversant with modeling techniques, the model can be described as one where side conditions are set by the user analyst and within these bounds the model is driven by goals of public and private growth. The side conditions can be visualized as a membrane defined by the limiting factors set by the ecosystem's ability to support the needs of the population. In this case, the model groups as the limiting factors, natural resources and demands for maintenance of life style. If a side condition is not met this will stretch or rupture the membrane (violate a parameter threshold in the set of minimum limits). When and if such a stress or rupture occurs, the model feedback controls attempt to correct the regional stress in ensuing time periods by introducing policies that would bring the demand trend back within the membrane or would relocate the membrane by modifying the limiting factors.

Assumptions and Simplifications

Since the model is expected to be operated as a regional model—where the region is national or subnational—the system does not have a high degree of closure. Hence the model must account for trade arrangements and other exogenous forces. At this point of the model development some of these

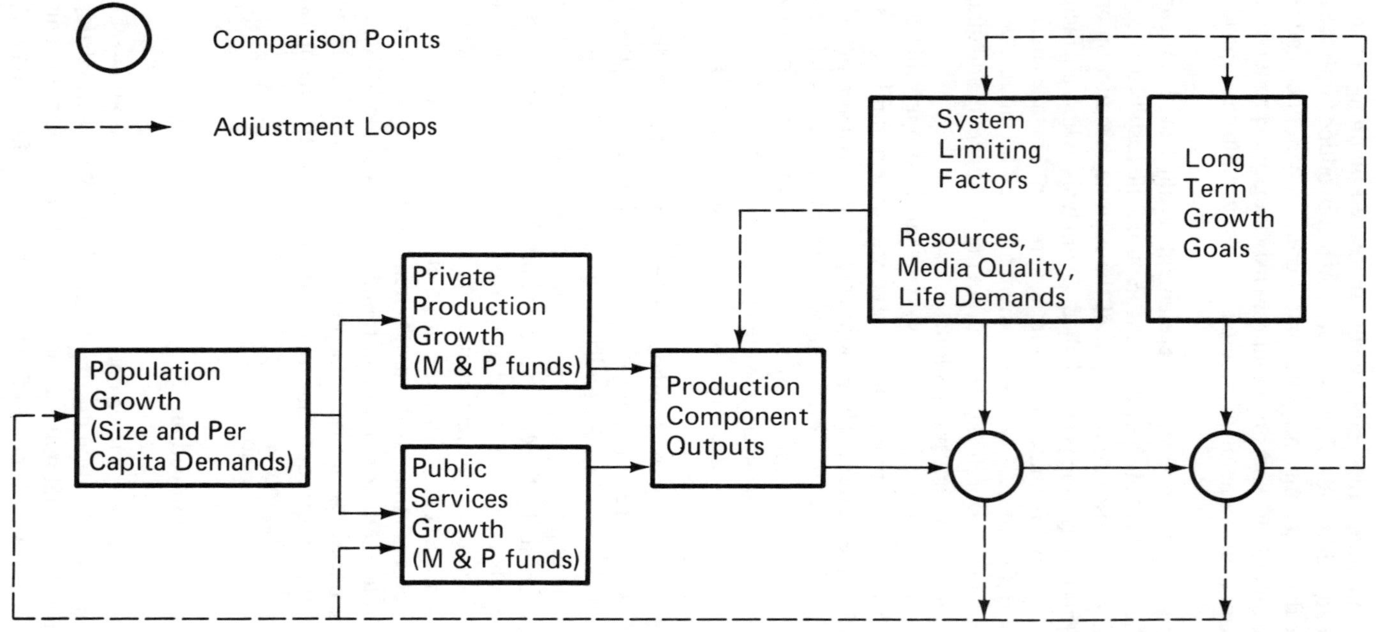

Figure 5-1. Conceptual Form of the State of the System Model.

questions are neglected. They will be considered in appropriate detail in the model formulation and data base discussions later in this volume.

Also, since the model is presently in a prototypical form, a number of difficulties in measurement of variables, primarily in determination of the dominant measures of quality of life and in selection of surrogate system limiting factors, are only briefly analyzed. These require in-depth analyses and are relegated to other research efforts.

The present model does not treat spatial dimensions. Rather, it uses the spatial hypotheses of human ecology as summarized by Quinn.[1] These have been further reduced to four general hypotheses.

Hypothesis of Minimum Costs

The hypothesis of minimum costs may be formulated as follows: Ecological units tend to distribute themselves throughout an area so that the total costs of gaining maximum satisfaction in adjusting population to environment (including other men) are reduced to the minimum. Or, stated in another way, ecological units tend to distribute themselves throughout an area so that costs are constant, the total net satisfactions that result from the adjustments of the population to environment (including other men) are raised to the maximum.

Hypothesis of Minimum Ecological Distance

The hypothesis of minimum ecological distance is a corollary of the hypothesis of minimum costs. It refers only to the costs involved in transporting men and materials from place to place, and it assumes that the economic costs of extraction, manufacture, and selling, as well as social and cultural influences, are held constant over the region.

This hypothesis may be stated as follows: If other factors are constant within an area, ecological units tend to distribute themselves throughout it so that the total ecological distance traversed in adjusting to limited environmental factors, including other ecological and social units, is reduced to the minimum.

Hypothesis of Median Location

The hypothesis of median location refers to the spatial location of an ecological unit within a functionally organized area. The hypothesis rests on the logically demonstrable assertion that less total distance will be traversed by all units in reaching the median than would be traveled by them in reaching any other spatial location in the area. The hypothesis may be stated tentatively as follows: Within a free competitive system, social and aesthetic factors being equal, a mobile ecological unit tends to occupy a median location with respect to: (1) the environmental resources it utilizes, (2) the other units on which it depends, and (3) the other units that it serves.

Hypothesis of Intensiveness of Utilization

Within an area, various types of ecological units may compete with one another for a given location. Several ecological units may find their respective medians located at the same place. Except for competition with others, each of these units could locate most advantageously at this median place. Under such conditions of competition, that ecological unit tends to occupy the common median which it can utilize most intensively.

Intensiveness of utilization may depend either on the direct utilization of resources located at the site under consideration, or on a special application of the hypothesis of median location or both.

Quinn recognizes some of the more obvious limitations on these laws. In general they can be paraphrased by stating that man generally acts predictably, but in specific places and at certain unexplained times, he violates this pattern. The reasons for the deviation include tradition, local culture, prejudice, and accidents of time.

Alternate Systemic Descriptors and Adjustment Loops

The dynamics of the model structure outlined earlier are expanded on in Figure 5-2. This figure emphasizes the cyclic descriptors of the system that are routinely modified, either by cyclical growth (if there are no "problems"), or by ecosystem adjustment reflected in the problem feedback loops.

The descriptive element of each cycle projects the elements and relationships shown earlier in Figure 5-1. This step consists of:

1. Projecting growths of the population size and demands, and the levels of funds available for operating the private and public output sectors
2. Generating the expected levels of goods and services outputs for each component of the private and public sectors
3. Determining the status of resource depletion, quality of ecosystem media, and the level and quality of life measures

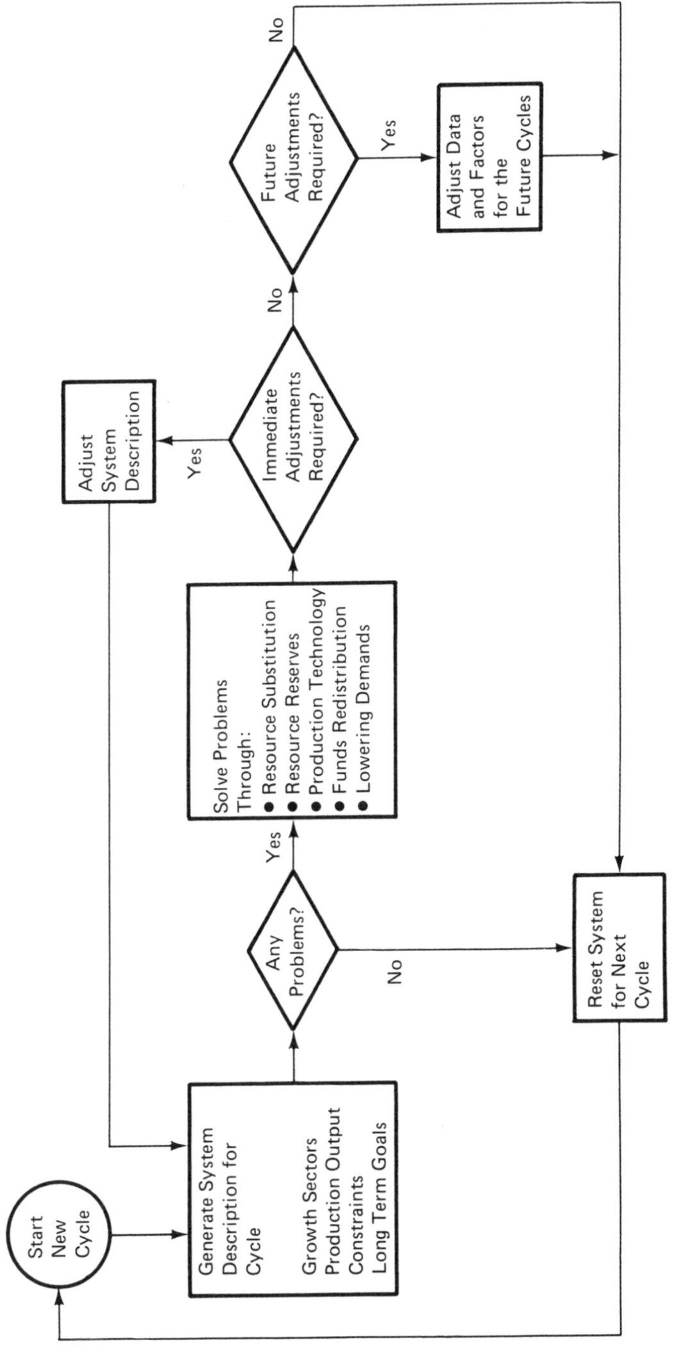

Figure 5-2. Model Procedural Flow.

This procedure describes the system status annually in terms of the regional carrying capacity—the ability of the regional output production to meet the demands of a growing (or stabilized) consumer population under the constraints and limitations of both availability of resources and maintenance of environmental quality.

If the status of the regional carrying capacity shows one or more demand measures indicating short term failure, the systemic element of the model is entered to determine if the system adjustment capabilities over the short term or the long term can relieve the failures, or, alternatively, can alter the population demands. This portion of the model can, but need not, be cognizant of regional planning processes. Hence, the adjustment forms can be of several types to reflect the intensiveness of regional management. Thus the model can consider fully planned societies that attempt to meet detailed preset comprehensive output plans, or, at the other extreme, laissez faire or natural systems that require only sufficient societal maintenance levels to reflect minimal regional life-support as growth and demand thresholds. Two regional processes will be discussed below as examples: these are the two processes most likely to be considered for applying SOS to analysis of regions of the United States as ecosystems.

The Comprehensive Planning Procedure

One useful environmental planning system is an extension of many past study efforts carried out as municipal and regional planning studies. This system is characterized by the specification of a comprehensive plan that reflects prediction of long term growth sector demands. From this an objective function is derived that is expected to be achievable. Included in the adjustment methods is a procedure that attempts to perform an overall system optimization that will maximize an objective function based on the information generated in the model operation up to that cycle.

The set of adjustments are put into operation primarily because of the status of resource stockpiles for the particular cycle. Resources are available at discrete points in time; thus some shortages may be localized or time dependent, not necessarily reflecting a permanent resource depletion but, perhaps, only inertial drag in the expansion of extraction methods as reacting to new growth demands. Thus, the management system can react to warning signals and "brownouts" by effecting adjustment over the short and/or the long run.

If the projected output of the system is maintained within the regional carrying capacity by simple adjustment of short run supply factors, no long term adjustment of system demand levels or of sector growth rates need be made. Otherwise, the projected growth rates and/or long term demand requirements will be adjusted based on maintenance of minimal degradation of the objective function. The system description procedures will then be repeated to determine if the new output projections are within the carrying capacity limits of the regional resource allocations and environmental requirements.

An operational model depicting the regional goals of a comprehensive plan as the operating system can be used to evaluate the value or practicality of the plan based on the type of analysis that is to be performed.

If the analysis is a capability study of the ecosystem without regard to a prescribed time limit, then an initial set of growth rates for the three growth sectors can be set. The model will then be operated to determine the timing and level of internal system adjustments that are made to the individual growth rates in order to maintain the system in a regenerative form, or alternatively, to extend the time frame of the ecosystem as a viable support system.

On the other hand, for a given time span and as a requirements study, the levels of the output required at that ending time can provide trend lines to indicate intermediate values to which the outputs generated each time period can be compared. This annual comparison determines which demand levels and growth rates must be adjusted and by how much in order to maintain the trend line. The model adjustment loops will attempt to recover to the trend lines as soon as possible or, if recovery is not feasible, to make the minimum degradation of trend goals.

The Operational System

A second representation of the regional system is closer to the ecological and economic management patterns observed in most U.S. regions today. This procedure suggests that, while there are many system thresholds that must be met, many of the growth and output adjustment choices are not developed in an "optimal" fashion, but reflect existent "policy" and other regional desires and initiatives after satisfying the natural system thresholds. The model then must first determine the area of acceptability of demands and output by interpreting a set of side conditions—resource constraints, demand thresholds, ecosystem minimums, output increase maximums, etc. Given that the outputs for a time frame occur within the area of acceptability and meet all demand thresholds, no further adjustment of outputs toward an optimal or growth-maximizing result is made, but, rather, output and input export patterns of the past periods are maintained.

This model description and adjustment form remains within our earlier definition of carrying capacity where the area of acceptability is equivalent to the range in which the ecosystem "remains healthy and productive." It also provides a definition of the level at which local desires and mores can prevail—any area-specific pattern is allowed as long as the end result is expected to be within the area of healthy productivity of the ecosystem.

If at any time, the projections for the ecosystem suggest that the full set of population demands is not met, then the ecosystem resilience is lost and adjustments must be made using the feedback adjustment schemes. These adjustments combine several of the items that are characteristic of the existing regional adjustment mechanisms:

- No overall optimization of the individual component production processes to meet total society goals under normal (healthy) conditions
- A capability in crisis situations to intensify and unify planning within the public-private processes to meet minimum demand standards
- An attempt by each component of growth and of output individually to adjust productivity not only to meet minimum standards (the society thresholds) but also to increase the resiliency and the stability of system by suboptimization of components in the total systems

It is worth noting that the second management process can be made to approach the first in the regional comprehensive plan by raising society minimum demand thresholds toward the realizable goals of the exacting comprehensive production plan.

Summary

In general terms the State of the System model, described in its most general conceptual form, will allow the user to iterate through time until it is projected that one or another of the system resources will be exhuasted or that costs of media treatment will become prohibitive. This means that the system can be conceived of as having several independent limits or thresholds, any of which will modify its further growth. As one, or all, of the system resources begins to be scarce and relatively expensive, there is a tendency first to skimp on maintenance to a given level and then to curtail affected growth. The indicators of public-private output levels compared to system demands begin to decline consistently. Unless drastic steps are taken to circumvent the seriousness of the shortage(s), the system may be in terminal decline.

A model of only this descriptive form, however, is of limited use to the policy maker who must make day to day decisions based on little information. Consequently, the State of the System model is seen to have a number of adjustment loops representing local and partial system reactions, permitting it to serve as a policy analysis device. In particular, a large set of resource adjustment capabilities exist to provide a reasonable representation of resource constraints by using economic decisions to effect adjustments.

One application of a model of this type is to test the operating or comprehensive plan of a specific region. The test is of the type which makes the assumption that the plan has represented the appropriate set of recommended changes within the data base, and that the region will make whatever adjustments are necessary to implement the plan. With this design in mind, the model iterates through time constrained by the desires of the local inhabitants. Whenever a specific value (or series of values) is out of phase with the desired plan, the model will adjust itself to refocus the subsequent iterations toward the end goal.

The questions addressed by the model then are whether the region has the capability of arriving at the desired goals of the population given the existing resource problems and the area-specific adjustment processes to manage the region's resources.

6 Model Formulation

General

This chapter examines the principal variables and functional relationships of the State of the System model. These present the general model structure and the type of data required for model operation, and thus will serve as a basis for subsequent research efforts. The relationships are presented in four groups paralleling the four model elements discussed in the preceeding chapter (see Figure 6-1). The groupings are:

System Inputs—These relationships are associated with the sectors of growth, specifying the total sector change. The inputs include total regional funds and allocation of expenditures to the private and public sector, plus the population size, age distribution, and quality of life demands.

System Outputs—These requirements translate the input to an overall demographic and economic description of the region for the year considered.

State of the System—These relationships are associated with the system limiting factors or demand constraints. They define resource availability and utilization, the quality of the environment, and the satisfaction of quality of life demands within the system.

System Adjustments—The last group of relationships are associated with the long term goals. They provide the necessary adjustments and feedbacks to reorient system outputs and demands when the state of the system is found to be incompatible with the ultimate goals.

Cycle Calculations and Adjustments

In essence, the dynamics of the SOS model can be visualized as follows (see Figure 6-2):

The particular system under study can be expected, on the basis of known patterns, to grow at a given rate. This growth includes changes in population and goods demand levels plus the funds used by the public and private sectors. During a cycle the desired growth rates project a produc-

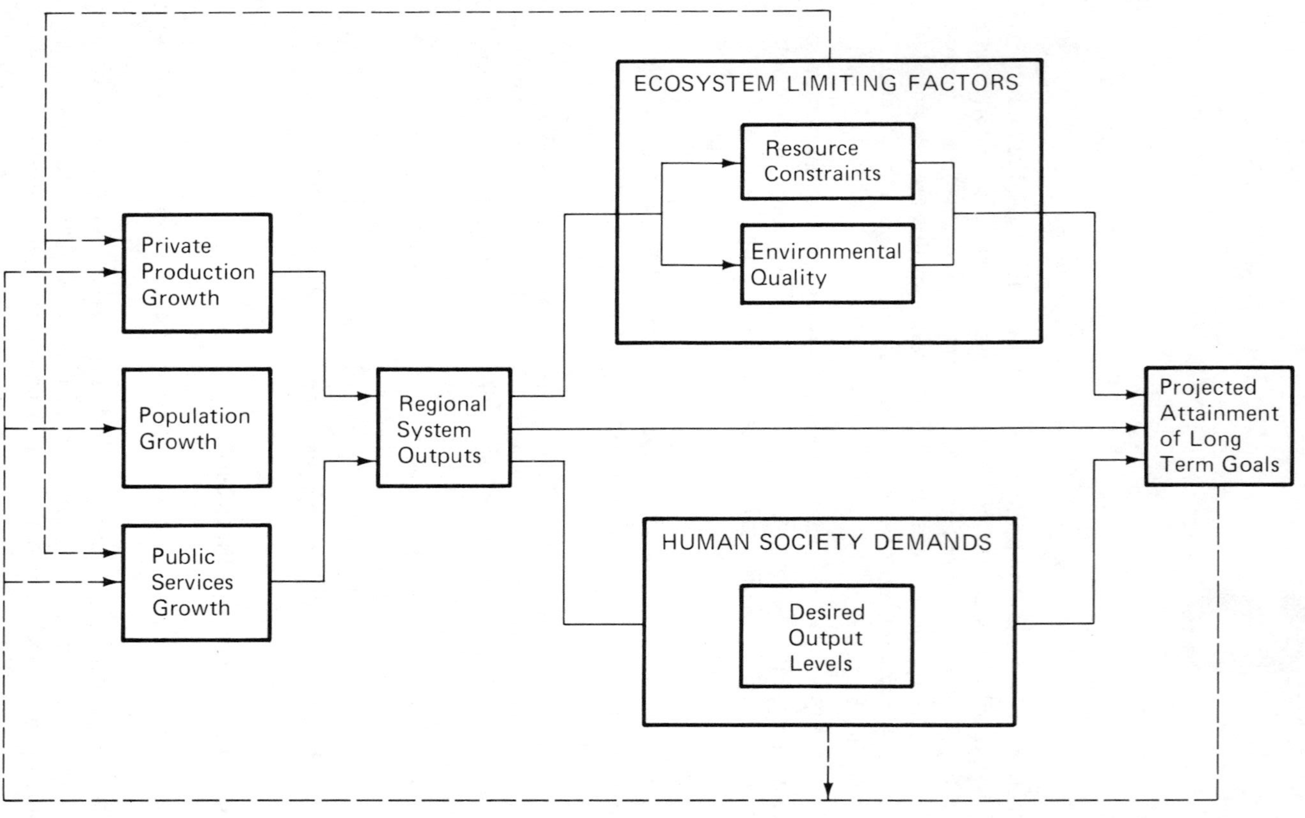

Figure 6-1. Elements of the Model.

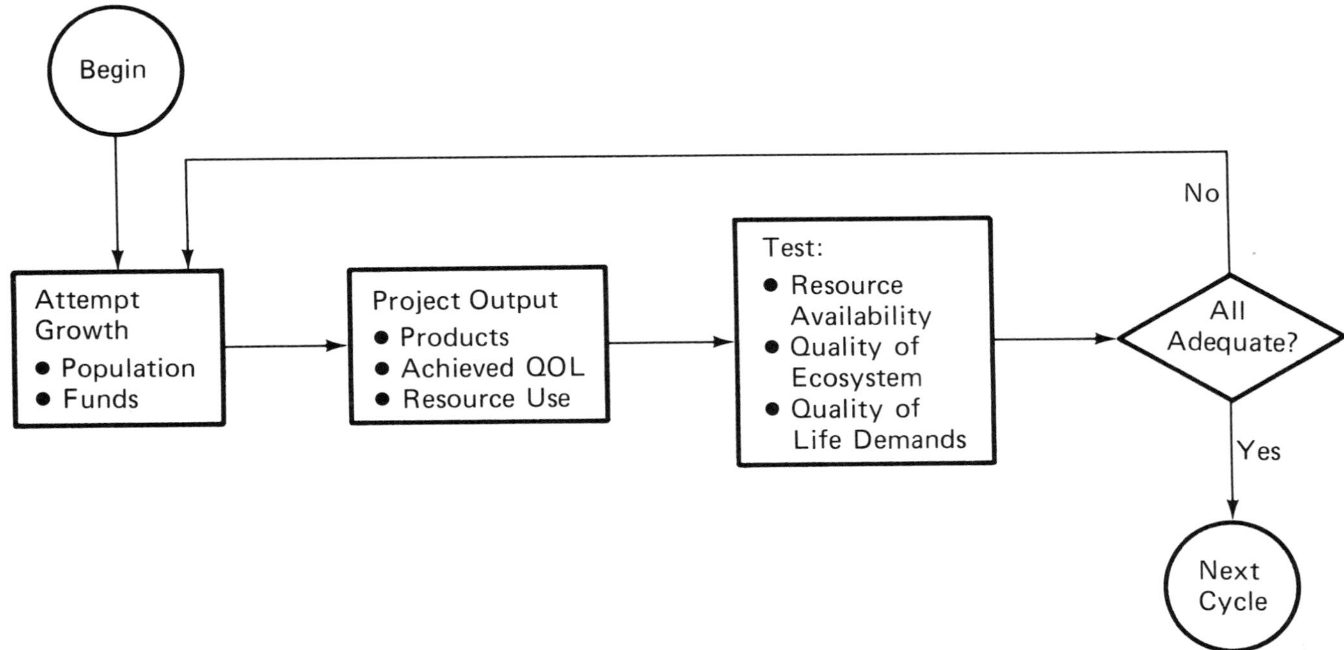

Figure 6-2. One Cycle of the Model.

tion output level. From this set of output levels a set of factors can be checked against the carrying capacity of the system. This carrying capacity can be seen to have two types of limits—those set by the desires of its local inhabitants for output (quality of life) and those set by the human ecosystem. The human desires tend to be of a short run nature and are changeable through time but they can not change instantaneously. The ecosystem limiting factor constraints are, of course, more enduring and consist of the availability of natural resources—energy, food, and the like—plus additional elements such as environmental quality. The model is so conceived that the amounts of resource reserves are set for discrete points in time (normally a yearly increment). Shortages can be due to circumstances that are localized and time dependent, but that do not necessarily reflect a permanent depletion of a resource. On the other hand, because the system reacts to shortages and "brownouts," such occurrences will be handled as system warnings, which may product short and long run adjustments of resource supply and utilization, substitutions for critical resources, and modification of demands for resources.

If the projected output of the system during a particular time period is within the limits set by its carrying capacity and meets the population demands then the model will continue to the next cycle. If the output demands are beyond the system capacity, the projected growth rates will be adjusted and the projections repeated until the projected output is within system limits. Throughout this process, the growth of the regional system is measured against the stated goals of the inhabitants—the quality of life demands.

The model can also respond to the whim of political pressure and public fancy. In addition to the "rational" feedbacks of the model itself, it responds to exogenous perturbation. This extrarational procedure reviews the areas of public expenditure (education, transportation, etc.) and checks to see whether each public area (1) has recently had an infusion of public funds, and (2) is an area where more funds would have a noticeable effect on the quality of life. The resultant output from the algorithm is a vector of weights for the public services components as an index of popularity.

System Inputs

Total Production Growth

The model takes its impetus for iteration from yearly growth rates. These rates are determined by forces endogenous and exogenous to the system. The closer the regional system is to closure, i.e., the more it represents a worldwide system rather than a regional one, the more the rate of change is endogenously determined. The efficacy with which the growth rates are changed by the feedback loops is the key to the success of the adjustment portions of the model. However, while the growth rates can change, the total input to the regional system cannot. The input to growth sectors other than population is in terms of funds available for conversion to real goods production plus the maintenance of the physical (developed and undeveloped) elements of the system. The total amount of funds available for a cycle includes two sources—the endogenous funds generated based on consumption of the past period production and capital expansion needs, and exogenous funds allocated on a nonhistorical trend, popularity basis. The exogenous funds could represent national to regional transfers and can be negative. The total funds for a region for any time are:

$$TFUND(t) = PRIVFD(t) + PUBLFD(t) + EXOGFD(t)$$

where $TFUND(t)$ is the total funds available for use by all production components in the public and private sectors for year t, $PRIVFD(t)$ is funds generated endogenously by the private sector activities for time t, $PUBLFD(t)$ is the funds generated endogenously for the public sector use, and $EXOGFD(t)$ is the net funds transferred to the region from outside sources through importation, subsidies, net taxation transfers, etc., plus the popularity vector contribution.

For either the private sector or the public sector, the basic funds for the cycle are equal to the funds generated by each component for the cycle based on its rate of growth. For example, in the private sector:

$$PRIVFD(t) = \sum_{c \text{ in } c'} XNVST(c, t-1) * (1 + RGJ(c, t-1))$$

where $XNVST(c, t-1)$ is the level of funds available to component c in the component's operation last cycle and c' is set of private components, and $RGJ(c, t-1)$ is the rate of funds growth attained by component c in the cycle. This rate of growth is described later in this section. It can undergo further modification in system adjustment processes, also described later.

The exogenous funds are made up of two elements, the net transferred funds balance and a cash transfer capability that is not wholly a function of the previous period. This second factor can be set to vary in a probabilistic range about an expected transfer value that is region-specific. For example, for the United States, the value could represent the outflow to other nations of funds with a range of variability consistent with the past trends of Congressional appropriations. As a second case, for a region of the United States receiving significant assistance within one of the public component areas, a mean transfer level modified by an annual stochastic variance might be applied.

$$EXOGFD(t) = \sum_{\text{all } c} NEXP(c, t-1) + f(RN, t) * TRNFD(t-1) * (1 + RGT)$$

where $NEXP(c, t-1) = [XEPORT(c, t-1) - XMPORT(c, t-1)] * [1 + RGJ(c, t-1)]$

$XEPORT(c, t-1)$ is the funds received for exports for component c in the last cycle

$XMPORT(c, t-1)$ is the funds paid out for imports of component c in the last cycle

$f(RN, t)$ is a weighted random function distribution of transfer fund variability

$TRNFD(t-1)$ is the level of funds transferred into the region last cycle

RGT is the mean rate of total funds growth for all components expected over the long term, and

finally:

$$RGJ(c, t) = [XNVST(c, t) - XNVST(c, t-1)]/XNVST(c, t-1)$$

This level of total available regional funds sets an upper constraint on inputs to the production sectors and components for the current cycle. The process of allocating funds to production components is done subject to the condition: the funds available to the components must equal to the total regional funds.

The allocation process has two major steps. First, an expected (or median) allocation of funds is made assuming the relative growth rates set and adjusted for each component in the past cycle. Thus, the general form of the growth of funds for a sector or a component can be represented as:

$$XNVST(c, t) = XNVST(c, t-1) * [1 + RGJ(c, t-1)] + EXOGFD(t) * f(CONPRF(c, t))$$

where $XNVST(c, t)$ is the funds for component c in year t and $f(CONPRF(c, t))$ is a function of the regional preference to add or delete funds from component c to adjust to exogenous funding levels in all components. The function is subject to the property that:

$$\sum_{c} f(CONPRF(c, t)) = 1$$

and includes components of

$f(CONPRF(c, t)) = f($Maintenance and expansion of capital plus preservation of quality of environmental media, and exogenous or endogenous preference to invest in component c for this $t)$

The fund allocation produced by the process above is described below, using the newly generated rates of fund growth for production components, *RGJ*(c, t). First, however, a static representation of the production sectors appears useful.

The Production Sectors

The sectors of regional growth, other than regional population and demands, are the production and services components of the private sector and the public sector. The dimension of growth for both of these sectors, and hence their input to the system, is the level of funds used annually by each component to procure and transform resources into capital and ecosystem maintenance[a] and sector production outputs (maintenance and production funds).

Due to the need to partition the sectors into more meaningful elements, both the private sector and the public sector are decomposed into components that represent natural regional subdivisions. For the private sector, production components are established—e.g., agricultural, mining, durable goods, nondurable goods, wholesale and retail trade, transportation and communications, and services. In the public sector and a·national region, typical service components could be education, public transport and communications, health and welfare, public safety, and administration. In SOS each of these components has related to it a rate of yearly funds growth as defined above.

For static representation of the production elements of the system, the funds expected are:

$$TFUND(t) = TEXPN(t) = EXPPUB(t) + EXPPRI(t)$$

All funds available to the region will be expended since overproduction is transformed into exports and increased stimuli to population demand. *EXPPUB*(t) is expenditures in the components of the public sector, and *EXPPRI*(t) is expenditures in the components of the private sector.

Further decomposition of the expenditures yields:

$$EXPPUB(t) = \sum_{c \text{ in } c''} EXPCOM(c, t)$$

$$EXPPRI(t) = \sum_{c \text{ in } c'} EXPCOM(c, t)$$

where *EXPCOM*(c, t) is the expenditures of component c, c' is the set of private components, and c'' is the set of public components.

[a] Capital maintenance here is expansion and maintenance of the facility and equipment of the production element.

Thus, for any time period, the funds available to the region are balanced by the production expenditures of there region.

$$TFUND(t) = \sum_c EXPCOM(c, t)$$

Expanding the consideration to annual increase or reduction of funds available to the components, for any component, the funds can be calculated from:

$$XNVST(c, t) = XNVST(c, t-1) * [1 + RGJ(c, t)]$$

where $RGJ(c, t)$ was defined earlier and represents the investment growth of new regional funds that come into (or out of) the area due to exogenous effects, and due to growth in regional components.

These rates are constructed such that:

$$TFUND(t) = \sum_c XNVST(c, t) = \sum_c XNVST(c, t-1) * [1 + RGJ(c, t)]$$

As implied in the above formulation, the model is visualized as being responsive to changes in many parameters of the public and private sectors. The model takes direct note of endogenous "rational" changes through the adjustment feedback mechanism discussed later in this section. In addition, the model can also reflect exogenous and endogenous economic and political pressures and public fancy to produce growth in the various components. Generally the latter will be reflected through the preference function within the growth rates.

Total Population

Demographers have noted that population levels and the composition of the population in terms of its basic characteristics do not change drastically in the short run. The growth of the population each year can best be described by the reasonably constant relationship between the birth and death rates plus the changes in the net migration rates. The migration rate is postulated to change in accordance with the basic desirability of a specific area. For SOS the area desirability is a function of employment opportunities and the prevailing level of attainment of the population demands.

The size of the regional population for any year t can be calculated by:

$$TPOP(t) = TPOP(t-1) * [1 + BRTH(t) - DETH(t) + ATTR(t) * NTMG]$$

where $TPOP(t)$ is the total population of the region for year t
$BRTH(t)$ is the birth rate for year t

$DETH(t)$ is the death rate for year t

$NTMG$ is the normal net immigration rate for the region

$ATTR(t)$ is the region attractiveness function for migration during year t, reflecting current system conditions

Population Characteristics

The demographic structure of the population is of interest in SOS for two reasons. First, the population is grouped into age cohorts. These age cohorts allow a representation of the resource of labor in terms of level and ability of the regional population to expand rapidly or to reduce the work-unit supply as a function of production sector demands for the labor resource. Secondly, the population age cohorts are further partitioned to determine the expected consumption rates of the population for types of output; the level of specific demands are affected by the size of the various partitions.

Typical partition characteristics include:

Length of immaturity/educational time
Mean rates of short term and long term infirmity
Ratio of educational units to work units in each age cohort
Death rates by age grouping
Size of work force, further partitioned as:
  Employed, paid workers
  Unemployed, paid workers
  Workers in unpaid status (housewives, volunteers)

The population characteristics are assumed to change directly with the production and services output levels of the private and public sectors. These changes are shifts of population elements from one partition to another, e.g., from unemployed to employed. This is reflected by:

$$RPOP(j, t) = CJ(j, t) * XJOT(c, t-1)$$

where $RPOP(j, t)$ is the "relative" (unnormalized) population of cohort partition j in year t, $XJOT(c, t-1)$ is the total output of production component c in year $t - 1$ in real goods, and $CJ(j, c)$ is the factor relating production output to population partitioning of a specific cohort.

To obtain actual population values, rather than relative values, the current total population must be used as a control total. Thus:

$$POP(j, t) = TPOP(j) * (RPOP(j, t)/ \sum_j RPOP(j, t))$$

where $POP(k, t)$ is the size of cohort population partition j in year t.

System Outputs

The major inputs used for setting system output are the expenditures by the various production components to produce the output. The input, i.e., the investments discussed earlier, includes not only production funds but also capital and environmental maintenance funds. Thus:

$$XNVST(c, t) = XNVOUT(c, t) + XMAIN(c, t)$$

where $XNVOUT(c, t)$ is the funds devoted to production output in year t, and $XMAIN(c, t)$ is the funds devoted to maintenance in year t. This yields:

$$XNVOUT(c, t) = XNVST(c, t) - XMAIN(c, t)$$

Maintenance is considered here to have three major elements and thus differs from the usual maintenance expressions that consider only offsetting plant and equipment depreciation. In addition to the capital depreciation offset, the model considers the ecosystem equivalent, the expenditure to restore the environmental media (water and air) to a "clean" state—i.e., the costs of effluent treatment; these ecomedia treatment costs are related to the component output level. The third maintenance element represents the annual expenditure of capital investment to increase the production facilities of the component. Thus:

$$\begin{aligned} XMAIN(c, t) = {} & XNVOUT(c, t) * [XMNORM(c, t) + XMPOLL(c, t)] \\ & + [XJOT(c, t) - XJOT(c, t-1)] * XMNCAP(c, t) \end{aligned}$$

where $XMNORM(c, t)$ is cost per unit of output at time t by component c to offset depreciation of capital equipment, $XMPOLL(c, t)$ is the cost per unit of output to restore environmental media damaged by production of component c goods, and $XMNCAP(c)$ is cost per added unit of output to expand capital facilities and equipment.

With the unit production cost $OCST(c, t)$ known, the last two equations can be combined to yield:

$$XNVOUT(c, t) = \frac{XNVST(c, t) + XJOT(c, t-1) * XMNCAP(c, t)}{1 + XMNORM(c, t) + XMPOLL(c, t) + XMNCAP(c, t)/OCST(c, t)}$$

It will be noted in the above expressions that the maintenance components are not constant over time. The depreciation offset costs may vary with time since these costs can be deferred to future times to allow needed short term increases in production funds. The effluent treatment costs vary over time based on the variation of overall media pollution quantities compared to the system's natural regeneration capacity.

Specifically, for this last consideration:

$$XMPOLL(c, t) = \sum_{m} KXMPOLL(c, m) * f(m, t)$$

where m is an index over the media types (e.g., air and water), $KXMPOLL(c, m)$ is the cost of totally treating the effluent of one output unit released into media m, and $f(m, t)$ is the fraction of the effluent to media m that must be treated in year t.

The fraction to be treated is determined by first calculating:

$$f'(m, t) = [POLL(m, t) - CLEAN(m)]/POLL(m, t)$$

where $POLL(m, t)$ is the overall pollution level expected if there were no natural regeneration treatment, and $CLEAN(m)$ is the level of pollution cleanable by natural processes. Then:

$$f(m, t) = \text{Max}[0, f'(m, t)]$$

State of the System

The major measures to describe the state of the system are the levels of available resources and the level and quality of life. Only resource levels will be discussed in detail here. Development of appropriate formulations for quality of life measures is a major part of the future effort for the model. The example model described in the next section illustrates one approach to QOL treatment as a set of scalar system demand measures.

Resource Utilization

In addition to the utilization of capital funds and volumes of ecomedia within the maintenance element of the expenditures, the outputs of the various growth components use resources in a production-transfer system that is postulated in the model as being directly related to the units of real goods output. Thus for any component, there is operating at any time one or more input/output functions which relate consumption of a combination of resource units to the production of one output unit for the component. For any of the production components, this resource utilization vector has as its components:

$$RU(r, c, t) = \sum_{n} RSIN(r, n, c) * FRTH(n, c, t)$$

where $RU(r, c, t)$ is the number of units of resource r used in year t to produce one output unit by component c; n is an index over a series of possible resource mixes (input/output functions) that can be used by production component c; $RSIN(r, n, c)$ is the number of units of resource r used to produce one output unit by component c, if the nth resource mix is employed; and $FRTH(n, c, t)$ is the fraction of component c that uses mix n in year t.

The use coefficients, *RSIN*, could also be treated as functions of time. This would allow consideration of the effects of technological developments and their staged implementation on resource usage levels as a function of breakthrough in research and development.

The cost for production of a unit of a production component can be developed as:

$$OCST(c, t) = \sum_{r} RUCST(r, t) * RU(r, c, t)$$

where $RUCST(r, t)$ is the cost to purchase one unit of resource r.

Given the output of a component in terms of expenditures, $XNVOUT(c, t)$, and the unit production cost, the output of a component in real goods is:

$$XJOT(c, t) = XNVOUT(c, t)/OCST(c, t)$$

The total usage of each resource can now be obtained from:

$$RESOR(r, t) = \sum_{c} XJOT(c, t) * RU(r, c, t)$$

Effect of Technology on Resource Utilization

A major consideration for this more general form of resource use is the determination of when, and at what cost, technology changes are allowed. The model as conceived admits as future facts that institutional and technological change occurs. To provide for an "idea whose time has come" requires an appropriate treatment of the timing and impetus for change.

The procedures included in the model for incorporation of technological change are driven by the cumulative expenditure of capital toward research and development. The model assumes that R&D expenditures for technological improvements in utilization of natural resources, energy resources, agricultural resources, and land density are made at a rate relative to the level a component expends to secure the resource. These R&D investments are cumulated for each resource category, and as the threshold of cumulated capital is passed that would cause a technological improvement, the production processes for all components are then adjusted to reflect the improvements due to technology.

Effect of Consumer Preference on Resource Utilization

A second reason for changes in the component production function is a more gradual trend over the time limits of the model. This is the shift in production output mix as demanded by the population to maintain a production level that is considered constant over time. Unlike the change due to technological improvement, this change in consumer education and preference for materials, and its resultant change in types of resources utilized, is considered to be continuous and reasonably linear over a model run of one or two generations. For longer periods of analysis more complex functional forms may be required.

Resource Availability

In general, new resource levels are determined by subtracting the total annual usage, *RESOR*, from reserves remaining from the previous year and then adding on the level of replenishment for renewable resources. A key feature of the model's consideration of such resources is that the "available" reserve level is the amount that can be extracted (or otherwise obtained) at a relatively fixed unit cost (see the earlier discussion of resources). Thus resource reserve levels can be increased by improved processing techniques or by accepting a higher unit cost, thus making more ores economically accessible. The latter process is discussed in the section on system adjustment that follows. Determination of resource availability levels for fixed unit costs are discussed below for each of the various resource categories.

Energy. At any given time, the total energy stock available to a region is the sum of the amounts of the various energy sources. At the present level of the model no distinction between energy utilization types (for example, stationary consumption vis-a-vis moving energy consumers) is made. However, by properly defining levels of substitution of fuel types in the data base, cognizance of consumer types can be made.

The total level is determined as:

$$TSTKE(t) = \sum_e STKE1(e, t) + \sum_f STKE2(f, t) + HISTKE - NEXPE(t)$$

where $TSTKE(t)$ is the total energy resource for the region in year t; $STKE1(e, t)$ is the amount of energy that is available for the region by the fuel type e, where the fuel source is a nonrenewable ore, e.g., a fossil fuel; $STKE2(f, t)$ is the amount of energy that is available for the region by the energy type that is renewable but limited in terms of annual recovery rate (These energy types include hydroelectric power, geothermal wells, etc.); $NEXPE(t)$ is the net export level of energy sources (processed or unprocessed) from the region; $HISTKE$ is additional energy available through a technological breakthrough, e.g., new energy source that requires minor depletion of other regional resources or eco-support media, e.g., magnetic power sources or solar conversion.

Natural Resources. Natural mineral resources, like energy, are normally viewed as a nonrenewable category. However, there are two important hedges in considering the actual stock reserve at any one time. First, for many of the ores, substitution of other resources within production processes is possible. These substitutions can be caused by technological improvement or simply by a tradeoff of one element for another similar material. This process is defined here to be substitution within resource strata, and the resources within the natural ores category are assumed to have several strata. Examples of strata include trace metals, structural metals, nonmetallic minerals, etc.

A second hedge available dealing with natural resources, but not available to any great degree in the most often used energy sources, is the ability to recycle debris from processed and consumed goods to substitute for virgin ore. This procedure, tempered by the mobility of the various component products in passing from the system status of ore to that of goods to that of debris, sets a resource reserve that is once again variable by cost, i.e., the recycling costs that will determine the level of ore salvage from the system debris.

The following equation is used to set the stock levels of each strata:

$$TSTKN(s, t) = \sum_{n \in s} [EXTR(n, t) + RECY(n, t) - NEXPN(n, t)]$$

where $TSTKN(s, t)$ is the level of natural resources in strata s for year t; $EXTR(n, t)$ is the amount of natural resource of type n extracted in the region; $RECY(n, t)$ is the amount of natural resource n salvaged in the region through recycling; and $NEXPN(t)$ is the net export of natural resource n from the region; and the summation is over all resources in strata s.

The mix of extraction to recycling is a function of the relative costs associated with preparation and distribution of each mode. This adjustment is assumed to be a continuous process of cost minimization.

Land. Within a given region the total amount of land does not change significantly. While it is possible to create some new acreage from surface water areas or to lose minor amounts of land due to erosion, the relative change in total land form is judged insignificant for consideration from the total land stock perspective.

The major considerations with respect to land availability is availability by land use type, and the potential conversion costs between land use types. Thus:

$$TSTKL(t) = \sum_{u} STKL(u, t) + RCLM(t)$$

where $TSTKL(t)$ is the total available stock of land; $STKL(u, t)$ is the stock of type u (e.g , residential, industrial, commercial, agricultural, recreational, and undeveloped); and $RCLM(t)$ is the land under reclamation.

Methods for expanding reserves of land use category are developed similar to those for other resource categories. The maximum potential for transformation at various cost levels is defined. If the potential land that can be transformed is added to the existent stock of land, the sum represents the total stock level for a given land use in a region at a given land cost. From these data a resource reserve generation procedure, as used in nonrenewable resources, is possible. In this procedure land use succession adjustments are activated for a given land use type as the unused land use reserve reaches a stock depletion warning level. At that time additional reserves for that land use are generated by a minimum cost algorithm. The major difference in the land category procedure from that of ores is that generation of new reserves in one land use category requires their removal from others.

To generate new land of a specific category requires developing a minimum cost transformation from all other land categories. Thus, the cost to produce one unit of land stock u is:

$$CSTL(u) = f(TCP, STKL(u'))$$

where T is a matrix of transformation costs by land use, C is a matrix of indices representing the amount of $STKL(u')$ that is as aesthetically acceptable as $STKL(u)$, and P is a matrix of indices representing the amount of $STKL(u')$ that is topographically consistent with conversion on use $STKL(u)$.

Application of this expression in a cost minimization routine will generate the amount and sources of new land of type u for a given cost.

The matrix of transformation costs T is simply a table of coefficients which relates, in the form of a square matrix, an index of the relative costs for transforming a unit of land to any of the defined land uses from any other. In general form, the coefficients employed on these cells can be subject to price and technological change. Taken in conjunction with the topographical and aesthetic matrices which modify availability to reflect physical, legal, and cultural constraints, the cost matrix defines the potential maximum for any particular land use in an area at a point in time for a given cost.

Agricultural Resources. Based on research in the field of resource availability and national needs, specific emphasis should be placed on the agricultural portion of the resource base. Availability of agricultural products to the regional system is given by:

$$TSTKA(t) = F(DRTL(u), STKL(u, t)) + IMPTA(t) + SEA(t)$$

where $TSTKA(t)$ is the total available agricultural resource u is the land use index representing agriculture use; $DRT(u)$ is the depreciation rate for land use type u; $IMPTA(t)$ is the net import level for agricultural products; $F(\ )$ is an agricultural production related to resource costs per agricultural land unit; and $SEA(t)$ is the amount of the resource obtained from the sea.

Capital. Capital is also an important renewable resource used as an intermediate step between raw materials and final consumption. This resource is measured by:

$$TSTKK(t) = \sum_k STKK(k, t-1) * (1 + MNTK(k, t) - DRTK(k)) + \sum_c (RDK(c, t) + INVK(c, t))$$

where $TSTKK(t)$ is the total capital stock in year t; $STKK(k, t-1)$ is the stock of capital type k for the previous year; $DRTK(k)$ is the depreciation rate of capital type k; $MNTK(k, t)$ is the maintenance rate of capital type k to offset decay; $RDK(c, t)$ is the capital investment in R&D by production component c; and $INVK(c, t)$ is the investment in capital goods by production component c.

Labor. Labor as a resource is measured in work units. The population partition representing paid workers determines at any time the instantaneous maximum labor supply level (the labor resource reserve). The labor cost unit is a function of the rate at which this level is utilized at that time—the full labor force employment rate. Additional labor units can be generated as a function of this rate by transferring, in later time periods, work units from the population partitions of in-training or in-unpaid-work partitions.

This resource is measured using:

$$TSTKW(t) = g(POP(j,t-1), EMPR(t-1))$$

where $TSTKW(t)$ is the total labor resource for year t; j is the population partition representing paid workers; $EMPR(t-1)$ is the previous year employment rate. $g(\ )$ is a function which adjusts work force size based on the full employment rate reference point.

Air. Unlike the case of other resources, the model is not concerned with the quantity of the air media. Rather, it is the pollution levels in the air that are of concern. This is determined from:

$$POLL(a, t) = POLL(a, t-1) * \left[\sum \frac{XJOT(c, t)}{XJOT(c, t-1)} - Ba * KLNA \right]$$

where $POLL(a, t)$ is the air pollution level, $KLNA$ is the percent of total expenditures devoted to perfect air clean up, and Ba is a pollution coefficient indicating the efficiency of cleanup.

This value is used in the ecosystem maintenance function discussed earlier under system outputs.

Water. Water, like air, is measured in terms of pollution generated. This level is expressed in a manner similar to the air formulation:

$$POLL(w, t) = POLL(w, t-1) * \left[\sum \frac{XJOT(c, t)}{XJOT(c, t-1)} - Bw * KLNW \right]$$

where the parameters are defined similar to their air pollution analogs.

Level and Quality of Life

The major elements of the state of the system are measured in terms of societal perceptions—a set of judgments dealing with various components of material output and quality of life. Our particular system must be area-specific, plus it must represent the planning system that would accomplish the adjustments of growth and output to achieve an acceptable quality of life. Hence, only a general formulation of the quality of life measures can be presented here. First, consider each of the two planning systems discussed earlier as they relate to selection of these state of the system indicators.

In the first alternative—achievement of the comprehensive plan goals—the procedure is reasonably straightforward. Each production goal by itself is a specific threshold to be realized. The relative importance assigned the production goals in the plan determines a set of weighting coefficients to determine priorities in establishing excess production tradeoffs, given that total achievement of goals cannot be accomplished. Thus, the only requirement in setting of goals is to restate the production component output goals in terms of parameters that measure population demands. These parameters will be primarily measures of real growth—

e.g., production component outputs as related to total system population growth, and sizes of specific population partitions.

The second alternative is the system that requires achievement of certain minimum values giving a marginally acceptable life state. It involves supplementary measures relating to the resiliency of the production system in remaining above these per capita demand minimums. Each of the collection of demand measures is a dissatisfaction threshold. The resiliency of the system measures ecosystem adjustment capability in terms of the relative demand satisfaction above the threshold for that demand.

Unlike the first system, where the measures are generated directly from the comprehensive goals, a set of measures must be selected in terms of the area-specific needs and desires of the society in the region. The general forms of these measures will be similar to those of the plan above with the exception that a minimum acceptable demand value rather than a maximum achievement goal is set.

Of greater difficulty for both systems is the setting of relative weights to combine the composite set of measures. This need not be accomplished as part of the SOS model, however. Instead an iterative process can be carried out which measures the state of the system as a set of criteria and then adjusts production fund levels among the production components until all thresholds are met or a suboptimized minimum miss distance is projected.

An extension of the procedure of setting thresholds of minimum acceptable values is to have the threshold values change based on population expectations. If for any period of time a value of a demand measure remains high compared to its threshold, experience suggests that the consumer changes his level of want to a level of need. This is equivalent to increasing the threshold to a new level of demand threshold representing society desires rather than a more basic set of subsistance needs. In a similar vein, if for a period of time a population must go without a level of goods or services that it desires, a reduction of the consumer preference is likely. To account for this phenomenon, the thresholds of each measure can be automatically set in the SOS model as a function of simulated historic output trends.

$$TMEAS(n, t) = f(MEASn(\tau); \quad \tau = 1, 2, \ldots, t-1)$$

where $TMEAS(n, t)$ is the threshold value of QOL measure n at t and $MEASn(\tau)$ is the achieved value of the measure at a previous time $\tau > t$.

System Adjustments

For any method of measuring the state of the system, if the present state is found unacceptable, a set of adjustments should be effected in SOS to allow future system states to become more acceptable. The adjustments are performed in the following order until the projected trends indicate acceptability:

(1) Short term adjustments: short term deferral of capital maintenance for each output component having a deficient output level

(2) Long term adjustments:

   (a) Changing input/output production functions to achieve the minimum cost mix for components having deficient output contributing to unacceptable values of demand satisfaction

   (b) Reallocating the total projected funds level within a sector to better balance projected growth rates and needed outputs of deficient production components (the adjustment of $RGJ(c, t-1)$)

   (c) Rescheduling the annual transfer of funds from one sector to the other where deficiencies exist and then repeating procedure (b) (This, of course, is used only if all components of one sector are not delinquent and hence can give up growth funds.)

   (d) Adjusting the rates and direction of net migration to reduce per capita consumption needs if significant unemployment exists in the region

If none of the long term adjustments produces a satisfactory correction of the projected state of the system, one final form of adjustment is made to permit the simulation to continue. In this situation the system goals (for the comprehensive plan analysis simulation) or the level of dissatisfaction thresholds (for the operating system alternative) are modified to lower levels. This will allow a possibility of maintaining the regional growth projections as a stable situation at the cost of a less acceptable level and quality of life.

Figure 6-3 illustrates the adjustment procedure.

Resource Base Adjustments

Finally, the resource base adjustments are melded into the general carrying capacity model. The diagram of the adjustment algorithm is illustrative (Figure 6-4).

The system reaching a natural limit to its carrying capacity may merely suggest a short run imbalance of the demand and supply of a specific resource. This imbalance can be corrected by changing the rate of extraction and distribution of the resource in question. If, on the other hand, the reaching of a depletion symptom at a particular point in time heralds the

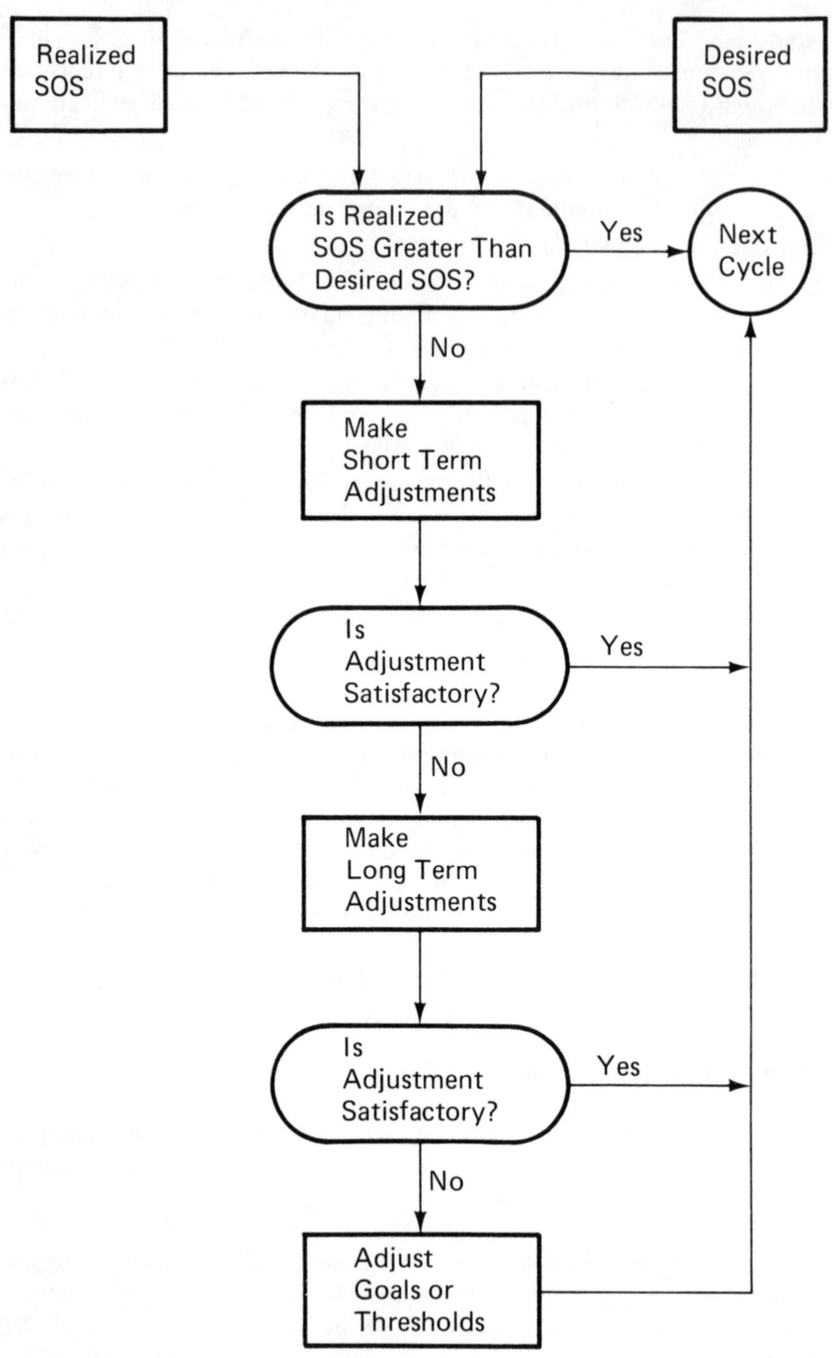

Figure 6-3. System Adjustment Procedure.

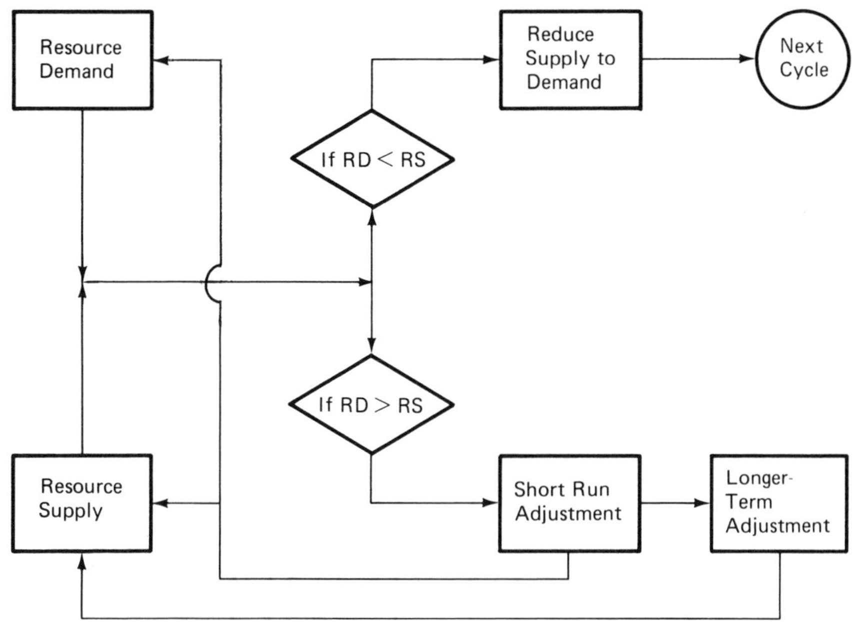

Figure 6-4. Resource Base Adjustment Process.

beginning of a serious shortage of a particular resource, there are several possible responses:

The rate of extraction could be increased, because increasing costs increase economically available reserves.

More supplies could be demanded from other regional systems at higher costs.

Adjustments may lower resource use by substituting a more available and lower cost resource mix.

7 The Basic Model (SOS-2)

The State of the System model offers a new capability to examine a national region, or subnational areas for large countries, as a human ecosystem. To represent an ecosystem, the model has a rather complete description of the present state of the regional carrying capacity plus feedback procedures for adjusting growth as a function of resource and ecomedia utilization, and area-specific societal value judgments and demands. Additionally, it allows for a stable adjustment of processes within the region to account for limitations of resources while maintaining viable historical trends.

Model Characteristics

As a first step in determining the utility of the general SOS model of chapter 6 the present operational form of the model, SOS-2, has been developed and programmed to have the following major characteristics.

- Three growth sectors are represented: the population of the region with its growth in terms of both size and per capita demands, seven production components of the private sector, and five services components of the public sector.
- Up to fifteen level and quality of life demand measures can be set. They must be of the form of satisfaction in terms of output production per capita for various combinations of output components.
- Up to twenty resources can serve as surrogates for representing the characteristics of the resource categories and two ecosystem media. It is not required that all categories be represented nor need any specific resource be included.
- Any number of substitution formulations for any resource can be set. These individual substitutions can include up to five resources. Since the resource for which the substitution is to be carried out can be included in the substitution set, partial substitution is possible. The substitution algorithm includes the setting of a time length (in years) to perform an activated substitution, thus allowing build-up of changeover impact and a capability of overreaction of adjustments.
- At least one, and in many cases, more than one input/output function to represent the mix of resources consumed in the production of each

component output can be set. One of these functions for each component is marked as active at the initiation of the simulation. Also, each production function has an associated time that is required for the sector to complete retooling for full application of the function. The resource assumptions are as given in the discussion of resources earlier, except that no R&D breakthrough is considered in the example model. These assumptions are listed at the end of chapter 4.

- The methods for measuring the state of the system and for adjusting operating funds levels between production components, substitution of resource allocation and utilization functions, and modification of society demands, are modeled on the second system form (laissez faire suboptimization) discussed earlier. This includes consideration of ecosystem concepts that include society demand thresholds and system resiliency, plus historical trend maintenance of the division of maintenance and production funds among the components given that the minimum demand thresholds are met.
- Model data characteristics for the simulation are operational for thirty annual cycles using data for a region similar to the United States with the beginning situation data similar to 1970 statistics.
- Since the model is expected to be operated as a regional model—where the region is national or subnational—the region does not require a high degree of closure. Elements that may be candidates for crossing system boundaries are resource imports, finished goods exports and imports, population migrants, and flow of investment funds. The model must account for each of these and must scale the level of the exogenous activity using model data. Thus the algorithms and data base can be varied to represent trade agreements, the state of the system in other regions, other region resource shortages, import and immigration quotas, etc.
- The present model structure is not at detailed levels of resolution but represents its various elements at aggregate levels. Many of the elements such as population demands and resource types are depicted by the use of indicators and surrogates. It is anticipated that later model versions will include critical elements and relationships as determined from empirical analysis of early model results. A major assumption in the model is the representation of many functions, such as the output coefficients that produce changes in consumer-need partitions, as linear or constant—when even the most cursory analysis refutes this assumption when the entire range of possible data values is considered. In this experimental model, general trends in expected ranges of data are to be explored and in these ranges, small compared to the total possible ranges, much of the empirical data suggests that the assigned forms of fit

are reasonable. A corollary to these assumptions is the set of assumptions that suggests constancy of many of the relationships over time. Once again the range of the practical analysis is limited by this assumption, but in the first applications of the model, using total simulation periods of about 30 to 50 years, the assumption provides an appropriate level of structural detail.

Model Structure

The model describes the state of the regional system and then processes required system adjustments on an annual basis. The general procedure is to operate on the existent data base and the state of the system descriptors as developed in the last cycle in order to, first, describe the system for the current cycle and, second, to affect needed short term (this year) and long term (affecting future years only) system adjustments. The general steps required in an SOS cycle are:

Descriptive Module

- Describe the population.
- Describe the availability of maintenance facilities, expansion and operating funds, resource utilization, output levels of the production components, and export/import levels.
- Describe the state of the system, in terms of:
  - Resource depletion levels
  - Quality of ecosystem media
  - Attainment of social demand goals (measures of level and quality of life)

Systemic Module

- Adjust critical resource usage by substitution of lower cost replacement resource mixes and, if appropriate, expansion of ore extraction and/or recycling facilities in subsequent cycles.
- Adjust short term procurement for additional goods by deferring maintenance funds that offset depreciation.
- Adjust long term M&P funds growth trends to meet projected demands for increased output of components and sectors.
- Adjust demand thresholds in future cycles to realizable levels.
- Reset the data base for the next annual cycle.

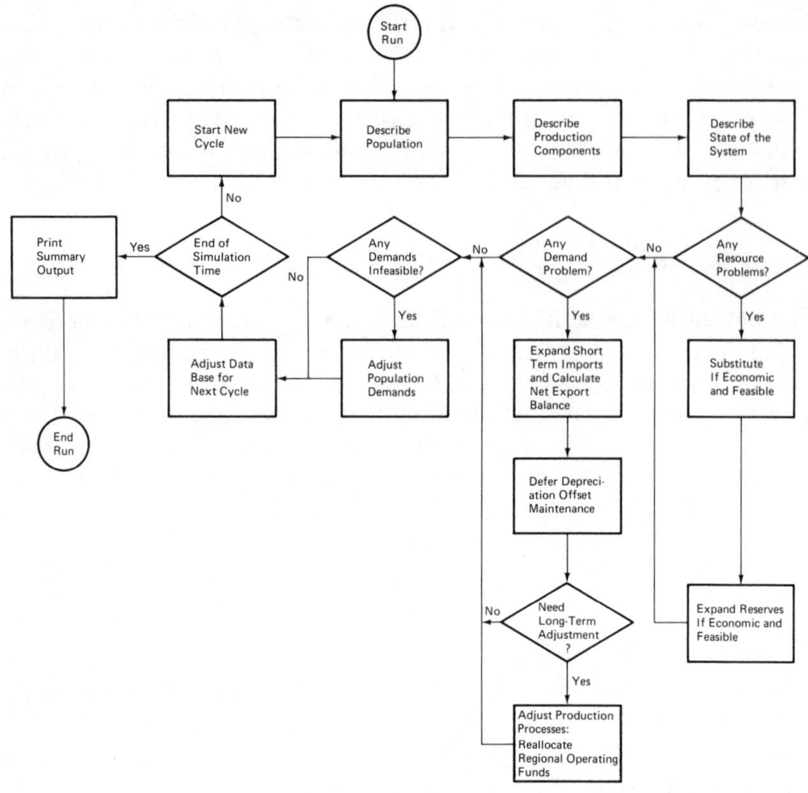

Figure 7-1. Example Model System Flowchart.

The logic flow through these eight steps is shown in Figure 7-1. Each step of the example model, SOS-2, is discussed in turn below. Additionally, the appendixes present detailed narrative flow charts of the steps of the model, and the detailed program listings.

The Descriptive Module of a Cycle

A full description of the regional human ecosystem for a year is developed by the first three steps of the model simulation. The data base used in development of this description has loaded the initial information. After the first cycle, nearly all data are modified as part of the last step operation to reset for the next cycle. The description of the system includes:

Population Growth

- Total population
- Total net immigration
- Population in each of four age cohorts
- Annual births
- Annual deaths by age cohort
- Annual net immigration by age cohort
- Cohort populations, each partitioned into six activity/consumption groups.

Public and Private Sector Components

- Expenditure of funds for generalized maintenance and production processes for each production component
- Output units produced by each component
- Unsatisfied regional demand for output units of each component
- Unit production costs for each component

State of the System

- Attainment of demand satisfaction for each measure
- Resilience level above threshold levels of demands
- Unsatisfied demand levels
- Resources in a reserve depletion warning status
- Treatment level required for ecosystem media

The detailed procedures for calculating each of these values and other parameters are discussed in the descriptions of model steps 1-3.

Step 1: Describe the Population

This first step of an SOS cycle compiles the full description of the human population of the region for the year of interest *t*. The general system flowchart for Step 1 is shown in Figure 7-2. All data requirements and their sources are listed in Table 7-1.

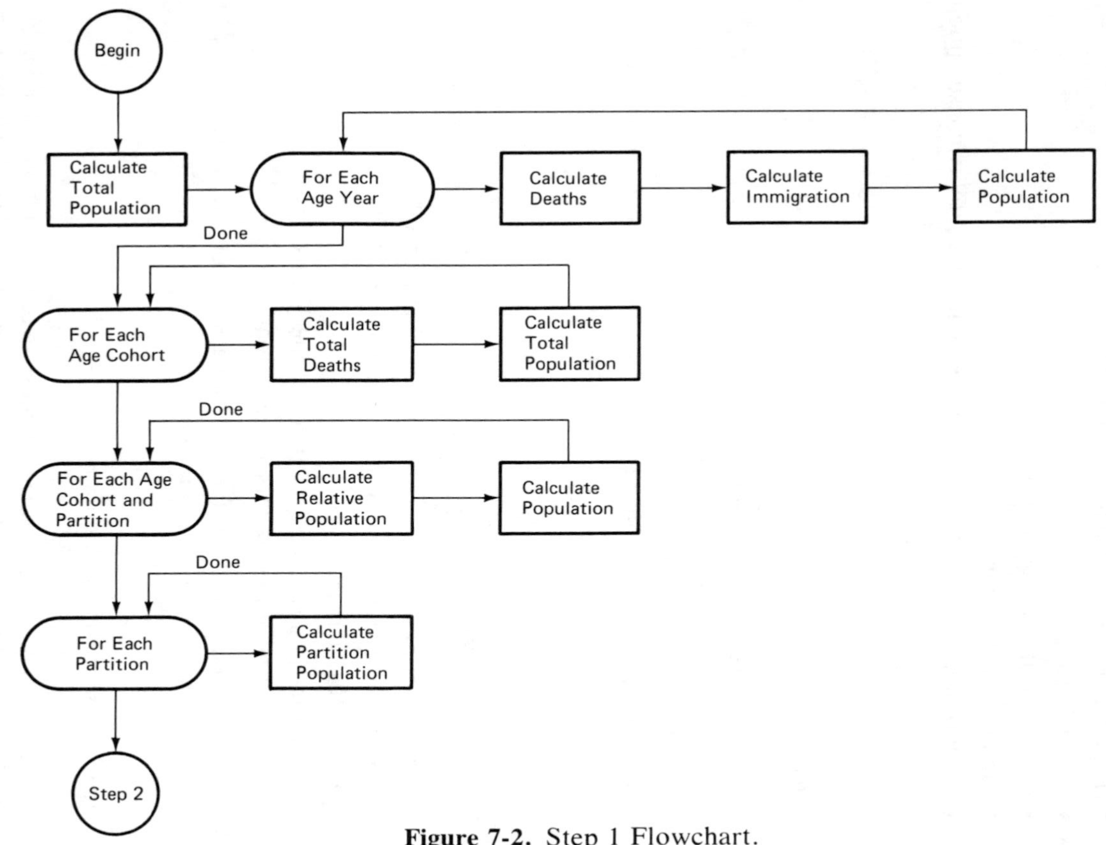

Figure 7-2. Step 1 Flowchart.

Table 7-1
Step 1 Parameters

Name	*Definition*	*Source*
TOPT(t)	Total population at year t	Calculated
TOPTM1(t)	Total population at year $t - 1$	Step 8 ($t-1$)
BR	Normal birth rate (births/1000 people)	Constant
FBR(t)	Birth rate modifier for year t due to demand satisfaction	Step 8 ($t-1$)
BRTHT(t)	Birth rate for year t (births/1000 people)	Calculated
DT	Normal death rate (deaths/1000)	Constant
FDT(t)	Death rate modifier for year t due to demand satisfaction	Step 8 ($t-1$)
DETHT(t)	Death rate for year t (deaths/1000)	Calculated
XMG	Normal immigration rate (immigration/1000)	Constant
FMG(t)	Net immigration modifier for year t due to demand satisfaction	Step 8 ($t-1$)
XNTMGT(t)	Net immigration rate for year t (immigrants/1000)	Calculated
TOTMIG(t)	Number of net immigrants in year t	Calculated
AGEPT(y, t)	Population in region of age y at t	Calculated
AGEPT1(y, t)	Population of age y in year $t - 1$	Step 1 ($t-1$)
AGRIT($\bar{y}$, t)	Population of age group $\bar{y}$ in year t	Calculated
PDTH(y)	Fraction of deaths that occur in age year y population	Constant
DTHPT(y, t)	Deaths that occur in age year y population in t	Calculated
DTHPTA($\bar{y}$, t)	Deaths that occur in age cohort $\bar{y}$ population in t	Calculated
DTHPTB(t)	Total deaths in year t	Calculated
CJK#(j, k, $\bar{y}$); # = 1, 2, 3, or 4	Coefficient of output j contribution to kth partition size for $\bar{y}$ age cohort	Constant
XJOT(j, $t-1$)	Units of production of component j last year	Step 2 ($t-1$)
C#($\bar{y}$, k, t)	Population of kth partition of age cohort $\bar{y}$ in t (unnormalized)	Calculated
XNOR($\bar{y}$, k, t)	Unnormalized population of age cohort $\bar{y}$ of kth partition in t calculated from C#($\bar{y}$, k, t)	Calculated
POPKT($\bar{y}$, k, t)	Normalized population of kth partition of age cohort $\bar{y}$ in t	Calculated
TOTKT(k, t)	Normalized population of partition k over all cohorts in t	Calculated
XPMG(y)	Fraction of immigrants that are of age-year y	Constant

Assumptions. The primary assumptions for developing the demographic data are:

(1) The distribution of death rates among age cohorts over time is assumed to be proportional to the relative population of the group. Hence,

throughout the period of simulation a constant death rate for an age cohort is set.

(2) Change in the size of the six consumption partitions of each age cohorts has been related directly only to the annual output levels of private and public components. While this indicates no explicit direct tie to the quality of life measures of the system capability to meet population demands as defined in Step 3, following, these are also related to the same component outputs, usually on a per capita basis. Thus, the reaction of population partition sizes do reflect the system reaction to level of attainment of quality of life demand thresholds since the reactions have the same independent variables.

Algorithms. The total population within the area for the current year t is last year's population plus its increases due to the birth rate and net migration rate minus the loss due to the annual death rate.

$$TOPT(t) = TOPTM1(t-1) * [1 + BRTHT(t) - DETHT(t) + XNTMGT(t)] \quad (7.1)$$

where
$$BRTHT(t) = BR * FBR(t)$$
$$DETHT(t) = DT * FDT(t)$$
$$XNTMGT(t) = XMG * FMG(t)$$

All normal rates can be adjusted due to the present capability of the system outputs to meet the population demands; these adjustments are performed in Step 8 of the previous cycle.

The next calculations develop for each age-year of the population, the total deaths and the age-year populations. An age-year represents, for $i = 1, 2, \ldots, 64$, all population at an age in the range $(i-1, i)$ and for $i = 65$, is the range ($i-1$, greatest age). The death population is:

$$DTHPT(1, t) = TOPTM1 * [1 + XNTMGT(t)] * BRTHT(t) * DETHT(t) \quad (7.2)$$

where
$$DETHT(t) = 0.0204 * FDT(t)$$
$$DTHPT(y, t) = AGEPT1(y, t-1) * PDTH(y) * 0.01 * FDT(t) \quad \text{for } y = 2, \ldots, 64$$
$$DTHPT(65, t) = (AGEPT1(64, t) + AGEPT1(65, t)) * PDTH(65) * 0.01 * FDT(t)$$

The living age-year population at t is:

$$AGEPT(1, t) = TOPTM1 * [1 + XNTMGT(t)] * BRTHT(t) - DTHPT(1) \quad (7.3)$$

$$AGEPT(y, t) = AGEPT1(y, t-1) - DTHPT(y, t) + TOTMIG(t) * XPMG(t-1) \text{ for } y = 2, \ldots, 64$$

$$AGEPT(65, t) = [AGEPT1(64, t-1) + AGEPT1(65, t-1)] - DTHPT(65, t) + TOTMIG(t) * XPMG(64)$$

For the model use in other procedures, most population data is in terms of four age-cohorts. The age cohorts $\bar{y}$ used in the SOS-2 model data base are:

Cohort $\bar{y}$	Range of age-years
1	1-17
2	18-24
3	25-64
4	> 64

The cohort annual death totals and living cohort populations are simply summations over the included age years.

$$DTHPTA(\bar{y}, t) = \sum_{y_1}^{y_2} DTHPT(y, t) \tag{7.4}$$

where $\bar{y} = [y_1, y_2]$

$$AGRIT(\bar{y}, t) = \sum_{y_1}^{y_2} AGEPT(y, t) \tag{7.5}$$

As a final set of calculations of Step 1 the cohort populations, $AGRIT(\bar{y}, t)$ are divided into six partitions. These partitions serve two roles in other steps of the model. First, the resource of work units of paid workers and the potential to expand the work unit size is represented by setting the numbers of population in each cohort that are workers-in-training, paid workers, and unpaid workers. Second, the six partitions can be used to represent differing demand levels for the public and private component outputs.

The changes in distribution of cohort population among the partitions are based on weighted linear combinations of the production component outputs of the past period. The relative (or unnormalized) distribution among the partitions within a cohort are:

$$XNOR(\bar{y}, k, t) = \sum_k \sum_j (CJK\#(j, k, \bar{y}) * XJOT(j, t-1)) \tag{7.6}$$

where k is the partition index, $k = 1, 2, \ldots, 6$, and j is the production component index.

The actual population of a partition in a cohort is:

$$POPKT(\bar{y}, k, t) = TOPT(t) * [XNOR(\bar{y}, k, t) / \sum_k XNOR(\bar{y}, k, t)] * AGRIT(\bar{y}, k, t) \quad (7.7)$$

Finally, the total population within a partition is the sum of the partition populations over all cohorts.

$$TOTKT(k, t) = \sum_y POPKT(\bar{y}, k, t) \quad (7.8)$$

Step 2: Describe the Production Components

The first calculations of Step 2 (see Figure 7-3 and Table 7-2) generate the new level of component funds available in the time period t, and then determine the level spent on the maintenance component with the residue available as the production funds. Note that the maintenance is the generalized form discussed in the general model formulation (chapter 6), and includes capital expansion funds, capital maintenance—both current and previously deferred—and ecosystem effluent treatment costs.

Available operating funds for component j are:

$$XNVST(j, t) = XNVST1(j, t-1) * [1 + RGJ(j, t)] + XMDUR(j, t) \quad j = 1, 2, \ldots, 12 \quad (7.9)$$

The second term on the right hand side represents funds used to purchase capital facilities and equipment by all components from component j. It is obtained from purchases scheduled in the past cycle $(t-1)$ for capital expansion and for pollution control, plus replacement of depreciated capital. The levels for the first two elements, $XMCAP(j, t-1)$ and $XMPOLL(j, t-1)$, are developed later in this section. The third element is developed to cover capital replacement purchases to offset this year's depreciation plus any deferred depreciation from last year. These funds levels for all production components are:

$$XNVCAP(t-1) = \sum_j XMCAP(j, t-1) \quad (7.10)$$

for capital expansion,

$$XNVPOL(t) = \sum_j XMPOLL(j, t-1) \quad (7.11)$$

for pollution control, and

$$XNVDUR(t) = \sum_j XMNDUR(j, t) \quad (7.12)$$

for capital maintenance.

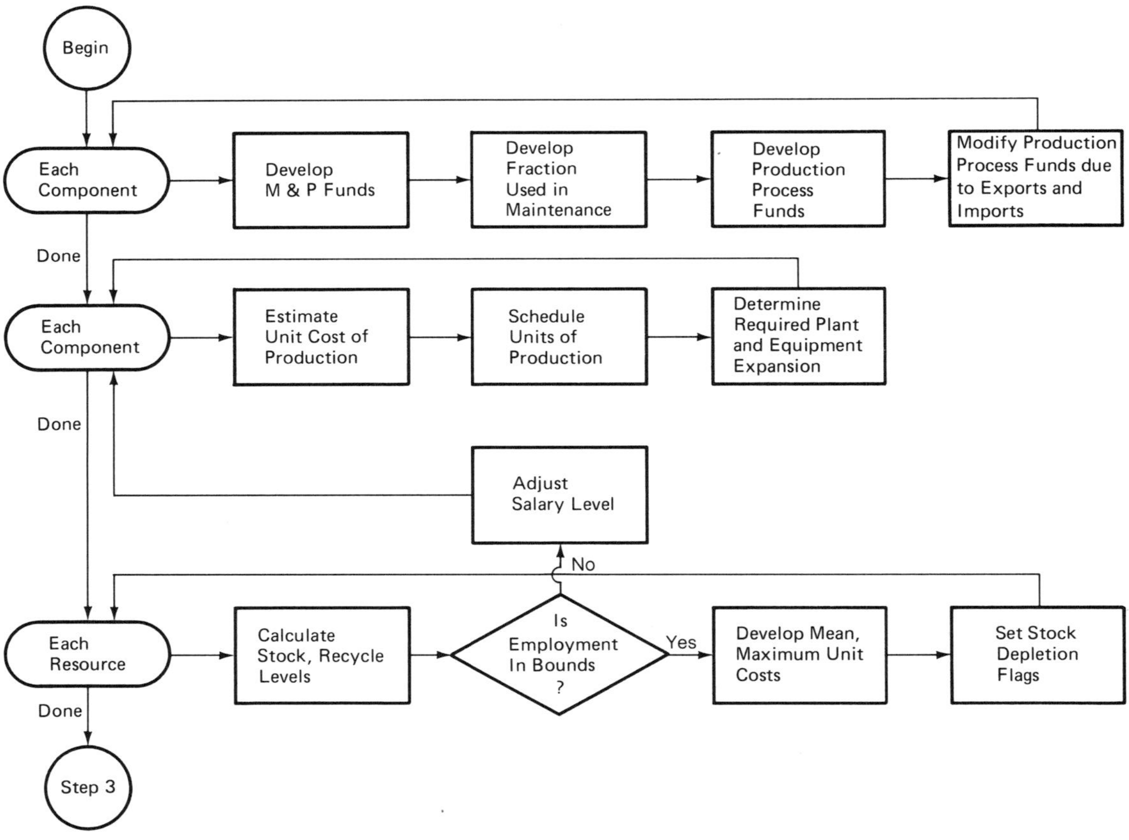

Figure 7-3. Step 2 General Flowchart.

Table 7-2
Step 2 Parameters

Name	*Definition*	*Source*
POPKT($\bar{y}$, k, t)	Normalized population of kth partition of age cohort y in t	Step 1
XMAINR(j, t)	Rate of funds used to maintain ecosystem media prorated for j at t	Step 8 ($t-1$)
QOLT(j)	Fraction of funds of production required to maintain ecosystem quality from damage caused by one unit of output of component j	Constant
XMDUR(j, t)	Funds credited to j for purchase of goods to maintain ecosystem plus used to expand production capital	Calculated
XNVST(j, t)	Funds available to component j at t	Calculated
XNVST1(j, $t-1$)	Funds available to last year	Step 2 ($t-1$)
RGJ(j, t)	Rate of personal consumption funds growth for j and t	Steps 5, 6 ($t-1$)
RATVST(j, t)	Fraction of funds used for capital investment, both for media protection and for component expansion	Calculated
XMNORM(j, t)	Rate of funds used for maintenance of j at t	Calculated
XMRNOR(j, t)	Normal rate used to maintain facilities of j	Constant
XIDFMN(j, $t-1$)	Amount of facility maintenance of j deferred last year	Step 5 ($t-1$)
XMANT(j, t)	Percentage of XNVST required to offset depreciation, maintain ecosystem media, plus increase capital expansion	Calculated
XNVOUT(j, t)	Funds to be used for production of j at t	Calculated
XMPORT(j, t)	Funds, in millions of dollars, required to be used from production funds to pay for imports of component j at t	Calculated
XEPORT(j, t)	Funds, paid for goods exported by component j at t	Calculated
XMPOLL(j, t)	Amount of funds required for component j to repair environmental damage at t	Step 2 ($t-1$)
SUMIUT(t)	Total of all production funds for t	Calculated
RUCST(r, t)	Mean resource unit cost for r at t	Calculated
RUCST1(r, $t-1$)	Mean resource unit cost for r last year	Step 2 ($t-1$)
RUCST2(r, $t-2$)	Mean resource unit cost for r in year $t-2$	Step 2 ($t-2$)
UTIL(r, j, t)	Required amount of resources to output one unit of j using current production formula(s) mix	Step 8 ($t-1$)
XFACT(j)	Unit cost normalizing factor for j	Step 2, Cycle 1
OCST(j, t)	Unit cost to produce output of component j at t (normalized)	Calculated
XJOT(j, t)	Number of units produced by j at t	Calculated
RESOR(r, t)	Units of resource r used by all j at t	Calculated
STDEP(r, t)	Fraction of resource r reserves expended at start of cycle t	Step 8 ($t-1$)
ESTCK(r, t)	Fraction of resource of r reserve expended at end of t	Calculated

Table 7-2 (cont.)

Name	*Definition*	*Source*
PILE(r, t)	Amount of total reserve available at unit cost for t prior to depletion	Step 8, Previous t
REREC(r, t)	Ratio of resource recycled to extracted at t	Calculated
FLG(k, r)	Depletion levels of existent stockpile on which warnings are set	Constant
FLAGR(r, t)	Existence of depletion warning this year for resource t	Calculated
XMCST(r, t)	Maximum unit cost of resource at t	Calculated
XMCST1(r, $t-1$)	Maximum unit cost of resource, last year	Calculated
ECST(r, t)	Mean unit cost of r at t	Calculated
XMCSTR(r, t)	Maximum unit procurement cost of r at t	Calculated
ECSTR(r, t)	Mean unit procurement cost of r at t	Calculated
VAL(r, t)	Value in units of economic reserves of r remaining at the end of t	Calculated
XMJOT(j, $t-1$)	Maximum output level of j prior to t	Step 2, Previous t
CAPVL(j)	Cost for capital facilities expansion of one output unit for j	Constant
XMCAP(j, t)	Total cost for capital facilities expansion for j	Calculated
CAPUSE(j, t)	Use of present j capacity, in percent, for t	Calculated
XNVCAP(t)	Total expenditures for capital expansion in t	Step 2 ($t-1$)
XNVPOL(t)	Total expenditures for pollution control in t	Step 2 ($t-1$)
XNVDUR(t)	Total expenditures to offset capital depreciation in t	Step 2 ($t-1$)
EXPDUR(j)	Fraction of XNVCAP to be spent on output from component j	Constant
ECODUR(j)	Fraction of XNVPOL to be spent on output from component j	Constant
EXPMNT(j)	Fraction of XNVDUR to be spend on output from component j	Constant
RESPR(r, t)	Total cost for units of r used at t	Step 2
RAMAT(t)	Total cost for units of all mined ores used at t	Step 2

The funds are used for purchases from each of the components based on the proportions, $EXPDUR(j)$, $ECODUR(j)$, and $EXPMNT(j)$, where:

$$\sum_j EXPDUR(j) = 1$$

$$\sum_j ECODUR(j) = 1$$

$$\sum_j EXPMNT(j) \leq 1$$

Then,

$$XMDUR(j, t) = XNVCAP(t-1) * EXPDUR(j) + XNVPOL(t) * ECODUR(j) + XNVDUR(t) * EXPMNT(j) \quad (7.13)$$

The funds used for maintenance of existing facilities are taken as a fraction of the total available finds and are the sum of the fraction needed to offset depreciation in the current year plus the fraction representing the amount of deferred maintenance from the past year.

$$XMNORM(j, t) = XMRNOR(j, t) + XIDFMN(j, t-1)/XNVST(j, t) \quad (7.14)$$

The total funds for all forms of "maintenance" as a fraction of total available funds to component j are calculated from the sum of the fractions needed to offset depreciation and deferred maintenance, treat environmental media, and expand facilities. For environmental media treatment:

$$XMAINR(j, t) = QOLT(j) * [XJOT(j, t-1) - MEDNOR]/XJOT(j, t-1) \quad (7.15)$$

MEDNOR is the number of units of production whose accompanying pollution can be mitigated by natural processes; for SOS-2, $MEDNOR = 1000$. The associated level of funds for eco-repair is:

$$XMPOLL(j, t) = XMAINR(j, t) * XNVST(j, t) \quad (7.16)$$

The rate of funds required for capital expansion is:

$$XMCAP(j, t) = CAPVL(j, t-1)/XNVST(j, t) \quad (7.17)$$

The total rate is:

$$XMANT(j, t) = XMNORM(j, t) + XMAINR(j, t) + XMCAP(j, t) \quad (7.18)$$

The funds available for production costs are the total funds reduced by the maintenance funds plus the funds generated by net exports.

$$XNVOUT(j, t) = XNVST(j, t)/[1 + XMANT(j, t)] + [XEPORT(j, t-1) - XMPORT(j, t-1)] \quad (7.19)$$

where $XEPORT(j, t-1)$ and $XMPORT(j, t-1)$ will be developed in Step 5.

The second major set of calculations of Step 2 sets an estimated unit cost for producing one output unit of component j and then schedules the total level of output units that will be produced in the time cycle. Prior to these calculations the estimated mean procurement cost to components for each of the up to twenty resources must be made. The estimate is based on the assumption that the cost per resource unit will maintain the same rate of increase noted in the previous year.

$$RUCST(r, t) = 2 * RUCST1(r, t-1) - RUCST2(r, t-2) \quad \text{for all } r \tag{7.20}$$

For each component there is a current mix of resources that are required to produce one unit of output, the matrix $[UTIL(r, j, t)]$. An unnormalized unit cost to produce one level of output can be produced by:

$$UOCST(j, t) = \sum_{r} UTIL(r, j, t) * RUCST(r, t) \tag{7.21}$$

This value is then normalized (or scaled) using a normalizing factor developed by the SOS-2 program in the first cycle of each simulation. In order to be able to compare growth among the several components that produce diverse goods and services, a common form of output is required that gives a relative output volume rather than a strict listing of products. For this reason the normalizing procedure is based on the model scaling of all component output levels in the first cycle to be 1,000 units (see the data discussion of the next chapter). Under that condition the normalizing factor, $XFACT(j)$, is developed as:

$$XFACT(j) = XNVOUT(j, 1)/1000 * UOCST(j, 1) \tag{7.22}$$

Then the normalized output unit cost for component j, $OCST(j, t)$, of any cycle is:

$$OCST(j, t) = XFACT(j) * UOCST(j, t) \tag{7.23}$$

This use of a normalizing cost factor deserves further explanation in order to state its assumptions explicitly. The production formula for component j, $[UTIL(r, j, t)]$ includes only twenty surrogates of resources. It is decidedly easier to calculate present day resource costs in terms of the known present day costs of the resource surrogates than to determine in detail all resources and their costs for, say, the wholesale-retail component, and then to assign each resource to a surrogate category that has a single mean cost set. Therefore, under the assumption that the set of resource surrogates are appropriate, and under the second assumption that the mix of surrogates in the production equation is generally balanced for the course of the simulation, the alternate procedure of developing an unnormalized cost is used. This cost, if the resources are properly balanced, should have its component costs in approximately the ratios that are observed in the base year data. Then the normalization maintains this ratio and allows the scaling of the diverse set of component outputs to an output volume that is easy to interpret in terms of time trends.

The output scheduled for each component, scaled to the original value of 1,000, is:

$$XJOT(j, t) = XNVOUT(j, t)/OCST(j, t) \qquad (7.24)$$

where $XJOT(j, 1) = 1000$

Based on the scheduled output levels it is now possible to calculate the resources utilization requirements of the area, including the labor force, land use, and media treatment requirements. First the resource requirements for each production component are calculated and then these are summed to give the system's total requirements.

For each (j, r) combination; $j = 1, 2, \ldots, 12$; $r = 1, 2, 3, \ldots, 20$:

$$RESOR(r, j, t) = XJOT(j, t) * UTIL(r, j, t) \qquad (7.25)$$

and for each resource r:

$$RESOR(r, t) = \sum_{j=1}^{12} RESOR(r, j, t) \qquad (7.26)$$

At this point in the calculations, the model makes its first check of resource usage. It is assumed that the region will utilize its labor force between set limits and will cause any required adjustments in the labor force to be instituted by modifying the per unit resource cost (the workers salaries). A check is made to determine if $RESOR(18)$ is within the set limits. (The labor force is the eighteenth resource.) The program asks if

$$REMIN(18) \leq RESOR(18)/PILE(18) \leq REMAX(18) \qquad (7.27)$$

a. If the answer is yes, the program continues to the next calculation.
b. If no, and $REMIN(18) > RESOR(18)/PILE(18)$, then the program sets $RUCST1(18) = 0.99 * RUCST1(18)$, returns to process equation (7.20), and continues.
c. If no, and $RESOR(18)/PILE(18) > REMAX(18)$, the program sets $RUCST1(18) = 1.01 * RUCST1(18)$,returns to process equation (7.20), and continues. (For the U.S. data base $REMIN(18) = 0.93$ and $REMAX(18) = 0.97$.)

The status of resource data at the end of the cycle, and for mean values, can now be calculated. Data of interest are unit procurement costs, end-of-period stock status, stocks extracted, stocks obtained by recycling, and cost to extract a unit plus recycle the associated ratio of stocks from production debris. All of these calculations are based on the assumptions used in determining stock levels and costs discussed at the end of chapter 4 with the simplifying assumption on calculations that simple interpolation procedures will be used, rather than iteration for more exact solutions. Each of the following calculations is done for each resource. The information produced does not affect the scheduled production levels, which are set above but which are used for display of resources availability and costs for the year and in the resource adjustment calculations that appear in Step 4.

The end-of-cycle stock depletion level is the fraction of the total stockpile that was originally available to the system at the present unit extraction cost. This is not necessarily the stockpile available at $t = 0$. It is the fraction that was depleted by the beginning of the cycle plus the fraction of stock that is extracted for use during the present cycle.

$$ESTCK(r, t) = STDEP(r, t) + RESOR(r, t)/[PILE(r, t) * (1 + REREC(r, t-1))] \tag{7.28}$$

The actual sources of stocks and amount derived are:

Extracted:

$$PILE(r, t) * [ESTCK(r, t) - STDEP(r, t)] \tag{7.29}$$

Recycled:

$$RESOR(r, t) - PILE(r, t) * ESTCK(r, t) \tag{7.30}$$

The recycling rate associated with the end-of-cycle stock depletion levels for this cycle and used in the next cycle calculations is a function of the *ESTCK* value, since the unit costs are directly associated with *ESTCK*.

$$REREC(r, t) = K4(r) + K5(r) * ESTCK(r, t)^2 \tag{7.31}$$

where $K4(r)$ and $K5(r)$ are constants defined in the next chapter. The first is a minimum rate of recycling, while their sum is a maximum proportion of recycling to extraction that will be used in production processes.

The maximum unit extraction costs are also a function of the value of *ESTCK*. In order that the system not consume resource stocks that are not available, the regulatory mechanism is set within this function by causing rapidly escalating costs as the depletion of the existant stockpile is approached. Two escalating factors are included: one is a permanent unit cost increase, while the second, used only as overusage of present economic resources appears imminent, produces a temporary severe escalation of the unit costs. The general unit cost equation to represent the end of cycle or maximum unit costs is:

$$XMCST(r, t) = [K1(r) + (K2(r) * ESTCK(r, t))^{K3(r)}] * TEMP(r, t) \tag{7.32}$$

where $TEMP(r, t)$, the temporary escalatory factor is:

$$TEMP(r, t) = \text{Max}\,\langle 1.0, \{[1 - K6(r)]/[1 - ESTCK(r, t)]\}^{K7(r)}\rangle \tag{7.33}$$

In the present model data base $K6(r) = 0.90$, and $K7(r) = 3$ for nonrenewable resources, and $K7(r) = 1$ for renewable resources.

The mean unit extraction cost is derived from weighted values of the maximum values for the last cycle and the current cycle.

$$ECST(r, t) = [2 * XMCST(r, t) + XMCST1(r, t-1)]/3 \qquad (7.34)$$

Since it is assumed that the extraction unit costs include the cost for producing the associated recycled ores and these costs are balanced, the unit procurement costs are set as:

$$MECSTR(r, t) = XMCST(r, t)/[1 + REREC(r, t)] \qquad (7.35)$$

$$ECSTR(r, t) = ECST(r, t)/[1 + REREC(r, t)] \qquad (7.36)$$

An adjustment is made to $ECSTR(r, t)$ so that mean resource costs do not decrease from one cycle to another (except for salaries). Then the unit resource cost is reset. The program asks if:

$$ECSTR(r, t) < RUCST1(r, t-1) \qquad (7.37)$$

if the answer is no, it continues; if yes, it sets $ECSTR(r, t) = RUCST1(r, t-1)$, and

$$RUCST(r, t) = ECSTR(r, t) \qquad (7.38)$$

The final calculation that is general to all resource data is determination of whether the stock depletion level has reached a point where it is considered critical. Four critical points can be set for a test of the present range of depletion for each resource; if the value was passed during the current cycle, a critical depletion flag is set to signal the need in Step 4 to consider available, economic adjustments of stock availability and utilization. The form of the test is:

If

$$ESTCK(r, t-1) \geq FLG(k, r) \geq ESTCK(r, t) \qquad (7.39)$$

then

$$FLAGR(r, t) = 1.0 \quad \text{for } k = 1, 2, 3, \text{ or } 4$$

Also, if $ESTCK(r, t) > 0.985$

$$FLAGR(r, t) = 1.0$$

Otherwise, $FLAGR(r, t) = 0.0$.

For agricultural resource levels, if the requirement for component production increases above 90% annual production, then the total stockpile of food and fiber is increased at a rate equal to the production funds rate of growth.

$$PILE(1) = RESOR(1) * (1.1 + RGJ(6) * 0.01) \tag{7.40}$$

where food and fiber is resource 1 and agriculture is production component 6.

If, however, the required demand for food and fiber is not equal or greater than 90% of the available resource, the difference is exported so that:

$$ESTCK(1) = 0.90 \tag{7.41}$$

The usage of existent production facilities and the need to expand these facilities is also in the set of calculations in Step 2. Throughout the simulation, for each production component, the maximum output in any previous cycle is maintained $XMJOT(j, t)$. The first calculation tests the amount of facilities that are used in this cycle:

$$CAPUSE(j, t) = [XJOT(j, t)/XMJOT(j, t)] \tag{7.42}$$

If $CAPUSE(j, t)$ is greater than 1.0 the facilities must be expanded to account for the excess. The cost of expansion is:

$$XMCAP(j, t) = XJOT(j, t) * [CAPUSE(j, t) - 1] * CAPVL(j, t) \tag{7.43}$$

where $CAPVL(j, t)$ is the cost for capital expansion to produce one unit of component output.

A final set of calculations to relate demand for mining production to ore resource warnings is begun in this step and is completed in Step 7. The total cost of ore for resource r is:

$$RESPR(r, t) = RESOR(r, t) * RUCST(r, t) \tag{7.44}$$

The total cost of all ores is equal to:

$$RAMAT(t) = \sum_{r \in r'} RESPR(r, t) \tag{7.45}$$

where r' are the mined resources.

Step 3: Describe the State of the System

From Steps 1 and 2, much of the regional description is given in terms of population and production growth, plus usage and present stock and unit cost levels for system resources. Step 3 completes the evaluation by comparing the current demand levels for goods and services to the annual output of the production components. The form to express population demand is development of a set of area specific measures giving per capita usage for combinations of outputs. The users (the per capita size) are the total population or one of the partitions of the population (see Step 1 for

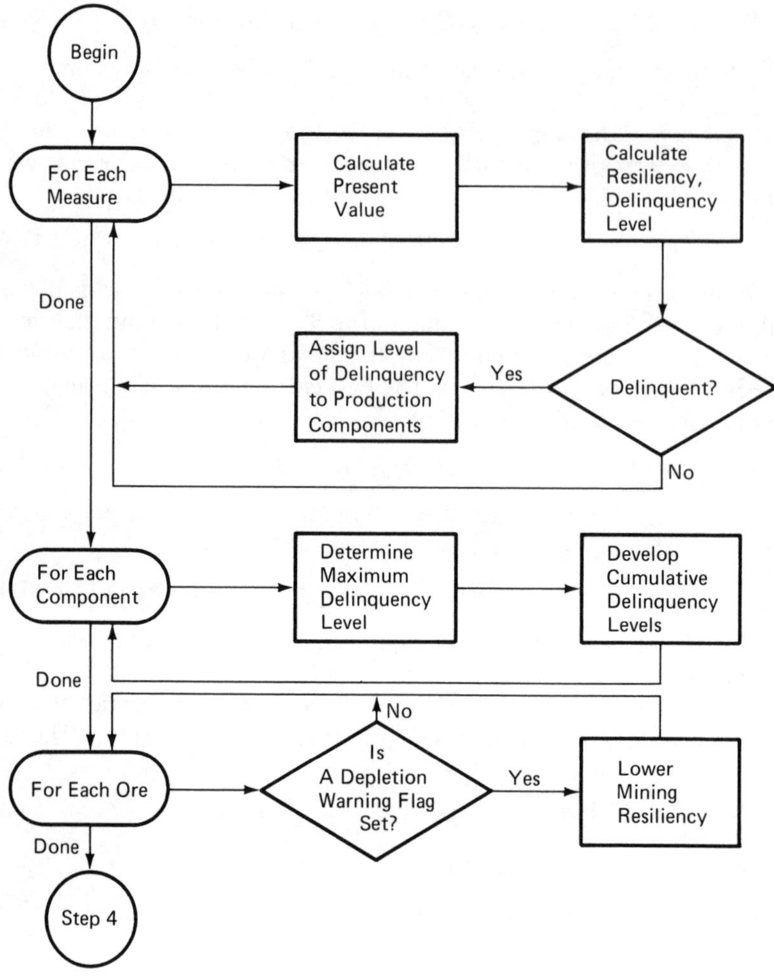

Figure 7-4. Step 3 Flowchart.

partition definitions). For each of these measures, a threshold, or minimum acceptable per capita output level, is set initially and adjusted as appropriate during the model operation. Comparison of the actual annual values of the measures to the thresholds allows expression of the quality of the region in terms of an ecosystem. Data produced can show:

System resilience for each measure

System processes acting as limiting factors

The severity of the limiting processes

Table 7-3
Step 3 Parameters

Name	*Definition*	*Source*
POP(k, t)	For k = 1, 2, 3, 4, 5, 6, total population in partition k at t	Calculated
	For k = 7, total population at t	Step 1
	For k = 8, total initial population	Constant
POPKT($\bar{y}$, k, t)	Population of partition k in age cohort $\bar{y}$ at t	Step 1
DN(n)	Index value for k to be used to select value of POP(k, t) for demand measure n	Constant
CNJ(j, n)	Coefficient relating output of production component j to impact on demand measure n	Constant
XJOT(j, t)	Units of output of component j at t	Step 2
XMEAS(n, t)	Value of the nth demand measure at t	Calculated
TMEAS(n, t)	Minimum threshold value for measure n at t	Step 7 ($t-1$)
RESIL(n, t)	Relative level of value of measure n above threshold at t (If XMEAS(n, t) $\leq$ TMEAS(n, t), RESIL(n, t) = 0)	Calculated
DEL(n, j, t)	Required additional (pro rata) output of component j needed to meet threshold of measure n at t	Calculated
DNJ(n, j, t)	Cumulative deficient level of output required for component j to meet threshold n since last time threshold n was met	Calculated
DNJ1(n, j, $t-1$)	Last year value of DNJ	Step 3 ($t-1$)
COUNT(n, t)	Years since threshold of measure n was met, at year t	Calculated
COUNT1(n, $t-1$)	Last year value of COUNT	Step 3($t-1$)
XMDEL(j, t)	Required maximum additional output of component j needed to meet all affected thresholds at t	Calculated
XMDNJ(j, t)	Maximum cumulative deficient output required for component j to meet all thresholds since last time no affected thresholds were missed	Calculated
XCONT(j, t)	Years since all thresholds affected by component j were met, at t	Calculated
FLAG(r, t)	Existance of a depletion warning at t for resource r	Step 2
PILE(r, t)	Amount of total reserve r available at unit cost for t prior to depletion	Step 8 ($t-1$)
CPILE(r, t)	Amount of increase of reserve possible at t to add to reserves due to escalating unit costs	Constant

Insight for adjustment of relative levels of the system processes to increase resilience

The general flowchart of the step calculations and examples is presented in Figure 7-4. Table 7-3 gives data requirements and sources.

Assumptions. It is assumed that all demands of the population can be translated into a series of demand levels for production goods and services. Hence, all measures can be set up as linear combinations of output levels divided by the consuming population size.

The form of the population demand thresholds is assumed to represent perceived needs; the level of need that is perceived is assumed to be a function of the past satisfaction of the demand. Therefore, if oversatisfaction has been maintained for a period of time (in SOS-2 set as two years) the threshold level will be increased to that past value. Similarly, if all adjustment of resources and funds distribution cannot produce a system that appears to regain resiliency, the level of thresholds may be lowered until a minimum threshold level is reached.

It should be noted that the *description* of the State of the System does not require an arbitrary combination of the several measures into a single value. On the contrary, each measure allows measurement of a selected area of quality of life as described in demand satisfaction terms. Since later steps include adjustments within and between component outputs based on the relative resiliency shown for each measure value, it is appropriate to use a large set of measures, each measuring a discrete and narrow segment of demand satisfaction. Thus, although the set of measures will include demand for all component outputs, each measure should show demands for only one to three component outputs in order that the later adjustment processes can diagnose the problems as they exist in discrete components.

While the set of measures must cover the spectrum of interests, it is not necessary that the measures be independent of each other. In fact, since the measures are not combined into a single scalar value, if one measure were the exact duplicate of another, no added weight would be produced in the adjustment processes of the later steps.

Algorithms. The first procedure of Step 3 calculates the present value assigned to each of the active measures for this time t. All measures are of the form:

$$XMEAS(n, t) = \sum_{j} [CNJ(n, j) * XJOT(j, t)/POP(DN(n), k, t)] \tag{7.46}$$

where $POP(DN(n), k, t)$ is the assigned partition of population for measure n by index $DN(n)$ and $n = 1, . 2, 3, \ldots, 15$.

To determine how well the value of the measure satisfies the population demands a test is made of the form:

$$\text{Is } kn = XMEAS(n, t) - TMEAS(n, t) \geq 0 \tag{7.47}$$

If kn is greater than or equal to zero, all required demand is satisfied and the system resiliency for measure n is set equal to the excess in output available to required output; this is computed as:

$$RESIL(n, t) = kn/TMEAS(n, t) \tag{7.48}$$

If kn is less than zero the production system was unable to satisfy all required demands associated with measure n. For the unsatisfied values a set of calculations is carried out to be used in later step adjustment procedures. First, for each component having a nonzero value for CNJ, there is assigned a pro rata delinquency of output:

$$\begin{aligned} DEL(n, j, t) &= [kn * POP(DN(n), k, t)]/TMEAS(n, t), \\ &\quad \text{if } CNJ(j, n) \neq 0 \\ &= 0, \quad \text{if } CNJ(j, n) = 0 \end{aligned} \tag{7.49}$$

The cumulative delinquency and number of years since $XMEAS(n, t)$ was resilient is calculated as:

$$DNJ(n, j, t) = DNJ1(n, j, t-1) + DEL(n, j, t) \tag{7.50}$$

$$COUNT(n, t) = COUNT1(n, t-1) + 1 \tag{7.51}$$

For all measures where $kn \geq 0$, the values, $DNJ(n, j, t)$ and $COUNT(n, t)$ are also set to zero.

After all calculations associated with the individual measures are complete, a set of calculations to determine the maximum unsatisfied demand for output of each production component is carried out. For each component j, a test is made to determine the largest value of delinquency in output and the value of n associated with that value

$$N(j) = n\{\text{Max}[DEL(n, j, t)]\} \tag{7.52}$$

Then for that value of n, the period deficiency, the cumulated deficiency and years of delinquency are calculated:

$$XMDEL(j, t) = DEL(N(j), j, t) \tag{7.53}$$

$$XMDNJ(j, t) = DNJ(N(j), j, t) \tag{7.54}$$

$$XCONT(j, t) = COUNT(N(j), t) \tag{7.55}$$

It should be noted that if no level of delinquency was noted for j in any measure where $CNJ \neq 0$ then (7.53), (7.54), and (7.55) all equal zero.

A subsidiary calculation in this step is taken to stimulate natural ore production if any resources were signalled as possible problem areas. For each natural ore r' the following tests are made.

Is a resource depletion flag set, that is, does

$$FLAGR(r', t) = 1.0\ ? \tag{7.56}$$

If so, continue to 7.51; if not, process the next r'.

Is a mining expansion possible, that is, does

$$CPILE(r') > 0 \ ? \tag{7.57}$$

If so, continue to 7.58; if no, process the next r'.

Then the value of the mining component's ($j = 12$) demand measure is lowered as follows:

$$XMEAS(12, t) = XMEAS(12, t)/[1 + k] \tag{7.58}$$

where $k = RESPR(r', t)/RAMAT(t) * CPILE(r')/PILE(r', t)$ thus, reducing the resiliency level or triggering a measure delinquency.

The Systemic Module of a Cycle

General Procedure

Within the first three steps of a cycle a number of elements may have been described as unsatisfactory when the system values were compared to its warning signals, goals, or thresholds. The next four steps comprise a set of mechanisms for adjusting these components of our human ecosystem in order to adjust values in this cycle or to reorient the system processes for subsequent cycle adjustments. Of these four steps, the next step, adjustment of the resource base, operates independently of the other adjustments. It is driven by its own special set of diagnostic signals, the resource stock depletion warnings, as developed in Step 2.

Steps 5, 6 and 7 are processed in a hierarchical order to reduce the level of dissatisfaction of population demands within the human ecosystem. The hierarchy represented to meet these unsatisfied demands are:

(1) Generate short term remedies by delay of certain maintenance expenditures. Additionally, exports and imports are generated based on system resilience.

(2) Generate long term solutions by modifying production processes to use more economical production functions and by redistribution of funds among sectors and among components.

(3) Lower the per capita demands of the consumers to reflect recognition that specific demands cannot be met at future times by the production sectors, and hence perceived needs will diminish until they fall to the subsistence level.

If a previous step is forecast to reduce the problem area to an acceptable level, then the adjustments within the subsequent steps are not processed.

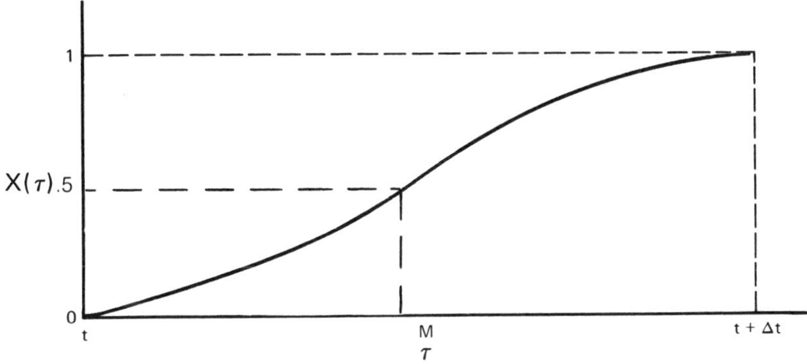

Figure 7-5. Time Change Interpolation Function.

If, however, the previous step does not appear to reduce the level of unsatisfied demand sufficiently, then the step is processed and the attempt to reduce stress levels is done independently of forecast adjustments of the previous steps, thus allowing the incidence of system overreaction.

Simulation of Long Term Adjustment Timing

The procedures common to Step 4 and Step 6 include introduction of changes that do not occur at once but begin in the next cycle and undergo cumulative change to a maximum value over several annual cycles. The rate of introduction of these changes (or changeovers) is represented by a normalized cumulative normal distribution using the range $(-2\sigma, 2\sigma)$. The present time is equated to $t = M - 2\sigma$ while the final time, $t + \Delta t = M + 2\sigma$. The amount of change for any $t \leq \tau \leq t + \Delta t$ is provided as shown on the next page. A change from a level of procedure X_1 to X_2 would be set at time τ by:

$$X(\tau) = X_2 * (L - T(\tau)) + X_1 * T(\tau)$$

This function is illustrated in Figure 7-5.

Specific processes using this several year structural relationship in the SOS model are:

Substitution of resources for a critical resource

Expansion of resource reserves due to increased unit extraction prices

Conversion from one production process to an expected lower cost process for a production component

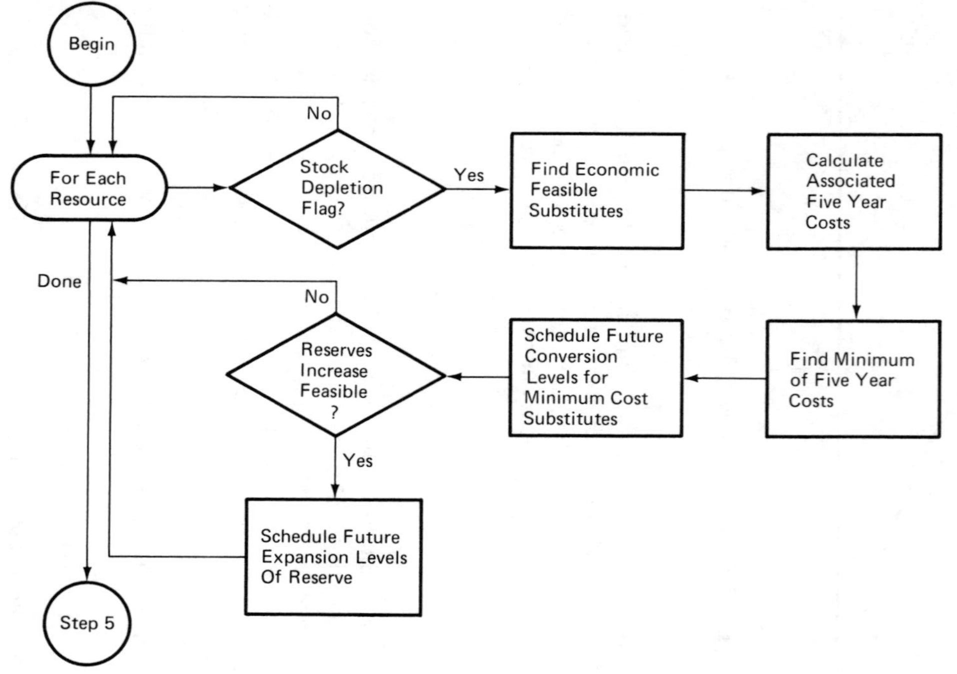

Figure 7-6. Step 4 Flowchart.

Table 7-4
Step 4 Parameters

Name	*Definition*	*Source*
T(τ)	Degree (fractional) of process transformation at time τ	Calculated
FLAGR(r, t)	Condition of stock level signal of r at t	Step 2, t
SUBDAT(n, m)	nth substitution formula available, made up of $m = 1, 2, \ldots, 13$	Constant
SUM(r, n, t)	Unit cost of nth substitution at t	Calculated
SUBDAT(r, $2n$)	Resource index for substituting resource r'	Constant
SUBDAT(r, $2n$+1)	Units of resource r' in substitution for one unit of r	Constant
XMCST(r', t)	Maximum unit cost of r' at t	Step 2, t
SCST(n, r, t)	Five-year estimated cumulated unit cost for affecting substitution r at t	Calculated
CPILE(r, t)	Level of expansion of resource reserve stock given that expansion is feasible at t	Constant

Elements of adjustment that do not require significant time delays (occur at least by next cycle) are:

Deferral of capital maintenance for expansion of production funds

Transfer and reallocation of rates of component funds growth

Increase or reduction of demand measures

Step 4: Adjust Resource Reserves and Utilization Factors

The fourth step of the cycle is processed only for those resources for which a critical stock depletion signal was set in Step 2 (i.e., $FLAGR(r) = 1.0$). For each such resource, the feasibility and economic utility of substitution, in whole or in part, and expansion of the reserve stockpile in reaction to increased unit extraction prices is simulated.

There exists a third adjustment of resource availability in SOS for durable resources not considered in this step but which was automatically introduced in the Step 2 calculation. The level of recycling of durable ores from production debris is changed from cycle to cycle as a function of change in unit procurement costs of the resource (see equations (7.30-7.31)).

Figure 7-6 represents the general flowchart of Step 4 while Table 7-4 lists the parameters of the algorithms and their sources.

Assumptions. Within any resource projection, the adjustment procedure will forecast data based on the maximum values at time t, rather than attempting to make nonlinear projections of future values.

If a substitution for a resource by a mix of resources occurs in this step it affects the resources utilization in all production components equally.

Once a substitution is initiated, the procedure will continue until it is completed. However, other substitutions can be initiated involving this resource and total change will be constructed across the chronological hierarchy of initiated substitution changes.

A substitution need not completely replace the use of a resource; in fact, it generally does not. Typically a substitution includes the original resource in its formulation but at a lower level than the amount for which the substitution is made.

If two substitutions are available and economically feasible, only one is initiated in a given cycle. The choice is based on a forecast of a minimum mean unit cost for an arbitrary period of time. In SOS-2 the time period is set as five years.

Algorithms. For each resource a test is made to determine if it has a critical stock depletion warning. For those resources in this condition the other algorithms of Step 4 are processed; for other resources no further action is taken in this step.

For each resource r the program tests whether:

$$FLAGR(r, t) = 1.0 \tag{7.59}$$

If the answer is yes, it continues Step 4 for r; otherwise it processes the next r.

For each resource for which the test is positive, the prógram determines which, if any, of the substitution equations apply. For each applicable formula, it checks to make sure the substitution process is not presently underway. Additionally, for some resources the substitution can be done one time only. For those meeting the feasibility criteria, the program calculates the present costs to substitute the new mix for a unit of resource and the projected five-year resource unit costs for time-phased conversion. This procedure is stated below:

$$\text{Is substitution } SUBDAT(n) \text{ for } r?\ n = 1, 2, \ldots, m \tag{7.60}$$

If yes, continue the process; if no, do the test for the next n.

$$\text{Is } SUBDAT(n) \text{ not presently underway?} \tag{7.61}$$

If yes, continue the sequence; if no, do the test above for the next n. Calculate the two costs cited above.

$$SUM(r, n, t) = \sum_{r'} \sum_{n=1}^{5} SUBDAT(r, 2n+1) * XMEST(r', t) \quad (7.62)$$

where $r' = SUBDAT\ (r, 2n)$

$$SCST(r, n, t) = \sum_{r=1}^{5} [XMCST(r, t) * (1 - T(n, \tau)) + SUM(r, n\ t) * T(n, \tau)] \quad (7.63)$$

After all substitutions are tested and the successful ones have values for equations (7.62) and (7.63) developed, the appropriate substitution is selected or all are judged unacceptable. The acceptability is set if any cost is smaller than the original resource procurement costs, then the substitution selected is the minimum of the five-year cost alternatives.

The test for an economical substitution candidate is:

$$SUM(r, n, t) < XMCST(r, t)\ ? \quad (7.64)$$

If yes, n is considered in set $[N]$ below; if no, n is dropped from further consideration.

For the minimum cost feasible substitution, find:

$$n = n \left\{ \underset{n \in N}{\text{Min}} [SCST(r, n, t)] \right\} \quad (7.65)$$

Store in the Future Actions File (used in Step 8) for all times $t + 1 \leq \tau \leq t + \Delta t$, the vector:

$$[r, n, \tau, T(\tau)] \quad (7.66)$$

After the procedure for substitution for a resource is complete, for each r in a stock depletion warning condition, the program checks the feasibility of expanding the reserve stock level and if feasible, expands the stocks by the prescribed amount.

$$\text{Is } CPILE(r, t) > 0 \text{ and expansion not now underway?} \quad (7.67)$$

If yes, continue; if no, return to the initial action of Step 4 (test (7.59)) and the next r.

Store in the Future Actions File for all times $t + 1$ to $t + \Delta t$, the vector:

$$[r, CPILE, \tau, T(\tau)] \quad (7.68)$$

Also, set expansion of stocks to be infeasible until the cycle time equals $t + \Delta t$.

After test (7.59) and indicated subsequent actions of Step 4 are completed for each resource r, the SOS-2 program exits to Step 5.

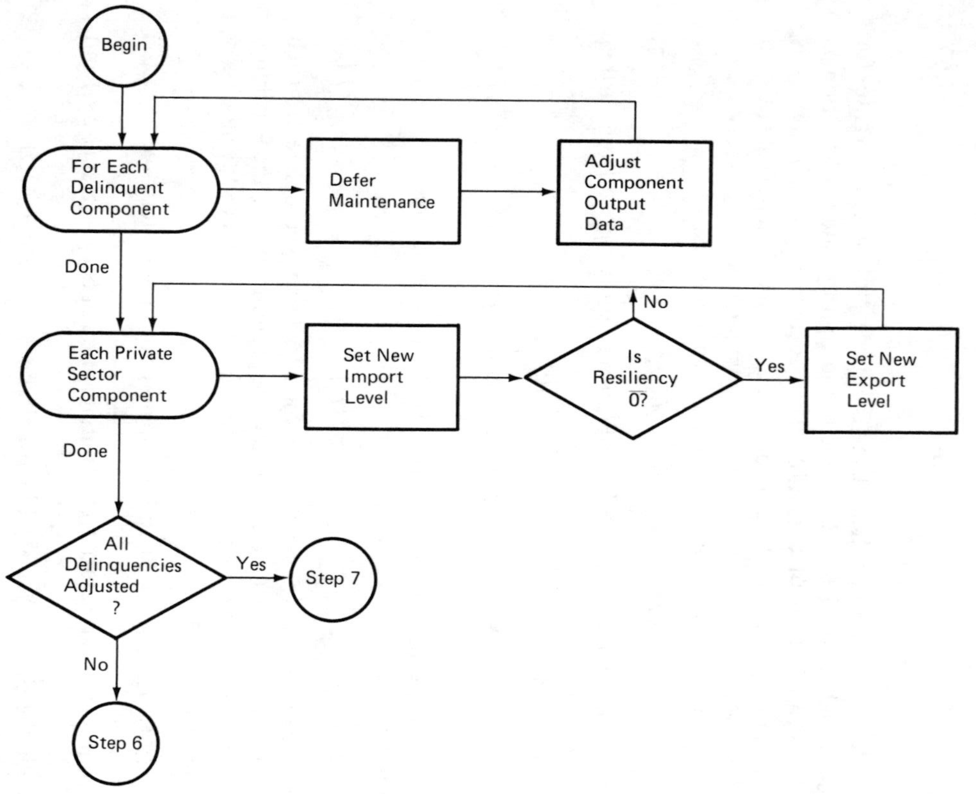

Figure 7-7. Step 5 General Flowchart.

Table 7-5
Step 5 Parameters

Name	*Definition*	*Source*
XMDEL(j, t)	Required additional goods of j at t	Calculated
XIDFMN(j, t)	Maximum maintenance funds of j that can be deferred at t	Calculated
XMRNOR(j)	Normal maintenance level for offset depreciation for j	Calculated
XNVST(j, t)	Total funds available to j at t	Step 2, t
CST(j, t)	Total funds need to supplement j at maximum resource price	Calculated
UTIL(r, j, t)	Units of r used in one unit of j at t	Step 2, t
XMESTR(t)	Maximum unit cost for r at t	Calculated
XFACT(j)	Normalizer of unit costs for component j	Step 2, Cycle 1
CMIN(j, t)	Fraction of XIDFMN for j actually deferred	Calculated
XKT(t)	Total cost to import required additional goods for all components	Calculated
XJOT(j, t)	Units of component j produced at t	Step 2, t
CNJ(n, j)	Get from Step 2 table	Step 2
RESIL(n, t)	Relative level of value of measure n above threshold at t (If XMEAS(n, t) $\leq$ TMEAS(n, t), RESIL(n, t) = 0)	Calculated
RESMN(j, t)	Resiliency of j in measure n at $t = 0$	Calculated
RESMN1(j, $t-1$)	Resiliency of j in measure n at $t - 1$	Calculated
EJOT(j, t)	Units of component j exported at t	Calculated
XEPORT(j, t)	Value of exports of j at t	Calculated
OCST(j, t)	Unit cost to produce output of component j at t (normalized)	Calculated
EJOT1(j)	Units of component j exported in initial year	Step 5, $t = 1$
UTILI(r, j, t)	Amount of foreign r used in one unit of j at t	Constant
XMPORT(j, t)	Value of imports of j at t	Calculated
XINJO(j, t)	Number of units of j imported at t	Calculated
SNCST	Net export value at t	Calculated

Step 5: Perform Short Term Output Adjustments

A check is made to determine if the output levels of any component produced unsatisfied demand. For each component that had a delinquent output level a short term adjustment by deferring maintenance is performed. If some components remain delinquent after these actions, Step 6 is processed: otherwise, the systemic module is complete and Step 7 is initiated to upgrade measure thresholds only. Additionally this step performs calculations of levels and dollar volume of exports and imports of private sector components.

Figure 7-7 depicts the general flowchart of Step 5, while Table 7-5 includes all parameters used in the step.

Assumptions. Deferred maintenance can be accomplished only on that element of maintenance associated with plant and equipment depreciation; facility expansion and ecosystem maintenance costs cannot be deferred. This deferral is allowed for only one year.

No resilient components will defer maintenance.

Algorithms. The first short term adjustments are performed within the delinquent components only. Up to the level of required funds or to the level of funds used to offset plant depreciation this cycle, the maintenance funds are deferred and the funds are used to purchase needed imports for that component.

To determine the maximum funds needed for the component, first a maximum unit cost for the cycle is calculated:

$$SUM(j, t) = XFACT(j) * \sum_{r} UTIL(r, j, t) * XMESTR(r, t) \quad (7.69)$$

Then the total funds required by the component to supplement its production in the system is:

$$CST(j, t) = XMDEL(j, t) * SUM(j, t) \quad (7.70)$$

The maximum funds available by deferring maintenance is:

$$XIDFMN(j, t) = XMRNOR(j) * XNVST(j, t) \quad (7.71)$$

If sufficient funds exist for the total adjustment, sufficient deferral is made to produce the necessary adjustment; otherwise, all maintenance funds are deferred and the funds are used to reduce demands for that component's output prior to entering the next set of adjustments. If

$$XIDFMN(j, t) \geq CST(j, t) \quad (7.72)$$

then the deferred funds are:

$$XIDFMN(j, t) = CST(j, t) \quad (7.73)$$

and the residues for further need are:

$$XMDEL(j, t) = 0 \quad (7.74)$$

$$CST(j, t) = 0 \quad (7.75)$$

Otherwise, if $CST(j, t) > XIDFMN(j, t)$ to the values are:

$$XIDFMN(j, t) = XIDFMN(j, t) \quad (7.73a)$$

Residual needed output for j is:

$$XMDEL(j, t) = XMDEL(j, t) * [1 - XIDFMN(j, t)/CST(j, t)] \quad (7.74a)$$

and residual funds that are needed are:

$$CST(j, t) = CST(j, t) - XIDFMN(j, t) \qquad (7.75a)$$

If $CST(j, t)$ is greater than zero for any output component, Step 6 will be entered for long term adjustments; otherwise, the model, after it finishes the rest of the Step 5 calculations, goes directly to Step 7 to determine if thresholds of demands should be upgraded in subsequent years.

The rest of the calculations of Step 5 set the levels of exports and imports for the components of the private sector. First, the levels of exports are developed based on past trends and the current internal requirements for the components output.

The initial check is to determine the minimum level of resilience for a measure associated with j. That is, does

$$CNJ(n, j) = 0.0 \quad \text{for all } n? \qquad (7.76)$$

If it does, $RESMN(j, t) = 5.0$ and the program goes to (7.78); if not, it continues.

$$RESMN(j, t) = \underset{n}{\text{Min}}\,[RESIL(n, t) | CNJ(n, j) \neq 0] \qquad (7.77)$$

The actual number of units exported for the component is:

$$EJOT(j, t) = EJOT1(j, t) * [RESMN(j, t)/RESMN1(j, t)] * XJOT(j, t) \qquad (7.78)$$

$$XEPORT(j, t) = EJOT(j, t) * OCST(j, t) * XFACT(j) \qquad (7.79)$$

The next phase of the subroutine is to calculate the amount of imports needed by the region.

If there has never been trade between the study region and the outside system, then a value is set for the initial imports based on relative unit prices.

$$XMPORT(j, t) = 0.5 * XNVOUT(j, t) * (OCST(j, t) - OCST1(j, t))^2 \qquad (7.80)$$

otherwise

$$XMPORT(j, t) = XMPORT\ (j, t-1) * (OCST1(j, t))^2$$

This monetary value is then normalized to an output value of units by:

$$XINJO(j, t) = XMPORT(j, t)/(OCSTI(j, t) * XFACT(j, t) \qquad (7.81)$$

The final calculation of Step 5 is the net balance of trade.

$$SNCST = \sum_j XEPORT(j, t) - \sum XMPORT(j, t) \qquad (7.82)$$

Step 6: Perform Long Term Component Output Adjustments

If some components, after Step 5 short term adjustments are performed, remain delinquent ($XMDEL(j, t) \neq 0$ at the end of Step 5), there is no further adjustment during this cycle that can be performed in order to meet the population demands. However, several adjustments can be made over the long term (succeeding periods) that are, over time, expected to reduce the level of delinquency. Three types of adjustments are possible:

Reduction of production costs by introduction of new production formulas

Reallocation of funds within sectors

Transfer of funds between sectors

Figure 7-8 presents the general flowchart and Table 7-6 defines the parameters in Step 6.

Assumptions. All adjustments or transfer of funds are performed in the smallest neighborhood possible—within the component (Step 5), within the sector, and then between the two sectors. Within each neighborhood the adjustments are performed without regard to other neighborhood adjustments.

In the present form of SOS-2, available funds are generated based on the prevailing rates of growth and fund levels for each component. The reallocation of funds calculates the total funds available for the next cycle and then changes the rates of growth of components appropriately so that the total funds growth from t to $t + 1$ is unchanged.

Algorithms. The long term adjustments are performed in the order of adjustment of input/output formulas and then reallocation of funds; both sets of adjustments are carried out if Step 6 is entered.

For any component that remains delinquent after Step 5, each of the available production formula alternatives are checked to determine if it is projected to lower unit production costs for that component. If a lower cost alternative exists, then a substitution process with timing as detailed in Step 4 is effected.

First, calculating the substitution cost and the five-year conversion costs for alternative production formulas:

$$XMOCST(n, j, t) = \sum_{r} UTIL(n, j, r) * XMESTR(r, t) \qquad (7.83)$$

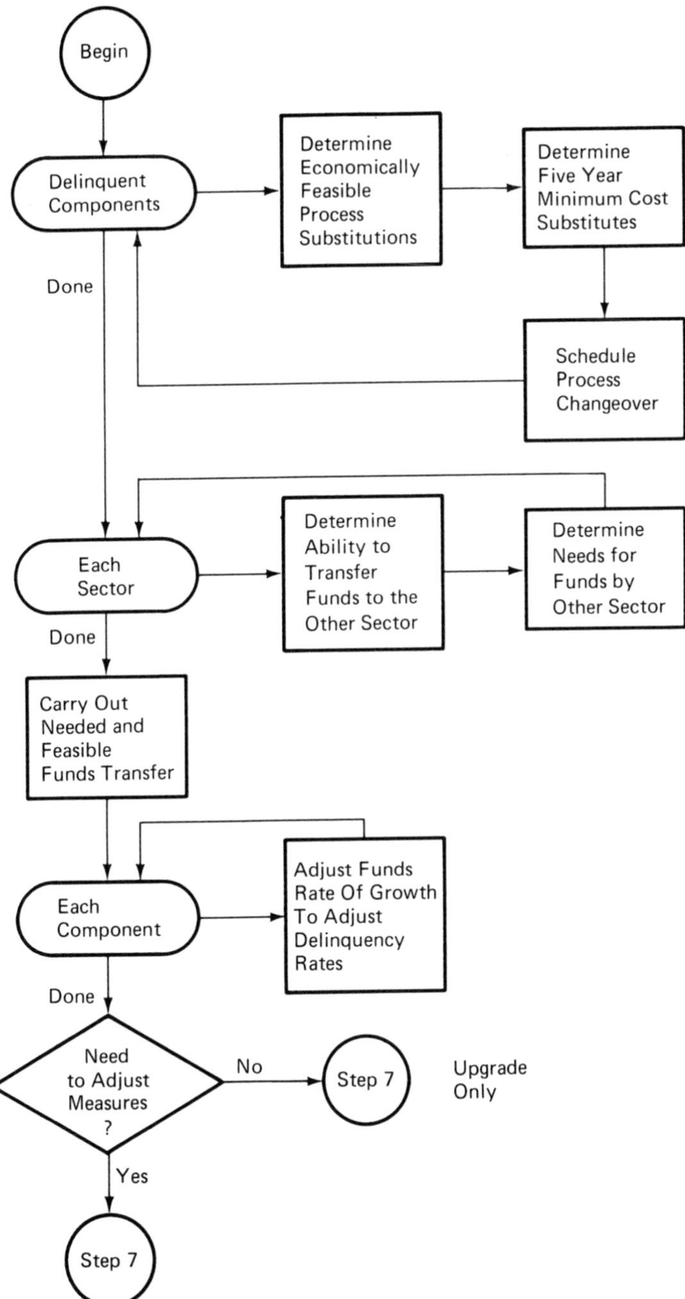

Figure 7-8. Step 6 General Flowchart.

Table 7-6
Step 6 Parameters

Name	*Definition*	*Source*
XOCST(n, j, t)	Unit cost of substitute process n at t	Calculated
XUTIL(n, j, r)	Amounts of resources r used by component j in any process n (both active and substitute processes)	Constant
XMESTR(r, t)	Maximum unit cost of r at t	Step 2, t
XMOCST(j, t)	Maximum unit output costs of j at t	Calculated
YOCST(n, n', j, t)	Five year cumulated mean unit cost beginning at t for time phasing process switch from process n to n'	Calculated
FPT(n', τ)	Change over time lag function to process n' for $t + 1 \leq \tau \leq t + \Delta t$	Calculated
XNVST(j, t)	Total funds used by j at t	Step 2, t
RGJ(j, t)	Current funds growth rate for j	Step 7, previous t
XNVST2(j, t+1)	Estimated available funds for j at $t + 1$	Calculated
XNEED2(j, t+1)	Estimated needed funds for j at $t + 1$	Calculated
XMDEL(j, t)	Additional output needed after short term adjustments of Step 5 for j at t	Step 5, t
TOPT(t)	Total population at t	Step 1, t
TOPTM1($t-1$)	Total population at $t - 1$	Step 1 ($t-1$)
XJOT(j, t)	Number of units produced by j at t	Calculated
XDWN2(s, t+1)	Additional funds needed by sector s components	Calculated
TRNFD(s, t)	Set level of funds transfer to s	Calculated
XNUP2(s, t+1)	Funds available from healthy components of s	Calculated
COMP(s)	Pro rata adjustment of funds levels of components in s	Calculated
TRINS(s, t+1)	Funds needed above available levels for s at $t + 1$	Calculated
XNED(s, t+1)	Total funds needed in s for delinquent j at $t + 1$	Calculated
DIFFS(s, t+1)	Total funds available in s for resilient j at $t + 1$	Calculated

if n is a substitute production formula for component j, then

$$YOCST(n, n', j, t) = \sum_{\tau=1}^{5} [(XOCST(n, j, t) * 1 - FPT(n', \tau)] + XMOCST(j, t) * FPT(n', \tau)] \qquad (7.84)$$

If $YOCST(n, n', j, t) < XMOCST(j, t)$ and if $YOCST(n, n', j, t)$ is the minimum for all candidates then it is introduced as a new production formula, and is stored in Future Actions File for all $t + 1 \leq \tau \leq t + \Delta t$ as the vector:

$$[j, n, \tau, FPT(n, \tau)] \tag{7.85}$$

In addition to the adjustments of production processes, if the long term adjustment processes are entered, the algorithms for adjustment of growth rates between components are entered. These include adjustment of growth between components of a sector, and between sectors. The first action in these procedures is to calculate for each component the expected level of funds and the estimated level of funds required to produce sufficient output for demands.

Estimated available funds are:

$$XNVST2(j, t+1) = XNVST(j, t) * [1 + RGJ(j, t)] \tag{7.86}$$

Estimated required funds are:

$$XNEED2(j, t+1) = XNVST2(j, t) * \frac{TOPT(t)}{TOPTM1(t-1)} * \left[\frac{1 + XMDEL(j, t)}{XJOT(j, t)}\right] \tag{7.87}$$

Then, for each component the required additional funds are:

$$TRINS(j, t+1) = XNEED2(j, t+1) - XNVST2(j, t+1) \tag{7.88}$$

If $TRINS(j, t+1)$ is negative, the amount represents the estimated level of funds that can be given up without causing component j to be delinquent in the next cycle. If it is positive, it is the amount of additional funds required by component j.

The funds needed by, or available for transfer from, the sectors can be calculated as:

$$XDWN2(\text{priv}, t+1) = \sum_{j=6}^{12} [XNEED2(j, t+1) - XNVST2(j, t+1)] \tag{7.89}$$

and

$$XDWN2(\text{publ}, t+1) = \sum_{j=1}^{5} [XNEED2(j, t+1) - XNVST2(j, t+1) \tag{7.90}$$

If both $XDWN2$ are negative, sufficient funds exist in each sector to perform needed adjustments. If both $XDWN2$ are positive, neither sector has sufficient funds for its own needs and hence cannot transfer funds to the other sector. In either of these cases, funds are not transferred and the process will skip to equation (7.94) for intrasector adjustments. For the case where one $XDWN2$ is positive and the other negative, intersector funds transfer is feasible. The level of funds transferred is the minimum value of the needed funds and the excess funds.

$$TRNFD(s, t+1) = \text{Min}[XDWN2(s, t+1), \; - XDWN2(s', t+1)] \tag{7.91}$$

where s is the receiving sector.

The funds are allocated to components in sector s on a pro rata basis using $XNVST(j, t+1)$ as the base.

$$XNVST(j, t+1) = XNVST2(j, t+1) * \left(\frac{1 + TRNFD(s, t+1)}{\sum_{j \in s} XNVST2(j, t+1)} \right) \tag{7.92}$$

The withdrawal of funds from sector s' are assigned on a similar pro rata basis:

For all j in s':

$$XNVST2(j, t+1) = XNVST2(j, t+1) * \left(\frac{1 - TRNFD(s, t+1)}{\sum_{j \in s'} XNVST2(j, t+1)} \right) \tag{7.93}$$

After these intersector transfers are completed, equation (7.88) is repeated for all j and then the process for intrasector transfers below is done.

Two totals are first calculated; the total funds required as an addition to delinquent components:

$$XNED(s, t+1) = \sum_{j \in s} \text{Max}[0, TRINS(j, t+1)] \tag{7.94}$$

and the total funds available as an addition to delinquent component funds:

$$DIFFS(s, t+1) = \sum_{j \in s} \text{Min}[0, TRINS(j, t+1)] \tag{7.95}$$

Within a sector there are sufficient funds for all adjustments if:

$$DIFFS(s, t+1) \geq XNED(s, t+1) \tag{7.96}$$

if so then

$$m = XNED(s, t+1)/DIFFS(s, t+1) \text{ and } n = 1 \qquad 7.97$$

otherwise,

$$m = 1 \quad \text{and } n = \frac{DIFFS(s, t+1)}{XNED(s, t+1)} \tag{7.98}$$

For components receiving additional funds:

$$XNVST2(j, t+1) = XNVST2(j, t+1) + TRINS(j, t+1) * n \tag{7.99}$$

and for components transferring funds:

$$XNVST2(j, t+1) = XNVST2(j, t+1) - TRINS(j, t+1) * m \qquad (7.100)$$

For all components the new rate of growth, as a fraction, is:

$$RGJ(j, t+1) = \frac{XNVST2(j, t+1)}{XNVST(j, t)} - 1 \qquad (7.101)$$

This action completes Step 6.

Step 7: Adjust Long Term Population Demands

The existing thresholds for a demand measure may be changed for either of two reasons. First, as a continuation of the system adjustment processes begun in Step 5, if the adjustments in Step 5 are not projected to fully meet the amount required for a specific measure, its threshold may be reduced in Step 7 to reduce stress on the system. Secondly, however, if a measure has been above its threshold for a period of time, SOS-2 adjusts the threshold higher to reflect increased perceived needs and their increase due to availability of outputs above the threshold. The general flowchart and the included parameters are displayed in Figure 7-9 and Table 7-7.

Assumptions. Although Step 6 may have adjusted data for long term change, Step 7 considers the data base as it exists at the end of the short term adjustments (at the end of Step 5). Hence, a Step 7 degradation adjustment, with or without a Step 6 adjustment, should normally overcompensate for the past delinquency, causing a chance for the ecosystem to become resilient again.

The simulation of changing perceived needs is performed in SOS-2 by increasing thresholds based on the arbitrary rule: If the measure has been above threshold for the last two cycles and has not decreased in that time, the new threshold is set to the measure value of two cycles ago.

Algorithms. If Step 7 is entered from Step 6 the following equations are processed in order for each measure. If another route of entry was followed, Step 7 will skip to test (7.105) for each measure in turn.

The first action is to estimate the value of the measure anticipated for next year. This is done using the same procedure as in Step 3, but the output level now includes the outputs imported as well as those produced internally. Secondly, a more severe requirement is set by assuming that the consuming population will grow by ten percent in the next year.

$$XMEAS(n, t+1) = \frac{CNJ(n, j) * XJOT(j, t)}{1.1 * POP(n, k, t)} \qquad (7.102)$$

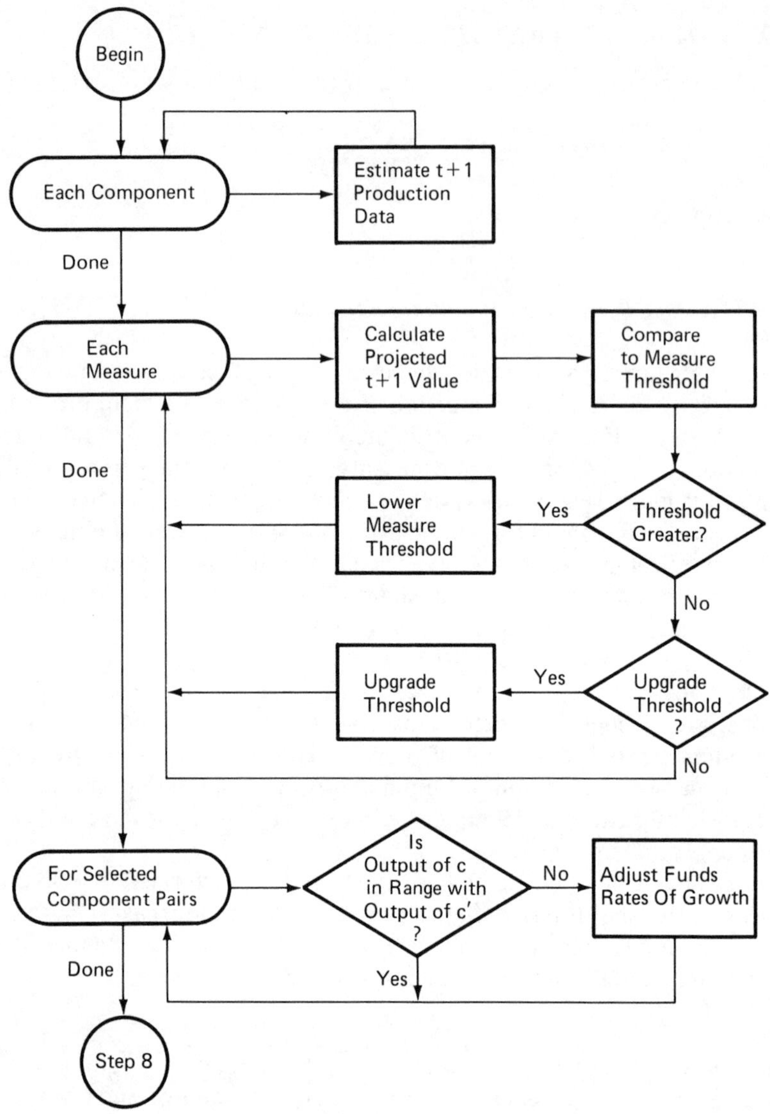

Figure 7-9. Step 7 General Flowchart.

As assessment of the acceptability of the measure threshold is made next using the following test: Is

$$XMEAS(n, t{+}1) < TMEAS(n) \text{ ?} \tag{7.103}$$

If so, proceed to test 7.104; otherwise, go to equation 7.105.

Table 7-7
Step 7 Parameters

Name	*Definition*	*Source*
XJOT(j, t)	Units of output for component j at t	Steps 2 and 5
XMEAS(n, t+1)	Value of measure n at $t + 1$	Calculated
CNJ(n, j)	Coefficient of output j in measure n	Constant
POP(k, n, t)	Size of the kth population at t used in n	Step 1, t
TMEAS(n)	Threshold of measure n	Step 7, previous t
XNVST(j, t)	Funds available to component j at t	Calculated
OCST(j, t)	Unit cost to produce output of component j at t (normalized)	Calculated
XFACT(j)	Unit cost normalizing factor for j	Step 2, Cycle 1
SA or SB(j, t+1)	Investment level of j for the following year	Calculated
SC or SD(j, t+1)	Output level of j for the following year	Calculated
SE(j, t+1)	Ratio of the output level of two sectors	Calculated
RGJ(j, t)	Growth rate of j at t	Step 2

Degrade the threshold of the measure n to:

$$TMEAS(n) = \text{Max}[0.05, XMEAS(n, t+1)] \qquad (7.104)$$

(For the purposes of the initial runs of SOS-2, for every measure the threshold of subsistance is set to 0.05).

At this point the next measure is processed without doing test (7.105).

A two-level test is done to determine if the measure threshold should be increased: Is

$$\left.\begin{array}{l} XMEAS(n, t-1) \geq XMEAS(n, t-2) \quad \text{and is} \\ XMEAS(n, t-2) \geq TMEAS(n)\ ? \end{array}\right\} \qquad (7.105)$$

If so, then set $TMEAS(n) = XMEAS(n, t-2)$; otherwise, $TMEAS(n)$ remains the same.

The final action in this Step 7 is to balance the ratio of the outputs of the durable, nondurable, service, and wholesale and retail trades sections. Next year's investment is estimated.

$$SA(j, t+1) = XNVST(j, t) * [1 + RGJ(j, t)] \qquad (7.106)$$

This level of investment is then transferred to units of output:

$$SC(j, t+1) = SA(j, t+1)/OCST(j, t) * XFACT(j, t) \qquad (7.107)$$

If the ratio of the output level of the two sectors (A, B) being composed is less than 80%, set it to 80%.

$$SE(j, t+1) = SA(j, t+1) * SD(j, t+1) * 0.8/SC(j, t+1) - SA(j, t+1) \qquad (7.108)$$

This output is then converted to a rate of growth for each sector.

$$RGJ(j, t) = \{[(SA(j, t+1) + SE(j, t+1))/XNVST(j, t)] - 1\} * 100 \quad (7.109)$$

If the ratio of the output level of the two sectors being compared is greater than 120%, set it to 120%.

$$SE(j, t+1) = SA(j, t+1) - [SA(j, t+1) * SD(j, t+1) * 1.20]/SC(j, t+1) \quad (7.110)$$

This output is then converted to growth rates for these sectors.

$$RGJ(j, t) = \{[(SA(j, t+1) - SE(j, t+1))/XNVST(j, t)] - 1\} * 100 \quad (7.111)$$

After all measures are processed, Step 7 is complete and Step 8 is initiated.

Cycle Bookkeeping

After Step 7 is completed, the systemic module of the cycle is complete. Step 8 is performed each cycle to do the required bookkeeping to set the data base for the next cycle. Since the initial data base is designed for immediate use in Step 1 for $t = 1$, the initializing of the data base for a cycle can be performed as the last cycle action, rather than as the initial cycle action. The general flowchart is given in Figure 7-10.

Step 8: Reset the Data Base for Next Cycle

Step 8 is entered after the completion of Step 7; it includes a number of bookkeeping chores as well as the performance of time-dependent data updates. These actions include:

Calculating modifiers of the birth, death and migration rates

Adjustment of the work force distribution among paid and unpaid workers

Performing time-delayed adjustments of substitutions and stockpile expansions

Additionally, Step 8 includes preparation of the output table/graph sets that are printed at the end of the run.

As part of the calculations for the birth, death, and immigration rates, a

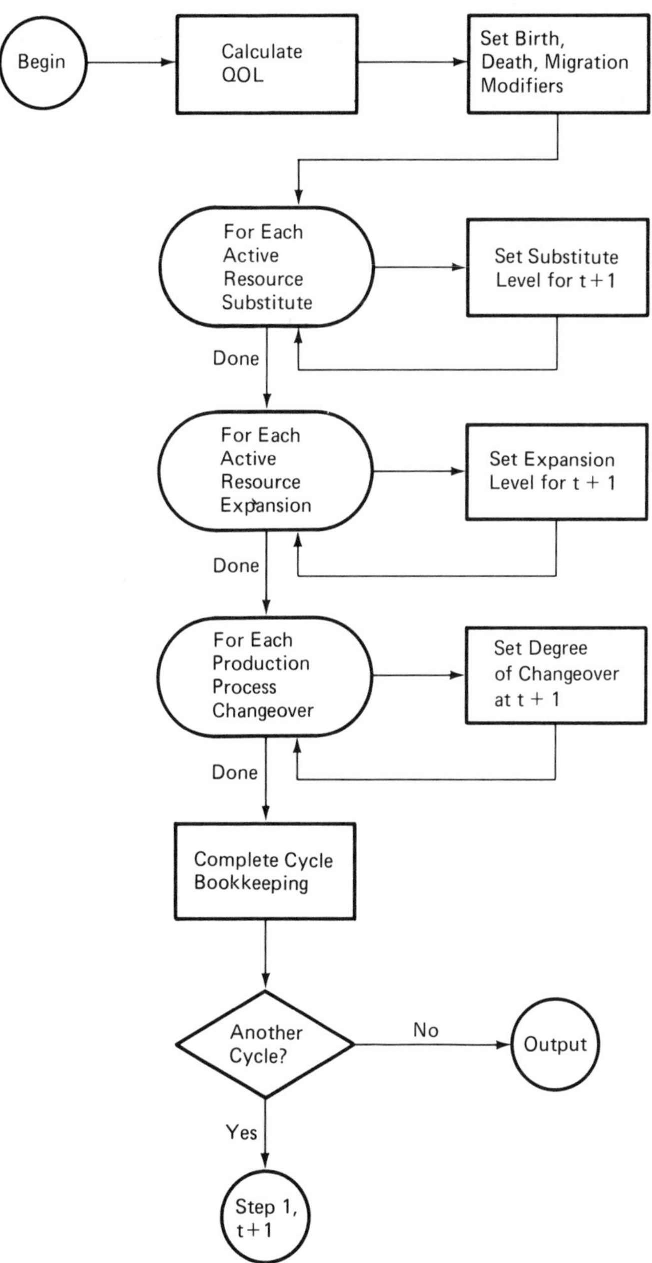

Figure 7-10. Step 8 General Flowchart.

linear combination of the demand measures into a quality of life scalar is used in SOS-2. The value is used only for this set of calculations, and then comes into play only when the values of the measures approach or pass below the subsistance thresholds.

Algorithms. The first set of calculations develop modifiers to the normal population rates based on the QOL scalar value, and for immigration based on the level of employment. These modifiers are applied as multipliers to the normal rates as defined as constants in the data base (see the next chapter).

The QOL scalar is a linear combination of the ratio of the individual measure values to their original thresholds.

$$VALLQL(t) = VN * [MEAS(n, t)/TMEAS(0)] \qquad (7.112)$$

The birthrate modifier is:

$$\begin{aligned} FBR &= 1.0 \text{ if } VALLQL \geq K/2 \\ &= 0.0 \text{ if } VALLQL \leq K/4 \\ &= [[K/2 - VALLQL]/K/4] \text{ otherwise} \end{aligned} \qquad (7.113)$$

The deathrate modifier is:

$$\begin{aligned} FDT &= 1.0 \text{ if } VALLQL \geq K/2 \\ &= 1.0 + K/4 \text{ if } VALLQL \geq K/8 \\ &= 1.0 + K/4 * [[K/2 - VALLQL]/3K/8] \text{ otherwise} \end{aligned} \qquad (7.114)$$

The net immigration modifier is:

$$\begin{aligned} FMG &= 1.0 * K \text{ if } VALLQL \geq 3K/4 \\ &= 0.0 \text{ if } VALLQL \leq K/2 \\ &= e * [1.0 - [3K/4 - VALLQL/K/4]] \text{ otherwise} \end{aligned} \qquad (7.115)$$

where $e = 20 * [ESTCK(r) - 0.9]$ and $r =$ labor.

Note that net immigration is the normal rate when employment is 95% and becomes outmigration if employment is less than 90%.

The next calculation adjusts the total work force units ratio of paid versus unpaid work units due to the reserve of employment becoming close to fully consumed. In Step 2, work unit salaries begin to escalate if unemployment is less than 4%. Additionally, the following calculation draws unpaid workers into the paid labor force if unemployment is less than 4%. This is done by adjusting the partition coefficients for these two population partitions.

The unpaid workers partition value is:

$$a(j, 6, y) = a(j, 6, y) - a(j, 5, y) * [ESTCK(r) - 0.96] \quad (7.116)$$

The paid workers partition value is:

$$a(j, 5, y) = a(j, 5, y) * [1 + ESTCK(r) - 0.96] \quad (7.117)$$

The remaining calculations of Step 8 involve adjustment of resource availability, resource usage, and production process changeover using the data stored in the Future Actions File for $t + 1$. These calculations were defined in Step 4 and Step 6.

As the final action of a cycle of SOS-2, the time clock is advanced to $t + 1$ and a check is made to see if the set of cycles is complete. If not, the next cycle is processed; otherwise, the summary data outputs are begun.

8 Data Requirements

Although often ignored, the data loaded for operation of a model is just as important as the structure of the equations. The first version of the model, SOS-1, proved to be very difficult to load and consequently was almost impossible to transfer. The principal reason for this problem was that the model was designed first and then data was scaled to fit the algorithms.

The present form of the model, SOS-2, included restructuring both to improve the theory and to make better use of available data sources. In the main, the data base is taken from sources that describe the United States around the beginning of this decade. The level, or value, numbers were usually from 1970. However, because this is a long range model, where inspection of the data led us to suspect that 1970 was an unusual year, the level was derived based on an average of several years before 1970. The rate, or growth, numbers were derived as averages of growth rates over the past twenty years or so; again review was done to capture the long term trend rather than reflect a short period cycle.

Following are the variables in the model for which initial values must be loaded. As the last chapter has shown, the remaining values are dynamically derived. The variables are arranged in the general order given in the *Block Data* subroutine of the FORTRAN listing (Appendix A). All of the data variables that can be modified as initial data are collected here for user ease. The variables will be presented with their mnemonic, the number of data items required, the code line number (see Appendix A) and the equation number where the data item is developed or used (chapter 7). Finally, there is an explanatory note for the parameter to assist in selectively modifying data.

Population Totals Data

At the beginning of each run of SOS, selected portions of the *Block Data* are printed out, both to specify the initial data assumptions of the variables and to facilitate data modifications for alternate scenarios. Table 8-1 specifies the initial birth, death, and migration rates.

Table 8-1
Population Totals Data

Mnemonic	*Number of Data Items*	*Code Line Number*	*Equation Number*
1. BR	1	82	7.1
2. DT	1	82	7.1
3. XMG	1	82	7.1
4. TOPTM1	1	84	7.1

Notes:

1. Birth Rate. Set at 0.0180; the United States birth rate for 1970.
2. Death Rate. Set at 0.0094; the United States rate for 1970.
3. Net migration rate deemed as normal, assuming an unemployment rate of 5%. Set at 0.0020, giving a first year level of 400 thousand immigrants.
4. Initial Total Population. Set at 204,000 thousand for 1970.

Age-Year Data

Because most demographic relationships are explained by the age of the population subsets, births and deaths are loaded in yearly amounts from ages 1 to 64 plus a last category for ages 65 and over. In each year, y, the ages covered are $(y - 1, y)$.

For presentation purposes, these age categories are summed in four cohorts:

1-17 (immature)
18-24 (young adults)
25-64 (working adults)
$\geq$ 65 (retired adults)

Tables 8-2 and 8-3 summarize the age-year data requirements.

Population Partitions

Within each of the four age cohorts, the resident population is subdivided into six mutually exclusive partitions:

(1) In Education
(2) In Institutions
(3) Nonworkers
(4) In Training or Welfare
(5) Paid Workers
(6) Unpaid Workers

Table 8-2
Age-Year Population Data

Mnemonic	*Number of Data Items*	*Code Line Number*	*Equation Number*
1. PDTH	65	91-92	7.2
2. AGEPT1	65	85-86	7.2, 7.3
3. XPMG	65	89-90	7.3

Notes:

1. Fraction of deaths for age year for all 65 age years covered in the model.
2. Number of people in each of the 65 age years for the previous year $(t-1)$ in thousands.
3. Fraction of people in each of the 65 age years for the previous year $(t-1)$ for immigration.

Table 8-3
Example Age-Year Data

Age-Year	*Population of Age-Year for Previous Year (thousands)*	*Age-Year Death Rate Fraction*	*Age-Year*	*Age-Year Migrant Fraction*
1	(calculated)	0.0204	1-4	0.01473
2-5	3430.8	0.0008	5-11	0.01434
6	3430.8	0.0004	12-16	0.00955
7-14	4581.3	0.0004		
15	3959.8	0.0004	17-18	0.01684
16-18	3959.8	0.0013		
19-21	3505.7	0.0013	19-24	0.07254
22-25	3505.0	0.0013	25-29	0.03465
26-35	2390.7	0.0016		
36-45	2308.8	0.0031	30-35	0.01567
46-55	2322.0	0.0072	36-45	0.01062
56-64	1859.0	0.01660	46-65	0.00279
≥ 65	21925.0	0.05775	> 65	0.01704

The partition selection is performed from the top; i.e., if a person qualifies in education he is not considered for any other partitions. Partition coefficient data is presented in Table 8-4.

The development of the number of people in each partition requires a coefficient matrix. These coefficients are multiplied by the output of goods (*XJOT*) of the appropriate component produced in the previous cycle. These data are printed out in Table 8-5, Example Partition Coefficients. The values are 1970 data scaled to thousands of people for each partition and output component. The columns are the twelve public and private

Table 8-4
Partition Coefficient Data

Mnemonic	*Number of Data Items*	*Code Line Number*	*Equation Number*
1. CJK1	72 (6×12)	94-96	7.6
2. CJK2	72 (6×12)	98-101	7.6
3. CJK3	72 (6×12)	103-106	7.6
4. CJK4	72 (6×12)	108-110	7.6

Note: The population is partitioned into four cohorts: age 1-17, 18-24, 25-64, and greater than 65. Within each of these the resident population is divided into six mutually exclusive partitions; in education, in institutions, nonworkers, in training or welfare (but not employed), paid workers and unpaid workers.

components of SOS-2. As an example value: in age cohort 1, for each of the education units produced, there is associated a population of 45,863 people. Since (by design) there are 1,000 public education units produced in 1970, the unnormalized public education population size is 45,683 thousand school children less than 18 years old.

The matrix is used to relate the output of the seven private and five public components to the resulting population partition in each of the four cohorts. Coefficients are set so that for each unit of output from the twelve components, the resulting number of people in the partitions in each age segment is equal to the 1970 partition population. In future years, coefficients may be altered and the partition sizes are normalized to cohort population sizes.

Resources Status

The resource data available today are of questionable validity as long term dynamic reserve forecasts. Consequently, the approach taken in SOS-2 represents a compromise to reconcile the quality of the present data with the data needs for a long range model. The five general data items required are: (1) initial reserves, (2) resource unit cost, (3) schedule and amount of additional supply available, (4) other resource substitution possibilities, and (5) recycling potential.

The calibration of the model resources was done by setting the initial reserves of each particular resource at 10,000 units, except the resource of labor. A ratio of present known reserves historically used to the present levels is calculated to arrive at the amount of the original 10,000 units still remaining. This ratio is applicable only to those resources considered

Table 8-5
Example Partition Coefficients

						Age Cohort 1					
Education	45863.	0.	0.	0.	0.	0.	0.	0.	0.	5528.	0.
Institutions	0.	0.	372.	0.	0.	0.	0.	0.	0.	104.	0.
Nonworkers	1435.	1175.	937.	3150.	201.	903.	6090.	3150.	276.	107.	30.
Train & Welfare	0.	0.	122.	0.	0.	0.	0.	0.	0.	0.	0.
Paid Workers	0.	0.	0.	0.	0.	0.	0.	0.	0.	0.	0.
Unpaid Workers	0.	0.	0.	0.	0.	0.	0.	0.	0.	0.	0.
						Age Cohort 2					
Education	5550.	0.	0.	0.	0.	0.	0.	0.	0.	0.	0.
Institutions	0.	0.	153.	0.	0.	0.	0.	0.	0.	0.	0.
Nonworkers	0.	0.	0.	0.	0.	0.	0.	0.	0.	0.	0.
Train & Welfare	0.	0.	415.	0.	0.	0.	0.	0.	0.	0.	0.
Paid Workers	825.	675.	539.	1300.	580.	519.	3500.	2546.	546.	2000.	17.
Unpaid Workers	134.	122.	88.	211.	94.	84.	553.	414.	89.	309.	3.
						Age Cohort 3					
Education	0.	0.	0.	0.	0.	0.	0.	0.	0.	0.	0.
Institutions	0.	0.	415.	0.	0.	0.	0.	0.	0.	0.	0.
Nonworkers	0.	0.	0.	0.	0.	0.	0.	0.	0.	0.	0.
Train & Welfare	0.	0.	743.	0.	0.	0.	0.	0.	0.	0.	0.
Paid Workers	4675.	3825.	3052.	10000.	655.	2943.	19836.	10000.	900.	349.	97.
Unpaid Workers	1901.	1555.	1241.	4068.	266.	1198.	8067.	4068.	366.	142.	40.
						Age Cohort 4					
Education	0.	0.	0.	0.	0.	0.	0.	0.	0.	0.	0.
Institutions	0.	0.	496.	0.	0.	0.	0.	0.	0.	726.	0.
Nonworkers	0.	0.	18836.	0.	0.	0.	0.	0.	0.	0.	0.
Train & Welfare	0.	0.	0.	0.	0.	0.	0.	0.	0.	0.	0.
Paid Workers	0.	0.	0.	0.	0.	0.	0.	0.	0.	0.	0.
Unpaid Workers	0.	0.	0.	0.	0.	0.	0.	0.	0.	0.	0.

Table 8-6
Resource Status Data

Mnemonic	*Number of Data Items*	*Code Line Number*	*Equation Number*
1. STDEP	20	117	7.28
2. K1	20	147-148	7.32
3. K2	20	149-150	7.32
4. K3	20	151	7.32
5. K4	20	152	7.31
6. K5	20	153	7.31
7. RUCST1	20	158-160	7.20
8. REREC	20	119	7.31

Notes:

1. Stock of resources of raw materials that have been used to the date when the model begins. It is the fraction of the 10,000 units of a resource that have been consumed and are nonrenewable at the present time. For annually renewable resources, this value is zero since each is assumed annually renewable in its entirety.

2-4. The values for *K*1, *K*2, and *K*3 are set to produce changes in costs during the first few cycles that appear to be appropriate for the surrogates in the next few real time years. For example, for the case of silver (nor a resource in the current SOS model), when the stockpile is 5000 units the initial cost is $(948 * 0.5)^2$; after another 1000 units are used, then the cost is $(0.948 * 0.6)^2$, an increase of 44%. The unit cost values are scaled so that the costs in production for a given resource would be typical of its share in the present production cost structure in the component processes.

*K*1 is the minimum unit cost to extract a unit of ore at its richest grade and cheapest extraction.

*K*2 is selected such that the maximum extraction unit cost is *K*1 + *K*2.

*K*3 is the value of the exponent to shape the function between the minimum and maximum values.

5-6. The parameters *K*4 and *K*5 are used to set the recycling levels for ores that can be obtained from the debris of products developed and consumed by earlier production/consumption processes. The function, like the unit cost function, depends on the level of reserves consumed to date.

*K*4 is the minimum level of ore reclaimed by recycling without regard to scarcity or unit price.

*K*5 is set such that *K*4 + *K*5 is the maximum ratio of recycled ores to extracted ores based on engineering feasibility.

(Note: in program listings, Appendix A, all K# are XK# to allow easier transferability to other computers).

7. The mean unit cost is calculated for the first year based on the present *STDEP* plus the level of stocks that are estimated to be consumed. Using these values and the unit cost equation a first estimate can be developed.

8. The recycling level for the first year can be developed by procedures similar to developing the first year unit costs.

Table 8-7
Example Resource Parameters

	K1	*K2*	*K3*	*K4*	*K5*
1 Fibre & Food	24.600	26.400	2.000	0.0	0.0
2 Iron & Steel	49.000	49.000	2.000	0.540	0.460
3 Copper	40.000	320.000	2.000	0.250	0.500
4 Non-Ferrous	8.000	52.000	2.000	0.090	0.410
5 Coal	0.0	1686.000	2.000	0.0	0.0
6 Petro-Nat Gas	7.200	58.700	2.000	0.0	0.0
7 Stone & Clay	8.000	52.000	2.000	0.0	0.0
8 Chemicals	0.790	1.580	2.000	0.0	0.0
9 Lead & Zinc	8.000	52.000	2.000	0.120	0.880
10 Aluminum	49.900	49.000	2.000	0.010	0.990
15 Urban Land	7.200	8.000	2.000	0.0	0.0
16 Arable Land	9.600	9.000	2.000	0.0	0.0
17 Capital	4.900	5.900	2.000	0.0	0.0
18 Work Units	5.000	5.900	2.000	0.0	0.0

nonrenewable. For renewable resources, the data value is reset each year to provide anew the 10,000 reserve units plus the expansion of production levels since 1970. For paid workers, the reserve level is the paid work partition size, in thousands; this is done to allow a simpler interpretation of demographic data.

The stock-level-used-to-date, *STDEP*, is the fraction of the 10,000 units that have been consumed that are nonrenewable at the present time. For annually renewable resources this value is zero since each of these is assumed annually renewable in its entirety.

Present unit cost for a resource is set by first determining the maximum unit price at the level of use for the cycle, and then developing a mean unit price from this maximum value and the previous year's maximum value. The level of usage for any cycle can be calculated from the projected levels of production output for the cycle (see the production data discussion). From this the used stockpile fraction at the end of the cycle, $ESTCK(r)$, can be obtained. The maximum unit price is:

$$[K1(r) + K2(r) * ESTCK(r)]^{K3(r)} * TEMP$$

when *TEMP* is set by equation 7.33, and $K1(r)$, $K2(r)$ are constants listed in Tables 8-6 and 8-7.

The values for $K1(r)$ and $K2(r)$, as well as the initial stock level were selected primarily to produce changes in costs during the first few cycles that appear to be appropriate for the next few real-time years after 1970.

Additionally, the initial values were scaled so that the costs in production for a given resource type would be typical of its share in the present production-costs structure in the component outlays, using data from the *U.S. Statistical Abstracts*.

The recycling rate for a nonrenewable ore represents that fraction of the ore that can be obtained from recycling debris from earlier production processes (output no longer in use). The recycling rate used at any time is:

$$K4(r) + K5(r) * ESTCK(r)^2$$

The example values for $K4$ and for $K5$ are given in Table 8-7 and represent conservative estimates of recycling capabilities with today's technologies. Note that no recycling is considered for renewable resources in the example data; in the general case this restriction can be lifted without altering the model algorithms.

The present annual use rate for resources is a function of the production process requirements. The determination of the level of resources that are withdrawn from the existing reserve stockpile vis-a-vis those produced by the recycling process from production debris is obtained from the values of the initial stockpile for the cycle, the associated recycling ratio, and the projected level of use of ores during the cycle.

These and other required data elements are presented in Table 8-6 and have example data in Table 8-7.

Resource Usage Adjustment Date

As resources are used, thus depleting the available stockpile, a set of tests are made to determine if the level of resources have reached a depletion level that is critical enough to project an expansion of the available stockpile; (i.e., extraction of neglected ores that now become economic due to a rise in unit sales prices) or to have all production processes substitute, partially or completely, for a resource in short supply. Data needed to implement these adjustments are defined in Table 8-8.

To select the times when a resource is considered to be in short supply, four points of stockpile depletion are set for each nonrenewable and renewable resource. In any cycle where one of these points, $FLAG(4)$, is past or if the stock depletion is greater than 0.985, the search for resource usage adjustments is initiated. The four values used for the test case are given in Table 8-9.

If a stock depletion point is past, two contingencies are checked. One of the resource checks determines whether the existing stockpile reserve can be increased. This can occur if the incremental size of the stockpile is greater than zero and if an increase is not presently underway. The increase

Table 8-8
Resource Usage Adjustment Data

Mnemonic	*Number of Data Items*	*Code Line Number*	*Equation Number*
1. FLAG	80 (20×4)	155-157	7.39, 7.59
2. CPILE	20	236-237	7.67
3. SUBDAT	130 (10×13)	190-194	7.60, 7.61

Notes:

1. For each resource, four fractional levels of resource depletion are provided to set off a signal that checks to make resource adjustments that should now be made. If the value of *FLAG* is greater than the last year *ESTCK* but less than this year's *ESTCK*, the adjustment test is positive.
2. If an adjustment test is positive and if reserve stockpile increase is not presently underway, the level of reserves will be increased by this value, phased over the next five years.
3. The matrix allows up to 10 substitutions to be stored for consideration. For each substitution, 13 values are stored.

   1—the number of the resource to be adjusted.

   2—a code set equal to −1.

   3, 5, 7, 9, 11—a resource number that is used in the substitution process or zero if all are placed in earlier cells.

   4, 6, 8, 10, 12—the amount of the resource ($n-1$) that is used in this substitution to replace one unit of ore of resource (1).

   13—the number of years that is required to fully change over to the new substitution formula.

Table 8-9
Example Resource Depletion Warnings

Resource	*Increment to Stockpile CPILE(r)*	*Warning Levels FLAG(r, t)*			
1 Fibre & Food	0.0	0.80	0.87	0.92	0.95
2 Iron & Steel	5000.00	0.30	0.60	0.92	0.95
3 Copper	2000.00	0.30	0.60	0.92	0.95
4 Non-Ferrous	5000.00	0.60	0.75	0.92	0.95
5 Coal	5000.00	0.30	0.60	0.92	0.95
6 Petro-Nat Gas	5000.00	0.30	0.60	0.92	0.95
7 Stone & Clay	10000.00	0.30	0.60	0.92	0.95
8 Chemicals	10000.00	0.30	0.60	0.92	0.95
9 Lead & Zinc	2500.00	0.30	0.60	0.92	0.95
10 Aluminum	2500.00	0.30	0.60	0.92	0.95
15 Urban Land	0.0	0.80	0.80	0.92	0.95
16 Arable Land	5000.00	0.50	0.55	0.60	0.95
17 Capital	0.0	0.0	0.0	0.0	0.0
18 Work Units	0.0	0.85	0.90	0.92	0.95

Table 8-10
Example Substitution Formulas

1. Copper	0.15 units of iron and 0.6 units of copper
2. Copper	0.15 units iron, 0.1 units other non-iron, 0.6 units copper
3. Fibers	0.5 units fiber, 0.1 units chemicals
4. Oil	0.02 units coal, 0.3 units oil
5. Urban Land	0.9 units urban land, 0.05 units arable land
6. Lead	0.05 units of iron, 0.8 units of lead

of stocks to the new level is assumed to take five years. The incremental stockpile size *CPILE*(*r*) assumed for this data base is shown in Table 8-9.

The second resource check determines if there are one or more substitutions available to reduce the usage of the resource, and that is projected to be less cost over the next five years. If any exist, the least costly for the next five years is selected. In this case, once a substitution for a nonrenewable resource is done, it cannot be made again. Each substitution that is activated is initiated during the next cycle and takes several years to be implemented fully. Table 8-10 displays the initial set of substitutions and the associated time factor. As an example, substitution 5 allows a change in use of urban land by any production process that uses urban land. The substitution is, for every unit of urban land (as existant in 1970) that is used formerly, 0.9 units of urban land plus 0.05 units of arable land can be used. (Note that the unit sizes of land are not equal.)

Component Production Data

The resource utilization and production of component output for regional consumption and for export requires data including:

- Annual funds projected for maintenance and production
- Maintenance rates for capital expansion, capital maintenance, and environmental maintenance
- Historical export and import amounts in millions of dollars
- Resource utilization formulas for production of one unit of output (both active and alternative production formulas)

Component Funds Data

The initial level of funds and the initial annual rate of funds growth are input

Table 8-11
Component Funds Data

Mnemonic	*Number of Data Items*	*Code Line Number*	*Equation Number*
1. XNVST1	12	121-122	7.9
2. RGJ	12	114	7.9
3. XEPORT	12	203	7.19
4. XMPORT	12	248	7.19
5. CAPVL	12	239	7.17
6. EXPDUR	12	168	7.13
7. QOLT	12	115	7.15
8. ECODUR	12	167	7.13
9. XMRNOR	12	202	7.14

Notes:

1. The 1970 value of production and maintenance funds in each of the five public and seven private components in millions of dollars. The total is equal to the GNP.
2. Initial annual growth rate in percent of funds for each of the five public and seven private production components.
3. The initial export level of the component in millions of dollars.
4. The initial import level of the component in millions of dollars.
5. Funds, in millions of dollars, required to expand the capital facilities of a component sufficient for one unit of output.
6. Fraction of each capital expansion dollar spent to purchase durable goods from each component.
7. Fraction of one unit of production costs required to repair one unit of environmental damage.
8. Fraction of each environmental damage repair dollar spent to purchase goods from each component.
9. Percentage of each investment dollar required to offset depreciation.

for each production component. The Component Funds Data is summarized in Table 8-11. These values are shown in Table 8-12. Investment funds are in millions of dollars for 1970; rate of growth is a percentage using 1950-1970 data in 1970 dollars. Data are taken from U.S. Department of Commerce figures. Additional funds available, or taken from the component production are the value of exports in millions of dollars, imports in millions of dollars, and funds used for capital goods for both expansion and environmental controls. The values for capital goods include a unit cost for one unit of expansion and a unit cost to offset one unit of environmental damage plus a distribution fraction indicating which components are paid these costs for producing the needed capital goods. The trade example data are also shown in Table 8-12 while the capital data are in Table 8-13.

Table 8-12
Example Component Funds Data

No.	*Name*	*Growth Rates (%)*	*Funds ($10^6$$)*	*Exports*	*Imports*
1	Education	3.20	15579.	0.0	0.0
2	Trans. & Commun.	4.30	6361.	0.0	0.0
3	Health & Welfare	6.50	29988.	0.0	0.0
4	Public Safety	3.70	18175.	0.0	0.0
5	Admin. & Other	4.80	19992.	0.0	0.0
6	Agriculture	1.00	41016.	7800.	6500.0
7	Non-Dur. Manuf.	3.10	113215.	2200.	17900.0
8	Durable Manuf.	3.10	182127.	43400.	22700.0
9	Commun. & Trans.	3.20	96295.	6200.	4800.0
10	Whol.-Ret. Trade	3.30	161871.	0.0	0.0
11	Services	3.60	149576.	4300.	6400.0
12	Mining	1.00	12086.	2200.	7000.0

Table 8-13
Example Durable Goods Expenditure Data

Component		*CAPVL*	*EXPDUR*	*ECODUR*	*XMRNOR*	*QOLT*
No.	*Name*	(%)	(%)	(%)	(%)	(%)
1	Education	9	0	0	3	0
2	Trans. & Commun.	15	1	1	6	4
3	Health & Welfare	20	0	0	4	0
4	Public Safety	20	0	0	3	0
5	Admin. & Other	20	0	0	3	0
6	Agriculture	50	0	5	7	30
7	Non-Dur. Manuf.	60	30	25	9	40
8	Durable Manuf.	100	49	46	9	30
9	Commun. & Trans.	50	5	7	8	4
10	Whol.-Ret. Trade	25	5	10	6	10
11	Service	35	10	1	6	20
12	Mining	25	0	5	7	30

Resource Utilization Data

For each production component a present production formula—usage of each resource type to produce one unit of output—plus alternative production formulae are entered. Each entry consists of the number of units of each resource to be used for one unit of output (scaled by 1000), and indication as to whether the formula is initially in use, and a time in years

Table 8-14
Resource Utilization Data

Mnemonic	*Number of Data Items*	*Code Line Number*	*Equation Number*
1. UTIL	240 (20×12)	249-269	7.25, 7.83
2. XUTIL	380 (20×19)	210-225	—
3. XMARK	12	228	—

Notes:

1. Required amount of resources to output one unit of *j* using current production formula's mix.
2. For each production component there is a present production formula (which relates the use of each resource type to the production of one unit of output) plus alternate production formulas. Each entry consists of the number of units of each of the twenty resources to be used for one unit of output (scaled by 1000).
3. Marker, set as 0 for no, 1 for yes, that sets the current production function for the beginning time period. (No denotes nonactive.)

required to fully implement a change to a nonactive formula. Table 8-14 summarizes the organization of this data, while Table 8-15 presents the actual input.

The computer output from *Block Data* (Table 8-15) lists all of the possible production functions *XUTIL* and the active ones this period *UTIL*.

Demand Measures Data

The calculation of eleven demand measures used in SOS-2 (Table 8-16) runs requires development of the coefficients associated with production output, an initial threshold value for the measure *TMEAS*, and selection of the population base *DN* to be used in selecting the per capita size. When the set of measures are combined into a scalar to set the birth, death, and immigration modifiers, a weighting factor *VN* is required. All data are given in Table 8-17.

As examples of the measure construction, measure 1 reflects education satisfaction. For measure 1 the population considered *DN* is school attendance. The relative contributions of the 12 production components are 80.6% from government operated education, 19.4% from private schools (assigned to the services sector) and none from other components. In 1970 when all component output was 1000 units and total population is about 200 million, the measure 2 value is 50.

Since the threshold is 0.35, education is exceeding its lowest required value; here, by a resilience level of $(0.50 - 0.35)/0.35 = 0.42$.

Table 8-15
Production Formulas

(XUTIL)

	COMPONENT NUMBER	1.	1.	2.	3.	4.	5.	5.	6.	6.	7.	7.	8.	8.	8.	9.	10.	10.	11.	12.
	IF ACTIVE,=1 *	1.	0.	1.	1.	1.	1.	0.	1.	0.	1.	0.	1.	0.	0.	1.	1.	0.	1.	1.
1	FIBRE & FOOD	1.	1.	1.	29.	24.	12.	12.	3266.	3266.	4848.	4848.	0.	0.	0.	60.	90.	90.	199.	10.
2	IRON & STEEL	0.	0.	0.	0.	0.	0.	0.	0.	0.	8.	8.	191.	191.	205.	2.	0.	0.	0.	1.
3	COPPER	0.	0.	0.	1.	0.	1.	1.	0.	0.	2.	1.	228.	200.	200.	0.	0.	0.	0.	18.
4	NON-FERROUS	0.	0.	0.	1.	0.	1.	1.	0.	0.	4.	6.	86.	100.	95.	0.	0.	0.	0.	8.
5	COAL	0.	0.	0.	0.	0.	11.	11.	0.	0.	15.	20.	0.	0.	0.	0.	0.	0.	0.	4.
6	PETRO-NAT GAS	0.	0.	0.	0.	0.	0.	0.	0.	0.	408.	300.	1.	2.	1.	0.	0.	0.	20.	3.
7	STONE & CLAY	0.	0.	0.	0.	0.	1.	1.	0.	0.	15.	15.	29.	33.	30.	0.	0.	0.	88.	6.
8	CHEMICALS	0.	0.	0.	0.	0.	0.	0.	0.	0.	22.	30.	24.	25.	25.	0.	0.	0.	0.	4.
9	LEAD & ZINC	0.	0.	0.	0.	0.	0.	0.	0.	0.	40.	40.	279.	300.	280.	0.	0.	0.	0.	1.
10	ALUMINUM	0.	0.	0.	0.	1.	0.	0.	0.	0.	4.	4.	193.	193.	193.	0.	0.	0.	0.	2.
15	URBAN LAND	0.	0.	750.	0.	0.	0.	0.	0.	0.	750.	750.	750.	750.	750.	750.	750.	750.	1875.	0.
16	ARABLE LAND	0.	0.	0.	0.	0.	0.	0.	6750.	6500.	0.	0.	0.	0.	0.	0.	0.	0.	0.	250.
17	CAPITAL	0.	0.	0.	0.	0.	0.	0.	0.	0.	0.	0.	0.	0.	0.	0.	0.	0.	0.	0.
18	WORK UNITS	2650.	2133.	4078.	2344.	917.	2854.	2346.	5235.	4265.	6752.	6752.	10177.	10177.	10177.	6282.	16589.	12796.	21593.	517.
19	AIR UNITS	0.	0.	2000.	0.	0.	0.	0.	0.	0.	0.	0.	2000.	1000.	500.	200.	0.	0.	1000.	0.
20	WATER UNITS	0.	0.	0.	0.	0.	0.	0.	0.	0.	1000.	625.	625.	1250.	625.	0.	0.	0.	1250.	875.

*Statistic *XMARK*

Table 8-16
Demand Measure Data

Mnemonic	*Number of Data Items*	*Code Line Number*	*Equation Number*
1. CNJ	132 (12×11)	176-180	7.46
2. TMEAS	12	182	7.49
3. VN	12	185	7.112
4. DN	12	181	7.46

Notes:

1. Multiplier of component output (*j*) to assign weight of each output to satisfaction of measure (*k*).
2. Minimum threshold value for measure (*k*) required to assign system satisfaction of the measure.
3. Weighting multiplier for combining of all measures into an aggregate measure, constrained by the requirement $\Sigma VN = 1.00$.
4. Partition number for population size to be used with measure (*k*). DN = 7 is total population; other DN indices are discussed earlier in the section entitled Population Partitions.

These measures comprise a major driving force for adjustments of funds and resource usage in SOS-2. Because of this, in a policy analysis, considerable care is needed in setting each measure to reflect a discrete population goal or interest that is representative of the region under analysis. In measure development the following guidelines should be observed:

(1) Each of the measures should represent a discrete area of the production processes. If a measure is set up that includes all or many component outputs as contributors and, during a run, it becomes delinquent, this forces each of the included components to attempt to expand output. Thus, a general measure can cause attempts that overcompensate and that signal that the majority of the output areas are in trouble when the actual cause may be much more localized.

(2) Not all components need to be included in the set of measures; however, if a component measure is not included in at least one measure, then there is no driving force to make it boost funds for output as resource costs grow. On the other hand, even if it is not included it does contribute to adjustments in terms of adjusting output formulas or resource substitutions. Thus it acts as a component having a set pattern of growth that is not changed by population preferences but that does act as a user of resource and a recipient of technological change.

(3) Each measure has equal weight in the adjustment process and is independent of all other measures; hence, each measure can be constructed without regard to other measures as long as the set of measures in-

Table 8-17
Demand Functions

******DEMAND FUNCTIONS******

COMPONENT		CNJ (measure, component)											
No.	Name												
1	EDUCATION	806.	0.	0.	0.	0.	0.	0.	0.	0.	0.	0.	0.
2	TRANS & COMMUN	0.	0.	500.	0.	0.	0.	0.	0.	0.	0.	0.	0.
3	HEALTH&WELFARE	0.	0.	0.	1000.	1000.	0.	0.	0.	0.	0.	0.	0.
4	PUBLIC SAFETY	0.	0.	0.	0.	0.	1000.	0.	0.	0.	0.	0.	0.
5	ADMIN & OTHER	0.	0.	0.	0.	0.	0.	0.	0.	0.	0.	200.	0.
6	AGRICULTURE	0.	45.	0.	0.	0.	0.	0.	0.	20.	1000.	0.	0.
7	NON-DUR MANUF	0.	130.	0.	0.	0.	0.	500.	0.	130.	0.	0.	0.
8	DURABLE MANUF	0.	260.	0.	0.	0.	0.	500.	0.	240.	0.	0.	0.
9	COMMUN & TRANS	0.	70.	500.	0.	0.	0.	0.	1000.	60.	0.	0.	0.
10	WHOL-RET TRADE	0.	180.	0.	0.	0.	0.	0.	0.	250.	0.	0.	0.
11	SERVICES	194.	310.	0.	0.	0.	0.	0.	0.	290.	0.	800.	0.
12	MINING	0.	0.	0.	0.	0.	0.	0.	0.	0.	0.	0.	1000.
	TMEAS THRESHOLD	1.65	1.00	0.40	68.00	40.00	0.40	1.00	0.40	0.35	0.40	0.40	0.40
	WN (measure) WEIGHT	0.10	0.11	0.06	0.06	0.12	0.10	0.07	0.08	0.08	0.08	0.07	0.07
	POPULATION BASE	1.00	5.00	7.00	4.00	2.00	7.00	5.00	7.00	7.00	7.00	7.00	7.00

cludes a nonzero coefficient for each output component that should be sensitive to regional desires.

(4) Initial threshold values for measures should be set relative to the known initial measure values to represent the level of initial relative stress patterns. For example, if all output areas other than education are considered adequate, the example data thresholds might have been set so that the resilience of measures 1 and 2 were −0.10 and all others were 0.15. This would have caused in cycle 1 immediate pressure to boost educational input funds.

9 Model Output

The output of a specific scenario of the SOS-2 model is dependent on the data entries discussed in chapter 8 and has been constructed to be a complete documentation of the variable input information, the annual status of the system, and the set of system adjustments performed endogenously for that year. A third section tabulates and presents time history graphs of the values of output for all major system status variables. Each of these three sections of output are discussed in subsequent paragraphs. Examples of each can be taken from Appendix B, which is a complete output listing of the basic scenario described in chapter 2 and which uses the example data given in chapter 8.

Input Data Verification

The first eight pages of output from the computer run is no more than formatting of the *Block Data* files. This is done both to specify the beginning data assumptions and to facilitate the loading of a new data base to run scenario variations. A description of this output and the data base is found in chapter 8.

Annual System Status

The next repeating pattern of two pages, headed, "YEAR IS ----" is a record of the results of the yearly iteration results of the model. The total number of years is controlled by setting a value for NCYCLE in the MAIN subroutine (line 13). In some of the runs presented in this book there are 40 cycles, carrying the model from 1970 to the year 2010; other runs span 30 years extending to the year 2000.

Yearly Output

The first page of the yearly output is divided into four areas: Population, Production, Resources, and System Resilience. We shall now describe each of these in turn.

Population

The Population section, found in the upper left hand quadrant of the page, contains two types of output. The first reports on the number of people in each of the six partitions used in the model. Each of these partitions are utilized elsewhere in the model. For example, the education and institutional partitions are used as the denominator in the calculation of the present value of some of the QOL measures. The unemployed partition plus yearly unemployment number is also used in the same fashion. The unpaid worker partition constitutes a potential labor pool for transfer to paid workers in the system. The number of people in these partitions is summed to the total population each year.

The second section prints the actual number of births, deaths, and net in-migrants.

Production

The second grouping, labeled Production and located in the upper right quadrant of the page, reports on selected variables related to the productive elements of the system. The first column, Production Fund, shows the amount of capital (in 1970 dollars) available for each of the twelve sectors for producing the goods and services desired by the system. This figure gives the funds spent for expansion and maintenance of the capital and equipment plus the amount necessary to maintain existing ambient air and water quality and to purchase imports. These funds are also presented as a total and approximate the National Income parameter on our National Income Accounts. The next column, Maintenance, is the percentage of total funds available that is taken up by all maintenance activities.

The Output column for the twelve sectors is scaled to 1000 units in the beginning year (here 1970). The Imports and Exports columns are also based on the same scale. The relationship between the three values is relatively straightforward. The amount of Imports in any given year is a function of the relative (external/internal) unit price of the goods and services of a sector. These Imports have a degree of historical rigidity, so it takes time for the system to adjust to price savings. Consequently, the supply of goods and services available for consumption in any one year is the units produced in a sector of Output plus the units Imported. If this is less than desired by the system, adjustments are attempted (see chapter 7). If it is more than sufficient, then the model attempts to export some or all of the excess.

The final column is the cumulative annual growth rate of each sector's output from the start to the present iteration.

Resources

The Resources section, in the lower left hand area of the first annual states page, deals with the disposition of the resources to be used by the system in the production of its goods and services. Although the model is currently designed to take 20 resource categories, only 16 are used in this example (air and water, categories 19 and 20, are not printed).

The Stockpile number represents the amount of a resource available at the end of the cycle. The Percent Used is a simple calculation of the amount of the stockpile used to produce the goods and services of the year divided by the total stockpile available in the run to date.

A declining Stockpile, particularly in those resources which are non-renewable, is a cause for some concern. The model, as noted earlier, allows for three resource based methods (plus an I/O change discussed below) of adding to or stretching the resource base. The first method, Recycle Ratio, allows a given percentage of the resource previously used to be recycled. If adding to the base is not sufficient to overcome the crisis, then the system is able to begin to substitute the mix of raw materials among themselves while still making use of the same production processes. The Substitution Number refers to the numbered substitutions produced on the *Block Data* output described above. A third method of stockpile increase can occur due to ores becoming economic at higher unit prices. When this occurs the increase is shown in Stockpile Increase. The Year Completed parameter tells us how long it will take for all of the processes in the system to switch from the current resource mix to the new one or to implement mining of stockpile increases.

System Resilience

The final quadrant of the page, the lower right hand side, is labeled System Resilience. These eleven measures are reported as the per capita expenditures of the production measures. For example, the Education measure takes the output of the Education Sector (1000 units) and after multiplying it by the earned weights, divides it by the number of people being educated (Education in the Population section):

$$\frac{(1000) * (1.)\ N * 10^5}{58{,}825{,}930} = 1.70$$

The education, employment, welfare, and health measures make use of closely related population partitions. The remainder of the measures use total population.

Total System Expenditure

The second page of the yearly output is more closely akin to the statistics that economists deal with. The final lines report the yearly expenditures in the maintenance of capital and the environment, together with a section that reports on the amount of previously deferred maintenance done that year.

The initial section is a presentation of a generalized production function and reports the amount of the material, the unit price, and the total cost for the resources. These resources are reported in the familiar categories of land, labor, capital, and raw materials. The total amount spent in production is also calculated. This total and the one reported on the previous page are not exactly the same due to where they are calculated in the routine. If there are no serious shortages of raw materials or other major traumas, then they will be quite close. However, because the total on the previous page is a gross estimate of production capacity at the beginning of a year and the second calculation is the actual expenditures after any price adjustments that occur during a year, the numbers may vary greatly for years that are at the turning points of major system adjustments.

Summary Scenario Data

Capital Credits

After the yearly reports are completed (here at year 2000), there is a table which reports the amounts of new production funds available to the twelve sectors because of various types of maintenance or capital expansion carried out in a given year; this prevents the subtraction of maintenance from productive capital from being a leakage from the system.

Tabular Output

The setting of the PPLOT to 1.0 will result in the printing of a summary graph for Population (nP), Natural Resources (two sets, N and E), Private (I) and Public (G) Sectors, Employed Workers (W), QOL (Q), and Land (F), and Air and Water Damage (M). In addition to the graph, a table is shown which lists the indicator values for the number of years specified in NCYCLE. If DETAIL is set to 1.0, then each of the 41 indices are printed in individual graphs.

All graphs conform to the following rules:

(a) The absolute amount of the parameters in question is converted to an index, with the beginning year (1970 here) as base = 1.00.

(b) The ordinate of the graph is scaled from the lowest to the highest value of the variable(s) covered in the graph. This means that the shape of the function described by a single variable (say population) may not be obvious when reported with other variables and so has to be studied in the DETAIL graphs if such information is important.

(c) The abscissa is scaled (automatically) to the number of years specified in NCYCLE (here 40).

Other Scenario Input Options

There are a number of things that can be done with the model beyond those automatically produced in a base case run. There are three types of possibilities: (1) changing the data base, (2) specifying printed output and, (3) introducing exogenous variables to the model.

Changing the Data Base

SOS-2 has been designed as a computer program with maximum flexibility of data specification in mind. All of the model variables are put in common and are gathered in the subroutine labeled *Block Data*. None of the significant variables are embedded in the code. The user who wishes to change all or some portion of these variables merely has to refer to this subroutine to change the necessary data card images.

Specifying Printed Output

There are three options available for the user in terms of the amount and kind of output he desires. (1) PPLOT is a switch that may be set as 0 or 1. If it is set at 1, the model prints out summary maps and tables. If at 0, no summary graphs are printed. (2) DETAIL if set at 1, prints individual graphs of the indices; zero supresses these graphs. (3) PRINTX is set to a number. This number specifies the number of sets of output to be printed.

Exogenous Specifications

Unfortunately, at least for those who desire models to be crystal balls, we shall never be able to specify a model which encompasses all of the parameters that could cause a system to change. Therefore, if SOS is to be used over a period of years and it becomes necessary to introduce time-series calibrations into the model there has to be a method available to accomplish the task. Further, many of the scenarios that can be specified to create alternate futures of interest to a researcher, teacher, or decision maker require changes not only in present levels and rates but in future ones as well. Some scenarios might even require the specification of a full function which overrides the model results. To accomplish these desired ends, the variable EXOG was created.

Procedure. One is able to make two general types of changes. The first type of changes is in the level of expenditure or item. The second is in the rate of growth. Each change card has four items to add: (1) year of change, (2) change code, (3) index of items to be changed, and (4) the multiple of the change.

The change codes presented are as follows:

1. Level of Production Sector Investment
2. Rate of Growth of Sector Funds
3. Rate of Environmental Unit Cost
4. Increase of Available Resource Stockpile
5. Level of Demand Measure Threshold
6. Level of Lowest Resource Unit Cost
7. Rate of Growth of Resource Cost

The index of the parameter to be changed allows specification of the absolute value desired. For example, if a (1) is specified as the change code (the level of production sector investment), then a (7) in the index area would specify that the level of investment to be changed was light industry.

Appendix A
Source FORTRAN Listings for SOS-2 Including Example Case Data

MAIN

```
C**     PROGRAM MASTER AS OF 1 MAY 1975,
C**     FOR FUBLICATION AS CODE FOR SOS-2.
        COMMCN/YEAR/NCYCLE,RESPR(20),DEGRAC(12),UPGRAD(12),IYEAR
        WRITE (6,1)
      1 FORMAT(1H1,51H<<<  S T A T E   O F   T H E   S Y S T E M   R U N   >>>)
C**     PRINT INITIAL GROWTH DATA FOR RUN
        CALL SETUP
        DO 100 NCYCLE = 1,30
        IYEAR = NCYCLE +1970.
C**     POPULATION DATA FOR CYCLE
        CALL STEP1
C**     PRODUCTION DATA FOR CYCLE
        CALL STEP2
C**     QOL MEASURES FOR CYCLE
        CALL STEP3
C**     ADJUSTS RESOURCE AVAILABILITY
        CALL STEP4
C**     EXPORTS, IMPORTS AND DCES NEEDED SHORT TERM MAINT DEFERRAL
        CALL STEP5(S8)
C**     IF S8=0 THEN SHORT TERM FUNDS WERE SUFFICIENT TO ADJUST
C**     COMPCNENT OUTPUT; OTHERWISE DO LONG TERM ADJUSTMENT IN STEP6
        IF (S8.EQ.0.0)  GO  TC  200
        CALL STEP6(PSUM1,PSUM2,S8)
C**     STEP7 ENTERED TO LOWER AND UPGRADE THRESHOLD LEVELS
        GO TO 400
C**     STEP7 ENTERED ONLY TC UPGRADE THRESHOLD
    200 PSUM1=1.0
        PSUM2=0.0
    400 CALL STEP7(PSUM1,PSUM2,S8)
C**     SET UP FOR NEXT CYCLE
     50 CALL STEP8(S8)
    100 CONTINUE
C**     SIMULATION COMPLETE; ENTER SUMMARY OUTPUT SUBROUTINE
        CALL OTPUT
        STOP
        END
```

```
0001              BLOCK DATA
           C**
           C      INITIALIZATION  STEP1
           C**
           C**
0002              COMMCN/TWC/XMCST1(20),PILE(20)
0003              COMMCN/PRINT/XPRNT1,XPRNT2,PRINTX,DETAIL,PPLOT
0004              COMMON/YEAR/NCYCLE,RESPR(20),DEGRAD(12),UPGRAD(12),IYEAR
0005              COMMCN/POPSCA/BR,DT,XMG,XXBR,DTHPTB,TOTMIG,XPMG(64)
0006              COMMCN/INTER/FMG,TOPTM1,AGEPT1(65)
                 1 ,TOPT,POPKT(4,6),AGRIT(4),FBR,FDT,PDTH(65)
0007              COMMON/CHAR/CJK1(6,12),CJK2(6,12),CJK3(6,12),CJK4(6,12)
0008              CCMMCN/INTER2/RGJ(12),QOLT(12),RESOR(20),TOTKT(12),
                 1 ESTCK(20),STDEP(20),RUCST(20),CAPREQ(12),
                 2 REREC(20),FLAGR(20),XMESTR(20),
                 3 XNVST1(12),XNVST(12),XJOT(12),UTIL(12,20)
0009              CCMMCN/COST/RUCST1(20),RUCST2(20),XFACT(12),OCST(12),OCSTI(12)
0010              CCMMON/OUTDIV/REDIV(20),XMPORT(12),UTILI(12,20),RUCSTI(20)
0011              COMMCN/DURBLE/XMDUR(110,12),ECODUR(12),EXPDUR(12),XMNDUR(12)
0012              COMMCN/INTER3/CNJ(12,12),DN(12),TMEAS(12),DNJT1(12,12),COUNT1(12),
                 1 XMDEL(12),RESIL(12),POP(8),VN(12),XMEAS(12),RATVST(12)
0013              COMMCN/INTER4/SUBDAT(10,13),SUBMAT(1000),SUBPIL(900),LST,LP
0014              COMMCN/TWORK/WORK(20),RESPRT(21)
0015              COMMCN/INTER5/XMRNOR(12),EJOT1(12),EXPO(12),EJOTX,SNCST,RESPR1(20)
                 1 ,XIDFMN(12),XINJO(12),EJOT(12),XFILE(3,12),RESMN1(12),XKTI(12),
                 2 XEPORT(12)
0016              COMMCN/INTER6/XUTIL(19,20),XMARK(19),TIME(19),ICTR,
                 1 SUBIOP(1000),KR5,LTNCY,INDX(19),XOCST(19),XMOCST(12)
0017              CCMMCN/INTER8/CPILE(20),CAPVL(12),OUTMAT(50,40),XMBRK(19),
                 1 SUMMAT(50,10),PUBDIV,PUBNUM,PRIDIV,PRINUM,SCAMSO
0018              CCMMCN/EXOG/B(100)
0019              CCMMCN/NAMES/TITLE(12,2),HEADG(20,2),XMETIT(12,2),POPGP(6,2)
0020              CCMMCN/XKDATA/XK1(20),XK2(20),XK3(20),XK4(20),XK5(20),FLG(20,4)
0021              COMMCN/TO/XNVOUT(12),XMAINR(12),XMANT(12),XNUMER,XLAND,XMNORM(12),
                 1 SUMIVT,RAMAT,RESPN,CAPUSE(12),VAL(20),XEXPR(12),
                 2 STCK1(20),CAPGR1(12)
0022              REAL*8 TITLE,HEADG,XMETIT,POPGP
0023              DATA  XPRNT1/1.0/,XPRNT2/1.0/,PRINTX/1.0/,DETAIL/1.0/
                 1 ,PPLCT/0.0/
0024              DATA NCYCLE/1/ , RESPR/20*0.0/
           C**
0025              DATA  BR/0.0180/,DT/0.0094/,XMG/0.0020/,XXBR/0.0/,DTHPTB/0.0/
           C**
0026              DATA  FMG /1.0/,TOPTM1/204000.0/,TOTKT/11*0./,
                 1 AGEPT1/5*3430.8,8*4581.3,4*3959.8,3*3505.7,4*3545.0,10*2390.7,
                 2 10*2308.8,10*2322.0,10*1859.0,20066.0/
0027              DATA TOPT/0.0/,  POPKT/24*0.0/,  AGRIT/4*0.0/
0028              DATA FBR /1.0/,TOTMIG/0./,  FDT/1.0/,
                 1 XPMG/4*.01473,10*.01134,4*.00955,2*.01684,5*.07254,4*.03465,
                 2 5*.01567,10*.01062,19*.00279,.01704/
0029              DATA PDTH/4*0.08,10*0.04,10*0.13,10*0.16,10*0.31,10*0.72,
                 1 10*1.66,5.775/
           C**
0030              DATA CJK1/45863.,0.,1467.,5*0.,1197.,4*0.,372.,958.,122.,4*0.,
                 1 3135.,5*0.,203.,5*0.,839.,5*0.,6214.,5*0.,3135.,5*0.,284.,
                 2 3*0.,5528.,104.,112.,5*0.,30.,5*0.,80.,3*0./
           C**
0031              DATA CJK2/5550.,3*0.,825.,133.,4*0.,675.,109.,0.,153.,0.,415.,
```

BLK DATA

```
          1 539.,87.,4*0.,1300.,209.,4*0.,580.,93.,4*0.,473.,76.,4*0.,
          2 3500.,564.,4*0.,2546.,410.,4*0.,546.,88.,4*0.,2000.,322.,
          3 4*0.,17.,3.,4*0.,46.,7./
      C**
0032        DATA CJK3/4*0.,4909.,1904.,4*0.,4007.,1554.,0.,415.,0.,743.,
          1 3208.,1244.,4*0.,10494.,4069.,4*0.,681.,264.,4*0.,2808.,1089.,
          2 4*0.,20798.,8065.,4*0.,10494.,4069.,2*0.,265.,0.,952.,369.,
          3 4*0.,375.,145.,4*0.,97.,38.,4*0.,265.,102./
      C**
0033        DATA CJK4/4*0.,279.,5*0.,217.,2*0.,496.,15736.,0.,186.,5*0.,
          1 589.,5*0.,31.,5*0.,155.,5*0.,1147.,5*0.,589.,5*0.,
          2 62.,2*0.,726.,2*0.,31.,13*0./
      C**
      C**   INITIALIZATION STEP2
      C**
C034        DATA RGJ/3.2,4.3,6.5,3.7,4.8,2.0,3.1,3.1,3.2,3.3,3.6,1.0/,
          1 QOLT/0.,.04,3*.0,.3,.4,.3,.04,.1,.2,.3/,
          2 RESOR/20*0.0/,  ESTCK/20*0.0/
0035        DATA STDEP/0.0,.01,2*.25,.05,.4,.01,.01,.3,.2,10*0./,
          4 RUCST/20*0.0/,CAPREQ/12*0./,
          1 REREC/0.,.01,2*.25,4*0.,.3,.2,10*0./
C036        DATA  FLAGR/20*0.0/,  XMESTR/20*0.0/,
          1 XNVST1/15579.,6361.,29988.,18175.,19992.,41016.,113215.,182127.,
          1 96295.,161871.,149576.,12068./,XNVST/12*0.0/
0037        DATA  UTIL/1.,1.,29.,24.,12.,3266.,4848.,0.,60.,90.,199.,10.,
          1 6*0.,8.,191.,2.,2*0.,1.,
          2 2*0.,1.,0.,1.,0.,2.,228.,3*0.,18.,
          3 2*0.,1.,0.,1.,0.,4.,86.,3*0.,8.,
          4 4*0.,11.,0.,15.,3*0.,20.,4.,
          5 5*0.,0.,408.,1.,2*0.,88.,3.,
          6 4*0.,1.,0.,15.,29.,3*0.,6.,
          7 6*0.,22.,24.,3*0.,4.,
          8 6*0.,40.,279.,3*0.,1.,
          9 3*0.,1.,2*0.,4.,193.,3*0.0,2.,
         1A 48*0.,
         11 0.,750.,4*0.,4*750.,1875.,0.,
         12 5*0.,6750.,5*0.,250.,
         13 12*00.,
         14 2650.,4078.,2344.,917.,2854.,5235.,6752.,10177.,6282.,16589.,
         15 21593.,517.,
         16 C.,2000.,5*0.,2000.,200.,0.,1000.,0.,
         17 6*0.,1000.,625.,2*0.,1250.,875./
      C**
0038        DATA  XMCST1/20*0./,KR5/0/,LTNCY/0/
C039        DATA PILE/10*10000.,4*0.,10000.,15000.,1000.,10000.,
          1 2*10000./
      C**
0040        DATA XK1/24.6,49.,40.,8.5,4.,7.2,9.,.79,9.,49.9,4*0.,7.2,9.6,
          1 .00,5.0,2*0./
0041        DATA XK2/26.4,49.,320.,23.,333.,58.7,15.,1.58,15.,49.,4*0.,
          1 8.,9.,.00,5.9,2*0./
0042        DATA XK3/20*2.0/
0043        DATA XK4/0.,.54,.25,.09,4*0.,.12,.01,10*0./
0044        DATA XK5/0.,.46,.50,.41,4*0.,.88,.99,10*0./
0045        DATA FLG/.87,2*.3,.6,6*.5,4*0.,.8,.50,0.,.85,2*0.,.90,
          1 2*.6,.75,6*.7,4*0.,.8,.55,0.,.9,2*0.,.92,9*.90,4*0.,.92,.6,
          2 0.,.92,2*0.,10*.95,4*0.,2*.95,0.,.95,2*0./
      C**
```

BLK DATA

```
0046          DATA RUCST1/.00045,.00031,.00050,.00009,.000050,.00020,
             1 .000085,.000008,.000078,.00047,4*0.,.000095,.00011,.0,.0001090,
             2 2*.0/
0047          DATA RUCST2/20*0.0/,XFACT/12*0.0/,OCST/12*0.0/,OCSTI/12*0.0/
        C**
0048          DATA REDIV/20*0.0/,RESPRT/21*0.0/
        C**
        C**   COMMCN AREA FOR DURABLE INVESTMENT AND INVESTMENT ONE-TIME GROWTH.
0049          DATA ECODUR/0.0,.01,3*0.,.05,.25,.46,.07,.1,.01,.05/,
             1 EXPDUR/0.,.01,3*0.,.0,.3,.49,2*.05,.1,0./,
             1 XMNDUR/0.,.01,3*0.,.0,.3,.49,2*.05,.1,0./,
             2 XMDUR/110*0.,19.0,21.0,438*0.,45.,50.,108*0.,534.,676.,108*0.,
             3 993.,1045.,108*0.,96.2,104.7,108*0.,97.,107.1,108*0.,
             4 187.3,198.1,108*0.,45.,50.,108*0.0/
        C**
        C**     INITIALIZATION STEP3
        C**
0050          DATA CNJ/806.,13*0.,500.,12*0.,1000.,1000.,12*0.,1000.,16*0.,
             1 200.,2*0.0,45.,6*0.,20.,1000.,3*0.0,130.,4*0.,500.,0.,
             2 130.,4*0.,260.,4*0.,500.,0.,240.,4*0.,70.,500.,4*0.,
             3 1000.,60.,4*0.,180.,6*0.,250.,3*0.,194.,310.,
             4 6*0.,290.,0.,800.,0.,11*0.0,1000./,
             5 DN/1.,5.,7.,4.,2.,7.,5.,5*7./,
             6 TMEAS/1.65,1.C0,.4,68.,40.,.4,1.,.4,.35,3*.4/,
             7 DNJT1/144*0.0/,                COUNT1/12*0.0/,
             8 XMDEL/12*0.0/,  RESIL/12*0.0/,    POP/8*0.0/,
             9 VN/.10,.11,2*.06,.12,.10,.07,3*.08,2*.07/
            1A , XMEAS/12*0.0/,RATVST/12*0.0/,XJOT/12*1000./
        C**
        C**    INITIALIZATION STEP4
        C**
0051          DATA SUBDAT/2*3.,1.,6.,15.,9.,4*0.,6*-1.,4*0.,2*2.,1.,
        CDELETE
             1 5.,15.,2.,4*0.,.15,.15,.8,.02,.9,.05,4*0.,
             2 3.,4.,8.,6.,16.,9.,4*0.,.6,.1,.001,.3,.05,.8,4*0.,
             3 0.,3.,9*0.,.6,48*0.,5.,10.,2*5.,1.,5.,4*0./
0052          DATA   SUBMAT/1.0,999*0.0/,SUBPIL/1.0,899*0.0/
        C**
0053          DATA  WORK/20*0.0/
        C**
        C**    INITIALIZATION STEP5
        C**
0054          DATA  XMRNOR/3.,6.,4.,3.,3.,7.,9.,9.,8.,6.,6.,7./,
             2 XEPORT/4*0.,1900.,7800.,2200.,43400.,6200.,0.,2400.,2200./,
             3 EJOT1/12*0./,EXPO/12*5.0/,XIDFMN/12*0.0/,XINJO/12*0.0/
             4 ,EJOT/12*0./,XFILE/33*.0/,INDX/19*0/, XMOCST/12*0./,XOCST/19*0./
0055          DATA RESMN1/5*10.,6*21.3,17.7/
        C**
        C**     INITIALIZATION STEP6
        C**
0056          DATA XUTIL/3*1.,29.,24.,2*12.,2*3266.,2*4848.,3*0.,60.,2*90.,199.,
             1 10.,7*0.,2*0.,2*8.,2*191.,205.,2.,3*0.,1.,3*0.,1.,0.,2*1.,2*0.,
             2 2.,1.,228.,2*200.,4*0.,18.,3*0.,1.,0.,2*1.,2*0.,4.,6.,86.,100.,
             3 95.,4*0.,8.,5*0.,2*11.,2*0.,15.,20.,6*0.,20.,4.,7*0.,2*0.,408.,
             4 300.,1.,2.,1.,3*0.,88.,3.,5*0.,2*1.,2*0.,2*15.,29.,33.,30.,4*0.,
             5 6.,7*0.,2*0.,22.,30.,24.,2*25.,4*0.,4.,7*0.,2*0.,2*40.,279.,300.,
             6 280.,4*0.,1.,4*0.,1.,4*0.,2*4.,3*193.,4*0.,2.,
             7 76*0.,
```

BLK DATA

```
           8 2*0.0,750.,6*0.0,8*750.,1875.,0.,
           9 7*0.,6750.,6500.,9*0.,250.,
          1A 19*.0,2650.,2133.,
          11 4078.,2344.,917.,2854.,2346.,5235.,4265.,2*6752.,3*10177.,
          12 6282.,16589.,12796.,21593.,517.,
          13 2*0.,2000.,8*C.,
          14 200C.,1000.,500.,200.,2*0.,100C.,10*0.,1000.,
          15 2*625.,1250.,625.,3*0.,1250.,875./
0057          DATA XMARK/1.,1.,2.,3.,4.,2*5.,2*6.,2*7.,3*8.,9.,2*10.,11.,12./
0058          DATA TIME/15.,2*10.,30.,20.,2*5.,2*20.,2*15.,5.,2*15.,10.,
           1 4*20./,
           2 ICTR/0/,     SUBIOP/1.0,999*0.0/
0059          DATA DEGRAD/12*0.0/,  UPGRAD/12*0.0/
      C**
      C**     INITIALIZATION STEPS
      C**
0060          DATA CPILE/0.,6000.,2000.,3*5000.,2*10000.,2000.,3000.,6*0.,
           1 4*0./,
      CDELETE
           2 CAPVL/9.,15.,3*20.,5C.,60.,100.,50.,25.,35.,25./
0061          DATA OUTMAT/2000*0.0/
0062          DATA XMBRK/1.,0.,4*1.,0.,1.,0.,1.,0.,1.,2*0.,2*1.,0.,2*1.0/
0063          DATA SUMMAT/500*0.0/, PUBNUM/0.0/,PRIDIV/0.0/,PRINUM/0.0/
0064          DATA PUBDIV/0.0/,SCAMSO/0.0/,LST/0/,LP/0/
0065          DATA XNVOLT/12*0.0/,XMAINR/12*0.0/,XMANT/12*0.0/,XNUMER/0.0/
0066          DATA XLAND/0.0/,SUMIVT/0.0/,RAMAT/0.0/,RESPN/0.0/
0067          DATA CAPUSE/12*0.0/,VAL/20*0.0/,STCK1/20*0.0/,CAPGR1/12*0.0/
0068          DATA XEXPR/12*.0/
0069          DATA XMPORT/4*0.,4800.,6500.,17900.,22700.,48C0.,0.,1600.,7000./
0070          DATA  UTILI/1.,1.,29.,24.,12.,3266.,4848.,0.,60.,90.,199.,10.,
           1 6*0.,8.,191.,2.,2*0.,1.,
           2 2*0.,1.,0.,1.,0.,2.,228.,3*0.,18.,
           3 2*0.,1.,0.,1.,0.,4.,86.,3*0.,8.,
           4 4*0.,11.,0.,15.,3*0.,20.,4.,
           5 5*0.,0.,408.,1.,2*0.,88.,3.,
           6 4*0.,1.,0.,15.,29.,3*0.,6.,
           7 6*0.,22.,24.,3*0.,4.,
           8 6*0.,40.,279.,3*0.,1.,
           9 3*0.,1.,2*0.,4.,193.,3*0.0,2.,
          1A 48*0.,
          11 0.,750.,4*0.,4*750.,1875.,0.,
          12 5*0.,6750.,5*0.,250.,
          13 12*00.,
          14 2650.,4078.,2344.,917.,2854.,5235.,6752.,10177.,6282.,16589.,
          15 21593.,517.,
          16 C.,2000.,5*0.,2000.,200.,C.,1000.,0.,
          17 6*0.,1000.,625.,2*0.,1250.,875./
      C       DATA RUCSTI/.00043,.00184,.00884,.00008,.000051,.00015,
      C      1 .00017,.000079,.0028,.00413,4*0.,.000089,.000116,.00005,.0001033,
      C      2 2*.0/
      C**
      C**     INITIALIZATION FOR OUTPUT
      C**
      C       THE B BLOCK ALLOWS CERTAIN CHANGES IN THE LEVELS OR RATES OF
      C       GROWTH USING A FOUR NUMBER CODE ENTRY; 1--YEAR TO INITIATE THE
      C       CHANGE, 2--THE CHANGE CODE, 3--THE INDEX OF THE PARAMETER TO BE
      C       CHANGED, 4--THE MULTIPLIER OF THE CHANGE.
      C       THE CHANGE CODES ARE; 1--LEVEL OF PRODUCTION SECTOR FUNDS
```

BLK DATA

```
            C      2--RATE OF GROWTH OF SECTOR FUNDS,3--RATE OF ENVIRONMENTAL
            C      MAINTENANCE UNIT COST, 4--INCREASE OF THE AVAILABLE RESOURCE
            C      STOCKPILE, 5--LEVEL OF THE DEMAND MEASURE THRESHOLD, 6--LEVEL
            C      OF THE LOWEST RESOURCE UNIT COST, 7--RATIO OF THE MAXIMUM
            C      RESOURCE UNIT COST TO THE LOWEST COST.
            C      PRESENT FIELD SIZE ALLOWS 25 CHANGES ENTERED SEQUENTIALLY.
0071               DATA B/12*0.,
                  1        00.,0.,00.,0.000,00.,0.,00.,0.000,00.,0.,00.,0.000,
                  2        00.,0.,00.,0.000,00.,0.,00.,0.000,00.,0.,00.,0.000,
                  3        00.,0.,00.,0.000,00.,0.,00.,0.000,00.,0.,00.,0.000,
                  4        00.,0.,00.,0.000,00.,0.,00.,0.000,00.,0.,00.,0.000,
                  5        00.,0.,00.,0.000,00.,0.,00.,0.000,00.,0.,00.,0.000,
                  6        00.,0.,00.,0.000,00.,0.,00.,0.000,00.,0.,00.,0.000,
                  7        00.,0.,00.,0.000,00.,0.,00.,0.000,00.,0.,00.,0.000,
                  8        00.,0.,00.,0.000/
0072               DATA TITLE/8H1       E,8H2 TRANS ,8H3 HEALTH,8H4  PUBLI,
                  1 8H5  ADMIN,8H6    AGR,8H7  NON-D,8H8  DURAB,8H9 COMMUN,
                  28H10WHOL-R,8H11       ,8H12       ,8HDUCATION,8H& COMMUN,8H&WELFARE,
                  3 8HC SAFETY,8H & OTHER,8HICULTURE,8HUR MANUF,8HLE MANUF,
                  4 8H & TRANS,8HET TRADE,8HSERVICES,8H  MINING/
0073               DATA HEADG/   8H 1  FIBR,8H 2  IRON,8H 3       ,8H 4   NON,
                  1 8H 5       ,8H 6 PETRO,8H 7  STON,8H 8     C,8H 9   LEA,
                  2 8H10       ,8H11       ,8H12       ,8H13       ,8H14       ,
                  3 8H15     UR,8H16    ARA,8H17       ,8H18     WO,8H19     A,
                  48H20    WAT,8HE & FOOD,8H & STEEL,8H  COPPER,8H-FERROUS,8H    COAL,
                  5 8H-NAT GAS,8HE & CLAY,8HHEMICALS,8HD & ZINC,8HALUMINUM,
                  6 8H       ,8H       ,8H       ,8H       ,8HBAN LAND,
                  7 8HBLE LAND,8H CAPITAL,8HRK UNITS,8HIR UNITS,8HER UNITS/
0074               DATA XMETIT/8H1       E,8H2      EM,8H3 TRANSP,8H4       ,
                  1 8H5       ,8H6 SFTY &,8H7  MANUF,8H8     CO,
                  28H9GROTH P,8H10    AGR,8H11       ,8H12       ,8HDUCATION,8HPLOYMENT,
                  4 8HORTATION,8H WELFARE,8H  HEALTH,8H DEFENSE,8HACTURING,
                  5 8HMMERCIAL,8HOTENTIAL,8HICULTURE,8HSERVICES,8H  MINING/
0075               DATA POPGP/8H       E,8H    INST,8H     NON,8HTRAIN & ,
                  1 8H     PAID,8H  UNPAID,8HDUCATION,8HITUTIONS,8H-WORKERS,
                  2 8H WELFARE,8H WORKERS,8H WORKERS/
0076               END
```

SETUP

```
      SUBRCUTINE SETUP
C**
      REAL*8 TITLE,HEADG,XMETIT,POPGP
      CCMMCN/POPSCA/BR,DT,XMG,XXBR,DTHPTB,TOTMIG,XPMG(64)
      COMMCN/INTER2/RGJ(12),QOLT(12),RESOR(20),TOTKT(12),
     1 ESTCK(20),STDEP(20),RUCST(20),CAPREQ(12),
     2 REREC(20),FLAGR(20),XMESTR(20),
     3 XNVST1(12),XNVST(12),XJOT(12),UTIL(12,20)
      COMMCN/INTER3/CNJ(12,12),DN(12),TMEAS(12),DNJT1(12,12),COUNT1(12),
     1 XMDEL(12),RESIL(12),POP(8),VN(12),XMEAS(12),RATVST(12)
      COMMCN/XKDATA/XK1(20),XK2(20),XK3(20),XK4(20),XK5(20),FLG(20,4)
      COMMCN/CHAR/CJK1(6,12),CJK2(6,12),CJK3(6,12),CJK4(6,12)
      COMMON/INTER6/XUTIL(19,20),XMARK(19),TIME(19),ICTR,
     1 SUBIOP(1000),KR5,LTNCY,INDX(19),XOCST(19),XMOCST(12)
      COMMCN/NAMES/TITLE(12,2),HEADG(20,2),XMETIT(12,2),POPGP(6,2)
      COMMCN/EXOG/B(100)
      COMMCN/INTER8/CPILE(20),CAPVL(12),CUTMAT(50,40),XMBRK(19),
     1 SUMMAT(50,10),PUBDIV,PUBNUM,PRIDIV,PRINUM,SCAMSO
C**
      COMMCN/INTER5/XMRNOR(12),EJOT1(12),EXPO(12),EJOTX,SNCST,RESPR1(20)
     1 ,XIDFMN(12),XINJO(12),EJOT(12),XFILE(3,12),RESMN1(12),XKTI(12),
     2 XEPORT(12)
      CCMMCN/OUTDIV/REDIV(20),XMPORT(12),UTILI(12,20),RUCSTI(20)
C**   WRITE BIRTH,DEATH, AND MIGRATION RATES
      WRITE (6,1) BR,DT,XMG
      DO 10 J=1,12
C**   WRITE GROWTH AND MAINTENANCE RATES AND EXPORTS AND IMPORTS
   10 WRITE(6,2) (TITLE(J,I),I=1,2),RGJ(J),XMRNOR(J),XEPORT(J),XMPORT(J)
      WRITE (6,3)
      WRITE (6,4) (XMARK(J),J=1,19)
      WRITE (6,5) (XMBRK(J),J=1,19)
      DO 4496 I=1,20
      IF (I.EQ.11.OR.I.EQ.12.OR.I.EQ.13.OR.I.EQ.14) GO TO 4496
C**   WRITE FULL PRODUCTION POSSIBILITIES
      WRITE(6,6) (HEADG(I,K),K=1,2),(XUTIL(J,I),J=1,19)
 4496 CONTINUE
      WRITE (6,7)
    7 FORMAT(1H1,//////,40X,37H*****ACTIVE PRODUCTION FUNCTIONS*****,//)
      DO 4498 I=1,20
      IF (I.EQ.11.OR.I.EQ.12.OR.I.EQ.13.OR.I.EQ.14) GO TO 4498
C**   WRITE PRESENT PRODUCTICN POSSIBILITIES
      WRITE (6,8) (HEADG(I,K),K=1,2), (UTIL(J,I), J=1,12)
    8 FORMAT(12X,2(A8),18(F6.0))
 4498 CONTINUE
      WRITE (6,201)
  201 FORMAT(1H1,///,T46,31H*****CONSUMPTION FUNCTIONS*****,///)
      DO 202 J = 1,6
      WRITE(6,203)(POPGP(J,K),K=1,2),(CJK1(J,L),L=1,12)
  203 FORMAT (12X,2(A8),12(2X,F6.0))
  202 CONTINUE
      WRITE (6,2137)
 2137 FORMAT (///)
      DO 212 J = 1,6
      WRITE(6,213)(POPGP(J,K),K=1,2),(CJK2(J,L),L=1,12)
  213 FORMAT (12X,2(A8),12(2X,F6.0))
  212 CONTINUE
      WRITE (6,2138)
 2138 FORMAT (///)
```

SETUP

```
      DO 222 J = 1,6
      WRITE(6,223)(POPGP(J,K),K=1,2),(CJK3(J,L),L=1,12)
  223 FORMAT (12X,2(A8),12(2X,F6.0))
  222 CONTINUE
      WRITE (6,2136)
 2136 FORMAT (///)
      DO 232 J = 1,6
      WRITE(6,233)(POPGP(J,K),K=1,2),(CJK4(J,L),L=1,12)
  233 FORMAT (12X,2(A8),12(2X,F6.0))
  232 CONTINUE
      WRITE (6,250)
  250 FORMAT(1H1,///,T46,26H*****DEMAND FUNCTIONS*****,///)
      DO 251 J = 1,12
      WRITE (6,252)(TITLE(J,I),I=1,2),(CNJ(L,J),L=1,12)
  252 FORMAT(15X,2(A8),12(1X,F6.0))
  251 CONTINUE
      WRITE(6,253) (TMEAS(N),N=1,12)
  253 FORMAT (22X,9HTHRESHOLD,12(1X,F6.2))
      WRITE (6,254) (VN(N),N=1,12)
  254 FORMAT (25X,6HWEIGHT,12(1X,F6.2))
      WRITE (6,255) (DN(N),N=1,12)
  255 FORMAT (16X,15HPOPULATION BASE,12(1X,F6.2))
      WRITE (6,351)
  351 FORMAT(1H1,///,T46,25H*****PRICE FUNCTIONS*****,///)
      DO 352 I = 1,20
      IF(I.EQ.11.OR.I.EQ.12.OR.I.EQ.13.OR.I.EQ.14) GO TO 352
      IF (I.EQ.19.OR.I.EQ.20)  GO TO 352
      WRITE(6,350) (HEADG(I,K),K=1,2),XK1(I),XK2(I),XK3(I),XK4(I),XK5(I)
  350 FORMAT(26X,2(A8),9X,5(F10.3))
  352 CONTINUE
      WRITE (6,353)
  353 FORMAT(///////,T46,37H*****RESOURCE DEPLETION WARNINGS*****,///)
      WRITE (6,361)
  361 FORMAT (36X,8HRESOURCE,11X,9HSTOCKPILE,19X,8HWARNINGS)
      DO 354 I = 1,20
      IF(I.EQ.12.OR.I.EQ.11.OR.I.EQ.13.OR.I.EQ.14) GO TO 354
      IF (I.EQ.17.OR.I.EQ.19.OR.I.EQ.20)  GO TO 354
      WRITE(6,355)(HEADG(I,K),K=1,2),CPILE (I),(FLG(I,J),J=1,4)
  355 FORMAT(30X,2(A8),9X,F9.2,9X,4(F6.2))
  354 CONTINUE
  951 WRITE(6,92)
   92 FORMAT(1H1,////,T46,31H*****SUBSTITUTION FORMULAE*****,////,
     1 T12,10H1.  COPPER,
     2 T46,40H.15 UNITS OF IRON AND .6 UNITS OF COPPER,/,
     3 T12,10H2.  COPPER,
     4 T46,55H.15 UNITS IRON,.1 UNITS OTHER NON-IRON ,.6 UNITS COPPER,/,
     5 T12,10H3.  FIBERS,
     6 T46,35H.8 UNITS FIBER,.001 UNITS CHEMICALS,/,
     7 T12,7H4.  OIL,T46,28H.02 UNITS COAL,.30 UNITS OIL,/,
     8 T12,14H5.  URBAN LAND,
     9 T46,41H.9 UNITS URBAN LAND,.05 UNITS ARABLE LAND,/,
    11 T12,8H7.  LEAD,
    12 T46,34H.05 UNITS OF IRON,.8 UNITS OF LEAD,/)
 4505 FORMAT(13X,F4.1,1X,F4.1,1X,F4.1,2X,F6.4)
 4503 FORMAT(20X,49H*****EXOGENOUS ADJUSTMENT ERROR IN NEXT LINE*****)
      DO 4511 J=1,97,4
      IF (B(J).EQ.0.0) GO TO 4510
 4511 CONTINUE
```

```
          WRITE(6,4501)
          DO 4510 J=1,97,4
          IF(B(J).EQ.0.0) GO TO 4510
          IF(B(J+1).LT.8.6.AND.B(J).NE.1.0) GO TO 4508
     4501 FORMAT(///,T46,29H*****EXOGENCUS OVERRIDES*****,////,
        1 13X,22HYEAR CODE INDEX  RATIO)
          WRITE(6,4503)
     4508 WRITE(6,4505) B(J),B(J+1),B(J+2),B(J+3)
     4510 CONTINUE
        1 FORMAT(//,40X,38H***** INITIAL SYSTEM GROWTH DATA *****,////////,
        1 5X,23HPOPULATION GROWTH RATES,//,20X,10HBIRTH RATE,2X,F6.4,/,
        2 20X,10HDEATH RATE,2X,F6.4,/,14X,16HIMMIGRATION RATE,2X,F6.4,////,
        3 38X,17HGROWTH RATES (%),3X,16HDEPRECIATION (%),3X,7HEXPORTS,12X,
        4 7HIMPORTS)
        2 FORMAT(14X,A8,A8,3(10X,F8.2),10X,F9.2)
        3 FORMAT(1H1,//////,40X,31H***** PRODUCTION FORMULAE *****,///)
        4 FORMAT(5X,13HSECTOR NUMBER,19(F6.0))
        5 FORMAT(6X,12HIF ACTIVE,=1,19(F6.0))
        6 FORMAT(2X,2(A8),19(F6.0))
          WRITE (6,11)
       11 FORMAT(1H1,////,40X,42H****INTERNATIONAL PRODUCTION FUNCTIONS****)
          DO 4488 I=1,20
          IF (I.EQ.11.OR.I.EQ.12.OR.I.EQ.13.OR.I.EQ.14) GO TO 4488
C**       WRITE PRESENT PRODUCTION PCSSIBILITIES
          WRITE (6,12)(HEADG(I,K),K=1,2), (UTILI(J,I), J=6,12)
       12 FORMAT(30X,2(A8),5X,18(F6.0))
     4488 CONTINUE
          RETURN
          END
```

```
      SUBROUTINE STEP1
C**
C**   POPULATION LEVEL, AGE DISTRIBUTION, CHARACTERISTICS, ARE DEVELOPED
      COMMON/YEAR/NCYCLE,RESPR(20),DEGRAD(12),UPGRAD(12),IYEAR
      COMMON/POPSCA/BR,DT,XMG,XXBR,DTHPTB,TOTMIG,XPMG(64)
      COMMON/PRINT/XPRNT1,XPRNT2,PRINTX,DETAIL,PPLOT
      COMMON/INTER/FMG,TOPTM1,AGEPT1(65),TOPT,
     1 POPKT(4,6),AGRIT(4),FBR,FDT,PDTH(55)
      COMMON/CHAR/CJK1(6,12),CJK2(6,12),CJK3(6,12),CJK4(6,12)
      COMMON/INTER2/RGJ(12),QOLT(12),RESCR(20),TOTKT(12),
     1 ESTCK(20),STDEP(20),RUCST(20),CAPREQ(12),
     2 REREC(20),FLAGR(20),XMESTR(20),
     3 XNVST1(12),XNVST(12),XJOT(12),UTIL(12,20)
      COMMON/INTER3/CNJ(12,12),DN(12),TMEAS(12),DNJT1(12,12),CCUNT1(12),
     1 XMDEL(12),RESIL(12),POP(8),VN(12),XMEAS(12),RATVST(12)
      COMMON/INTER8/CPILE(20),CAPVL(12),CUTMAT(50,40),XMBRK(19),
     1 SUMMAT(50,10),PUBDIV,PUBNUM,PRIDIV,PRINUM,SCAMSO
      DIMENSION XNOR(6),DTHPT(56),DTHPTA(4),AGEPT(55),C1(6),C2(6),
     1 C3(6),C4(6),PPLT(6,4),PPL(4,6)
C**
C**   CALCULATE TOTAL POPULATION
      BRTHT   =  BR * FBR
      XNTMGT   =  XMG * FMG
      DETHT=DT*FDT
      TOPT=TOPTM1*(1+BRTHT-DETHT+XNTMGT)
C**   STORE POP GROWTH IN SUMMARY TABLE
      IF (NCYCLE.GT.1) GO TO 20
      POP(8)=TOPT
   20 SUMMAT(NCYCLE,1)=NCYCLE
      SUMMAT(NCYCLE,2)=TOPT/POP(8)
C**
C**   AGEPT IS POP BY AGE - YEAR
C**   AGRIT IS POP BY AGE GROUP
C**   DTHPT IS DEATHS BY AGE-YEAR; DTHPTA IS DEATHS BY AGE GROUP
      DO 35 I=1,4
   30 AGRIT(I)=0
   35 DTHPTA(I)=0.0
C**   THE 4 AGE GROUPS ARE:   AGES 1   TO  17
C**                                18  TO  24
C**                                25  TO  64
C**                                65      AND ABOVE
C**
C**   XX IS BIRTHS DURING LAST YEAR
      XXBR =TOPTM1 * (1+XNTMGT) *BRTHT
      DTHPT(1)= XXBR * 2.04 *DETHT/.65
      DTHPTA(1)=DTHPTA(1)+DTHPT(1)
      AGEPT(1) = XXBR  -  DTHPT(1)
      AGRIT(1) = AGRIT(1) + AGEPT(1)
      TOTMIG=TOPTM1*XNTMGT
      DO 40 I=1,4
      IF (I.EQ.1) K=2
      IF (I.EQ.1) L=17
      IF (I.EQ.2) K=18
      IF (I.EQ.2) L=24
      IF(I.EQ.3) K=25
      IF (I.EQ.3) L=64
      DO 40 J=K,L
      DTHPT(J)=AGEPT1(J-1) * PDTH(J) *DETHT/.65
```

STEP1

```
      DTHPTA(I)=DTHPTA(I)+DTHPT(J)
      AGEPT(J) = AGEPT1(J-1) -DTHPT(J) + TOTMIG * XPMG(J-1)
   40 AGRIT(I) = AGRIT(I) + AGEPT(J)
      DTHPTB=DTHPTA(1)+DTHPTA(2)+DTHPTA(3)+DTHPTA(4)
C**   AGE GROUP 65 REPRESENTS ALL OVER AND EQUAL TO AGE 65
      DTHPT(65)=(AGEPT1(65)+AGEPT1(64))*PDTH(65)*DETHT/.65
      DTHPTA(4)=DTHPT(65)
      AGEPT(65)=(AGEPT1(65)+ AGEPT1(64)) -DTHPT(65) +TOTMIG * XPMG(64)
      AGRIT(4) = AGEPT(65)
      XX = 0.0
      DO 550 I=1,4
C**   AGRIT 'S ARE NORMALIZED TO PRESENT POPULATION
  550 XX=XX + AGRIT(I)
      XX = TOPT/XX
      DO 560 I =1,4
  560 AGRIT(I) = AGRIT(I)*XX
C**
C**
  509 CALL MATMPY(CJK1,XJOT,C1,6,12)
      CALL MATMPY(CJK2,XJOT,C2,6,12)
      CALL MATMPY(CJK3,XJOT,C3,6,12)
      CALL MATMPY(CJK4,XJOT,C4,6,12)
      XNOR(1) = C1(1) + C1(2) + C1(3) + C1(4) + C1(5) + C1(6)
      XNOR(2) = C2(1) + C2(2) + C2(3) + C2(4) + C2(5) + C2(6)
      XNOR(3) = C3(1) + C3(2) + C3(3) + C3(4) + C3(5) + C3(6)
      XNOR(4) = C4(1) + C4(2) + C4(3) + C4(4) + C4(5) + C4(6)
C**   POPKT(I,K) IS POPULATION OF AGE GROUP I IN PARTITION K
      DO 110 K=1,6
      POPKT(1,K) =(C1(K)/XNOR(1)) * AGRIT(1)
      POPKT(2,K) = (C2(K)/XNOR(2)) * AGRIT(2)
      POPKT(3,K) = (C3(K)/XNOR(3)) * AGRIT(3)
      POPKT(4,K) = (C4(K)/XNOR(4)) * AGRIT(4)
  110 TOTKT(K)=POPKT(1,K)+POPKT(2,K)+POPKT(3,K)+POPKT(4,K)
C**
      DO 350 J=1,65
  350 AGEPT1(J)=AGEPT(J)
  401 RETURN
      END
```

STEP2

```
            SUBROUTINE STEP2
      C**   THE RGJ(1) TO RGJ(5) IS PUBLIC SECTOR, RGJ(6) TO RGJ(12) IS PRIV
            REAL*8 TITLE,HEADG,XMETIT,POPGP
            COMMCN/INTER3/CNJ(12,12),DN(12),TMEAS(12),DNJT1(12,12),COUNT1(12),
           1 XMDEL(12),RESIL(12),POP(8),VN(12),XMEAS(12),RATVST(12)
            COMMCN/INTER2/RGJ(12),QOLT(12),RESOR(20),TOTKT(12),
           1 ESTCK(20),STDEP(20),RUCST(20),CAPREQ(12),
           2 REREC(20),FLAGR(20),XMESTR(20),
           3 XNVST1(12),XNVST(12),XJOT(12),UTIL(12,20)
            COMMON/TO/XNVOLT(12),XMAINR(12),XMANT(12),XNUMER,XLAND,XMNORM(12),
           1 SUMIVT,RAMAT,RESPN,CAPUSE(12),VAL(20),XEXPR(12),
           2 STCK1(20),CAPGR1(12)
            COMMCN/PRINT/XPRNT1,XPRNT2,PRINTX,DETAIL,PPLCT
            COMMCN/COST/RUCST1(20),RUCST2(20),XFACT(12),OCST(12),OCSTI(12)
            COMMCN/YEAR/NCYCLE,RESPR(20),DEGRAD(12),UPGRAD(12),IYEAR
            CCMMON/INTER6/XUTIL(19,20),XMARK(19),TIME(19),ICTR,
           1 SUBIOP(1000),KR5,LTNCY,INDX(19),XCCST(19),XMOCST(12)
            COMMCN/INTER5/XMRNOR(12),EJOT1(12),EXPO(12),EJOTX,SNCST,RESPR1(20)
           1 ,XIDFMN(12),XINJO(12),EJOT(12),XFILE(3,12),RESMN1(12),XKTI(12),
           2 XEPORT(12)
            COMMCN/TWO/XMCST1(20),PILE(20)
            CCMMCN/INTER/FMG,TOPTM1,AGEPT1(65)
           1 ,TOPT,POPKT(4,6),AGRIT(4),FBR,FDT,PDTH(65)
            CCMMCN/XKDATA/XK1(20),XK2(20),XK3(20),XK4(20),XK5(20),FLG(20,4)
            CCMMCN/INTER8/CPILE(20),CAPVL(12),OUTMAT(50,40),XMBRK(19),
           1 SUMMAT(50,10),PUBDIV,PUBNUM,PRIDIV,PRINUM,SCAMSO
            COMMCN/CHAR/CJK1(6,12),CJK2(6,12),CJK3(6,12),CJK4(6,12)
            COMMCN/OUTDIV/REDIV(20),XMPORT(12),UTILI(12,20),RUCSTI(20)
            COMMCN/DURBLE/XMDUR(110,12),ECODUR(12),EXPDUR(12),XMNDUR(12)
            COMMCN/NAMES/TITLE(12,2),HEADG(20,2),XMETIT(12,2)
            DIMENSION ECST(20),XMCST(20),ECSTR(20)
            DIMENSION XKOUT(12),RESCRD(20,12)
            DIMENSION XUTILT(20,12),UTILT(20,12),XMCAP(60,12),XMJCT(12)
            DATA XMJOT/12*1000.0/,XMCAP/5*250.,55*0.0,5*600.,55*.0,
           1 5*1500.,55*.0,5*700.,55*.0,5*1800.,55*.0,1000.,59*.0,1800.,59*0.,
           2 5*3000.,55*.0,5*1200.,55*.0,5*800.,55*.0,1200.,59*0.,2500.,59*0./
      C**
            IF(NCYCLE.GT.1) GO TO 7
            DO 6 J=1,10
            DO 6 I=1,12
          6 XMCAP(J,I)=XMCAP(1,I)*((11.-J)/10.)
          7 CONTINUE
      C**   STCCKPILE(WORK UNITS)=POPULATION CF PAID WORKERS
            PILE(18)=POPKT(1,5)+POPKT(2,5)+ POPKT(3,5) + POPKT(4,5)
      C**
      C**   CALCULATE FUNDS TO SECTORS TO CLEAN UP MEDIA AND
      C**   ADD TO GENERATED FUNDS DUE TO CAPITAL GROWTH.
            DC 4 J=1,12
            XMAINR(J)=5.*QOLT(J)*(XJOT(J)/1000.)
            IF (XMAINR(J).LT.0.0) XMAINR(J)=0.0
            DO 4 K=1,12
          4 XMDUR(NCYCLE,K)=XMDUR(NCYCLE,K) + XNVST(J)*XMAINR(J)*ECODUR(K)*.01
      C**
      C**   XNVST IS AMOUNT OF INVESTMENT AVAILABLE
            TEMP=0.
            XNUMER=0.
            SUM=0.
            DO 10 J= 1,12
```

STEP2

```
    5 XNVST(J)  = XNVST1(J)*(1.+RGJ(J)*.01)+XMDUR(NCYCLE,J)
C**   RATVST IS THE FRACTION OF COSTS THAT REQUIRE CAPITAL COSTS
      RATVST(J)=XMDUR(NCYCLE,J)/XNVST(J)
C**   TEMP IS THE GROWTH FUNCTION FOR CAPITAL COST STDEP
      XNUMER= XNUMER+XNVST(J)
C**   XNVST1 IS THE LEVEL OF FUNDS ACTING AS BASE FOR GROWTH RATE
      XNVST1(J)=XNVST(J)-XMDUR(NCYCLE,J)

C**   XMNORM IS SUM OF THIS CYCLE & DEFERRED LAST CYCLE CAPITAL
C**   MAINTENANCE (%); J IS CODE OF OUTPUT COMPONENT
      XMNORM(J) = XMRNOR(J) +  100*(XIDFMN(J)/XNVST(J))
      XIDFMN(J)=(XMRNOR(J)*XNVST(J))*0.01
   10  SUM=SUM + XNVST(J)*XMNORM(J)*.01
C**
C**   XMAINR IS MAINT RATE (%) TO REPAIR ENVIRONMENTAL MEDIA
C**   XMANT IS TOTAL MAINT RATE (%)=XMNORM+XMAINR+CAPITAL EXPANSION COSTS
C**   CAPITAL EXPANSION COSTS ARE FINANCED OVER 10 YEARS (SEE 45-74)
      DO 30  J= 1,12
      XMDUR(NCYCLE,J)=XMDUR(NCYCLE,J)+ SUM*XMNDUR(J)
       XNVST(J)=XNVST1(J)+XMDUR(NCYCLE,J)
       TEMP=TEMF+XMDUR(NCYCLE,J)
      XEXPR(J)=100.*(XMCAP(NCYCLE,J)/XNVST(J))
      XMANT(J) = XMNORM(J)+ XMAINR(J) +XEXPR(J)
C**
C***  XMPORT IS THE $ VALUE OF IMPORTED GOODS
C**   XNVOLT IS FUNDS FOR COMPONENT PRODUCTION
      XNVOLT(J) = XNVST(J)/(1 + XMANT(J) * 0.01)
   30 XNVOLT(J) = XNVOUT(J)+XEPORT(J)-XMPORT(J)


      IF(NCYCLE.EQ.1) PILE(17)=TEMP
      CAPNED=TEMP
      IF(CAPNED.GT.TEMP) GO TO 12
      DO 14 J=7,8
   14 XNVOLT(J)=XNVOLT(J)+(TEMP-CAPNED)/2
      GO TO 16
   12 DEFER =CAPNED-TEMP
      TEMP=.0
      DO 18 J=1,12
   18 TEMP=TEMP+XIDFMN(J)
      DO 17 J=1,12
   17 CAPREQ(J)=XIDFMN(J)*(DEFER/TEMP)
   16 CONTINUE
      SUMIVT = 0.0
      DO 423 J = 1,12
      IF(NCYCLE.GT.1) GO TO 9843
      IF(XNVOUT(J).LT.100.) XNVOUT(J) = 100.
      EJOT1(J) = 100.*XEPORT(J)/XNVOUT(J)
 9843 SUMIVT = SUMIVT + XNVOUT(J)
  423 CONTINUE
C**   STORE PRIV, PUB PROD GROWTH IN SUMMARY TABLE
C**   GROWTH MEASURED IN TERMS OF PRODUCTION GROWTH
      PUBNUM=0.0
      PRINUM=0.0
      IF (NCYCLE.GT.1) GO TO 20
C**   INITTALIZE RESOURCE UNIT COST DATA
      DO 21 NR=1,20
      XMCST1(NR)=RUCST1(NR)
```

```
   21 RUCST2(NR)=RUCST1(NR)
      PRIDIV=0.0
      PUBDIV=0.0
      DO 22 J=1,12
      IF (J.GE.6) GO TO 24
      PUBDIV=PUBDIV+XNVOUT(J)
      GO TC 22
   24 PRIDIV=PRIDIV+XNVOUT(J)
   22 CONTINUE
   20 DO 26 J=1,12
      IF (J.GE.6) GO TO 28
      PUBNUM=PUBNUM+XNVOUT(J)
      GO TC 26
   28 PRINUM=PRINUM+XNVOUT(J)
   26 CONTINUE
      SUMMAT(NCYCLE,3)=PUBNUM/PUBDIV
      SUMMAT(NCYCLE,4)=PRINUM/PRIDIV
C**
  488 DO 40 NR=1,20
C**   TEST MAINTAINS COST AT NOT LOWER THAN LAST YEAR (BUT SEE STEP # 8)
      IF (RUCST2(NR).GT.RUCST1(NR)) RUCST2(NR)=RUCST1(NR)
C**   THIS YEAR'S COST ESTIMATE BY LINEAR PRCJECTION
   40 RUCST(NR)  = 2* RUCST1(NR) - RUCST2(NR)
C**
C**   CALCULATE FOR EACH COMPONENT THE EST COST FOR ONE OUTPUT UNIT
C**
C**   UTIL(J,NR) IS MATRIX CF ACTIVE I/O PRODUCTION FUNCTIONS
C**   NEXT LINE MODIFIES CAPITAL COST UTILITY TO INCLUDE CAPITAL ADDS
      DO 90 J=1,12
      IF(UTIL(J,17).LT..5) UTIL(J,17)=0.
   90 UTIL(J,17)=UTIL(J,17)*RATVST(J)
      CALL MATMPY (UTIL,RUCST,OCST,12,20)
C**
C**   XJOT(J) IS SCHEDULED OUTPUT UNITS FOR COMPONENT
C**   (.001*XFACT) SCALES UNIT COSTS TO TRUE COMPONENT COSTS (SETS
C**   OTHER PRODUCTION COSTS AS MULTIPLIER OF RESOURCE COSTS)
C**   CALCULATE XFACT FOR NCYCLE = 1
      IF (NCYCLE.NE.1) GO TC 47
      DO 48 J=1,12
   48 XFACT(J)=XNVOUT(J)/(OCST(J)*1000.)
   47 DO 42 J=1,12
      XKOUT(J)=XNVOUT(J)/(XFACT(J))
   42 XJOT(J)=XKOUT(J)/OCST(J)
C**
C**   TRANSPOSING UTIL AND SCALING TO SINGLE UNIT VALUES
      DO 46 J=1,12
      DO 46 NR=1,20
      IF(UTIL(J,NR).LT..5) UTIL(J,NR)=0.
      UTILT(NR,J)=UTIL(J,NR)
   46 XUTILT(NR,J)=UTILT(NR,J) * 0.001
C**
C**   RESOR(20) IS THE RESOURCE REQUIREMENTS FOR EACH CYCLE
      CALL MATMPY (XUTILT,XJOT,RESOR,20,12)
      TEMP=PILE(18)
      IF(RESOR(18).LT.0.93*TEMP) RUCST1(18)=RUCST1(18)*.99
      IF(RESOR(18).GT.0.97*TEMP) RUCST1(18)=RUCST1(18)*1.01
      IF(RESOR(18).LT.0.93*TEMP.OR.RESOR(18).GT.0.97*TEMP) GO TO 488
      DO 473 J=1,12
```

STEP2

```
      DO 473 NR=1,20
  473 RESORD(NR,J)=XUTILT(NR,J)*XJOT(J)*1000.
C**   DEVELCP RESOURCE SUMMARY DATA
      IF (NCYCLE.GT.1) GO TO 480
      DO 482 NR=1,20
  482 REDIV(NR)=RESOR(NR)
  480 CONTINUE
      TEMP=0.0
      DO 484 NR=2,4
  484 TEMP=TEMP+(RESOR(NR)/REDIV(NR))
      SUMMAT(NCYCLE,6)=TEMP/3
      TEMP=0.0
      DO 486 NR=5,6
  486 TEMP=TEMP+(RESOR(NR)/REDIV(NR))
      SUMMAT(NCYCLE,7)=TEMP/2
      TEMP=0.0
      TEMP=TEMP+(RESOR(1)/REDIV(1))
      DO 490 NR=15,16
  490 TEMP=TEMP+(RESOR(NR)/REDIV(NR))
      SUMMAT(NCYCLE,8)=TEMP/3
      TEMP=0.0
      SUMMAT(NCYCLE,9)=RESOR(18)/REDIV(18)
      DO 492 NR=19,20
  492 TEMP=TEMP+(RESOR(NR)/REDIV(NR))
      SUMMAT(NCYCLE,10)=TEMP/2
C**
C**
C**   STDEP(20) IS THE STOCK DEPLETION LEVEL OF EACH RESOURCE
      DO 60 NR=1,18
      IF (PILE(NR).EQ.0.0) GO TO 59
C**   END OF CYCLE RESOURCE STOCK LEVEL IS ESTCK(% OF PILE(NR))
      ESTCK(NR) = STDEP(NR)+(RESOR(NR)/PILE(NR))*(1/(1+REREC(NR)))
      IF (NR.EQ.1) GO TO 53
      GO TO 54
C**   INCREASE AGRI BY ANNUAL PROD
   53 IF (ESTCK(1).GT.0.9) GO TO 52
      EJOTX=(ESTCK(1)-.1)*PILE(1)*.00001
      GO TO 54
   52 PILE(1) =  RESOR(1)*(1.1+RGJ(6)*0.01)
   54 PILE(1)=PILE(1)*1.005
      IF (ESTCK(NR).LE.1.0) GO TO 59
C**   NEED ONE TIME IMPORT CF RESOURCE DUE TO SCHEDULED PRODUCTION;
C**   NEXT CYCLE COSTS WILL ADJUST TO ELIMINATE IMPORTS
      ESTCK(NR)=0.999
   59 CONTINUE
C**   DETERMINE IF STOCK LEVELS ARE CRITICAL; FLAGR(NR)=1.0
      DO 64 I=1,4
      IF (STDEP(NR).LE.FLG(NR,I).AND.FLG(NR,I).LE.ESTCK(NR)) GO TO 65
      IF (ESTCK(NR).GE.0.985) GO TO 65
   64 CONTINUE
      FLAGR(NR)=0.0
      GO TO 60
   65 FLAGR(NR)=1.0
   60 CONTINUE
C**   FLAGR(20) ARE STOCK DEPLETION FLAGS OF EACH RESOURCE
C**   ESTCK(20) ARE THE NEW STOCK DEPLETION LEVELS CF EACH RESOURCE
C**
C**   CALCULATE RESOURCE UNIT COSTS - ECST(NR),XMCST(NR),XMESTR(NR)
```

STEP2

```
C**    XMCST IS THE MAX VALUE, ECST IS THE MEAN VALUE
C**    ECST(NR),XMCST(NR) ARE PURCHASE COSTS;ECSTR(NR),XMESTR(NR) ARE COSTS
C**    TO "MINE" ONE UNIT
       DO 70 NR=1,18
       TEMP=1.0
       IF (NR.NE.18) GO TO 413
  7411 TEMP=1.0+0.10*((ESTCK(18)-0.93)/0.04)
       GO TO 415
   413 CONTINUE
C**    IF STOCK LOW, RAPIDLY ESCALATE PRICE EXCEPT FOR CAPITAL,WORK UNITS
       IF (ESTCK(NR).LE.0.0)  ESTCK(NR)=0.000001
       IF (NR.EQ.1.OR.NR.GT.16) GO TO 417
       IF (ESTCK(NR).GT.0.9) TEMP=(0.1/(1.0-ESTCK(NR)))**3
       GO TO 415
   417 IF (ESTCK(NR).GE.0.9) TEMP=(0.1/(1.0-ESTCK(NR)))
   415 XMCST(NR) =0.00001*( XK1(NR)+(XK2(NR)*(ESTCK(NR)**XK3(NR))))*TEMP
       ECST(NR)  = 0.33 * ((2*XMCST(NR))+XMCST1(NR))
C**    REREC IS RATIO OF UNITS RECYCLED TO UNITS MINED,SET AS FUNCTION
C**    OF STOCK USED
       REREC(NR)=XK4(NR)+XK5(NR)*(ESTCK(NR)**2)
       ECSTR(NR)=ECST(NR)/(1+REREC(NR))
       XMESTR(NR) = XMCST(NR)/(1+REREC(NR))
       IF (ECSTR(NR).LT.RUCST1(NR)) ECSTR(NR)=RUCST1(NR)
       RUCST(NR)=ECSTR(NR)
C**
C**    VAL(NR) IS REMAINING AMOUNT OF STOCK PILE
       VAL(NR) = PILE(NR) * (1 - ESTCK(NR))
       XMCST1(NR)=XMCST(NR)
       STCK1(NR)=ESTCK(NR)*100.
       RUCST2(NR)=RUCST1(NR)
    70 RUCST1(NR)=RUCST(NR)
C**    CALCULATE CAPITAL EXPANSION COSTS IF OUTPUT PASSED MAXIMUM
C**    PLANT CAPACITY. ALLOCATE COSTS OVER NEXT 10 YEARS
       DO 74 J=1,12
       IF (XJOT(J).LE.XMJOT(J)) GO TO 74
C**    CAPITAL EXPANSION OF J EQUALS TEMP; NEW CAPITAL LEVEL IS XMJOT(J)
       TEMP=XJOT(J)-XMJOT(J)
       XMJOT(J)=XJOT(J)
C**    CAPITAL EXPANSION COST/YEAR IS TEMP
       TEMP=TEMP*CAPVL(J)*0.1
       DO 72 I=1,12
       K=NCYCLE+I
       IF (I.NE.1) GO TO 72
       DO 78 NR=1,12
    78 XMDUR(K,NR)=XMDUR(K,NR)+TEMP*EXPDUR(NR)*10.
    72 XMCAP(K,J)=XMCAP(K,J)+TEMP
    74 CONTINUE
C**
C**    DETERMINE USAGE OF EXISTANT FACILITIES
       DO 76 J=1,12
       CAPUSE(J)=(XJOT(J)/XMJOT(J))*100.0
       TEMP=(ALOG(XMJOT(J))-ALOG(1000.0))/NCYCLE
       CAPGR1(J)=EXP(TEMP)
    76 CONTINUE
       DO 310 J=1,12
   310 CAPGR1(J)=100*(CAPGR1(J)-1.0)
       CALL MATMPY (RESORD,XFACT,RESPR1,20,12)
       DO 606 NR= 1,20
```

```
 606  RESPR(NR) = RESPR1(NR)*RUCST(NR)
      XLAND = 0.0
      DO 8 NR= 15,16
   8  XLAND = XLAND + RESPR(NR)
      RAMAT = 0.0
      DO 9 NR= 1,10
   9  RAMAT = RAMAT + RESPR(NR)
      RESPN = RAMAT+XLAND+RESPR(18)
C**
 107  RETURN
      END
```

MATMPY

```
      SUBROUTINE MATMPY (XMAT,VEC,RVEC,I,J)
C**   MULTIPLIES A MATRIX WITH A VECTOR OF VARIABLE DIMENSIONS
      DIMENSION XMAT(I,J),VEC(J),RVEC(I)
      REST=0.0
      DO 10 M=1,I
      DO 10 N=1,J
      RES  =  XMAT(M,N) * VEC(N)
      REST = REST + RES
      IF (N.EQ.J) RVEC(M) = REST
   10 IF (N.EQ.J) REST = 0.0
      RETURN
      END
```

STEP3

```
      SUBROUTINE STEP3
C**   EVALUATING VALUES,RESILIENCY & ADJUSTMENTS IF REQD FOR EACH
C**   NTH MEASURE, WHERE N=12, AS THERE ARE 12 MEASURES
C**
      REAL*8 TITLE,HEADG,XMETIT,POPGP
      COMMON/INTER8/CPILE(20),CAPVL(12),CUTMAT(50,40),XMBRK(19),
     1 SUMMAT(50,10),PUBDIV,PUBNUM,PRIDIV,PRINUM,SCAMSO
      COMMON/YEAR/NCYCLE,RESPR(20),DEGRAD(12),UPGRAD(12),IYEAR
      COMMON/INTER2/RGJ(12),QCLT(12),RESOR(20),TOTKT(12),
     1 ESTCK(20),STDEP(20),RUCST(20),CAPREQ(12),
     2 REREC(20),FLAGR(20),XMESTR(20),
     3 XNVST1(12),XNVST(12),XJOT(12),UTIL(12,20)
      COMMON/PRINT/XPRNT1,XPRNT2,PRINTX,DETAIL,PPLOT
      COMMON/INTER3/CNJ(12,12),DN(12),TMEAS(12),DNJT1(12,12),COUNT1(12),
     1 XMDEL(12),RESIL(12),POP(9),VN(12),XMEAS(12),RATVST(12)
      COMMON/INTER/FMG,TOPTM1,AGEPT1(65),TOPT,
     1 POPKT(4,6),AGRIT(4),FBR,FDT,PDTH(65)
C**
      COMMON/NAMES/TITLE(12,2),HEADG(20,2),XMETIT(12,2)
      DIMENSION DEL(12,12),DNJ(12,12),XCONT(12),XMDNJ(12),
     1 COUNT(12)
      COMMON/TO/XNVOLT(12),XMAINR(12),XMANT(12),XNUMER,XLAND,XMNORM(12),
     1 SUMIVT,RAMAT,RESPN,CAPUSE(12),VAL(20),XEXPR(12),
     2 STCK1(20),CAPGR1(12)
C**   INITIALIZE STATE INDICATORS
      DO 11 N=1,12
   11 COUNT(N)=0.0
      DO 12 J=1,12
      XCONT(J)=0.0
      XMDNJ(J)=0.0
   12 XMDEL(J)=0.0
      POINT=0.0
      DO 15 J=1,6
   15 POP(J)   =   POPKT(1,J) + POPKT(2,J) + POPKT(3,J) + POPKT(4,J)
      POP(7)   =   TOPT
C**
C**   LOOP TO PROCESS EACH MEASURE IN TURN (TO 1000)
      DO 1000 N=1,12
      IF (N.EQ.13) GO TO 1000
      SUM=0.0
C**
C**   CALCULATE XNUMER OF MEASURE
      DO 10 J=1,12
   10 SUM = SUM + (CNJ(N,J)*XJOT(J) * 0.1)
C**   SELECT AFFECTED POPULATION
      I = DN(N)
C**   CALCULATE MEASURE VALUE
      XMEAS(N)   =SUM/POP(I)
C**
C**   CALCULATE RESIL; IF < 0.0 NEED OUTPUT ADJUSTMENTS
      RESIL(N)   = (XMEAS(N) - TMEAS(N))/TMEAS(N)
C**   TMEAS(N) IS THE THRESHOLD VALUE
C**
C**   IF RESIL >= 0.0 OUTPUTS O.K.,SET DEMANDS TO 0.0 & GO TO 1000
   16 IF(RESIL(N).GE.0.0) GO TO 20
C**   IF RESIL < 0.0; NEED ADJUSTMENTS
      GO TO 30
   20 DO 25 J=1,12
```

STEP3

```
      DEL(N,J)= 0.0
   25 DNJ(N,J)= 0.0
      COUNT(N)= 0.0
      GO TO 1000
C**
C**   SET RESIL ADJUSTMENTS FOR EACH APPROPRIATE J
   30 POINT=1.0
      DO 40 J=1,12
C**   IF CNJ=0.0 THEN COMPONENT OUTPUT DEMAND =0.0 (J NOT IN XMEAS)
      IF (CNJ(N,J).EQ.0.0) DEL(N,J)=0.0
      IF (CNJ(N,J).EQ.0.0) GO TO 40
C**   OUTPUT DEMAND SCALED TO J'S SHARE OF SETTING MEASURE VALUE
      DEL(N,J)=(1/ CNJ(N,J)) *(TMEAS(N) - XMEAS(N)) * POP(I)
C**   DNJT1 IS CUMULATIVE NEED SINCE RESIL LAST WAS >=0.0
   40 DNJ(N,J)= DNJT1(N,J) + DEL(N,J)
C**   COUNT IS YEARS SINCE RESIL LAST WAS >=0.0
      COUNT(N)  = COUNT1(N) + 1.0
 1000 CONTINUE
C**
C**   END OF MEASURES CALCULATIONS
C**
C**   MAXIMUM OUTPUT ADJUSTMENT FOR EACH OUTPUT SECTOR J
C**   DUE TO ADDITIONAL DEMANDS PLACED BY MEASURES WITH RESIL < 0.0
C**   IF NO RESIL < 0.0  SKIP TO STATEMENT 60
  504 IF (POINT.EQ.0.0) GO TO 70
C**
C**   FOR EACH J, FIND THE MAX OUTPUT DEMAND  (XMDEL(J)) AND ITS
C**   MEASURE NO(N)
      DO 60 J=1,12
      XMDEL(J) = DEL(1,J)
      DO 50 N=1,12
      IF (N.EQ.13) GO TO 55
      IF (DEL(N,J).GT.XMDEL(J))  XMDEL(J)=DEL(N,J)
      IF (DEL(N,J).GT.XMDEL(J)) I=N
   50 CONTINUE
C**
C**   SET PARAMETERS FOR MAXIMUM DEMAND LEVELS
   55 XMDNJ(J) =  DNJ(I,J)
   60 XCONT(J)  =  COUNT(I)
   70 CONTINUE
C**
C**   PREPARATION FOR NEXT CYCLE
      DO 90 N=1,12
      DO 80 J=1,12
   80 DNJT1(N,J)  = DNJ(N,J)
   90 COUNT1(N)  = COUNT(N)
   99 RETURN
      END
```

STEP4

```
      SUBRCUTINE STEP4
C**   ADJUSTS RESOURCE USAGE DUE TO SUBSTITUTION WITHIN THE AREA
C**
      COMMCN/INTER2/RGJ(12),QCLT(12),RESOR(20),TOTKT(12),
     1 ESTCK(20),STDEP(20),RUCST(20),CAPREQ(12),
     2 REREC(20),FLAGR(20),XMESTR(20),
     3 XNVST1(12),XNVST(12),XJOT(12),UTIL(12,20)
      COMMCN/YEAR/NCYCLE,RESPR(20),DEGRAD(12),UPGRAD(12),IYEAR
      COMMCN/PRINT/XPRNT1,XPRNT2,PRINTX,DETAIL,PPLOT
      COMMCN/INTER8/CPILE(20),CAPVL(12),CUTMAT(50,4C),XMBRK(19),
     1 SUMMAT(50,10),PUBDIV,PUBNUM,PRIDIV,PRINUM,SCAMSO
       COMMCN/TWO/XMCST1(20),PILE(20)
      CCMMCN/INTER4/SUBDAT(10,13),SUBMAT(1000),SUBPIL(900),LST,LP
      COMMCN/TWCRK/WORK(20),RESPRT(21)
      COMMCN/NAMES/TITLE(12,2),HEADG(20,2),XMETIT(12,2)
      DIMENSION SCST(10),FPT(50),MARK(10),ORES(10)
C**
      REAL*8 TITLE,HEADG,XMETIT,POPGP
      IT1=5
      DO 2000 I= 1,21
 2000 RESPRT(I) =  0.0
      RESPRT(1) = 2.01
C**
C**   LOOP 1000 CHECKS FOR EACH R IF SUBSTITUTION IS CALLED FOR AND
C**   EXISTS; EACH TEST IS LABELLED
  200 DO 1000 NR=1,20
C**   INITIALIZE VALUES FOR EACH NR
      DO 5 K=1,10
      ORES(K)=0.0
      SCST(K)=0.0
    5 MARK(K)=0
      POINT=0.0
C**
C**   TEST 1: IF FLAGR(NR)=0.0, NOT CALLED FCR THIS CYCLE; GO TO 1000
      IF (FLAGR(NR).EQ.0.0) GC TO 1000
C**   SEARCHING FOR SUBSTITUTION VECTORS, MARK(K) STORES THE INDEX
      K=1
C**
C**   TEST 2: IF SUBSTITUTICN (IV) IS FOR RESOURCE R, PUT MARK IN TEST
C**   VECTOR= TO IV POSITION & NUMBER; OTHERWISE LEAVE AS 0.0
      DO  10 M=1,10
      IF (SUBDAT(M,1).EQ.NR) GO TO 20
      GO TO 10
   20 MARK(K)=K
   10 K=K+1
C**
C**   TEST 3: CHECK IS OPTICNAL
C**   CHECKING FOR FLAGS TURNED ON IN THE SUBSTITUTING RESOURCES
C**   OF THE SUBSTITUTIN VECTORS
      DO 30 K=1,10
      IF (NCYCLE.GT.0) GO TC 53
C**   LOOP SUPPRESSED
      IF (MARK(K).EQ.0) GO TO 30
      M=MARK(K)
      DO  40 J=1,5
      N=2*J+1
      I=SUBDAT(M,N)
      IF (I.EQ.0) GO TO 30
```

STEP4

```
      IF( FLAGR(I).EQ.0.0) GO TO 40
      MARK(K)=0
   40 CONTINUE
   30 CONTINUE
   53 CONTINUE
C**
C**
C**   FOR ALL SUBSTITUTIONS WHICH PASSED THE FLAG TEST CALCULATE SCST;
C**   SCST IS THE ONE YEAR SUBSTITUTION COST
      LST=10000
      L=1
C**
      DO 75 K=1,10
C**   IDX TAKEN FROM TEST 2 RESIDUES
      M=MARK(K)
      IF (M.EQ.0) GO TO 70
C**
C**   SUBDAT CAN BE A FORMULA FOR UP TO 5 RESOURCES (MAY INCLUDE
C**   ORIGINAL RESOURCE)
      DO 60 J=1,5
      N=2*J+1
C**   IRN IS RESOURCE NUMBER TO BE SUBBED
      I=SUBDAT(M,N)
      IF (I.EQ.0) GO TO 60
C**   N+1 IS AMOUNT TO BE SUBBED
C**   SUM IS COST OF J+H COMPONENT
      SUM = SUBDAT(M,N+1) * XMESTR(I)
C**   SCST IS CUMULATED COSTS FOR UP TO # 5 SUBS
      SCST(L)=SCST(L)+SUM
   60 COMP=SCST(L)
C**   TEST 4: IF SUB COST >= RESOURCE COST,DROP FROM CONSIDERATION
      I=0
      IF (XMESTR(NR).GT.COMP) GO TO 68
      MARK(K)=0
      SCST(L)=0.0
      GO  TO 70
C**   SET LST TO STATE AT LEAST ONE SUB EXISTS
   68 LST=L
C**   I IS NUMBER OF ACCEPTABLE SUBS
      I=I+1
   70 L=L+1
   75 CONTINUE
C**
C**   TEST 5: IF IICTR IS <= 1 ALL NEEDED DATA IS GATHERED
      IF (I.LE.1) GO TO 105
C**
      L=1
C**
C**   STORE 5 YEAR COST OF SUBSTITUTION FOR ALL VECTORS STILL ACTIVE
      DO 80 I=1,10
      M=MARK(I)
      IF (M.EQ.0) GO TO 80
      POINT=1.0
C**   SUBDAT (M,13) IS TIME TO COMPLETE SUB IN YEARS
      IT1 = SUBDAT(M,13)
      CALL NORMAL(IT1,FPT)
      IT=SUBDAT(M,1)
C**   90 LOOP DEVELOPS TIME SUB 5 YEAR COST INTO ORES
```

STEP4

```
         DO 90 K=1,5
         SUM=XMESTR(IT)*(1-FPT(K))  + (SCST(I)*FPT(K))
      90 ORES(L) = ORES(L) + SUM
      80 L=L+1
         IF (POINT.EQ.0.0) GO TO 1000
         LST=10000
         CMP=10000.0
C**      SELECT LEAST 5 YEAR COST (MINIMUM OF ORES)
         I=1
         DO 110 K=1,10
         IF (ORES(K).EQ.0.0) GO TO 110
          IF (ORES(K).LT.CMP)  LST=I
         IF (ORES(K).LT.CMP) CMP=ORES(K)
     110 I=I+1
C**      LEAST COST OPTION IN LST IF IICTR IS .GE. 1;
C**      ELSE NO SUB AND LST=10000.0
     105 CONTINUE
         IF (LST.EQ.10000) GO TO 1000
C**
C**      FOR SUB LST STORE THE TIME PHASED SUBS INTO SUBMAT AS (YEAR OF
C**      SUB,RESOURCE SUBBED,SUB #, FRAC OF SUB COMPLETED)
         IT1 = SUBDAT(LST,13)
         CALL NORMAL(IT1,FPT)
         DO 900 K=1,IT1
         I=SUBMAT(1)
         IF (I.GE.995) GO TO 910
         SUBMAT(I+1) = NCYCLE + K
         SUBMAT(I+2) = NR
         SUBMAT(I+3) = LST
         SUBMAT(I+4) = FPT(K)
     900 SUBMAT(1) = I + 4
         LPP=RESPRT(1)
         RESPRT(LPP) = NR
         RESPRT(LPP+1) = 1.
         RESPRT(LPP+2) = LST
         RESPRT(LPP+3) = IYEAR + K
         RESPRT(1) = RESPRT(1) + 4.
         GO TO 915
     910 WRITE (6,911)
     911 FORMAT(5X,44HRESOURCE SUB NOT COMPLETED: STORAGE OVERFLOW,/)
     915 IF(NR.EQ.16.OR.NR.EQ.15) GO TO 914
C**      IF NR IS NOT LAND, SUB MARK SET SO SUB CANNOT BE DONE AGAIN
         SUBDAT(LST,1) = SUBDAT(LST,1) * (-1.0)
     914 LP=NCYCLE+K
C**
C**      PRINT RESOURCE SUBSTITUTION ACTION STATEMENT
    1000 CONTINUE
C**
C**      RESOURCE SUB LOOP COMPLETED
C**
C**
C**      BEGIN CHECK TO SEE IF STOCK PILE SHOULD BE INCREASED. THIS
C**      ACTION CAN BE REPEATED AFTER PRESENT INCREASE IS DONE
         DO 800 NR=1,20
C**      IF RESOURCE IS ANNUALLY RENEWABLE, GO TO 810
         IF (NR.EQ.16.OR.NR.EQ.15.OR.NR.EQ.17) GO TO 810
C**      IF RESOURCE IS AIR OR WATER GO TO 810
         IF (NR.EQ.19.OR.NR.EQ.20) GO TO 810
```

STEP4

```
               C**    IF NR IS FARM GOODS GC TO 800
0113                  IF (NR.EQ.1) GO TO 800
               C**    IF RESOURCE IS WORKERS, SKIP
0114                  IF (NR.EQ.18) GO TO 800
               C**    IF RESOURCE FLAG NOT SET, SKIP RESOURCE
0115                  IF (FLAGR(NR).EQ.0.0) GO TO 800
               C**    IF AMOUNT OF EXPANSION IS 0.0, SKIP
0116                  IF (CPILE(NR).LE.0.0) GO TO 800
               C**    IF AN INCREASE IS PRESENTLY BEING DONE, SKIP
0117                  IF(WORK(NR).GT.0.0) GC TO 800
               C**
               C**    DEVELCP TIME PHASED INCREASE FOR 5 YEAR COMPLETION PERIOD
0118                  NPP=0.0
0119                  CALL NORMAL(5,FPT)
               C**    STORE EXPANSION VALUES FOR NEXT 5 YEARS IN SUBPIL AS:
               C**    (RESOURCE,YEAR,AMOUNT ADDED)
0120                  DO 820 K=1,5
0121                  I=SUBPIL(1)
0122                  IF (I.GE.895) GO TO 830
0123                  SUBPIL(I+1) = NR
0124                  SUBPIL(I+2) = NCYCLE + K
0125                  SUBPIL(I+3) = CPILE(NR) * (FPT(K)-NPP)
0126                  NPP = FPT(K)
0127             820  SUBPIL(1) = I + 3
0128                  LPP=RESPRT(1)
0129                  RESPRT(LPP+1) = 0.0
0130                  RESPRT(LPP) = NR
0131                  RESPRT(LPP+2) = CPILE (NR)
0132                  RESPRT(1) = RESPRT(1) + 4.
0133                  GO TO 840
0134             830  WRITE (6,831)
0135             831  FORMAT(5X,50HRESOURCE STOCKPILE NOT INCREASED: STORAGE OVERFLOW,/)
               C**    SET COUNTER AS INACTIVE FOR 5 YEARS
0136             840  WORK(NR)=5.0
0137                  LP=NCYCLE+K
               C**
               C**    PRINT RESOURCE EXPANSION ACTION STATEMENT
0138                  GO TO 800
               C**
               C**    RENEWABLE STOCKS RESET TO LIMIT
0139             810  ESTCK(NR)=0.0
0140             800  CONTINUE
               C**
               C**    IF MAX WORK UNITS EXCEEDED BY 1.14 CUT OUTPUT
               C**    OF PUBLIC COMPONENTS
0141                  IF (ESTCK(18).LT.(1.14*PILE(18))) GO TO 700
0142                  TEMP=0.0
               C**    CALCULATE PUBLIC WORKERS
0143                  DO 710 J=1,5
0144             710  TEMP=XJOT(J)*UTIL(J,18)*0.001+TEMP
               C**    CALCULATE OVERAGE
0145                  COMP=ESTCK(18)-1.14*PILE(18)
               C**    REDUCE CONSUMED OUTPUT
0146                  DO 720 J=1,5
0147             720  XJOT(J)=XJOT(J)*(TEMP-CCMP)/TEMP
0148                  TEMP=100.0*(TEMP-COMP)/TEMP
0149             700  CONTINUE
0150                  RETURN
0151                  END
```

NORMAL

```
      SUBROUTINE NORMAL(IT1,FPT)
C**   NORMALIZED CUMULATIVE NORMAL
      DIMENSION FPT(50)
C**
      DATA A1,A2,A3,A4/0.278393,0.230389,0.000972,0.078108/
      DATA FT0,FT1/0.02275,0.97725/
      DATA IT0/0/
C**
C**   CALCULATING THE MEAN
      XMEW=(IT0+IT1)/2.0
C**   CALCULATING THE VARIANCE
      SIG= (IT1 - IT0)/4.0
C**
      DO  100  IT=1,IT1
      M = IT - 1
      TEMP=IT - XMEW
      X = ABS(TEMP)/(1.41421 * SIG)
      X2 = X*X
      X3 = X2 * X
      X4 = X3 * X
      IDEL = 1
      MEW=XMEW
      IF (M.LT.MEW) IDEL = -1
      PHI = 1 - (1/((1 + A1*X + A2*X2 + A3*X3 + A4*X4)**4))
      FT = 0.5 + ( IDEL * (PHI/2))
      FPT(IT) = (FT - FT0)/(FT1 - FT0)
  100 CONTINUE
      II=IT1-1
      DO 200 IT=1,II
  200 FPT(IT) = FPT(IT+1)
      FPT(IT1) = 1.0
      RETURN
      END
```

```
      SUBROUTINE STEP5(S8)
C**
C**   REALLOCATE INVESTMENTS TO MEET ANTICIPATED THRESHOLDS IN THE
C**   CYCLE
      REAL*8 TITLE,HEADG,XMETIT,POPGP
      COMMON/TO/XNVOUT(12),XMAINR(12),XMANT(12),XNUMER,XLAND,XMNORM(12),
     1 SUMIVT,RAMAT,RESPN,CAPUSE(12),VAL(20),XEXPR(12),
     2 STCK1(20),CAPGR1(12)
      COMMON/INTER2/RGJ(12),QOLT(12),RESOR(20),TOTKT(12),
     1 ESTCK(20),STDEP(20),RUCST(20),CAPREQ(12),
     2 REREC(20),FLAGR(20),XMESTR(20),
     3 XNVST1(12),XNVST(12),XJOT(12),UTIL(12,20)
      COMMON/PRINT/XPRNT1,XPRNT2,PRINTX,DETAIL,PPLOT
      COMMON/NAMES/TITLE(12,2),HEADG(20,2),XMETIT(12,2)
      COMMON/INTER3/CNJ(12,12),DN(12),TMEAS(12),DNJT1(12,12),COUNT1(12),
     1 XMDEL(12),RESIL(12),POP(8),VN(12),XMEAS(12),RATVST(12)
      COMMON/CCST/RUCST1(20),RUCST2(20),XFACT(12),OCST(12),OCSTI(12)
      COMMON/OUTDIV/REDIV(20),XMPORT(12),UTILI(12,20),RUCSTI(20)
      COMMON/INTER5/XMRNOR(12),EJOT1(12),EXPO(12),EJOTX,SNCST,RESPR1(20)
     1 ,XIDFMN(12),XINJO(12),EJOT(12),XFILE(3,12),RESMN1(12),XKTI(12),
     2 XEPORT(12)
      DIMENSION CST(12),XKT(12)
C**
C**   INITIALIZE DATA AREAS
      S8=0.
  111 DO 1 J=1,12
      XIDFMN(J)=0.0
      CST(J)=0.0
      XKT(J)=0.0
    1 XINJO(J)=0.0
C**   FOR EACH OUTPUT(J) DETERMINE IF MORE OUTPUT IS DEMANDED
C**   (XMDEL IS .GT. 0.0); OTHERWISE GO TO EXPORT ROUTINE
      DO 1000 J=1,12
      IF (XMDEL(J).GT.0.0) GO TO 10
      GO TO 35
C**
C**   CALCULATE LEVEL OF J MAINTENANCE THAT CAN BE DEFERRED
   10 XIDFMN(J)=(XMRNOR(J)*XNVST(J))*0.01
C**   DETERMINE COST TO IMPORT GOODS TO MEET DEMAND OF J
      SUM=0.0
      DO 20 NR=1,20
   20 SUM=SUM+UTIL(J,NR)*XMESTR(NR)
      CST(J)=XMDEL(J)*SUM*XFACT(J)
C**
C**   DETERMINE AMT OF MAINT TO BE DEFERRED & AMOUNT OF GOODS TO BE
C**   IMPORTED.
C**   CMIN IS FRACTION OF DEMAND MET BY MAINT DEFERRAL
      CMIN=XIDFMN(J)/CST(J)
      IF(CMIN.GT.1.0) CMIN=1.0
      XJOT(J)=(CMIN*XMDEL(J))+XJOT(J)
C**   XMDEL(J) IS RESIDUE OF IMPORT DEMAND
      XMDEL(J)=XMDEL(J)*(1-CMIN)
C**
C**   XKT IS COST TO IMPORT RESIDUE
      XKT(J)=XMDEL(J)*SUM*XFACT(J)
C**
C**   SKIP EXPORT ROUTINE -, ALL GOODS CONSUMED INTERNALLY FOR J
C     GO TO 1000
```

STEP5

```
C**
C**   CALCULATE AMT & FUNDS OF J COMPONENT EXPORT
C**
   35 RESMN=5.0
C**   DETERMINE MIN RESIL FOR J
      DO 36 N=1,12
      IF (CNJ(N,J).EQ.0.0) GO TO 36
      IF (RESIL(N).LT.RESMN) RESMN=RESIL(N)
   36 CONTINUE
      IF (RESMN.LE.0.) RESMN=.0
      IF (NCYCLE.GT.1) GO TC 37
      RESMN1(J)=RESMN
C**
C**   EJOT(J) IS OUTPUT UNITS OF J TO EXPORT (%)
   37 EJOT(J)=EJOT1(J)*(RESMN/RESMN1(J))*XJOT(J)
      IF (EJOT(J).GT..4*XJOT(J)) EJOT(J)=.4*XJOT(J)
 1000 CONTINUE
      DO 1002 J=1,12
 1002 XIDFMN(J)=XIDFMN(J)+CAPREQ(J)
      EJOT(6)=EJOT(6)+EJOTX
C**
C***  IMPORTS ARE A FUNCTION OF THE XJOT REQUIRED BY A SOCIETY.
C**   IF XMPORT IS SET TO A VALUE IN BLOC DATA,IT IS NOT CALCULATED
C**   BELOW BUT IS ADDED TO. FIRST, THERE IS A DOLLAR VALUE CALCULATED
C**   TO BE USED IN STEP2 TO DETERMINE THE FUNDS AVAILABLE: THEN THE
C**   DOLLAR VALUE IS CONVERTED TO OUTPUT UNITS. THE CODE IS SIMILAR
C **  TO THAT USED IN THE INTERNAL SYSTEM WITH MIRROR PRICES AND
C**   PRODUCTION FUNCTIONS LOADED IN BLOC DATA. THESE REMAIN CONSTANT.
C**   DIFFERENCES IN THESE VALUES CAUSE CHANGES IN IMPORTS.
C**   MAINT & EXPORT LOOP COMPLETE
      SNCST=0.
      DO 1051 J=5,12
      XEPORT(J)=EJOT(J)*OCST(J)*XFACT(J)
 1051 SNCST=SNCST+XEPORT(J)
      CALL MATMPY (UTILI,RUCST1,OCSTI,12,20)
      DO 1052 J = 6,12
      IF(OCSTI(J).GE.OCST(J)) OCSTI(J)=OCST(J)
      IF(XMPORT(J).NE.0.) GO TO 1055
      XMPORT(J) = XNVOUT(J) *(((OCST(J)-OCSTI(J))/OCST(J))**2)
      GO TO 1052
 1055 XMPORT(J) = XMPORT(J)*(1+((OCST(J)-OCSTI(J))/OCST(J))**2)
      IF(XMPORT(J).GT.XNVOUT(J)) XMPORT(J)=XNVOUT(J)
 1052 CONTINUE
      TEMP=0.
      DO 1054  J=5,12
      XKTI(J) =XMPORT(J)/XFACT(J)
      TEMP=TEMP+XMPORT(J)
      XINJO(J) = XKTI(J)/OCSTI(J)
      IF(XMDEL(J).GT.XINJO(J)) S8=1.0
 1054 CONTINUE
      SNCST=SNCST-TEMP
 1056 CONTINUE
      RETURN
      END
```

STEP6

```
      SUBROUTINE STEP6(PSUM1,PSUM2,S8)
      REAL*8 TITLE,HEADG,XMETIT,POPGP
      COMMCN/INTER2/RGJ(12),QOLT(12),RESOR(20),TOTKT(12),
     1 ESTCK(20),STDEP(20),RUCST(20),CAPREQ(12),
     2 REREC(20),FLAGR(20),XMESTR(20),
     3 XNVST1(12),XNVST(12),XJOT(12),UTIL(12,20)
      COMMCN/PRINT/XPRNT1,XPRNT2,PRINTX,DETAIL,PPLOT
      COMMCN/YEAR/NCYCLE,RESPR(20),DEGRAD(12),UPGRAD(12),IYEAR
      COMMON/INTER3/CNJ(12,12),DN(12),TMEAS(12),DNJT1(12,12),COUNT1(12),
     1 XMDEL(12),RESIL(12),POP(8),VN(12),XMEAS(12),RATVST(12)
      COMMON/INTER/FMG,TOPTM1,AGEPT1(65),TOPT,
     1 POPKT(4,6),AGRIT(4),FBR,FDT,PDTH(65)
       COMMCN/INTER6/XUTIL(19,20),XMARK(19),TIME(19),ICTR,
     1  SUBIOP(1000),KR5,LTNCY,INDX(19),XOCST(19),XMOCST(12)
      COMMCN/INTER5/XMRNOR(12),EJOT1(12),EXPO(12),EJOTX,SNCST,RESPR1(20)
     1 ,XIDFMN(12),XINJO(12),EJOT(12),XFILE(3,12),RESMN1(12),XKTI(12),
     2 XEPORT(12)
      COMMCN/INTER4/SUBDAT(10,13),SUBMAT(1000),SUBPIL(900),LST,LP
      COMMCN/INTER8/CPILE(20),CAPVL(12),OUTMAT(50,40),XMBRK(19),
     1 SUMMAT(50,10),PUBDIV,PUBNUM,PRIDIV,PRINUM,SCAMSO
      COMMCN/NAMES/TITLE(12,2),HEADG(20,2),XMETIT(12,2)
      DIMENSION XNVST2(12),XNEED2(12),XOVER2(12),XNUP2(2),XDWN2(2),
     1 TRINS(2),DIFFS(2),DELRGJ(12),YOCST(19)
      DIMENSION FPT(50) ,RGJKT(12)
C**
C**   FIND LOWER COST I/O PROCESS
C**   XMCCST IS PRESENT PROCESS MAX COST; XOCST IS OTHER PROCESS
C**   SUBSTITUTE COST
      CALL MATMPY(XUTIL,XMESTR,XOCST,19,20)
      CALL MATMPY(UTIL,XMESTR,XMOCST,12,20)
C**
C**
      S8=0.0
      DO 601 I=1,12
  601 XFILE(1,I)=0.0
C**   DC I/O SUB PROCESS CHECK FOR ALL J
  201 CO 1000 J=1,12
C**   INITIALIZE YOCST FOR EACH J
      DO 500 NP=1,19
      YOCST(NP)=0.0
      INDX(NP)=XMARK(NP)
C**
C**   IF PROCESS NOT FOR J OR IF STATUS IS NOT ALTERNATE PROCESS,
C**   DO NCT CONSIDER (GO TO 500)
      IF (INDX(NP).NE.J) GO TO 500
      IF (XMBRK(NP).NE.0.0) GO TO 500
      IF (XOCST(NP).GE.XMOCST(J)) GO TO 500
C**   SUB PROCESS TAKES TIME(NP) YEARS; GET SUBPROCESS VALUES
C**   FROM NORMAL
      LT=TIME(NP)
      CALL NORMAL(LT,FPT)
C**
C**   CALCULATE 5 YEAR COST IF XMARK(NP)=J
      DO 100 K5=1,5
  1CC YOCST(NP)=YOCST(NP)+0.2*(XMOCST(J)*(1-FPT(K5))+XOCST(NP)*FPT(K5))
  500 CONTINUE
C**   COST OF ALL I/O CANDIDATES STORED IN YOCST; IF
C**   YOCST=0.0, NOT A CANDIDATE
```

STEP6

```
      KR5=0
C**
C**   COMPARE YOCSTS TO COMP=XMOCST(J); IF YOCST IS .LT. XMOCST,
C**   SUB WILL BE DONE
      COMP=XMOCST(J)
      DO 95 NPP=1,19
      IF (YOCST(NPP).LE.0.0) GO TO 95
C**   P PASSES TEST; IN FUTURE TESTS SUB YOCST(NP) FOR XMOCST
      IF (YOCST(NPP).GE.COMP) GO TO 95
C**   NPP IS PRESENT SUBSTITUTE I/O PROCESS
      KR5=NPP
      COMP=YOCST(NPP)
C**   KR5 IS CHOSEN; IF 0 NO SUB CHOSEN
C**
   95 CONTINUE
      IF (KR5.EQ.0) GO TO 1000
      S8=1.0
C**
C**   STORE I/O SUB VALUES FOR LT YEARS IN SUBIOP MATRIX AS
C**   (COMPONENT,I/O LINE,VALUE DONE, YEAR)
      DO 900 K4=1,LT
      ICTR=SUBIOP(1)
      IF (ICTR.GE.995) GO TO 913
      SUBIOP(ICTR+1) = J
      SUBIOP(ICTR+2) = KR5
      SUBIOP(ICTR+3) = FPT(K4)
      SUBIOP(ICTR+4) = K4+NCYCLE
  900 SUBIOP(1) = ICTR + 4
      GO TO 904
  913 WRITE (6,914)
  914 FORMAT(5X,39HI/O SUB NOT COMPLETED: STORAGE OVERFLOW,/)
C**
C**   SET MARKER AS SUBSTITUTION IN PROCESS
C**
C**   PRINT I/O SUB ACTION STATEMENT
  904 LTNCY=NCYCLE+LT
      XMBRK(KR5)=-1.0
      DO 600 I=1,11
      IF (XFILE(1,I).NE.0.0) GO TO 600
      XFILE(1,I)=J
      XFILE(2,I)=KR5
      XFILE(3,I)=LTNCY
      GO TO 1000
  600 CONTINUE
 1000 CONTINUE
C**   I/O ROUTINE COMPLETE FOR ALL J
C**
C**   FUNDS TRANSFER ROUTINE TO ADJUST RATES OF GROWTH
C**
C**   INITIALIZE DATA FOR ROUTINE
      DO 907 J=1,12
  907 DELRGJ(J)=0.0
      XNUP2(1)=0
      XNUP2(2)=0
      XDWN2(1)=0
      XDWN2(2)=0
C**
C**   EXTRAPOLATE FUNDS EXPECTED (XNVST2) & NEEDED (XNEED2) FOR J
```

```
      DO 20 J=1,12
      XNVST2(J) =   XNVST(J)  * (1 + RGJ(J) * 0.01)
      XNEED2(J) =   XNVST(J) * (1 +XMDEL(J)/XJOT(J)) * (TOPT/TOPTM1)
C**   XOVER2 IS AMT OF FUNDS EXPECTED OVER NEEDED (IF .LT.0, NEED FUNDS)
      XOVER2(J) =  XNVST2(J) -  XNEED2(J)
C**
C**   XNUP2(1,2) ARE COMPONENT POSITIVE XOVER2;
C**   XDWN2(1,2) ARE COMPONENT NEGATIVE XOVER2
C**   J=6,12 WITH K=1, J=1,5 WITH K=2
      IF (XOVER2(J).GE.0.0) GO TO 21
      K=2
      IF (J.GE.6) K=1
      XDWN2(K)= XDWN2(K)-XOVER2(J)
      GO TO 20
   21 K=2
      IF (J.GE.6) K=1
      XNUP2(K)=XNUP2(K)+XOVER2(J)
C**   EXTRAPOLATION LOOP COMPLETED
C**
   20 CONTINUE
C**
C**   THERE ARE TWO POSSIBLE LOOPS TO INCREASE THE RATES OF
C**   GROWTH, ONE FOR PUBLIC (1-5) AND ONE FOR PRIVATE (6-12).
C**   FUNDS TRANSFER FIRST INTERSECTOR (TO 99) THEN INTRASECTOR (TO 999)
   34 DO 99 K= 1,2
C**   CASH TRANSFER BETWEEN SECTORS (TO 99)
C**   IF XDWN2=0 NO FUNDS NEEDED; IF XNUP2 .GE.XDWN2 NO INTERSECTOR
C**   TRANSFER NEEDED
      IF (XDWN2(K).EQ.0.0) GO TO 99
      IF (XNUP2(K).LT.XDWN2(K)) GO TO 37
      GO TO 99
   37 IF(K.EQ.1) K1=2
      IF(K.EQ.2) K1=1
C**
C**   FUNDS OF INTER NEEDED ARE TRINS(K)
      TRINS(K) = XDWN2(K)-XNUP2(K)
C**
C**   OTHER SECTOR HAS NO FUNDS FOR INTER
      IF (XNUP2(K1).LT.XDWN2(K1)) GO TO 99
C**   DIFFS(K1) ARE FUNDS AVAILABLE FOR INTER
      DIFFS(K1) = XNUP2(K1)-XDWN2(K1)
C**
C**   IF OD.GE. T, TRINS REQUIREMENT FULLY MET
      IF(DIFFS(K1).GE.TRINS(K))  GO TO 60
C**   LOWER TRINS TO FUNDS AVAILABLE
   85 TRINS(K)=DIFFS(K1)
C**   FUNDS ARE TRANSFERRED ON EQUAL % BASIS
C**   BETWEEN COMPONENTS OF SECTORS
C**   INTRASECTOR WILL COMPLETE REDISTRIBUTION
   60 CONTINUE
      COMP=0.0
      J2=5*(2-K)
C**   FOR RECEIVING SECTOR, INCREASE SECTION IS COMP
      K2=5
      IF(J2.EQ.2) K2=6
      DO 62 J3=1,K2
      J=J3+J2
   62 COMP=COMP+XNVST2(J)
```

STEP6

```
      COMP=TRINS(K)/COMP
C**   RESULT OF SECTOR INCREASES
      DO 64 J3=1,K2
      J=J3+J2
      XNVST2(J)=XNVST2(J)*(1+COMP)
      XOVER2(J)=XNVST2(J)-XNEED2(J)
   64 RGJ(J)=((XNVST2(J)-XNVST(J))/XNVST(J))*100.0
      COMP=0.0
      J2=5*(2-K1)
C**   FOR GIVING SECTOR, DECREASE FRACTION IS COMP
      DO 66 J3=1,K2
      J=J3+J2
   66 COMP=COMP+XNVST2(J)
      COMP=TRINS(K)/COMP
C**   RESULTS OF SECTOR DECREASES
      DO 68 J3=1,K2
      J=J3+J2
      XNVST2(J)=XNVST2(J)*(1-COMP)
      XOVER2(J)=XNVST2(J)-XNEED2(J)
   68 RGJ(J)=((XNVST2(J)-XNVST(J))/XNVST(J))*100
C**
C**   INITIALIZE RG FOR INTRA SECTOR
      DO 96 J=1,12
   96 DELRGJ(J)=0.0
   99 CONTINUE
C**
C**   INTERSECTOR ROUTINE CCMPLETE
C**
C**   BEGIN INTRASECTOR LOOP
C**   EACH SECTOR DONE IN TURN (K=1,2)
C**   RECALCULATE XNUP(K) AND XDWN(K)
      DO 999 K=1,2
      XNUP2(K)=0.0
      XDWN2(K)=0.0
      K2=5
      IF(K.EQ.1) K2=6
      J2=5*(2-K)
      DO 899 J3=1,K2
      J=J2+J3
      IF (XOVER2(J).GE.0.0) GO TO 898
      XDWN2(K)=XDWN2(K)-XOVER2(J)
      GO TO 899
  898 XNUP2(K)=XNUP2(K)+XOVER2(J)
  899 CONTINUE
C**
C**   IF XNUP2=0 NO ADJUSTMENT POSSIBLE
      IF (XNUP2(K).EQ.0.0) GO TO 999
      IF (XNUP2(K).GE.XDWN2(K)) GO TO 1010
C**   IF XNUP .GE. XDWN ALL FUND DEMANDS (XOVER2 .LT.0) CAN BE MET
      GO TO 1500
C**
C**   XKK2 IS AMT OF OVERAGE IN XOVER2 .GT.0 COMPONENTS THAT IS
C**           TAKEN FOR DEMANDS
 1010 XKK2=XDWN2(K)/XNUP2(K)
      J=5*(2-K)
      DO 1020 J3=1,K2
      J=J2+J3
C**
```

STEP6

```
C**    XKK3 IS ADJUSTMENT MULTIPLIER; =1 IF XOVER2.LT.0 AND # IS .LT.1
C**            IF XOVER2 IS .GE.0
       XKK3=XKK2
       IF (XOVER2(J).GE.0.0) GO TO 1015
       XKK3=1.0
C**    CHANGE IN RATE OF GROWTH
  1015 DELRGJ(J)=(XOVER2(J)*XKK3*(-100.0))/XNVST2(J)
C**    THE FOLLOWING RESTRICTION IS TO PREVENT THE GROWTH RATES FROM
C**    FLUCTUATING BEYOND A 10% CHANGE.
       RGJKT(J) = RGJ(J)*0.1
       IF (DELRGJ(J).LT.RGJKT(J)) GO TO  1020
  4264 DELRGJ(J) = RGJKT(J)
  1020 RGJ(J)=RGJ(J)+DELRGJ(J)
       GO TO 999
C**
C**    LOOP IF XDWN(K).GT.XNUP(K); ONLY PARTIAL MEETING OF DEMAND
C**          POSSIBLE
C**    XKK2 IS FRACTION OF DEMAND MET
  1500 XKK2=XNUP2(K)/XDWN2(K)
       J2=5*(2-K)
       DO 1510 J3=1,K2
       J=J2+J3
C**
C**    XKK3 IS ADJUSTMENT MULTIPLIER; =1 IF XOVER2.GE.0;
C**                                    .LT.1 IF XOVER2 IS .LT. 0.0
       XKK3=XKK2
       IF(XOVER2(J).LT.0.0) GO TO 1505
       XKK3=1.0
  1505 DELRGJ(J)=(XOVER2(J)*XKK3*(-100.0))/XNVST2(J)
  1510 RGJ(J)=RGJ(J)+DELRGJ(J)
C**
   999 CONTINUE
C**
C**    INTRASECTOR ROUTINE DONE
C**
C**    SET STEP6 END PARAMETERS TO SEE IF THRESHOLDS OF MEASURES NEED
C**          TO BE LOWERED
       PSUM1 = XNUP2(1) + XNUP2(2)
       PSUM2 = XDWN2(1) + XDWN2(2)
       RETURN
       END
```

STEP7

```
      SUBROUTINE STEP7(PSUM1,PSUM2,SB)
C**   ADJUST LOL,QOL MEASURES TO RESPOND TO LACK OF INVESTMENT
C**   FUNDS FOR PRIVATE AND/OR PUBLIC SECTOR IN FUTURE CYCLES
C**
      COMMCN/INTER2/RGJ(12),QOLT(12),RESOR(20),TOTKT(12),
     1 ESTCK(20),STDEP(20),RUCST(20),CAPREQ(12),
     2 REREC(20),FLAGR(20),XMESTR(20),
     3 XNVST1(12),XNVST(12),XJOT(12),UTIL(12,20)
      COMMCN/PRINT/XPRNT1,XPRNT2,PRINTX,DETAIL,PPLOT
      COMMCN/COST/RUCST1(20),RUCST2(20),XFACT(12),OCST(12),OCSTI(12)
      COMMCN/YEAR/NCYCLE,RESPR(20),DEGRAD(12),UPGRAD(12),IYEAR
      COMMCN/INTER3/CNJ(12,12),DN(12),TMEAS(12),DNJT1(12,12),COUNT1(12),
     1 XMDEL(12),RESIL(12),POP(8),VN(12),XMEAS(12),RATVST(12)
      COMMCN/NAMES/TITLE(12,2),HEADG(20,2),XMETIT(12,2)
      DIMENSION XMESB2(12),XMESB1(12)
      REAL*8 TITLE,HEADG,XMETIT,POPGP
C**
C**
C**   INITIALIZE MEASURES FCR UPGRADE CHECK
  102 DO 10 N=1,12
      IF (N.GE.12) GO TO 10
      IF (NCYCLE.NE.1) GO TC 11
      XMESB1(N)=XMEAS(N)
      XMESB2(N)=XMESB1(N)
      GO TC 12
   11 XMESB2(N)=XMESB1(N)
      XMESB1(N)=XMEAS(N)
   12 DEGRAD(N)=0.
      UPGRAD(N)=0.
   10 CONTINUE
C**
C**   MAJOR COMPUTATION LOOP
      J=1
      DO 1000 N = 1,12
      IF (N.GE.13) GO TO 1000
C**   SETS POPULATION AFFECTED (SEE STEP3)
      I=DN(N)
C**
C**   CALCULATE XNUMER OF MEASURE
      SUM = 0.0
      DO 40 J=1,12
   40 SUM = SUM + (CNJ(N,J)*XJOT(J)*0.1)
C**   EXTRAPOLATE XMEAS FOR NEXT CYCLE
      XX = SUM / (POP(I)  * 1.1)
C**
C**   IF XMEAS O.K. GO TO UPGRADE (200)
      IF (XX.GE.TMEAS(N)) GC TO 200
C**   IF STEP6 ANSWERED FUNDS, DONT ADJUST TMEAS NEEDS
      IF (PSUM1.GE.PSUM2) GC TO 1000
C**   TMEAS SET TO MAX(0.05,XX)
      TMEAS(N)=XX
      IF (TMEAS(N).LT.0.05) TMEAS(N)=0.05
C**
C**   PRINT TMEAS DEGRADE STATEMENT
      DEGRAD(N)=TMEAS(N)
      GO TC 1000
C**
C**   IF XMESB1 .GE. XMESB2 .GT. TMEAS, UPGRADE TMEAS TO XMESB2
```

STEP7

```
  200 IF(NCYCLE.LT.3) GO TO 1000
      IF (XMESB2(N).LE.TMEAS(N)) GO TO 1000
      IF (XMESB1(N).LT.XMESB2(N)) GO TO 1000
C***  SET THE RATE OF CULTURE CHANGE HERE
      TMEAS(N)=TMEAS(N)+((XMESB2(N)-TMEAS(N))/5)
C**
C**   PRINT TMEAS UPGRADE STATEMENT
      UPGRAD(N)=TMEAS(N)
 1000 CONTINUE
C**   AREA THAT ADJUSTS LEVEL OF INVESTMENT GROWTH TO KEEP
C**   OUTPUT BALANCES APPROPRIATE
      SA=XJOT(7)
      SB=XJOT(10)
      SC=XJOT(11)
      IF(SA.LE.SB.AND.SA.LE.SC) J=7
      IF(SB.LE.SA.AND.SB.LE.SC) J=10
      IF(SC.LE.SA.AND.SC.LE.SB) J=11
      K=8
      IF(XJOT(K).LT.XJOT(J)) GO TO 6103
      GO TO 6100
 6103 IF(SA.GE.SB.AND.SA.GE.SC) J=7
      IF(SB.GE.SA.AND.SB.GE.SC) J=10
      IF(SC.GE.SA.AND.SC.GE.SB) J=11
      IF(XJOT(8).GT.XJOT(J)) GO TO 6026
 6100 SA=XNVST(J)*(1.+RGJ(J)*.01)
      SB=XNVST(K)*(1.+RGJ(K)*.01)
      SC=SA/(OCST(J)*XFACT(J))
      SD=SB/(OCST(K)*XFACT(K))
      IF(SC.LT.SD*.8) GO TO 6101
      IF(SC.GT.SD*1.2) GO TO 6102
      GO TO 6026
 6101 SE=SA*SD*.8/SC -SA
      IF(.04*SB.LT.SE) SE = .04*SB
      RGJ(J)=(((SA+SE)/XNVST(J))-1.)*100.
      RGJ(K)=(((SB-SE)/XNVST(K))-1.)*100.
      GO TO 6026
 6102 SE=SA-SA*SD*1.2/SC
      IF(.04*SA.LT.SE) SE = .04*SA
      RGJ(J)=(((SA-SE)/XNVST(J))-1.)*100.
      RGJ(K)=(((SB+SE)/XNVST(K))-1.)*100.
 6026 CONTINUE
      RETURN
      END
```

STEP8

```
0001          SUBROUTINE STEP8(S8)
        C**   CALCULATE GROWTH MODIFICATION FACTORS FOR POPULATION AND
        C**   ADJUST RESOURCE STOCK PILES
0002          REAL*8 TITLE,HEADG,XMETIT,POPGP,TIT1
0003          COMMCN/POPSCA/BR,DT,XMG,XXBR,DTHPTB,TOTMIG,XPMG(64)
0004          COMMCN/OUTDIV/REDIV(20),XMPORT(12),UTILI(12,20),RUCSTI(20)
0005          CCMMCN/INTER/FMG,TOPTM1,AGEPT1(65)
             1             ,TOPT,POPKT(4,6),AGRIT(4),FBR,FDT,PDTH(65)
0006            COMMCN/TWO/XMCST1(20),PILE(20)
0007          COMMCN/DURBLE/XMDUR(110,12),ECODUR(12),EXPDUR(12),XMNDUR(12)
C008          COMMCN/CHAR/CJK1(6,12),CJK2(6,12),CJK3(6,12),CJK4(6,12)
0009          COMMCN/INTER2/RGJ(12),QOLT(12),RESOR(20),TOTKT(12),
             1 ESTCK(20),STDEP(20),RUCST(20),CAPREQ(12),
             CREREC(20),FLAGR(20),XMESTR(20),
             3 XNVST1(12),XNVST(12),XJOT(12),UTIL(12,20)
0010          COMMCN/YEAR/NCYCLE,RESPR(20),DEGRAD(12),UPGRAD(12),IYEAR
0011          COMMCN/COST/RUCST1(20),RUCST2(20),XFACT(12),OCST(12),OCSTI(12)
0012          COMMCN/XKDATA/XK1(20),XK2(20),XK3(20),XK4(20),XK5(20),FLG(20,4)
0013          COMMCN/INTER3/CNJ(12,12),DN(12),TMEAS(12),DNJT1(12,12),COUNT1(12),
             1 XMDEL(12),RESIL(12),POP(8),VN(12),XMEAS(12),RATVST(12)
0014            COMMCN/INTER6/XUTIL(19,20),XMARK(19),TIME(19),ICTR,
             1  SUBIOP(1000),KR5,LTNCY,INDX(19),XOCST(19),XMOCST(12)
C015          COMMCN/INTER4/SUBDAT(10,13),SUBMAT(1000),SUBPIL(900),LST,LP
0016          COMMON/INTER8/CPILE(20),CAPVL(12),CUTMAT(50,40),XMBRK(19),
             1 SUMMAT(50,10),PUBDIV,PUBNUM,PRIDIV,PRINUM,SCAMSO
0017          CCMMCN/INTER5/XMRNOR(12),EJOT1(12),EXPO(12),EJOTX,SNCST,RESPR1(20)
             1 ,XIDFMN(12),XINJO(12),EJOT(12),XFILE(3,12),RESMN1(12),XKTI(12),
             2 XEPORT(12)
0018          COMMCN/TWORK/WCRK(20),RESPRT(21)
0019          COMMCN/PRINT/XPRNT1,XPRNT2,PRINTX,DETAIL,PPLOT
0020          COMMCN/EXOG/B(100)
C021          COMMCN/TO/XNVOLT(12),XMAINR(12),XMANT(12),XNUMER,XLAND,XMNORM(12),
             1 SUMIVT,RAMAT,RESPN,CAPUSE(12),VAL(20),XEXPR(12),
             2 STCK1(20),CAPGR1(12)
C022          COMMCN/NAMES/TITLE(12,2),HEADG(20,2),XMETIT(12,2),POPGP(6,2)
0023          DIMENSION DPILE(20),XMPOL2(10),XUTIL1(19,20),TMEASO(12),RPILE(20)
0024          DIMENSION TIT1(11,2),LST1(18),LP1(18)
0025          DATA TIT1/8H     EDUC,8HINSTITUT,8H   NON-W,8H   UNEMP,
             1 8H  PAID W,8HUNPAID W,8H        ,8H        B,
             2 8H       D,8H    MIGR,8HATION   ,8HIONAL   ,8HORKER   ,
             3 8HLCYED   ,8HORKER   ,8HORKER   ,8HTOTAL   ,8H        ,
             4 8HIRTHS   ,8HEATHS   ,8HATION   /
0026          WRITE(6,500) IYEAR
0027     500  FORMAT(1H1,55X,20H********************,/,56X,12H*  YEAR  IS    ,I5,
             1 3H  *,/,56X,20H********************,///)
0028          WRITE(6,503)
0029     503  FORMAT(1H0,5X,16H***POPULATION***,T63,16H***PRODUCTION***,//,
             1 1H ,T63,6HINVST.,1X,7HDELAYED,1H ,T22
             2    ,17HPEOPLE          ***,T69,5HFUNDS,3X,6H MAINT,3X,6HOUTPUT,3X,
             3 7HIMPORTS,2X,7HEXPORTS,3X,6HGROWTH)
        C**   SUM COLUMNS OF THE REPORT
0030          IF(NCYCLE.EQ.1) T2=900000.
0031          T1 = 0.
0032          TOTKT(11)   = TOTMIG
        CDELETE
        CDELETE
0033          TOTKT(10) =DTHPTB
0034          TOTKT(7) = TOPT
```

STEP8

```
      TOTKT(9) = XXBR
      DO 5002 I=1,12
      IF (I.EQ.8.OR.I.EQ.12) GO TO 8001
      WRITE (6,6000) (TIT1(I,J),J=1,2),TOTKT(I),(TITLE(I,J),J=1,2),
     1 XNVST(I),XMNORM(I),XJOT(I),XINJO(I),EJOT(I),RGJ(I)
 6000 FORMAT(1H,A8,A5,4X,F11.3,6X,3H***,6X,2A8,2X,F11.3,5(1X,F8.2))
      GO TO 8003
8001  WRITE(6,8002) (TITLE(I,J),J=1,2),
     1 XNVST(I),XMNORM(I),XJOT(I),XINJO(I),EJOT(I),RGJ(I)
8002  FORMAT(1H ,T36,3H***,6X,2A8,T63,F11.3,5(1X,F8.2))
8003  T1 = XNVST(I)+T1
CDELETE
CDELETE
 5002 CONTINUE
       PILE(17)=PILE(17)*T1/T2
       T2=T1
      WRITE (6,6001) T1,SNCST
 6001 FORMAT(T36,3H***,17X,5HTOTAL,2X,F11.3,3X,21H  BALANCE OF PAYMENTS,
     1 2X,F11.3,//)
      WRITE(6,6010)
 6010 FORMAT(1H-,T27,15H***RESOURCES***,T89,23H***SYSTEM RESILIENCE***,
     1 //,T22,9HSTOCKPILE,2X,6H% USED,1X,7HRECYCLE,1X,6HSUBST.,2X,
     24HYEAR,3X,9HSTOCKPILE,T94,7HPRESENT,1X,9HTHRESHOLD,1X,
     310HRESILIENCE,2X,8HADJUSTED,/,T41,5HRATIO,2X,6HNUMBER,1X,
     4 7HCCMPLTD,1X,8HINCREASE,T94,5HVALUE,T124,9HTHRESHOLD)
      DO 7097 I= 1,18
      RPILE(I) = 0.0
      LST1(I) = 0.0
 7097 LP1(I) = 0.0
      IF(RESPRT(1).LT.3.0) GO TO 7090
      LPP = RESPRT(1)
      DO 7098 K = 2,LPP,4
      I =  RESPRT(K)
      IF  (RESPRT(K+1).EQ.1.0) GO TO  7091
      RPILE(I) = RESPRT(K+2)
      GO  TO 7098
 7091 LST1(I) = RESPRT(K+2)
      LP1(I) = RESPRT(K+3)
 7098 CONTINUE
 7090 CONTINUE
      DO 5015 I = 1,12
      IF (I.EQ.11.OR.I.EQ.12) LST1(I)=LST1(I+4)
      IF(I.EQ.11.OR.I.EQ.12) LP1(I) = LP1(I+4)
      IF(I.EQ.11.OR.I.EQ.12) RPILE(I) = RPILE(I+4)
      IF(I.EQ.11.OR.I.EQ.12) STCK1(I) =STCK1(I+4)
      IF(I.EQ.11.OR.I.EQ.12) REREC(I) = REREC(I+4)
       IF(I.EQ.11.OR.I.EQ.12) VAL(I) = VAL(I+4)
      DO 1 J =1,2
      IF (I.EQ.11.OR.I.EQ.12) HEADG(I,J) = HEADG(I+4,J)
    1 CONTINUE
      P = UPGRAD(I)
      IF(UPGRAD(I).EQ.0.0)  P=DEGRAD(I)
      M = LST1(I)
      K = LP1(I)
      F = RPILE(I)
      G = XMEAS(I)
      C = RESIL(I)
      Z = STCK1(I)
```

STEP8

```
      C = REREC(I)
      IF(VAL(I).EQ.0.0)  VAL(I) = 0.0
      A = VAL(I)
      H=TMEAS(I)
      IF(M.EQ.0.0)  GO TO 5013
      IF (F.EQ.0.0)  GO TO 5014
      WRITE(6,8411) (HEADG(I,J),J=1,2),A,Z,C,M,K,F,(XMETIT(I,J),J=1,2),
     1 G,H,O,P
 8411 FORMAT(1H ,2A8,T22,F9.2,2X,F6.2,1X,F7.3,1X,I3,5X,I4,1X,F9.2,1X,
     1 3H***,1X,2A8,2X,F7.3,1X,F9.3,1X,F10.3,2X,F8.3)
      GO TC 5015
 5013 IF(F.EQ.0.0)  GO TO 5C16
      WRITE(6,6211)  (HEADG(I,J),J=1,2),A,Z,C,F,(XMETIT(I,J),J=1,2),
     1 G,H,O,P
 6211 FORMAT(1H ,2A8,T22,F9.2,2X,F6.2,1X,F7.3,14X,F9.2,1X,3H***,1X
     1 2A8,2X,F7.3,1X,F9.3,1X,F10.3,2X,F8.3)
      GO TO 5015
 5016  WRITE(6,6311)  (HEADG(I,J),J=1,2),A,Z,C,(XMETIT(I,J),J=1,2),
     1 G,H,O,P
 6311 FORMAT(1H ,2A8,T22,F9.2,2X,F6.2,1X,F7.3,24X,3H***,1X,
     1 2A8,2X,F7.3,1X,F9.3,1X,F10.3,2X,F8.3)
      GO  TO 5015
 5014 WRITE(6,6411) (HEADG(I,J),J=1,2),A,Z,C,M,K,(XMETIT(I,J),J=1,2),
     1 G,H,O,P
 6411 FORMAT(1H ,2A8,T22,F9.2,2X,F6.2,1X,F7.3,1X,I3,5X,I4,11X,
     1 3H***,1X,2A8,2X,F7.3,1X,F9.3,1X,F10.3,2X,F8.3)
 5015 CONTINUE
      IF(UPGRAD(12).EQ.0.0) UPGRAD(12) = DEGRAD(12)
C6012 FORMAT(1H ,T71,3H***,1X,2A8,2X,F7.3,1X,F9.3,1X,F10.3,1X,F9.3)
      DO 5021 I = 17,18
      IF(VAL(I).EQ.0.0) VAL(I) = 0.0
      IF(I.EQ.17) GO TO 5021
      A = VAL(I)
      Z = STCK1(I)
      C = REREC(I)
      J = LST1(I)
      K = LP1(I)
      F = RPILE(I)
      IF(J.EQ.0.0)  GO TO 5113
      IF(F.EQ.0.0) GO TO 5114
 5113 IF(F.EQ.0.0) GC TC 5026
      WRITE (6,6221) (HEADG(I,J),J=1,2), A,Z,C,F
 6221 FORMAT(1H ,2A8,T22,F9.2,2X,F6.2,1X,F7.3,14X,F9.2,1X,3H***)
      GO TC 5021
 5026 WRITE(6,6321)  (HEADG(I,J),J=1,2), A,Z,C
 6321 FORMAT(1H ,2A8,T22,F9.2,2X,F6.2,1X,F7.3,24X,3H***)
      GO TO 5021
 5114 WRITE (6,6421) (HEADG(I,J),J=1,2), A,Z,C,J,K
 6421 FORMAT(1H ,2A8,T22,F9.2,2X,F6.2,1X,F7.3,1X,I3,5X,I4,11X,3H***)
 5021 CONTINUE
      IF (S8.EQ.0.0) GO TO 2095
      WRITE(6,9514)
 9514 FORMAT(1X,///)
      DO 4061 I=1,12
      IF (XFILE(1,I).EQ.0.0) GO TO 2096
      J=XFILE(1,I)
      KR5=XFILE(2,I)
      LTNCY=XFILE(3,I)+IYEAR
```

STEP3

```
0133          WRITE (6,2097) (TITLE(J,K),K=1,2),KR5,LTNCY
0134     2097 FORMAT(T6,A8,A8,T23,22H : NEW I/O FORMULA NO.,
             1 I4,T49,20H; COMPLETE IN YEAR  ,I4)
0135     4061 CONTINUE
0136     2096 CONTINUE
0137          WRITE (6,2013)
0138     2013 FORMAT(1H1,/////,T42,35H*****TOTAL SYSTEM EXPENDITURES*****,/,T49,
             1 21H(MILLIONS CF DCLLARS),//)
0139          XMANRS = 0.0
0140          ECODRS = 0.0
0141          XDFMNS = 0.0
0142          DO 2317 I=1,12
0143          XMANRS = XEXPR(I)*XNVST(I)*.01 + XMANRS
0144          IF (XMANRS.LE.0.00001)  XMANRS = 0.0
0145          ECODRS = XMAINR(I)*XNVST(I)*.01 + ECODRS
0146          IF (ECORDS.LE.0.00001)  ECORDS = 0.0
0147          XDFMNS = XMNORM(I)*XNVST(I)*.01+XDFMNS
0148     2317 CONTINUE
0149          RESPR(17)=XMANRS+ECODRS+XDFMNS
0150          RESPN = RESPR(17) + RESPN
0151          WRITE (6,2050)
0152     2050 FORMAT(T15,8HRESOURCE,T42,6HAMOUNT,T58,10HUNIT PRICE,
             1T76,4HCOST)
0153          WRITE(6,2017)
0154     2017 FORMAT(1H0,10H***LAND***,/)
0155          WRITE (6,2051) RESOR(15),RUCST(15),RESPR(15)
0156     2051 FORMAT(T15,10HURBAN LAND,T34,F14.3,T56,F12.8,T69,F14.3)
0157          WRITE(6,2052) RESOR(16),RUCST(16),RESPR(16)
0158     2052 FORMAT(T15,11HARABLE LAND,T34,F14.3,T56,F12.8,T69,F14.3)
0159          WRITE (6,2055)XLAND
0160     2055 FORMAT(T15,5HTOTAL,T77,F13.3,//)
0161          WRITE(6,2019)
0162     2019 FORMAT(1H0,19H***RAW MATERIALS***/)
0163          WRITE(6,2053)RESOR(1),RUCST(1),RESPR(1)
0164     2053 FORMAT(T15,12HFOOD & FIBER,T34,F14.3,T56,F12.8,T69,F14.3)
0165          WRITE(6,2040)RESOR(2),RUCST(2),RESPR(2)
0166     2040 FORMAT(T15,8HIRON ORE,T34,F14.3,T56,F12.8,T69,F14.3)
0167          WRITE (6,2041) RESOR(3),RUCST(3),RESPR(3)
0168     2041 FORMAT(T15,6HCOPPER,T34,F14.3,T56,F12.8,T69,F14.3)
0169          WRITE(6,2042)RESOR(4),RUCST(4),RESPR(4)
0170     2042 FORMAT(T15,14HOTHER NON-IRON,T34,F14.3,T56,F12.8,T69,F14.3)
0171          WRITE (6,2043) RESOR(5),RUCST(5),RESPR(5)
0172     2043 FORMAT(T15,4HCOAL,T34,F14.3,T56,F12.8,T69,F14.3)
0173          WRITE(6,2045)RESOR(6),RUCST(6),RESPR(6)
0174     2045 FORMAT(T15,13HPETRO-NAT GAS,T34,F14.3,T56,F12.8,T69,F14.3)
0175          WRITE(6,2046)RESOR(7),RUCST(7),RESPR(7)
0176     2046 FORMAT(T15,14HSTONE AND CLAY,T34,F14.3,T56,F12.8,T69,F14.3)
0177          WRITE (6,2047) RESOR(8),RUCST(8),RESPR(8)
0178     2047 FORMAT(T15,9HCHEMICALS,T34,F14.3,T56,F12.8,T69,F14.3)
0179          WRITE(6,2048)RESOR(9),RUCST(9),RESPR(9)
0180     2048 FORMAT(T15,9HLEAD,ZINC,T34,F14.3,T56,F12.8,T69,F14.3)
0181          WRITE (6,2049) RESOR(10),RUCST(10),RESPR(10)
0182     2049 FORMAT(T15,8HALUMINUM,T34,F14.3,T56,F12.8,T69,F14.3)
0183          WRITE (6,2054)RAMAT
0184     2054 FORMAT(T15,5HTOTAL,T77,F13.3,//)
0185          WRITE (6,2021)
0186     2021 FORMAT(1H0,11H***LABOR***,/)
0187          WRITE(6,2022) RESOR(18),RUCST(18),RESPR(18)
```

STEP8

```
 2022 FORMAT(T15,13HWORKERS COSTS,T40,F14.3,T58,F12.8,T76,F14.3)
      WRITE(6,2023)
 2023 FORMAT(1H0,13H***CAPITAL***,/)
      WRITE (6,2024)  XMANRS
 2024 FORMAT(T15,17HNEW CAPITAL GOODS,T76,F14.3)
      WRITE(6,2027)  ECODRS
 2027 FORMAT(T15,25HENVIRONMENTAL MAINTENANCE,T76,F14.3)
      WRITE(6,2028)  XDFMNS
 2028 FORMAT(T15,20HCAPITAL  MAINTENANCE,T76,F14.3)
      WRITE(6,2319)  RESPR(17)
 2319 FORMAT(T15,5HTOTAL,T76,F14.3)
      WRITE (6,2026) RESPN
 2026 FORMAT(1H0,11HTOTAL COSTS,T77,F13.3)
C**   DEVELCP SCALAR QOL VALUE FOR POP MODIFIER
      IF (NCYCLE.GT.1) GO TC 5
      DO 2 N=1,12
    2 TMEASO(N)=TMEAS(N)
    5 CONTINUE
      SUM = 0.0
      DO 10 N=1,12
C**   VN IS WGT OF XMEAS(N) IN VALLQL
      IF (N.EQ.13) GC TO 15
      IF(TMEASO(N).EQ.0.) PSUM=0.
      IF(TMEASO(N).EQ.0.) GC TO 10
      PSUM=VN(N)+(XMEAS(N)/TMEASO(N))
   10 SUM  = PSUM  + SUM
   15 VALLQL  =  SUM
      IF (NCYCLE.GT.1) GO TC 20
      SCAMSO=VALLQL
   20 SUMMAT(NCYCLE,5)=VALLQL/SCAMSO
C**   MAXIMUM WORK UNITS IS PAID WCRKER POP
      XMWU  =   POP(5)
C**
C**   SET FACTORS
      XKK=1.0
      XKK2=XKK/2.0
      XKK4=XKK/4.0
      XKK5 = XKK*2.0
      XKK8=XKK/8.0
C**
C**   BIRTHRATE MODIFIER
      IF(VALLQL.GE.XKK2) FBR= 1.0
      IF (VALLQL.LT.XKK4) FBR=0.0
      IF (VALLQL.GE.XKK4.AND.VALLQL.LT.XKK2) GO TO 30
      GO TO 40
   35 IF (VALLQL.GE.5.0) FBR=0.5
      IF (VALLQL.GE.5.0) GO TO 40
      FBR= 1.0 -.50*((VALLQL-2.)/3.)**2
      GO TO 40
   30 FBR= 1.0 - ((XKK2-VALLQL)/(XKK2-XKK4))**2
C**
C**   DEATHRATE MODIFIER
   40 IF (VALLQL.GE.XKK2) FDT=1.0
      IF (VALLQL.LT.XKK8) FDT=(1.0 + XKK4)
      IF (XKK2.GT.VALLQL.AND.VALLQL.GE.XKK8) GO TO 50
      GO TO 60
   50 FDT = 1.0 + (XKK4*(((XKK2-VALLQL)/(XKK2-XKK8))**2))
C**
```

STEP8

```
C**    NET IMMIGRATION MODIFIERS
   60  IF (VALLQL.GT.(3*XKK4)) FMG=1.0
       IF (VALLQL.LT.XKK2) FMG=0.0
       IF ((3*XKK4).GT.VALLQL.AND.VALLQL.GE.XKK2) GO TO 70
       GO TO 85
   70  FMG = 1.0 - (((3*XKK4-VALLQL)/XKK4)**2)
       MGRT = (20.*ESTCK(18)-18.)
       IF(ESTCK(18).LT.0.85) MGRT=-1.1
   80  FMG=FMG*(1+MGRT)
C**
   85  CONTINUE
C**    ADJUSTMENT OF WORK FORCE IF UNEMPLOYMENT IS LESS THAN 5%
       IF (ESTCK(18).LE.0.95) GO TO 76
       COMP=(ESTCK(18)-0.95)/0.95
       IF(ESTCK(18).GE.1.0)  COMP = COMP*(ESTCK(18)-1.0)/.020
       DO 72 J=1,12
       TEMP=CJK2(5,J)*COMP
       IF ((CJK2(6,J)-TEMP).LE.0.0) TEMP=0.0
       CJK2(5,J)=CJK2(5,J)+TEMP
   72  CJK2(6,J)=CJK2(6,J)-TEMP
       DO 74 J=1,12
       TEMP=CJK3(5,J)*COMP
       IF((CJK3(6,J)-TEMP).LE.0.0) TEMP=0.0
       CJK3(5,J)=CJK3(5,J)+TEMP
   74  CJK3(6,J)=CJK3(6,J)-TEMP
   76  CONTINUE
       COMP=(0.95-ESTCK(18))/0.95
       DO 78 J=1,12
       TEMP=CJK2(6,J)*COMP
       IF ((CJK2(5,J)-TEMP).LE.0.0) TEMP=0.0
       CJK2(6,J)=CJK2(6,J)+TEMP
   78  CJK2(5,J)=CJK2(5,J)-TEMP
       DO 79 J=1,12
       TEMP=CJK3(6,J)*COMP
       IF((CJK3(5,J)-TEMP).LE.0.0) TEMP=0.0
       CJK3(6,J)=CJK3(6,J)+TEMP
   79  CJK3(5,J)=CJK3(5,J)-TEMP
   77  CONTINUE
C**
C**    RESOURCE RESET
C**    INITIALIZE I/O PROCESS MATRIX
       DO 330 NR=1,20
       DO 330 J=1,19
  330  XUTIL1(J,NR) = XUTIL(J,NR)
C**
C**    EXPAND RESOURCE STOCK PILES
       NP=SUBPIL(1)
       DO 340 I=2,NP,3
       IF ((NCYCLE+1).NE.SUBPIL(I+1)) GO TO 340
       NR=SUBPIL(I)
       COMP=ESTCK(NR)
C**    NEW LEVEL OF USE (ESTCK) AND PILE
       ESTCK(NR) = (ESTCK(NR)*PILE(NR))/(PILE(NR)+SUBPIL(I+3))
       PILE(NR)=PILE(NR)+SUBPIL(I+2)
C**    ADJUST COSTS IF THEY WERE IN ESCALATION RANGE (PILE .GE. 0.9)
       IF (COMP.GT.0.9.AND.COMP.GT.ESTCK(NR)) GO TO 335
       GO TO 340
  335  COMP=0.9
```

STEP8

```
      IF (COMP.LT.ESTCK(NR)) COMP=ESTCK(NR)
      XMESTR(NR)=0.00001*(XK1(NR)+(XK2(NR)*COMP**XK3(NR)))
      XMCST1(NR)=XMESTR(NR)
      RUCST1(NR)=XMCST1(NR)/(1+REREC(NR))
      RUCST2(NR)=RUCST1(NR)
  340 CONTINUE
C**
C**   PHASE IN RESOURCE SUBSTITUTIONS
      NP=SUBMAT(1)
      DO 341 I=2,NP,4
      IF ((NCYCLE+1).NE.SUBMAT(I)) GO TO 341
      COMP=SUBMAT(I+3)
      IDX=SUBMAT(I+2)
      NR= SUBMAT(I+1)
C**   FOR (NR,IDX) COMBINATIONS, UPDATE EACH I/O PROCESS
      DO 342 J=1,19
      IF (XUTIL1(J,NR).EQ.0.0) GO TO 342
C**   LOWER RESOURCE BEING SUBSTITUTED FOR
      TEMP=XUTIL1(J,NR)
      XUTIL1(J,NR)=XUTIL1(J,NR)*(1-COMP)
C**   LOOP TO INCREASE SUBSTITUTION RESOURCES
      DO 343 NX=1,5
      NPP=2*NX+1
      NPPP=SUBDAT(IDX,NPP)
      IF(SUBDAT(IDX,NPP+1).EQ.0.0) GO TO 343
      XUTIL1(J,NPPP)=XUTIL1(J,NPPP)+(TEMP*COMP*SUBDAT(IDX,NPP+1))
  343 CONTINUE
C**
C**   IF SUB COMPLETE (COMP=1) ENTER INTO PERMANENT I.O PROCESS MATRIX
      IF (COMP.NE.1.0) GO TO 342
      DO 344 NRR=1,20
  344 XUTIL(J,NRR)=XUTIL1(J,NRR)
  342 CONTINUE
  341 CONTINUE
C**
C**   LOWER STOCK PILE COUNTER FOR FUTURE EXPANSIONS
      DO 349 NR=1,20
  349 IF(WORK(NR).GT.0.0) WORK(NR)=WORK(NR)-1.0
C**
C**   IN/OUT RESET
      I=0
C**   CONSTRUCT ACTIVE I/O PROCESS MATRIX
      DO 360 J=1,19
      NP = XMARK(J)
      IF (NP.LT.6) MULPRO=1.0
      IF (NP.GE.6) MULPRO=2.0
      IF (ESTCK(18).LT.95) MULPRO=0.5*MULPRO
      IF (ESTCK(18).LT.90) MULPRO=.0555*ESTCK(18)*MULPRO
      XUTIL(J,18)=XUTIL(J,18)/(1.+.01*MULPRO)
      XUTIL1(J,18)=XUTIL1(J,18)/(1.+.01*MULPRO)
      XUTIL(J,16)=XUTIL(J,16)/1.01
      XUTIL1(J,16)=XUTIL1(J,16)/1.01
      IF (XMBRK(J).EQ.0.0) GO TO 360
      IF (XMBRK(J).EQ.-1.0) GO TO 360
      I=I+1
      DO 361 NR=1,20
  361 UTIL(I,NR) = XUTIL1(J,NR)
  360 CONTINUE
```

STEP8

```
C**
C**   MAKE TIME PHASED I/O PROCESS ADJUSTMENTS
      ICTR=SUBIOP(1)
      DO 362 I=2,ICTR,4
      IF ((NCYCLE+1).NE.SUBIOP(I+3)) GO TO 362
      J=SUBIOP(I)
      KR5=SUBIOP(I+1)
      COMP=SUBIOP(I+2)
C**   ACTUAL COMPUTATION LOOP
      DO 363 NR=1,20
  363 UTIL(J,NR)=UTIL(J,NR)*(1-COMP)+XUTIL1(KR5,NR)*COMP
C**
C**   IF TIME PHASE COMPLETE, RESET ACTIVE I/O MARKER FILE
      IF(COMP.NE.1.0) GO TO 362
      XMBRK(J)=0.0
      XMBRK(KR5)=1.0
  362 CONTINUE
C**   ALL TIME STEPS FOR MATRICES DONE
C**
C**   RESET STOCK LEVELS, POP FOR NEXT CYCLE
      DO 370 NR=1,18
      IF (NR.EQ.1.OR.NR.EQ.15.OR.NR.EQ.16.OR.NR.EQ.17) GO TO 371
      IF (NR.EQ.18.OR.NR.EQ.12.OR.NR.EQ.13.OR.NR.EQ.14) GO TO 370
      STDEP(NR)=ESTCK(NR)
      GO TO 370
  371 STDEP(NR)=0.0
  370 FLAGR(NR)=0.0
      TOPTM1=TOPT
      WRITE(6,3999)
 3999 FORMAT(//)
      DO 4090 I=1,97,4
      J=B(I)-1
      IF (J.NE.NCYCLE) GO TO 4090
      J=B(I+2)
      IF (B(I+1).GT.1.1) GO TO 4020
      IF (J.EQ.0) GO TO 4012
      IF (J.GT.12) GO TO 4100
      XNVST1(J)=XNVST1(J)*B(I+3)
      GO TO 4010
 4012 DO 4014 N=1,12
 4014 XNVST1(N)=XNVST1(N)*B(I+3)
      GO TO 4010
 4020 IF (B(I+1).GT.2.1) GO TO 4030
      IF (J.EQ.0) GO TO 4022
      IF (J.GT.12) GO TO 4100
      RGJ(J)=RGJ(J)*B(I+3)
      GO TO 4010
 4022 DO 4024 N=1,12
 4024 RGJ(N)=RGJ(N)*B(I+3)
      GO TO 4010
 4030 IF (B(I+1).GT.3.1) GO TO 4040
      IF (J.EQ.0) GO TO 4032
      IF (J.GT.12) GO TO 4100
      QOLT(J)=QOLT(J)*B(I+3)
      GO TO 4010
 4032 DO 4034 N=1,12
 4034 QOLT(N)=QOLT(N)*B(I+3)
      GO TO 4010
```

STEP8

```
4040 IF (B(I+1).GT.4.1) GO TO 4050
     IF (J.GT.18) GO TO 4100
     PILE(J)=PILE(J)*B(I+3)
     STDEP(J)=STDEP(J)/B(I+3)
     GO TO 4010
4050 IF (B(I+1).GT.5.1) GO TO 4060
     IF (J.EQ.0) GO TO 4052
     IF (J.GT.12) GO TO 4100
     TMEAS(J)=TMEAS(J)*B(I+3)
     GO TO 4010
4052 DO 4054 N=1,12
4054 TMEAS(N)=TMEAS(N)*B(I+3)
     GO TO 4010
406C IF (B(I+1).GT.6.1) GO TO 4070
     IF (J.GT.18) GO TO 4100
     XK1(J)=XK1(J)*B(I+3)
     GO TO 4010
4070 IF (B(I+1).GT.7.1) GO TO 4080
     IF (J.GT.18) GO TO 41C0
     XK2(J)=XK1(J)+(XK2(J)-XK1(J))*B(I+3)
     GO TO 4010
408C IF(B(I+1).GT.8.6) GO TO 4100
     IF(B(I).EQ.B(I+2)) GO TO 4010
     IF(B(I+1).GT.8.2) GO TO 4082
     BR=((B(I+2)-1.-B(I))*BR+B(I+3))/(B(I+2)-B(I))
     IF(B(I).LT.B(I+2)) B(I)=B(I)+1.
     GO TO 4010
4082 IF(B(I+1).GT.8.4) GO TO 4083
     DT=((B(I+2)-1.-B(I))*DT+B(I+3))/(B(I+2)-B(I))
     IF(B(I).LT.B(I+2)) B(I)=B(I)+1.
9826 FORMAT(1X,'RRRRR',3(F5.3,1X))
     GO TO 4010
4083 CONTINUE
     XMG=((B(I+2)-1.-B(I))*XMG+B(I+3))/(B(I+2)-B(I))
     IF(B(I).LT.B(I+2)) B(I)=B(I)+1.
     GO TO 4010
4100 VALU=(I+3)/4
     WRITE (6,4101) VALU
4101 FORMAT(5X,21HEXOG ADJUSTMENT ERROR,2X,I2)
4010 CONTINUE
     WRITE(6,9826) BR,DT,XMG
C**
4090 CONTINUE
C**  STORE OUTPUT SUMMARY DATA
C**  HERE IS THE PLACE FOR OUTPUT OPTIONS
     I=NCYCLE
     OUTMAT(I,1)=I
     OUTMAT(I,2)=TOPT/208000.0
     DO 390 J=1,4
 390 OUTMAT(I,2+J)=AGRIT(J)/203210.0
     DO 391 J=1,12
 391 OUTMAT(I,6+J)=XJOT(J)/1000.0
     DO 392 NR=1,10
 392 OUTMAT(I,18+NR) = RESOR(NR)/REDIV(NR)
     OUTMAT(I,30) = RESOR(15)/REDIV(15)
     OUTMAT(I,31) = RESOR(16)/REDIV(16)
     OUTMAT(I,32)=(RESOR(19)-1000.0)/(REDIV(19)-1000.0)
     OUTMAT(I,33)=(RESOR(20)-1000.0)/(REDIV(20)-1000.0)
```

STEP8

```
CUTMAT(I,36) =1.0 - ESTCK(18)
CUTMAT(I,37)=VALLQL/SCAMSO
RETURN
END
```

PLOT

```
      SUBROUTINE PLOT(NO,A,M,N,ANG)
C**   THIS IS THE PLOT PROGRAM
C**   PURPOSE
C**   PLOT SEVERAL CROSS-VARIABLES VERSUS A BASE VARIABLE
C**   DESCRIPTION OF PARAMETERS
C**   NO - CHART NUMBER (3 DIGITS MAXIMUM)
C**   A - MATRIX OF DATA TO BE PLOTTED. FIRST COLUMN REPRESENTS
C**   BASE VARIABLE AND SUCCESSIVE COLUMNS ARE THE CROSS-
C**   VARIABLES (MAXIMUM IS 9).
C**   N - NUMBER OF ROWS IN MATRIX A
C**   M - NUMBER OF COLUMNS IN MATRIX A -EQUAL TO THE TOTAL
C**   NUMBER OF VARIABLES). MAXIMUM IS 10.
C     INTEGER*2 OUT(101,52)
      DIMENSION NO(7),XPR(11),ANG(9),A(1000),OUT(101,52)
      DATA BLANK/4H    /
C
    1 FORMAT(1H1,20H                    ,30X,7A4,//)
    2 FORMAT(1H ,4X,F7.3,5X,101A1)
    7 FORMAT(1H ,16X,101H'         '         '         '         '
     1 YEARS    '         '         '         '         ')
    8 FORMAT(1H0,9X,11F10.1)
    9 FORMAT(1H,16X,101A1)
C        PRINT TITLE
C
   20 WRITE(6,1)NO
C
C     SET HORIZONTAL SPACING
      NP=1
      IF(N.LT.51) NP=2
      IF(N.LT.34) NP=3
      IF(N.LT.26) NP=4
C
C     CLEAR MATRIX
      DO 10 J = 1,101
      DO 10 I = 1,52
   10 OUT(J,I) = BLANK
C
C     SET STORAGE COUNTERS
      VMAX=0.0
      MY=M*N
      MZ = N + 1
      DO 34 J=MZ,MY
      IF (A(J).LT.0.0) A(J)=0.0
   34 IF (VMAX.LT.A(J)) VMAX=A(J)
      IF (VMAX.LT.1.0) VMAX=1.0
      VINTER=VMAX/50.
      I=1
      II=1
      M=M-1
   22 DO 30 J=1,M
      JR=1
      L=I+J*N
      JP=(A(L)/VINTER)+1.0
      IF (JP.GT.51) JR=52
      IF (JR.EQ.52) GO TO 30
      JR=52-JP
   30 OUT(II,JR)=ANG(J)
      I = I + 1
```

PLOT

```
      II = II + NP
      IF (I.LE.N) GO TO 22
C
C     SET COUNTERS FOR ORDINATE PRINT
      L = 0
      YPR= VMAX + 5.0*VINTER
      WRITE(6,7)
      DO 40 J = 1,51
      IF (L) 50,50,60
   50 YPR= YPR -5.0* VINTER
      IF (YPR.LE.0.0) YPR=0.000
      L =5
      WRITE(6,2) YPR,(OUT(I,J),I = 1,101)
      GO TO 40
   60 WRITE(6,9)(OUT(I,J),I = 1,101)
   40 L = L - 1
C
C     PRINT ABSCISSA
      XPR(1) = 1.0
      DO 70 I = 1,10
   70 XPR(I+1) = XPR(I) + (10.0/NP)
      WRITE (6,7)
      WRITE (6,8)  (XPR(I),I =1,11)
      WRITE (6,9)  (OUT(I,52),I = 1,101)
      RETURN
      END
```

OTPUT

```
0001          SUBROUTINE OTPUT
         C**
         C**   SETS UP THE OUTPUT
0002          REAL*4 XMBRK,XMG
0003          INTEGER*4 ADD6,ADD7,ADD8,IIII
0004          COMMCN/PRINT/XPRNT1,XPRNT2,PRINTX,DETAIL,PPLOT
0005          COMMCN/INTER8/CPILE(20),CAPVL(12),OUTMAT(50,40),XMBRK(19),
             1 SUMMAT(50,10),PUBDIV,PUBNUM,PRIDIV,PRINUM,SCAMSO
0006          COMMCN/YEAR/NCYCLE,RESPR(20),DEGRAD(12),UPGRAD(12),IYEAR
0007          COMMCN/EXOG/B(100)
0008          COMMCN/DURBLE/XMDUR(110,12),ECODUR(12),EXPDUR(12),XMNDUR(12)
0009          DIMENSION LINE1(8)
0010          DIMENSION NO(7),N1(7),N2(7),N3(7),N4(7),N5(7),N6(7),N7(7)
0011          DIMENSION A(1000),PLTMAT(10,100)
0012          DIMENSION ANG1(9),ANG2(9),ANG3(9),ANG4(9),ANG5(9),ANG6(9),ANG7(9)
0013          DIMENSION ANG0(9),ANG8(9)
0014          DIMENSION NN1(8),NN2(8),NN3(8),NN4(8),NN5(8),NN6(8),NN7(8),
             1 NN8(8),NN9(8),NN10(8),NN11(8),NN12(8),NN13(8),NN14(8),NN15(8),
             2 NN16(8),NN17(8),NN18(8),NN19(8),NN20(8),NN21(8),NN22(8),
             3 NN23(8),NN24(8),NN25(8),NN26(8),NN27(8),NN28(8)
0015          DIMENSION LIST(224)
0016          DIMENSION ADD6(9),ADD7(9),ADD8(9)
0017          EQUIVALENCE(LIST(1),NN1(1)),(LIST(9),NN2(1)),(LIST(17),NN3(1)),
             1 (LIST(25),NN4(1)),(LIST(33),NN5(1)),(LIST(41),NN6(1)),(LIST(49),
             2 NN7(1)),(LIST(57),NN8(1)),(LIST(65),NN9(1)),(LIST(73),NN10(1)),
             3 (LIST(81),NN11(1)),(LIST(89),NN12(1)),(LIST(97),NN13(1)),
             4 (LIST(105),NN14(1)),(LIST(113),NN15(1)),(LIST(121),NN16(1)),
             5 (LIST(129),NN17(1)),(LIST(137),NN18(1)),(LIST(145),NN19(1)),
             6 (LIST(153),NN20(1)),(LIST(161),NN21(1)),(LIST(169),NN22(1)),
             7 (LIST(177),NN23(1)),(LIST(185),NN24(1)),(LIST(193),NN25(1)),
             8  (LIST(201),NN26(1)),(LIST(209),NN27(1)),(LIST(217),NN28(1))
0018          DATA NO/4HSTAT,4HE OF,4H THE,4H SYS,4HTEM ,4H    ,4H    /
0019          DATA N1/4HPOPU,4HLATI,4HON  ,4H    ,4H    ,4H    ,4H    /
0020          DATA N2/4HPUBL,4HIC S,4HECTO,4HR   ,4H    ,4H    ,4H    /
0021          DATA N3/4HPRIV,4HATE ,4HSECT,4HOR  ,4H    ,4H    ,4H    /
0022          DATA N4/4HNATU,4HRAL ,4HRESO,4HURCE,4HS   ,4H    ,4H    /
0023          DATA N5/4HNATU,4HRAL ,4HRESO,4HURCE,4HS CO,4HNT. ,4H    /
0024          DATA N6/4HEMPL,4HOYME,4HNT, ,4HQOL ,4H    ,4H    ,4H    /
0025          DATA N7/4HLAND,4H AIR,4H AND,4H WAT,4HER  ,4H    ,4H    /
0026          DATA ANG0/4HP   ,4HG   ,4HI   ,4HQ   ,4HN   ,4HE   ,4HF   ,
             1 4HW   ,4HM   /
0027          DATA ANG1/4HP   ,4H1   ,4H2   ,4H3   ,4H4   ,4H    ,4H    ,
             1 4H    ,4H    /
0028          DATA ANG2/4HE   ,4HT   ,4HH   ,4HS   ,4HA   ,4H    ,4H    ,
             1 4H    ,4H    /
0029          DATA ANG3/4HA   ,4HN   ,4HD   ,4HC   ,4HW   ,4HS   ,4HM   ,
             1 4H    ,4H    /
0030          DATA ANG4/4HF   ,4HI   ,4HK   ,4HO   ,4H    ,4H    ,4H    ,
             1 4H    ,4H    /
0031          DATA ANG5/4HK   ,4HT   ,4HS   ,4HC   ,4HL   ,4HA   ,4H    ,
             1 4H    ,4H    /
0032          DATA ANG6/4HU   ,4HQ   ,4H    ,4H    ,4H    ,4H    ,4H    ,
             1 4H    ,4H    /
0033          DATA ANG7/4HU   ,4HF   ,4HA   ,4HW   ,4H    ,4H    ,4H    ,
             1 4H    ,4H    /
0034          DATA NN1/4HEDUC,4HATIO,4HN   ,5*1H /
0035          DATA NN2/4HTRAN,4HSPOR,4HTATI,4HON  ,4*1H /
0036          DATA NN3/4HHEAL,4HTH &,4H WEL,4HFARE,4*1H /
```

```
0037          DATA NN4/4HPUBL,4HIC S,4HAFET,4HY    ,4*1H /
0038          DATA NN5/4HADMI,4HNIST,4HRATI,4HON &,4H OTH,4HER   ,2*1H /
0039          DATA NN6/4HAGRI,4HCULT,4HURE ,5*1H /
0040          DATA NN7/4HNON-,4HDURA,4HBLE ,4HGOOD,4HS    ,3*1H /
0041          DATA NN8/4HDURA,4HSLE ,4HGOOD,4HS    ,4*1H /
0042          DATA NN9/4HCOMM,4HUN. ,4H& TR,4HANS.,4*1H /
0043          DATA NN10/4HWHOL,4HESAL,4HE & ,4HRETA,4HIL   ,3*1H /
0044          DATA NN11/4HSERV,4HICES,6*1H /
0045          DATA NN12/4HMINI,4HNG   ,6*1H /
0046          DATA NN13/4HFOOD,4H & F,4HIBRE,5*1H /
0047          DATA NN14/4HIRON,7*1H /
0048          DATA NN15/4HCOPP,4HER   ,6*1H /
0049          DATA NN16/4HNON-,4HFERR,4HOUS ,4HMETA,4HLS   ,3*1 H /
0050          DATA NN17/4HCOAL,7*1H /
0051          DATA NN18/4HOIL  ,7*1H /
0052          DATA NN19/4HSTON,4HE & ,4HCLAY,5*1H /
0053          DATA NN20/4HCHEM,4HICAL,4HS & ,4HFERT,4HILIZ,4HERS ,2*1H /
0054          DATA NN21/4HLEAD,4H & Z,4HINC ,5*1H /
0055          DATA NN22/4HALUM,4HINUM,6*1H /
0056          DATA NN23/4HUNEM,4HPLOY,4HMENT,5*1H /
0057          DATA NN24/4HQUAL,4HITY ,6*1H /
0058          DATA NN25/4HURBA,4HN    ,4HLAND,5*1H /
0059          DATA NN26/4HARAB,4HLE L,4HAND ,5*1H /
0060          DATA NN27/4HTREA,4HTED ,4HUNIT,4HS OF,4H AIR,3*1H /
0061          DATA NN28/4HTREA,4HTED ,4HUNIT,4HS OF,4H WAT,4HER   ,2*1H /
0062          DATA ADD6/4HPOPU,4HPUBL,4HPRIV,4HQOL ,4HNATU,4HENER,4HFARM,
             1 4HEMPL,4HECO-/
0063          DATA ADD7/4HLATI,4HIC F,4HATE ,4H    ,4HRAL ,4HGY O,4HLAND,
             1 4HOYME,4HMEDI/
0064          DATA ADD8/4HON   ,4HUNDS,4HFUND,4H    ,4HORES,4HRES ,4H    ,
             1 4HNT  ,4HA    /
        C**   IF DETAIL = 0.0, THEN DETAILED GRAPHS WILL NOT PRINT
        C**   SET THE NUMBER OF COPIES OF TOTAL  SUMMARY OUTPUT.
0065          IIII=PRINTX
0066          DO 950 KOPYNO = 1,IIII
0067          DO 10 I=1,1000
0068       10 A(I)=0.0
        C**
0069          WRITE (6,92)
0070       92 FORMAT(1H1,///,2X,45HCAPITAL CREDITS TO SECTOR FOR PLANT EXPANSION
             1 32H, ENVIRONMENTAL TREATMENT COSTS,//,1X,4HYEAR,45X,9H<SECTORS>)
0071          DO 90 I=1,NCYCLE
0072          J = I+1970
0073       90 WRITE(6,91) J,(XMDUR(I,J),J=1,12)
0074       91 FORMAT(1X,I4,12(F10.3))
        C**
        C**   PRINT SUMMARY DATA
0075          WRITE(6,1001)
0076     1001 FORMAT(1H1,46X,35HSUMMARY TABLE - STATE OF THE SYSTEM,/,
             1 51X,26H(SCALED TO ORIGINAL VALUE),//,29X,6HPUBLIC,5X,7HPRIVATE,
             2 5X,7HQUALITY,3X,7HNATURAL,7X,5HENERGY,5X,8HFARM AND,3X,
             3 8HEMPLOYED,4X,7HTREATED,/,9X,4HYEAR,3X,10HPOPULATION,6X,5HFUNDS,
             4 6X,5HFUNDS,7X,5HLEVEL,3X,9HORE USAGE,9X,5HUSAGE,2X,10HLAND USAGE,
             5 3X,7HWORKERS,3X,9HECO-MEDIA,/,19X,4H(NP),8X,3H(G),8X,3H(I),
             6 9X,3H(Q),9X,3H(N),9X,3H(E),9X,3H(F),9X,3H(W),9X,3H(M),/)
0077          DO 1500 I=1,NCYCLE
0078     1500 WRITE(6,1003) (SUMMAT(I,J),J=1,10)
0079     1003 FORMAT(8X,F4.0,4X,F7.4,5X,F7.4,4X,F7.4,6(5X,F7.4))
```

```
      KK=1
      DO 1510 J=1,11
      DO 1510 I=1,NCYCLE
      A(KK)=SUMMAT(I,J)
 1510 KK=KK+1
      M1=10
      NS1=1
      CALL PLOT(NO,A,M1,NCYCLE,ANGO)
      IF (DETAIL.EQ.0.0) GO TO 203
      M1=2
      J=2
  204 DO 201 I = 1,NCYCLE
      KK = NCYCLE + I
  201 A(KK) = SUMMAT(I,J)
C
      JJ=J-1
      ANG8(1)=ANGO(JJ)
      LINE1(4) = ADD8(4)
      LINE1(5) = ADD8(4)
      LINE1(6) = ADD9(4)
      LINE1(7) = ADD8(4)
      LINE1(8) = ADD8(4)
      LINE1(1)=ADD6(JJ)
      LINE1(2)=ADD7(JJ)
      LINE1(3)=ADD8(JJ)
      CALL PLOT2(LINE1,A,M1,NCYCLE,ANG8)
      IF(J.GT.9) GO TO 203
      J = J + 1
      GO TO 204
  203 CONTINUE
C**
      DO  20 I=1,NCYCLE
      DO 20 J=1,6
 20   PLTMAT(J,I)=OUTMAT(I,J)
      WRITE(6,26)
 26   FORMAT(1H1,T37,29HTABLE NUMBER ONE - POPULATION,/,
     1 T39,26H(SCALED TO ORIGINAL VALUE),//,T23,5HTOTAL,T40,5HUNDER,
     2 T57,5H18-24,T73,5H25-64,T88,4HOVER,/,T10,4HYEAR,
     3 T20,10HPOPULATION,T38,8H18 YEARS,T57,5HYEARS,T73,5HYEARS,
     4 T86,8H64 YEARS,/,T25,4H(NP),T41,3H(1),T57,3H(2),T73,3H(3),
     5 T89,3H(4),/)
      DO 25 I=1,NCYCLE
 25   WRITE(6,27) (PLTMAT(J,I),J=1,6)
 27   FORMAT(8X,F4.0,5(9X,F8.4))
      IF (FPLOT.EQ.0.0) GO TO 2000
      KK=1
      DO 28 J=1,6
      DO 28 I=1,NCYCLE
      A(KK)  = OUTMAT(I,J)
      KK=KK+1
   28 CONTINUE
      M1=6
      NS1=1
      CALL PLOT (N1,A,M1,NCYCLE,ANG1)
C**
 2000 DO 30 I=1,NCYCLE
      DO 30 J=7,11
      K=J-5
```

OTPUT

```
   30  PLTMAT(K,I)=OUTMAT(I,J)
       WRITE(6,35)
   35  FORMAT(1H1,T31,45HTABLE NUMBER TWO - PUBLIC SECTOR OUTPUT UNITS,/,
      1 T39,26H(SCALED TO ORIGINAL VALUE),//,
      2 T10,4HYEAR,T23,9HEDUCATION,T36,14HTRANSPORTATION,T56,6HHEALTH,
      3 T69,13HPUBLIC SAFETY,T86,14HADMINISTRATION,/,T26,3H(E),T42,3H(T),
      4 T58,3H(H),T73,3H(S),T90,3H2A),/)
       DO 36 I=1,NCYCLE
   36  WRITE(6,37) (PLTMAT(K,I),K=1,6)
   37  FORMAT(8X,F4.0,5(9X,F8.4))
       IF (PPLOT.EQ.0.0) GO TO 4001
C**
       KK=1+NCYCLE
       M1=6
       DO 38 J=7,11
       DO 38 I=1,NCYCLE
       A(KK)  = OUTMAT(I,J)
       KK=KK+1
   38 CONTINUE
      CALL PLOT (N2,A,M1,NCYCLE,ANG2)
      IF (DETAIL.EQ.0.0) GO TO 5101
C**
 4001 M1 = 2
      JJ = 1
      J=7
      III = 1
 5099 DO 5100 I = 1,NCYCLE
      KK = NCYCLE + I
 5100 A(KK) = OUTMAT(I,J)
      ANG8(1) = ANG2(JJ)
      CALL PLOT2(LIST(III),A,M1,NCYCLE,ANG8(1))
      III = III + 8
      IF(J.GT.10) GO TO 5101
      J = J + 1
      JJ = JJ + 1
      GO TO 5099
 5101 CONTINUE
 4000 DO 40 I=1,NCYCLE
      DO 40 J=12,18
      K=J-10
   40  PLTMAT(K,I)=OUTMAT(I,J)
       WRITE(6,45)
   45  FORMAT(1H1,T29,48HTABLE NUMBER THREE - PRIVATE SECTOR OUTPUT UNITS,
      1 /,T38,26H(SCALED TO ORIGINAL VALUE),//,T38,11HNON-DURABLE,T57,
      2 7HDURABLE,T90,12HWHOLE & RET.,/,T10,4HYEAR,T21,11HAGRICULTURE,
      3 T38,11HMANUFACTURE,T57,11HMANUFACTURE,T74,10HCOMMERCIAL,T93,
      4 5HTRADE,T109,8HSERVICES,T123,8H  MINING,/,T25,3H(A),T42,3H(N),
      5 T60,3H(D),T77,3H(C),T94,3H(W),T112,3H(S),T128,3H(M),/)
       DO 46 I=1,NCYCLE
   46  WRITE(6,47) (PLTMAT(K,I),K=1,8)
   47  FORMAT(8X,F4.0,7(9X,F8.4))
       IF (PPLOT.EQ.0.0) GO TO 5001
C**
       KK=1+NCYCLE
       M1=8
       DO 48 J=12,18
       DO 48 I=1,NCYCLE
       A(KK)  = OUTMAT(I,J)
```

```
      KK=KK+1
   48 CONTINUE
      CALL PLOT (N3,A,M1,NCYCLE,ANG3)
      IF (DETAIL.EQ.0.0) GO TO 5201
C**
 5001 M1 = 2
      JJ = 1
      J = 12
      III = 41
 5199 DO 5200 I = 1,NCYCLE
      KK = NCYCLE + I
 5200 A(KK) = OUTMAT(I,J)
      ANG8(1) = ANG3(JJ)
      CALL PLOT2(LIST(III),A,M1,NCYCLE,ANG8(1))
      III = III + 8
      IF(J.GT.17) GO TO 5201
      J = J + 1
      JJ = JJ+1
      GO TO 5199
 5201 CONTINUE
 5000 DO 50 I=1,NCYCLE
      DO 50 J=19,22
      K=J-17
 50   PLTMAT(K,I) = OUTMAT(I,J)
      WRITE (6,55)
 55   FORMAT(1H1,T39,43HTABLE NUMBER FOUR - NATURAL RESOURCES USAGE,/,
     1 T47,26H(SCALED TO ORIGINAL VALUE),//,T74,5HOTHER,/,
     2 T10,4HYEAR,T26,4HFOOD,T42,4HIRON,T57,6HCOPPER,T73,11HNON-FERROUS,
     3 /,T26,3H(F),T43,3H(I),
     4 T60,3H(K),T77,3H(O),/)
      DO 56 I=1,NCYCLE
 56   WRITE(6,57) (PLTMAT(K,I),K=1,5)
 57   FORMAT(8X,F4.0,6(9X,F8.4))
      IF (PPLOT.EQ.0.0) GO TO 6001
C**
      KK=1+NCYCLE
      M1=5
      DO 58 J=19,22
      DO 58 I=1,NCYCLE
      A(KK)  = OUTMAT(I,J)
      KK=KK+1
   58 CONTINUE
      CALL PLOT (N4,A,M1,NCYCLE,ANG4)
      IF (DETAIL.EQ.0.0) GO TO 5301
C**
 6001 M1 = 2
      JJ = 1
      J = 19
      III = 97
 5399 DO 5300 I = 1,NCYCLE
      KK = NCYCLE + I
 5300 A(KK) = OUTMAT(I,J)
      ANG8(1) = ANG4(JJ)
      CALL PLOT2(LIST(III),A,M1,NCYCLE,ANG8(1))
      III = III + 8
      IF(J.GT.20) GO TO 5301
      J = J + 1
      JJ = JJ+1
```

```
      GO TO 5399
 5301 CONTINUE
 6000 DO 60 I = 1,NCYCLE
      DO 60 J = 23,28
      K = J-21
      PLTMAT(K,I) = OUTMAT(I,J)
   60 CONTINUE
      WRITE (6,65)
 65   FORMAT(1H1,T29,46HTABLE NUMBER FIVE - RAW MATERIAL USAGE; CONT.,/
     1 ,T39,26H(SCALED TO ORIGINAL VALUE),//,
     2 T10,4HYEAR,T25,4HCOAL,T41,3HOIL,T52,12HSTONE & CLAY,T70,
     3 9HCHEMICALS,T88,4HLEAD,T101,8HALUMINUM,/,T25,3H(K),T41,
     4 3H(T),T56,3H(S),T73,3H(C),T89,3H(L),T104,3H(A),/)
      DO 66 I=1,NCYCLE
 66   WRITE (6,67) (PLTMAT(K,I),K=1,7)
 67   FORMAT(8X,F4.0,6(8X,F8.4))
      IF (PPLOT.EQ.0.0) GO TO 7001
C**
      KK=1+NCYCLE
C     DO 16 II=KK,1000
C 16  A(II)=0.0
      M1=7
      DO 68 J=23,28
      DO 68 I=1,NCYCLE
      A(KK) = OUTMAT(I,J)
      KK=KK+1
   68 CONTINUE
      CALL PLOT (N5,A,M1,NCYCLE,ANG5)
      IF (DETAIL.EQ.0.0) GO TO 5401
 7001 M1 = 2
      JJ=1
      J = 23
      III = 129
 5499 DO 5400 I = 1,NCYCLE
      KK = NCYCLE + I
 5400 A(KK) = OUTMAT(I,J)
      ANG8(1) = ANG5(JJ)
      CALL PLOT2(LIST(III),A,M1,NCYCLE,ANG8(1))
      III = III + 8
      IF(J.GT.26) GO TO 5401
      J = J + 1
      JJ = JJ+1
      GO TO 5499
 5401 CONTINUE
C**
 7000 DO 70 I=1,NCYCLE
      PLTMAT(2,I) = OUTMAT(I,36)
 70   PLTMAT(3,I) = OUTMAT(I,37)
      WRITE(6,75)
 75   FORMAT(1H1,T24,15HTABLE NUMBER SIX,/,
     1 T19,27HUNEMPLOYMENT AND QOL VALUES,//,
     2 T10,4HYEAR,T26,12HUNEMPLOYMENT,T50,7HQUALITY,/,
     3 T30,3H(U),T53,3H(Q),/)
      DO 76 I=1,NCYCLE
 76   WRITE(6,77) (PLTMAT(K,I),K=1,3)
 77   FORMAT(8X,F4.0,2(14X,F8.4))
      IF (PPLOT.EQ.0.0) GO TO 8000
C**
```

```
                                OTPUT
      KK=1+NCYCLE
      DO 17 II=KK,1000
   17 A(II)=0.0
      M1=3
      DO 71 I=1,NCYCLE
      A(KK)=OUTMAT(I,36)
      KK=KK+1
   71 CONTINUE
      DO 72 I=1,NCYCLE
      A(KK)=OUTMAT(I,37)
      KK=KK+1
   72 CONTINUE
      CALL PLOT (N6,A,M1,NCYCLE,ANG6)
      IF (DETAIL.EQ.0.0) GO TO 5501
      M1 = 2
      III = 178
      DO 5500 I = 1,NCYCLE
      KK = NCYCLE + I
 5500 A(KK) = OUTMAT(I,34)
      ANG8(1) = ANG6(1)
      CALL PLCT2(LIST(III),A,M1,NCYCLE,ANG8(1))
      M1 = 2
      III = 177
      DO 5503 I = 1,NCYCLE
      KK = NCYCLE + I
 5503 A(KK) = OUTMAT(I,37)
      ANG8(1) = ANG6(2)
      CALL PLCT2(LIST(III),A,M1,NCYCLE,ANG8(1))
 5501 CONTINUE
C**
 8000 DO 80 I=1,NCYCLE
      DO 81 J=30,33
      K=J-28
81    PLTMAT(K,I) = OUTMAT(I,J)
 80   CONTINUE
      WRITE (6,85)
85    FORMAT(1H1,T29,40HTABLE NUMBER SEVEN - LAND, AIR AND WATER,
     1 6H USAGE,/,T39,26H(SCALED TO ORIGINAL VALUE),//,
     2 T10,4HYEAR,T23,5HURBAN,T41,6HARABLE,T58,
     3 22HTREATED UNITS OF MEDIA,/,T25,3H(U),
     4 T43,3H(F),T61,3H(A),T77,3H(W),/)
      DO 86 I=1,NCYCLE
86    WRITE(6,87) (PLTMAT(K,I),K=1,5)
87    FORMAT(8X,F4.0,4(9X,F8.4))
      IF (PPLOT.EQ.0.0) GO TO 9989
C**
      KK=1+NCYCLE
      M1=5
      DO 88 J=30,33
      DO 88 I=1,NCYCLE
      A(KK) = OUTMAT (I,J)
      KK=KK+1
   88 CONTINUE
      CALL PLOT (N7,A,M1,NCYCLE,ANG7)
      IF (DETAIL.EQ.0.0) GO TO 950
 9989 M1 = 2
      JJ = 1
      J = 30
```

OTPUT

```
      III = 193
 5699 DO 5600 I = 1,NCYCLE
      KK = NCYCLE + I
 5600 A(KK) = OUTMAT(I,J)
      ANG8(1) = ANG7(JJ)
      CALL PLOT2(LIST(III),A,M1,NCYCLE,ANG8(1))
      III = III + 8
      IF(J.GT.32) GO TO 950
      J = J + 1
      JJ = JJ+1
      GO TO 5699
  950 CONTINUE
C**
 9999 RETURN
      END
```

PLOT2

```
      SUBROUTINE PLOT2(NO,A,M,N,ANG)
C**    MODIFIED FROM SUBROUTINE PLOT; SEE PLOT FOR DEFINITIONS
C     INTEGER*2 OUT(101,52)
      DIMENSION NO(8),XPR(11),ANG(1),A(200),OUT(101,52)
      CATA BLANK/4H    /
C
    1 FORMAT(1H1,50X,20HDETAIL GRAPH ------ ,8A4,//)
    2 FORMAT(1H ,4X,F7.3,5X,101A1)
    7 FORMAT(1H ,16X,101H'         '         '         '         '
     1 YEARS   '         '         '         '         ')
    8 FORMAT(1H0,9X,11F10.1)
    9 FORMAT(1H,16X,101A1)
C**   PRINT TITLE
C
   20 WRITE(6,1)NO
C
C     SET HORIZONTAL SPACING
      NP=1
      IF(N.LT.51) NP=2
      IF(N.LT.34) NP=3
      IF(N.LT.26) NP=4
C
C     CLEAR MATRIX
      DO 10 J = 1,101
      DO 10 I = 1,52
   10 OUT(J,I) = BLANK
C
C     SET STORAGE COUNTERS
      VMAX=0.0
      VMIN=10000.0
      MY=2*N
      MZ = N + 1
      DO 34 J=MZ,MY
      IF (A(J).LT.0.0) A(J)=0.0
      IF (VMAX.LT.A(J)) VMAX=A(J)
   34 IF (VMIN.GT.A(J)) VMIN=A(J)
      IF(VMAX.LT.(VMIN+0.5)) VMAX =VMIN+0.5
      VINTER=(VMAX-VMIN)/50.
      I=1
      II=1
      M=M-1
   22 CO 30 J=1,M
      JR=1
      L=I+J*N
      JP=((A(L)-VMIN)/VINTER)+1.0
      IF (JP.GT.51) JR=52
      IF (JR.EQ.52) GO TO 30
      JR=52-JP
   30 OUT(II,JR)=ANG(1)
      I = I + 1
      II = II + NP
      IF (I.LE.N) GO TO 22
C
C     SET CCUNTERS FOR ORDINATE PRINT
      L = 0
      YPR= VMAX + 5.0*VINTER
      WRITE(6,7)
      DO 40 J = 1,51
```

PLOT2

```
      IF (L) 50,50,6C
   5C YPR= YPR -5.0* VINTER
      IF (YPR.LE.0.0) YPR=0.000
      L =5
      WRITE(6,2) YPR,(OUT(I,J),I = 1,101)
      GO TC 40
   6C WRITE(6,9)(OUT(I,J),I = 1,101)
   40 L = L - 1
C
C     PRINT ABSCISSA
      XPR(1) = 1.0
      DO 7C I = 1,10
   70 XPR(I+1) = XPR(I) + (10.0/NP)
      WRITE (6,7)
      WRITE (6,8) (XPR(I),I =1,11)
      WRITE (6,9) (OUT(I,52),I = 1,101)
      RETURN
      END
```

Appendix B
Base Case Scenario

<<< S T A T E O F T H E S Y S T E M R U N >>>

***** INITIAL SYSTEM GROWTH DATA *****

POPULATION GROWTH RATES

BIRTH RATE	0.0180
DEATH RATE	0.0094
IMMIGRATION RATE	0.0020

		GROWTH RATES (%),	DEPRECIATION (%)	EXPORTS	IMPORTS
1	EDUCATION	3.20	3.00	0.0	0.0
2	TRANS & COMMUN	4.30	6.00	0.0	0.0
3	HEALTH&WELFARE	6.50	4.00	0.0	0.0
4	PUBLIC SAFETY	3.70	3.00	0.0	0.0
5	ADMIN & OTHER	4.80	3.00	1900.00	4800.00
6	AGRICULTURE	2.00	7.00	7800.00	6500.00
7	NON-DUR MANUF	3.10	9.00	2200.00	17900.00
8	DURABLE MANUF	3.10	9.00	43400.00	22700.00
9	COMMUN & TRANS	3.20	8.00	6200.00	4800.00
10	WHOL-RET TRADE	3.30	6.00	0.0	0.0
11	SERVICES	3.60	6.00	2400.00	1600.00
12	MINING	1.00	7.00	2200.00	7000.00

***** PRODUCTION FORMULAE *****

	SECTOR NUMBER	1.	1.	2.	3.	4.	5.	5.	6.	6.	7.	7.	8.	8.	8.	9.	10.	10.	11.	12.
	IF ACTIVE,=1	1.	0.	1.	1.	1.	1.	0.	1.	0.	1.	0.	1.	0.	0.	1.	1.	0.	1.	1.
1	FIBRE & FOOD	1.	1.	1.	29.	24.	12.	12.	3266.	3265.	4848.	4848.	0.	0.	0.	60.	90.	90.	199.	10.
2	IRON & STEEL	0.	0.	0.	0.	0.	0.	0.	0.	0.	8.	8.	191.	191.	205.	2.	0.	0.	0.	1.
3	COPPER	0.	0.	0.	1.	0.	1.	1.	0.	0.	2.	1.	228.	200.	200.	0.	0.	0.	0.	18.
4	NON-FERROUS	0.	0.	0.	1.	0.	1.	1.	0.	0.	4.	6.	86.	100.	95.	0.	0.	0.	0.	8.
5	COAL	0.	0.	0.	0.	0.	11.	11.	0.	0.	15.	20.	0.	0.	0.	0.	0.	0.	20.	4.
6	PETRO-NAT GAS	0.	0.	0.	0.	0.	0.	0.	0.	0.	408.	300.	1.	2.	1.	0.	0.	0.	88.	3.
7	STONE & CLAY	0.	0.	0.	0.	0.	1.	1.	0.	0.	15.	15.	29.	33.	30.	0.	0.	0.	0.	6.
8	CHEMICALS	0.	0.	0.	0.	0.	0.	0.	0.	0.	22.	30.	24.	25.	25.	0.	0.	0.	0.	4.
9	LEAD & ZINC	0.	0.	0.	0.	0.	0.	0.	0.	0.	40.	40.	279.	300.	280.	0.	0.	0.	0.	1.
10	ALUMINUM	0.	0.	0.	0.	1.	0.	0.	0.	0.	4.	4.	193.	193.	193.	0.	0.	0.	0.	2.
15	URBAN LAND	0.	0.	750.	0.	0.	0.	0.	0.	0.	750.	750.	750.	750.	750.	750.	750.	750.	1875.	0.
16	ARABLE LAND	0.	0.	0.	0.	0.	0.	0.	6750.	6500.	0.	0.	0.	0.	0.	0.	0.	0.	0.	250.
17	CAPITAL	0.	0.	0.	0.	0.	0.	0.	0.	0.	0.	0.	0.	0.	0.	0.	0.	0.	0.	0.
18	WORK UNITS	2650.	2133.	4078.	2344.	917.	2854.	2346.	5235.	4265.	6752.	6752.	10177.	10177.	10177.	6282.	16589.	12796.	21593.	517.
19	AIR UNITS	0.	0.	2000.	0.	0.	0.	0.	0.	0.	0.	0.	2000.	1000.	500.	200.	0.	0.	1000.	0.
20	WATER UNITS	0.	0.	0.	0.	0.	0.	0.	0.	0.	1000.	625.	625.	1250.	625.	0.	0.	0.	1250.	875.

*****ACTIVE PRODUCTION FUNCTIONS*****

1	FIBRE & FOOD	1.	1.	29.	24.	12.	3266.	4848.	0.	60.	90.	199.	10.
2	IRON & STEEL	0.	0.	0.	0.	0.	0.	8.	191.	2.	0.	0.	1.
3	COPPER	0.	0.	1.	0.	1.	0.	2.	228.	0.	0.	0.	18.
4	NON-FERROUS	0.	0.	1.	0.	1.	0.	4.	86.	0.	0.	0.	8.
5	COAL	0.	0.	0.	0.	11.	0.	15.	0.	0.	0.	20.	4.
6	PETRO-NAT GAS	0.	0.	0.	0.	0.	0.	408.	1.	0.	0.	88.	3.
7	STONE & CLAY	0.	0.	0.	0.	1.	0.	15.	29.	0.	0.	0.	6.
8	CHEMICALS	0.	0.	0.	0.	0.	0.	22.	24.	0.	0.	0.	4.
9	LEAD & ZINC	0.	0.	0.	0.	0.	0.	40.	279.	0.	0.	0.	1.
10	ALUMINUM	0.	0.	0.	1.	0.	0.	4.	193.	0.	0.	0.	2.
15	URBAN LAND	0.	750.	C.	0.	0.	0.	750.	750.	750.	750.	1875.	0.
16	ARABLE LAND	0.	0.	0.	0.	0.	6750.	0.	0.	0.	0.	0.	250.
17	CAPITAL	0.	0.	0.	0.	0.	0.	0.	0.	0.	0.	0.	0.
18	WORK UNITS	2650.	4078.	2344.	917.	2854.	5235.	6752.	10177.	6282.	16589.	21593.	517.
19	AIR UNITS	0.	2000.	0.	0.	0.	0.	0.	2000.	200.	C.	1000.	0.
20	WATER UNITS	0.	0.	0.	0.	0.	0.	1000.	625.	0.	0.	1250.	875.

*****CONSUMPTION FUNCTIONS*****

EDUCATION	45863.	0.	0.	0.	0.	0.	0.	0.	0.	5528.	0.	0.
INSTITUTIONS	0.	0.	372.	0.	0.	0.	0.	0.	0.	104.	0.	0.
NON-WORKERS	1467.	1197.	958.	3135.	203.	839.	6214.	3135.	284.	112.	30.	80.
TRAIN & WELFARE	0.	0.	122.	0.	0.	0.	0.	0.	0.	0.	0.	0.
PAID WORKERS	0.	0.	0.	0.	0.	0.	0.	0.	0.	0.	0.	0.
UNPAID WORKERS	0.	0.	0.	0.	0.	0.	0.	0.	0.	0.	0.	0.

EDUCATION	5550.	0.	0.	0.	0.	0.	0.	0.	0.	0.	0.	0.
INSTITUTIONS	0.	0.	153.	0.	0.	0.	0.	0.	0.	0.	0.	0.
NON-WORKERS	0.	0.	0.	0.	0.	0.	0.	0.	0.	0.	0.	0.
TRAIN & WELFARE	0.	0.	415.	0.	0.	0.	0.	0.	0.	0.	0.	0.
PAID WORKERS	825.	675.	535.	1300.	580.	473.	3500.	2546.	546.	2000.	17.	46.
UNPAID WORKERS	133.	109.	87.	209.	93.	76.	564.	410.	88.	322.	3.	7.

EDUCATION	0.	0.	0.	0.	0.	0.	0.	0.	0.	0.	0.	0.
INSTITUTIONS	0.	0.	415.	0.	0.	0.	0.	0.	0.	0.	0.	0.
NON-WORKERS	0.	0.	0.	0.	0.	0.	0.	0.	265.	0.	0.	0.
TRAIN & WELFARE	0.	0.	743.	0.	0.	0.	0.	0.	0.	0.	0.	0.
PAID WORKERS	4909.	4007.	3208.	10494.	581.	2808.	20798.	10494.	952.	375.	97.	265.
UNPAID WORKERS	1904.	1554.	1244.	4069.	264.	1089.	8065.	4069.	369.	145.	38.	102.

EDUCATION	0.	0.	0.	0.	0.	0.	0.	0.	0.	0.	0.	0.
INSTITUTIONS	0.	0.	496.	0.	0.	0.	0.	0.	0.	726.	0.	0.
NON-WORKERS	0.	0.	15736.	0.	0.	0.	0.	0.	0.	0.	0.	0.
TRAIN & WELFARE	0.	0.	0.	0.	0.	0.	0.	0.	0.	0.	0.	0.
PAID WORKERS	279.	217.	186.	589.	31.	155.	1147.	589.	62.	31.	0.	0.
UNPAID WORKERS	0.	0.	0.	0.	0.	0.	0.	0.	0.	0.	0.	0.

*****DEMAND FUNCTIONS*****

1 EDUCATION	806.	0.	0.	0.	0.	0.	0.	0.	0.	0.	0.	0.
2 TRANS & COMMUN	0.	0.	500.	0.	0.	0.	0.	0.	0.	0.	0.	0.
3 HEALTH&WELFARE	0.	0.	0.	1000.	1000.	0.	0.	0.	0.	0.	0.	0.
4 PUBLIC SAFETY	0.	0.	0.	0.	0.	1000.	0.	0.	0.	0.	0.	0.
5 ADMIN & OTHER	0.	0.	0.	0.	0.	0.	0.	0.	0.	0.	200.	0.
6 AGRICULTURE	0.	45.	0.	0.	0.	0.	0.	0.	20.	1000.	0.	0.
7 NON-DUR MANUF	0.	130.	0.	0.	0.	0.	500.	0.	130.	0.	0.	0.
8 DURABLE MANUF	0.	260.	0.	0.	0.	0.	500.	0.	240.	0.	0.	0.
9 COMMUN & TRANS	0.	70.	500.	0.	0.	0.	0.	1000.	60.	0.	0.	0.
10WHOL-RET TRADE	0.	180.	0.	0.	0.	0.	0.	0.	250.	0.	0.	0.
11 SERVICES	194.	310.	0.	0.	0.	0.	0.	0.	290.	0.	800.	0.
12 MINING	0.	0.	0.	0.	0.	0.	0.	0.	0.	0.	0.	1000.
THRESHOLD	1.65	1.00	0.40	68.00	40.00	0.40	1.00	0.40	0.35	0.40	0.40	0.40
WEIGHT	0.10	0.11	0.06	0.06	0.12	0.10	0.07	0.08	0.08	0.08	0.07	0.07
POPULATION BASE	1.00	5.00	7.00	4.00	2.00	7.00	5.00	7.00	7.00	7.00	7.00	7.00

*****PRICE FUNCTIONS*****

1	FIBRE & FOOD	24.600	26.400	2.000	0.0	0.0
2	IRON & STEEL	49.000	49.000	2.000	0.540	0.460
3	COPPER	40.000	320.000	2.000	0.250	0.500
4	NON-FERROUS	8.500	23.000	2.000	0.090	0.410
5	COAL	4.000	333.000	2.000	0.0	0.0
6	PETRO-NAT GAS	7.200	58.700	2.000	0.0	0.0
7	STONE & CLAY	9.000	15.000	2.000	0.0	0.0
8	CHEMICALS	0.790	1.580	2.000	0.0	0.0
9	LEAD & ZINC	9.000	15.000	2.000	0.120	0.880
10	ALUMINUM	49.900	49.000	2.000	0.010	0.990
15	URBAN LAND	7.200	8.000	2.000	0.0	0.0
16	ARABLE LAND	9.600	9.000	2.000	0.0	0.0
17	CAPITAL	0.0	0.0	2.000	0.0	0.0
18	WORK UNITS	5.000	5.900	2.000	0.0	0.0

*****RESOURCE DEPLETION WARNINGS*****

	RESOURCE	STOCKPILE	WARNINGS			
1	FIBRE & FOOD	0.0	0.87	0.90	0.92	0.95
2	IRON & STEEL	6000.00	0.30	0.60	0.90	0.95
3	COPPER	2000.00	0.30	0.60	0.90	0.95
4	NON-FERROUS	5000.00	0.60	0.75	0.90	0.95
5	COAL	5000.00	0.50	0.70	0.90	0.95
6	PETRO-NAT GAS	5000.00	0.50	0.70	0.90	0.95
7	STONE & CLAY	10000.00	0.50	0.70	0.90	0.95
8	CHEMICALS	10000.00	0.50	0.70	0.90	0.95
9	LEAD & ZINC	2000.00	0.50	0.70	0.90	0.95
10	ALUMINUM	3000.00	0.50	0.70	0.90	0.95
15	URBAN LAND	0.0	0.80	0.80	0.92	0.95
16	ARABLE LAND	0.0	0.50	0.55	0.60	0.95
18	WORK UNITS	0.0	0.85	0.90	0.92	0.95

*****SUBSTITUTION FORMULAE*****

1.	COPPER	.15 UNITS OF IRON AND .6 UNITS OF COPPER
2.	COPPER	.15 UNITS IRON,.1 UNITS OTHER NON-IRON ,.6 UNITS COPPER
3.	FIBERS	.8 UNITS FIBER,.001 UNITS CHEMICALS
4.	OIL	.02 UNITS COAL,.30 UNITS OIL
5.	URBAN LAND	.9 UNITS URBAN LAND,.05 UNITS ARABLE LAND
7.	LEAD	.05 UNITS OF IRON,.8 UNITS OF LEAD

****INTERNATIONAL PRODUCTION FUNCTIONS****

1	FIBRE & FOOD	3266.	4848.	0.	60.	90.	199.	10.
2	IRON & STEEL	0.	8.	191.	2.	0.	0.	1.
3	COPPER	0.	2.	228.	0.	0.	0.	18.
4	NON-FERROUS	0.	4.	86.	0.	0.	0.	8.
5	COAL	0.	15.	0.	0.	0.	20.	4.
6	PETRO-NAT GAS	0.	408.	1.	0.	0.	88.	3.
7	STONE & CLAY	0.	15.	29.	0.	0.	0.	6.
8	CHEMICALS	0.	22.	24.	0.	0.	0.	4.
9	LEAD & ZINC	0.	40.	279.	0.	0.	0.	1.
10	ALUMINUM	0.	4.	193.	0.	0.	0.	2.
15	URBAN LAND	0.	750.	750.	750.	750.	1875.	0.
16	ARABLE LAND	6750.	0.	0.	0.	0.	0.	250.
17	CAPITAL	0.	0.	0.	0.	0.	0.	0.
18	WORK UNITS	5235.	6752.	10177.	6282.	16589.	21593.	517.
19	AIR UNITS	0.	0.	2000.	200.	0.	1000.	0.
20	WATER UNITS	0.	1000.	525.	0.	0.	1250.	875.

```
                              ********************
                              *  YEAR  IS  1971  *
                              ********************

     ***POPULATION***                              ***PRODUCTION***

                     PEOPLE      ***                     INVST.FUNDS   MAINT   OUTPUT   IMPORTS  EXPORTS   GROWTH
     EDUCATION     58188.035     ***  1        EDUCATION  16077.520    3.00  1000.00      0.0      0.0      3.20
 INSTITUTIONAL      2334.945     ***  2 TRANS & COMMUN     7273.398    5.00  1000.00      0.0      0.0      4.30
    NON-WORKER     33760.348     ***  3 HEALTH&WELFARE    31937.207    4.00  1000.00      0.0      0.0      6.50
    UNEMPLOYED      1425.050     ***  4   PUBLIC SAFETY   18847.469    3.00  1000.00      0.0      0.0      3.70
   PAID WORKER     83056.187     ***  5   ADMIN & OTHER   20951.602    3.00  1000.00    297.55   254.49    4.80
 UNPAID WORKER     27357.590     ***  6     AGRICULTURE   41881.297    7.00  1000.00    166.37   185.64    2.00
         TOTAL    206162.187     ***  7  NON-DUR MANUF   135855.062    9.00  1000.00    170.07    19.43    3.10
                                 ***  8  DURABLE MANUF   219140.062    9.00  1000.00    104.81   186.25    3.10
        BIRTHS      3679.343     ***  9 COMMUN & TRANS   102571.875    8.00  1000.00     50.43    60.54    3.20
        DEATHS      1936.932     *** 10WHOL-RET TRADE    170408.937    6.00  1000.00      0.0      0.0      3.30
     MIGRATION       408.000     *** 11        SERVICES  161346.687    6.00  1000.00     10.63     3.11    3.60
                                 *** 12          MINING   12233.668    7.00  1000.00   1000.00   400.00    1.00
                                 ***              TOTAL  938524.625    BALANCE OF PAYMENTS    -1204.004


               ***RESOURCES***                                              ***SYSTEM RESILIENCE***

                   STOCKPILE  % USED RECYCLE SUBST.  YEAR   STOCKPILE                      PRESENT THRESHOLD RESILIENCE  ADJUSTED
                                      RATIO  NUMBER COMPLTD INCREASE                       VALUE                         THRESHOLD
 1  FIBRE & FOOD    1565.59    85.40  0.0                        *** 1         EDUCATION    1.719     1.650     0.042      0.0
 2  IRON & STEEL    9700.00     3.00  0.540                      *** 2        EMPLOYMENT    1.198     1.000     0.198      0.0
 3        COPPER    7300.00    27.00  0.286                      *** 3 TRANSPORTATION       0.485     0.400     0.213      0.0
 4   NON-FERROUS    7420.00    25.80  0.117                      *** 4           WELFARE   70.173    68.000     0.032      0.0
 5          COAL    9450.00     5.50  0.0                        *** 5            HEALTH   42.827    40.000     0.071      0.0
 6 PETRO-NAT GAS    5500.00    45.00  0.0                        *** 6 SFTY & DEFENSE       0.485     0.400     0.213      0.0
 7  STONE & CLAY    9849.00     1.51  0.0                        *** 7   MANUFACTURING      1.204     1.000     0.204      0.0
 8     CHEMICALS    9850.00     1.50  0.0                        *** 8        COMMERCIAL    0.485     0.400     0.213      0.0
 9   LEAD & ZINC    6753.84    32.46  0.213                      *** 9GRCTH POTENTIAL       0.480     0.350     0.372      0.0
10      ALUMINUM    7833.33    21.67  0.056                      *** 10   AGRICULTURE       0.485     0.400     0.213      0.0
15    URBAN LAND    4375.00    56.25  0.0                        *** 11         SERVICES    0.485     0.400     0.213      0.0
16   ARABLE LAND    8000.01    46.67  0.0                        *** 12           MINING    0.485     0.400     0.213      0.0
18    WORK UNITS    3068.32    96.31  0.0                        ***
```

*****TOTAL SYSTEM EXPENDITURES*****
(MILLIONS OF DOLLARS)

	RESOURCE	AMCUNT	UNIT PRICE	COST	
LAND					
	URBAN LANC	5624.996	0.00009558	38718.469	
	ARABLE LAND	6999.992	0.00011260	11980.230	
	TCTAL				50698.699
RAW MATERIALS					
	FCOD & FIBER	8539.980	0.00045000	110542.437	
	IRON ORE	202.000	0.00031000	8858.137	
	CCPPER	250.000	0.00050000	17251.723	
	CTHER NON-IRON	100.000	0.00009000	1195.269	
	COAL	50.000	0.00005000	119.435	
	PETRO-NAT GAS	499.999	0.00020000	3848.032	
	STONE ANC CLAY	51.000	0.00008747	445.641	
	CHEMICALS	50.000	0.00000800	35.659	
	LEAD,ZINC	320.000	0.00007881	3335.976	
	ALUMINUM	200.000	0.00047291	13569.680	
	TCTAL				159201.687
LABOR					
	WCRKERS COSTS	79987.875	0.00011080		656682.312
CAPITAL					
	NEW CAPITAL GOODS				16349.965
	ENVIRCNMENTAL MAINTENANCE				9501.113
	CAPITAL MAINTENANCE				67238.750
	TCTAL				93089.812
TCTAL COSTS					959672.500

****
* YEAR IS 1972 *
****

POPULATION

	PEOPLE
EDUCATION	58329.531
INSTITUTIONAL	2351.802
NON-WORKER	33828.684
UNEMPLOYED	1449.929
PAID WORKER	85994.875
UNPAID WORKER	26392.422
TOTAL	208347.312
BIRTHS	3718.340
DEATHS	1942.855
MIGRATION	412.324

PRODUCTION

		INVST.FUNDS	MAINT	OUTPUT	IMPORTS	EXPORTS	GROWTH
1	EDUCATION	16591.992	3.00	1000.99	0.0	0.0	3.20
2	TRANS & COMMUN	7683.871	6.00	1036.65	0.0	0.0	4.30
3	HEALTH&WELFARE	34013.109	4.00	1039.62	0.0	0.0	6.50
4	PUBLIC SAFETY	19544.816	3.00	1011.74	0.0	0.0	3.70
5	ADMIN & OTHER	21957.262	3.00	1167.47	297.53	328.54	4.80
6	AGRICULTURE	43198.051	7.00	1002.50	163.94	157.66	2.00
7	NON-DUR MANUF	142836.250	9.00	1051.00	169.12	17.30	3.10
8	DURABLE MANUF	230764.500	9.00	1008.78	102.90	159.15	3.10
9	COMMUN & TRANS	106566.375	8.00	1005.16	49.64	51.55	3.20
10	WHCL-RET TRADE	177027.875	6.00	1007.69	0.22	0.0	3.30
11	SERVICES	167312.750	6.00	994.82	10.46	2.89	3.60
12	MINING	12835.594	7.00	1528.17	977.85	611.27	1.00
	TOTAL	980332.312	BALANCE OF PAYMENTS			-5711.152	

RESOURCES

		STOCKPILE	% USED	RECYCLE RATIO	SUBST. NUMBER	YEAR COMPLTD	STOCKPILE INCREASE
1	FIBRE & FOOD	2057.64	82.10	0.0			
2	IRON & STEEL	9567.16	4.33	0.541			
3	COPPER	7096.48	29.04	0.292			
4	NON-FERROUS	7325.67	26.74	0.119			
5	COAL	9395.38	6.05	0.C			
6	PETRO-NAT GAS	4978.05	50.22	0.0	4	1977	5000.00
7	STONE & CLAY	9793.64	2.06	0.C			
8	CHEMICALS	9796.55	2.03	0.C			
9	LEAD & ZINC	6485.84	35.14	0.229			
10	ALUMINUM	7641.21	23.59	0.065			
15	URBAN LAND	4302.77	56.97	0.0			
16	ARABLE LAND	7921.85	47.19	0.C			
18	WORK UNITS	4505.44	94.76	0.C			

SYSTEM RESILIENCE

		PRESENT VALUE	THRESHOLD	RESILIENCE	ADJUSTED THRESHOLD
1	EDUCATION	1.714	1.650	0.039	0.0
2	EMPLOYMENT	1.168	1.000	0.168	0.0
3	TRANSPORTATION	0.490	0.400	0.225	0.0
4	WELFARE	71.701	68.000	0.054	0.0
5	HEALTH	44.205	40.000	0.105	0.0
6	SFTY & DEFENSE	0.486	0.400	0.214	0.0
7	MANUFACTURING	1.198	1.000	0.198	0.0
8	COMMERCIAL	0.482	0.400	0.206	0.0
9	GROTH POTENTIAL	0.480	0.350	0.371	0.0
10	AGRICULTURE	0.481	0.400	0.203	0.0
11	SERVICES	0.494	0.400	0.235	0.0
12	MINING	0.733	0.400	0.834	0.0

*****TOTAL SYSTEM EXPENDITURES*****
(MILLIONS OF DOLLARS)

RESOURCE	AMCUNT	UNIT PRICE	COST
LAND			
URBAN LAND	5697.234	0.00009677	39493.336
ARABLE LAND	7078.148	0.00011473	12811.871
TOTAL			52305.207
RAW MATERIALS			
FOOD & FIBER	8804.160	0.00045000	114643.437
IRON ORE	204.624	0.00031531	9100.012
COPPER	261.818	0.00050384	17763.102
OTHER NON-IRCN	105.392	0.00009000	1224.705
COAL	54.616	0.00005096	132.455
PETRO-NAT GAS	521.946	0.00020821	4164.246
STONE AND CLAY	55.356	0.00008915	473.758
CHEMICALS	53.445	0.00000800	37.000
LEAD,ZINC	325.018	0.00008671	3709.956
ALUMINUM	202.967	0.00048784	14147.652
TCTAL			165396.062
LABOR			
WORKERS COSTS	81489.437	0.00011080	665945.875
CAPITAL			
NEW CAPITAL GOODS			14714.965
ENVIRCNMENTAL MAINTENANCE			9945.441
CAPITAL MAINTENANCE			70296.437
TCTAL			94956.812
TOTAL COSTS			978603.937

```
********************
*  YEAR  IS  1973  *
********************
```

POPULATION

	PEOPLE
EDUCATION	57942.422
INSTITUTIONAL	2365.467
NON-WORKER	34287.730
UNEMPLOYED	1493.859
PAID WORKER	87523.125
UNPAID WORKER	26942.781
TOTAL	210555.562
BIRTHS	3757.750
DEATHS	1950.266
MIGRATION	416.695

PRODUCTION

		INVST.FUNDS	MAINT	OUTPUT	IMPORTS	EXPORTS	GROWTH
1	EDUCATION	17122.926	3.00	1011.03	0.0	0.0	3.20
2	TRANS & COMMUN	8232.777	6.00	1090.84	0.0	0.0	4.30
3	HEALTH&WELFARE	36223.945	4.00	1087.28	0.0	0.0	6.50
4	PUBLIC SAFETY	20267.969	3.00	1030.43	0.0	0.0	3.70
5	ADMIN & OTHER	23011.195	3.00	1274.33	291.74	418.84	4.80
6	AGRICULTURE	44037.660	7.00	992.69	163.26	166.31	2.00
7	NON-DUR MANUF	154025.562	9.00	1139.64	168.36	20.33	3.10
8	DURABLE MANUF	249045.000	9.00	1033.22	100.88	176.72	3.10
9	COMMUN & TRANS	111119.687	8.00	1018.83	48.73	56.65	3.20
10	WHOL-RET TRADE	184018.562	6.00	1024.21	0.22	0.0	3.30
11	SERVICES	175552.375	6.00	1023.31	10.26	4.60	3.60
12	MINING	12944.859	7.00	1602.77	961.75	641.11	1.00
	TOTAL	1035602.37	BALANCE OF PAYMENTS			2712.703	

RESOURCES

		STOCKPILE	% USED	RECYCLE RATIO	SUBST. NUMBER	YEAR COMPLTD	STOCKPILE INCREASE
1	FIBRE & FOOD	2449.90	80.13	0.0			
2	IRON & STEEL	9430.81	5.69	0.541			
3	COPPER	6888.25	31.12	0.298	2	1983	2000.00
4	NON-FERROUS	7228.65	27.71	0.121			
5	COAL	9333.62	6.66	0.0			
6	PETRO-NAT GAS	5391.73	53.86	0.0			
7	STONE & CLAY	9735.69	2.64	0.0			
8	CHEMICALS	9740.27	2.60	0.0			
9	LEAD & ZINC	6212.82	37.87	0.246			
10	ALUMINUM	7445.73	25.54	0.075			
15	URBAN LAND	4101.24	58.99	0.0			
16	ARABLE LAND	8038.60	46.41	0.0			
18	WORK UNITS	3542.57	95.95	0.0			

SYSTEM RESILIENCE

		PRESENT VALUE	THRESHOLD	RESILIENCE	ADJUSTED THRESHOLD
1	EDUCATION	1.749	1.650	0.060	0.0
2	EMPLOYMENT	1.182	1.034	0.182	1.034
3	TRANSPORTATION	0.501	0.418	0.252	0.418
4	WELFARE	72.783	68.000	0.070	0.0
5	HEALTH	45.965	40.841	0.149	40.841
6	SFTY & DEFENSE	0.489	0.417	0.223	0.417
7	MANUFACTURING	1.241	1.040	0.241	1.040
8	COMMERCIAL	0.484	0.416	0.210	0.416
9	GRCTH POTENTIAL	0.489	0.376	0.398	0.376
10	AGRICULTURE	0.471	0.400	0.179	0.0
11	SERVICES	0.510	0.419	0.275	0.419
12	MINING	0.761	0.400	0.903	0.0

*****TOTAL SYSTEM EXPENDITURES*****
(MILLIONS OF DOLLARS)

RESOURCE	AMCUNT	UNIT PRICE	COST	Total
LAND				
URBAN LAND	5898.762	0.00009822	41143.793	
ARABLE LAND	6961.402	0.00011473	12678.020	
TCTAL				53821.812
RAW MATERIALS				
FOOD & FIBER	9213.691	0.00045000	121435.937	
IRON ORE	210.103	0.00031557	9333.355	
COPPER	269.065	0.00053106	19198.727	
OTHER NON-IRCN	108.599	0.00009027	1260.760	
CCAL	61.762	0.00005338	154.416	
PETRO-NAT GAS	428.568	0.00023251	3800.603	
STONE AND CLAY	57.949	0.00008919	489.608	
CHEMICALS	56.280	0.00000800	38.332	
LEAD,ZINC	335.457	0.00008780	3855.005	
ALUMINUM	208.206	0.00048784	14495.863	
TCTAL				174062.312
LABOR				
WORKERS COSTS	83980.562	0.00011302		697476.062
CAPITAL				
NEW CAPITAL GOCDS				15345.262
ENVIRCNMENTAL MAINTENANCE				10879.070
CAPITAL MAINTENANCE				74483.875
TOTAL				100708.187
TOTAL COSTS				1026068.37

```
*********************
*  YEAR  IS  1974   *
*********************
```

POPULATION

	PEOPLE
EDUCATION	57475.973
INSTITUTIONAL	237C.548
NCN-WORKER	34775.391
UNEMPLOYED	1528.377
PAID WORKER	90318.125
UNPAID WORKER	26318.297
TOTAL	212787.250
BIRTHS	3797.579
DEATHS	1959.086
MIGRATICN	421.111

PRODUCTION

		INVST.FUNDS	MAINT	OUTPUT	IMPORTS	EXPORTS	GROWTH
1	EDUCATION	17670.852	3.00	1044.35	0.0	0.0	3.20
2	TRANS & COMMUN	8503.223	6.00	1123.21	0.0	0.0	4.30
3	HEALTH&WELFARE	38578.484	4.00	1161.37	0.0	0.0	6.50
4	PUBLIC SAFETY	21017.875	3.00	1071.03	0.0	0.0	3.70
5	ADMIN & OTHER	24115.715	3.00	1433.37	288.86	463.79	4.80
6	AGRICULTURE	44962.957	7.00	1033.63	163.90	138.64	2.00
7	NON-DUR MANUF	156620.250	9.00	1163.68	168.89	16.33	3.10
8	DURABLE MANUF	253244.750	9.00	1068.75	99.61	143.79	3.10
9	COMMUN & TRANS	114328.812	8.00	1053.15	48.23	46.06	3.20
10	WHOL-RET TRADE	189761.875	6.00	1055.45	0.22	0.0	3.30
11	SERVICES	181042.125	6.00	1056.79	10.15	8.21	3.60
12	MINING	13123.977	7.00	1684.26	959.42	673.70	1.00
	TCTAL	1062969.00	BALANCE OF PAYMENTS			-5876.086	

RESOURCES

		STOCKPILE	% USED	RECYCLE RATIC	SUBST. NUMBER	YEAR COMPLTD	STOCKPILE INCREASE
1	FIBRE & FOOD	3054.31	76.90	0.0			
2	IRON & STEEL	9287.28	7.13	0.542			
3	COPPER	7146.98	33.04	0.305			
4	NON-FERRCUS	7125.80	28.74	0.124			
5	COAL	9264.93	7.35	0.C			
6	PETRO-NAT GAS	6618.05	55.88	0.C			
7	STONE & CLAY	9675.71	3.24	0.0			
8	CHEMICALS	9682.29	3.18	0.C			
9	LEAD & ZINC	5934.84	40.65	0.265			
10	ALUMINUM	7245.32	27.55	0.085			
15	URBAN LAND	3920.33	60.80	0.0			
16	ARABLE LAND	7819.49	47.87	0.0			
18	WORK UNITS	3215.19	96.44	0.C			

SYSTEM RESILIENCE

		PRESENT VALUE	THRESHOLD	RESILIENCE	ADJUSTED THRESHOLD
1	EDUCATION	1.821	1.670	0.104	1.670
2	EMPLOYMENT	1.181	1.034	0.143	0.0
3	TRANSPORTATION	0.511	0.435	0.223	0.435
4	WELFARE	75.987	68.957	0.117	68.957
5	HEALTH	48.983	41.866	0.199	41.866
6	SFTY & DEFENSE	0.503	0.432	0.207	0.432
7	MANUFACTURING	1.236	1.040	0.189	0.0
8	COMMERCIAL	0.495	0.430	0.188	0.430
9	GROTH POTENTIAL	0.499	0.399	0.328	0.399
10	AGRICULTURE	0.486	0.414	0.214	0.414
11	SERVICES	0.532	0.437	0.270	0.437
12	MINING	0.792	0.400	0.979	0.0

*****TOTAL SYSTEM EXPENDITURES*****
(MILLIONS OF DOLLARS)

RESOURCE	AMCUNT	UNIT PRICE	COST	
LAND				
URBAN LAND	6079.668	0.00003998	43228.695	
ARABLE LAND	7160.503	0.00011505	13126.031	
TCTAL				56354.727
RAW MATERIALS				
FCOD & FIBER	9481.434	0.00045000	124697.125	
IRON CRE	221.249	0.00031593	9835.199	
CCPPER	268.101	0.00055868	20098.434	
CTHER NCN-IRCN	115.339	0.00009122	1352.522	
COAL	68.691	0.00005636	179.851	
PETRO-NAT GAS	307.541	0.00024844	2917.191	
STONE AND CLAY	59.988	0.00008924	507.199	
CHEMICALS	57.988	0.00000800	39.598	
LEAD,ZINC	346.413	0.00008895	4038.290	
ALUMINUM	215.363	0.00048784	14994.949	
TCTAL				178660.125
LABOR				
WORKERS COSTS	87102.937	0.00011415		730459.375
CAPITAL				
NEW CAPITAL GOODS				15300.961
ENVIRCNMENTAL MAINTENANCE				11555.594
CAPITAL MAINTENANCE				76285.812
TCTAL				103142.312
TCTAL COSTS				1068616.00

****
* YEAR IS 1975 *
****

POPULATION

	PEOPLE
EDUCATION	57319.488
INSTITUTIONAL	2401.079
NON-WORKER	34714.180
UNEMPLOYED	1616.677
PAID WORKER	93902.125
UNPAID WORKER	25088.848
TOTAL	215042.562
BIRTHS	3837.829
DEATHS	1969.013
MIGRATION	425.574

PRODUCTION

		INVST.FUNDS	MAINT	OUTPUT	IMPORTS	EXPORTS	GROWTH
1	EDUCATION	18236.309	3.00	1088.47	0.0	0.0	3.20
2	TRANS & COMMUN	8883.734	6.00	1184.31	0.0	0.0	4.30
3	HEALTH&WELFARE	41086.066	4.00	1250.75	0.0	0.0	6.50
4	PUBLIC SAFETY	21795.527	3.00	1121.03	0.0	0.0	3.70
5	ADMIN & OTHER	25273.254	3.00	1553.14	288.80	510.82	4.80
6	AGRICULTURE	45880.246	7.00	1027.65	164.44	130.68	2.00
7	NON-DUR MANUF	162261.062	9.00	1215.85	170.11	16.18	-1.02
8	DURABLE MANUF	262390.750	9.00	1076.79	99.62	137.34	5.65
9	COMMUN & TRANS	118119.812	8.00	1084.33	48.15	44.96	3.20
10	WHOL-RET TRADE	196157.687	6.00	1100.32	0.22	0.0	3.30
11	SERVICES	187760.312	6.00	1109.25	10.19	11.26	3.60
12	MINING	13278.922	7.00	1757.28	965.29	702.91	1.00
	TOTAL	1101122.00	BALANCE OF PAYMENTS			-6706.047	

RESOURCES

		STOCKPILE	% USED	RECYCLE RATIO	SUBST. NUMBER	YEAR COMPLTD	STOCKPILE INCREASE
1	FIBRE & FOOD	3736.01	73.65	0.0			
2	IRON & STEEL	9135.69	8.60	0.543			
3	COPPER	7836.71	34.69	0.310			
4	NON-FERROUS	7019.10	29.81	0.126			
5	COAL	9189.57	8.10	0.0			
6	PETRO-NAT GAS	8394.30	56.99	0.0			
7	STONE & CLAY	9614.14	3.86	0.0			
8	CHEMICALS	9622.66	3.77	0.0			
9	LEAD & ZINC	5657.61	43.42	0.286			
10	ALUMINUM	7045.05	29.55	0.096			
15	URBAN LAND	3673.95	63.26	0.0			
16	ARABLE LAND	7911.85	47.25	0.0			
18	WORK UNITS	3322.44	96.46	0.0			

SYSTEM RESILIENCE

		PRESENT VALUE	THRESHOLD	RESILIENCE	ADJUSTED THRESHOLD
1	EDUCATION	1.906	1.700	0.141	1.700
2	EMPLOYMENT	1.174	1.034	0.136	0.0
3	TRANSPORTATION	0.527	0.450	0.214	0.450
4	WELFARE	77.366	70.363	0.122	70.363
5	HEALTH	52.091	43.289	0.244	43.289
6	SFTY & DEFENSE	0.521	0.446	0.208	0.446
7	MANUFACTURING	1.221	1.040	0.174	0.0
8	COMMERCIAL	0.504	0.443	0.173	0.443
9	GROTH POTENTIAL	0.511	0.419	0.282	0.419
10	AGRICULTURE	0.478	0.414	0.153	0.0
11	SERVICES	0.557	0.456	0.275	0.456
12	MINING	0.817	0.400	1.043	0.0

*****TOTAL SYSTEM EXPENDITURES*****
(MILLIONS OF DOLLARS)

RESOURCE	AMCUNT	UNIT PRICE	COST	
LAND				
URBAN LAND	6326.047	0.00010217	45606.953	
ARABLE LAND	7088.152	0.00011511	13034.246	
TCTAL				58641.199
RAW MATERIALS				
FOOD & FIBER	9737.227	0.00045000	129244.125	
IRON ORE	227.631	0.00031639	10110.848	
COPPER	259.991	0.00058428	20321.781	
OTHER NCN-IRCN	119.926	0.00009225	1417.304	
COAL	75.354	0.00005997	208.697	
PETRO-NAT GAS	220.321	0.00025758	2156.050	
STONE AND CLAY	61.562	0.00008930	515.341	
CHEMICALS	59.621	0.00000800	40.247	
LEAD, ZINC	350.817	0.00009017	4129.895	
ALUMINUM	217.320	0.00048784	15116.668	
TCTAL				183260.625
LABOR				
WCRKERS COSTS	90579.687	0.00011415		756946.312
CAPITAL				
NEW CAPITAL GOODS				15517.797
ENVIRONMENTAL MAINTENANCE				12317.824
CAPITAL MAINTENANCE				78979.937
TOTAL				106815.500
TCTAL COSTS				1105663.00

****
* YEAR IS 1976 *
****

POPULATION

	PEOPLE
EDUCATION	57258.055
INSTITUTIONAL	2437.309
NON-WORKER	34583.691
UNEMPLOYED	1714.294
PAID WORKER	97564.687
UNPAID WORKER	23763.617
TOTAL	217321.812
BIRTHS	3878.506
DEATHS	1980.179
MIGRATION	430.085

PRODUCTION

		INVST.FUNDS	MAINT	OUTPUT	IMPORTS	EXPORTS	GROWTH
1	EDUCATION	18819.859	3.00	1122.81	0.0	0.0	3.20
2	TRANS & COMMUN	9233.629	6.00	1225.19	0.0	0.0	4.30
3	HEALTH&WELFARE	43756.641	4.00	1333.51	0.0	0.0	6.50
4	PUBLIC SAFETY	22601.953	3.00	1162.06	0.0	0.0	3.70
5	ADMIN & CTHER	26486.352	3.00	1663.13	288.74	522.81	4.80
6	AGRICULTURE	46824.516	7.00	1046.62	164.94	121.46	2.00
7	NON-DUR MANUF	161240.500	9.00	1206.53	170.38	14.65	-1.02
8	DURABLE MANUF	274957.062	9.00	1119.05	99.52	130.25	5.65
9	COMMUN & TRANS	121803.562	8.00	1114.02	48.05	42.15	3.20
10	WHOL-RET TRADE	202540.687	6.00	1134.73	0.22	0.0	3.30
11	SERVICES	194239.812	6.00	1148.39	10.17	10.63	3.60
12	MINING	13444.344	7.00	1825.90	969.18	730.36	1.00
	TOTAL	1135948.00	BALANCE OF PAYMENTS			-8880.543	

RESOURCES

		STOCKPILE	% USED	RECYCLE RATIO	SUBST. NUMBER	YEAR COMPLTD	STOCKPILE INCREASE
1	FIBRE & FOOD	4723.71	68.93	0.C			
2	IRON & STEEL	8982.81	10.17	0.545			
3	COPPER	8823.67	36.09	0.315			
4	NON-FERROUS	6904.97	30.95	0.129			
5	COAL	9110.93	8.89	0.C			
6	PETRO-NAT GAS	10370.15	57.70	0.C			
7	STONE & CLAY	9550.98	4.49	0.0			
8	CHEMICALS	9561.96	4.38	0.0			
9	LEAD & ZINC	5375.87	46.24	0.308			
10	ALUMINUM	6839.27	31.61	0.109			
15	URBAN LAND	3497.13	65.03	0.0			
16	ARABLE LAND	7843.86	47.71	0.0			
18	WORK UNITS	4077.50	95.82	0.0			

SYSTEM RESILIENCE

		PRESENT VALUE	THRESHOLD	RESILIENCE	ADJUSTED THRESHOLD
1	EDUCATION	1.970	1.741	0.159	1.741
2	EMPLOYMENT	1.161	1.034	0.124	0.0
3	TRANSPORTATION	0.538	0.465	0.196	0.465
4	WELFARE	77.788	71.763	0.106	71.763
5	HEALTH	54.712	45.050	0.264	45.050
6	SFTY & DEFENSE	0.535	0.461	0.199	0.461
7	MANUFACTURING	1.192	1.040	0.146	0.0
8	COMMERCIAL	0.513	0.455	0.157	0.455
9	GROTH POTENTIAL	0.520	0.437	0.242	0.437
10	AGRICULTURE	0.482	0.427	0.162	0.427
11	SERVICES	0.576	0.476	0.263	0.476
12	MINING	0.840	0.400	1.100	0.0

*****TOTAL SYSTEM EXPENDITURES*****
(MILLIONS OF DOLLARS)

RESOURCE	AMCUNT	UNIT PRICE	COST	
LAND				
URBAN LAND	6502.867	0.00010417	47941.230	
ARABLE LAND	7156.137	0.00011519	13198.891	
TOTAL				61140.121
RAW MATERIALS				
FOOD & FIBER	9772.117	0.00045000	129587.062	
IRON ORE	242.125	0.00031697	10778.566	
COPPER	253.871	0.00060692	20616.043	
CTHER NCN-IRCN	128.556	0.00009337	1541.517	
COAL	78.642	0.00006419	233.567	
PETRO-NAT GAS	179.558	0.00026317	1801.776	
STONE ANC CLAY	63.169	0.00008937	533.607	
CHEMICALS	60.704	0.00000800	41.483	
LEAD, ZINC	362.302	0.00009143	4344.891	
ALUMINUM	225.617	0.00048784	15705.875	
TCTAL				185184.187
LABOR				
WCRKERS COSTS	93487.187	0.00011415		783419.187
CAPITAL				
NEW CAPITAL GOODS				15560.129
ENVIRCNMENTAL MAINTENANCE				12993.047
CAPITAL MAINTENANCE				81369.125
TCTAL				109922.250
TCTAL COSTS				1139665.00

```
********************
*  YEAR  IS  1977  *
********************
```

POPULATION

	PEOPLE
EDUCATION	57316.230
INSTITUTIONAL	2481.153
NON-WORKER	34364.340
UNEMPLOYED	1825.905
PAID WORKER	100473.687
UNPAID WORKER	23163.651
TOTAL	219625.187
BIRTHS	3919.615
DEATHS	1992.522
MIGRATION	434.644

PRODUCTION

		INVST.FUNDS	MAINT	OUTPUT	IMPORTS	EXPORTS	GROWTH
1	EDUCATION	19422.086	3.00	1158.78	0.0	0.0	3.20
2	TRANS & COMMUN	9606.797	6.00	1274.01	0.0	0.0	4.30
3	HEALTH&WELFARE	46600.801	4.00	1422.14	0.0	0.0	6.50
4	PUBLIC SAFETY	23438.215	3.00	1205.53	0.0	0.0	3.70
5	ADMIN & OTHER	27757.680	3.00	1746.94	288.68	504.47	4.80
6	AGRICULTURE	47778.449	7.00	1062.27	165.34	121.98	2.00
7	NON-DUR MANUF	160505.125	9.00	1199.57	170.29	14.41	-1.02
8	DURABLE MANUF	288635.187	9.00	1166.24	99.61	134.32	5.65
9	COMMUN & TRANS	125643.250	8.00	1144.60	47.96	42.85	3.20
10	WHOL-RET TRADE	209166.375	6.00	1170.95	0.22	0.0	3.30
11	SERVICES	201053.562	6.00	1186.16	10.16	10.87	3.60
12	MINING	13602.586	7.00	1895.73	973.65	758.29	1.00
	TOTAL	1173209.00	BALANCE OF PAYMENTS			-8063.629	

RESOURCES

		STOCKPILE	% USED	RECYCLE RATIO	SUBST. NUMBER	YEAR COMPLTD	STOCKPILE INCREASE
1	FIBRE & FOOD	5784.96	64.51	0.0			
2	IRON & STEEL	8815.01	11.85	0.546			
3	COPPER	9917.49	37.26	0.319			
4	NON-FERROUS	6782.14	32.18	0.132			
5	COAL	9030.43	9.70	0.0			
6	PETRO-NAT GAS	10192.04	58.43	0.0			
7	STONE & CLAY	9486.04	5.14	0.C			
8	CHEMICALS	9500.00	5.00	0.0			
9	LEAD & ZINC	5089.01	49.11	0.332			
10	ALUMINUM	6627.46	33.73	0.123			
15	URBAN LAND	3309.43	66.91	0.0			
16	ARABLE LAND	7798.73	48.01	0.0			
18	WORK UNITS	4045.50	95.97	0.C			

SYSTEM RESILIENCE

		PRESENT VALUE	THRESHOLD	RESILIENCE	ADJUSTED THRESHOLD
1	EDUCATION	2.031	1.787	0.166	1.787
2	EMPLOYMENT	1.160	1.034	0.122	0.0
3	TRANSPORTATION	0.551	0.480	0.183	0.480
4	WELFARE	77.887	71.763	0.085	0.0
5	HEALTH	57.317	46.982	0.272	46.982
6	SFTY & DEFENSE	0.549	0.476	0.191	0.476
7	MANUFACTURING	1.177	1.040	0.133	0.0
8	COMMERCIAL	0.521	0.467	0.145	0.467
9	GROTH POTENTIAL	0.529	0.454	0.211	0.454
10	AGRICULTURE	0.484	0.438	0.133	0.438
11	SERVICES	0.591	0.496	0.241	0.496
12	MINING	0.863	0.400	1.158	0.0

*****TOTAL SYSTEM EXPENDITURES*****
(MILLIONS OF DOLLARS)

RESOURCE	AMCUNT	UNIT PRICE	COST
LAND			
URBAN LAND	6690.566	0.00010608	50361.109
ARABLE LAND	7201.270	0.00011549	13351.898
TCTAL			63713.008
RAW MATERIALS			
FOOD & FIBER	9807.535	0.00045000	130045.750
IRON ORE	259.215	0.00031770	11568.402
CCPPER	244.475	0.00062657	20506.137
CTHER NON-IRCN	138.709	0.00009451	1690.367
COAL	80.506	0.00006895	257.808
PETRO-NAT GAS	179.848	0.00026803	1844.096
STONE AND CLAY	64.936	0.00008946	553.886
CHEMICALS	61.963	0.00000800	42.874
LEAD,ZINC	375.258	0.00009275	4586.078
ALUMINUM	234.879	0.00048784	16363.504
TOTAL			187458.625
LABOR			
WCRKERS COSTS	96428.187	0.00011415	810796.875
CAPITAL			
NEW CAPITAL GOODS			15515.445
ENVIRONMENTAL MAINTENANCE			13639.754
CAPITAL MAINTENANCE			83942.812
TOTAL			113098.000
TOTAL COSTS			1175066.00

```
*********************
*  YEAR  IS  1978  *
*********************
```

POPULATION

	PEOPLE
EDUCATION	57256.270
INSTITUTIONAL	2524.729
NCN-WORKER	34141.887
UNEMPLOYED	1936.254
PAID WORKER	103689.625
UNPAID WORKER	22403.859
TOTAL	221953.000
BIRTHS	3961.158
DEATHS	2007.217
MIGRATION	439.250

PRODUCTION

		INVST.FUNDS	MAINT	OUTPUT	IMPORTS	EXPORTS	GROWTH
1	EDUCATION	20043.582	3.00	1195.82	0.0	0.0	3.20
2	TRANS & COMMUN	10011.746	6.00	1325.61	0.0	0.0	4.30
3	HEALTH&WELFARE	49629.832	4.00	1516.25	0.0	0.0	6.50
4	PUBLIC SAFETY	24305.418	3.00	1250.40	0.0	0.0	3.70
5	ADMIN & CTHER	29090.027	3.00	1806.54	288.61	474.56	4.80
6	AGRICULTURE	48755.031	7.0C	1087.15	165.57	120.81	2.00
7	NON-DUR MANUF	160278.437	9.00	1198.14	170.17	14.66	-1.02
8	DURABLE MANUF	303841.500	9.00	1230.97	99.76	144.42	5.65
9	COMMUN & TRANS	129686.875	8.00	1180.40	47.88	45.02	3.20
10	WHOL-RET TRADE	216093.562	6.00	1208.78	0.22	0.0	3.30
11	SERVICES	208265.812	6.00	1227.03	10.15	11.45	3.60
12	MINING	13766.277	7.00	1966.37	977.97	786.55	1.00
	TOTAL	1213767.00	BALANCE OF PAYMENTS			-5896.680	

RESOURCES

		STOCKPILE	% USED	RECYCLE RATIO	SUBST. NUMBER	YEAR COMPLTD	STOCKPILE INCREASE
1	FIBRE & FOOD	6863.60	60.74	0.C			
2	IRON & STEEL	8633.50	13.66	0.549			
3	COPPER	9738.29	38.39	0.324			
4	NON-FERROUS	6648.76	33.51	0.136			
5	COAL	8948.12	10.52	0.C			
6	PETRO-NAT GAS	10011.22	59.17	0.C			
7	STONE & CLAY	9418.77	5.81	0.0			
8	CHEMICALS	9436.23	5.64	0.C			
9	LEAD & ZINC	4793.77	52.06	0.359	6	1983	2000.00
10	ALUMINUM	6406.95	35.93	0.138			
15	URBAN LAND	3091.39	69.09	0.0			
16	ARABLE LAND	7696.91	48.69	0.C			
18	WORK UNITS	3970.19	96.17	0.C			

SYSTEM RESILIENCE

		PRESENT VALUE	THRESHOLD	RESILIENCE	ADJUSTED THRESHOLD
1	EDUCATION	2.099	1.836	0.175	1.836
2	EMPLOYMENT	1.162	1.059	0.125	1.059
3	TRANSPORTATION	0.565	0.494	0.176	0.494
4	WELFARE	78.308	71.763	0.091	0.0
5	HEALTH	60.056	49.049	0.278	49.049
6	SFTY & DEFENSE	0.563	0.490	0.184	0.490
7	MANUFACTURING	1.171	1.040	0.127	0.0
8	COMMERCIAL	0.532	0.478	0.140	0.478
9	GROTH POTENTIAL	0.541	0.469	0.193	0.469
10	AGRICULTURE	0.490	0.447	0.118	0.447
11	SERVICES	0.605	0.515	0.219	0.515
12	MINING	0.886	0.400	1.215	0.0

*****TOTAL SYSTEM EXPENDITURES*****
(MILLIONS OF DOLLARS)

RESOURCE	AMOUNT	UNIT PRICE	COST
LAND			
URBAN LAND	6908.609	0.00010830	53314.961
ARABLE LAND	7303.086	0.00011597	13618.047
TOTAL			66933.000
RAW MATERIALS			
FOOD & FIBER	9900.859	0.00045000	131148.937
IRON ORE	280.699	0.00031862	12570.559
COPPER	236.437	0.00064506	20450.648
OTHER NON-IRON	151.045	0.00009600	1875.618
COAL	82.304	0.00007425	284.734
PETRO-NAT GAS	180.816	0.00027303	1894.436
STONE AND CLAY	67.275	0.00008957	581.157
CHEMICALS	63.768	0.00000800	44.793
LEAD,ZINC	393.333	0.00009413	4903.711
ALUMINUM	247.554	0.00048784	17264.008
TOTAL			191018.250
LABOR			
WORKERS COSTS	99719.437	0.00011415	842356.125
CAPITAL			
NEW CAPITAL GOODS			15518.191
ENVIRONMENTAL MAINTENANCE			14386.801
CAPITAL MAINTENANCE			86772.687
TOTAL			116677.625
TOTAL COSTS			1216984.00

* YEAR IS 1979 *

POPULATION

	PEOPLE
EDUCATION	57134.945
INSTITUTIONAL	2565.544
NON-WORKER	33950.289
UNEMPLOYED	2045.220
PAID WORKER	107267.562
UNPAID WORKER	21341.312
TOTAL	224305.500
BIRTHS	4003.142
DEATHS	2022.966
MIGRATION	443.906

PRODUCTION

		INVST.FUNDS	MAINT	OUTPUT	IMPORTS	EXPORTS	GROWTH
1	EDUCATION	20684.965	3.00	1234.01	0.0	0.0	3.20
2	TRANS & COMMUN	10456.121	6.00	1380.57	0.0	0.0	4.30
3	HEALTH&WELFARE	52855.750	4.00	1616.20	0.0	0.0	6.50
4	PUBLIC SAFETY	25204.711	3.00	1296.82	0.0	0.0	3.70
5	ADMIN & OTHER	30486.328	3.00	1860.68	298.53	448.53	4.80
6	AGRICULTURE	49759.969	7.00	1109.72	165.76	104.65	2.00
7	NON-DUR MANUF	160764.750	9.00	1202.90	170.03	11.87	-1.02
8	DURABLE MANUF	320956.187	9.00	1307.50	99.84	123.66	5.65
9	COMMUN & TRANS	133975.437	8.00	1218.75	47.77	37.47	3.20
10	WHOL-RET TRADE	223369.750	6.00	1248.13	0.22	0.0	3.30
11	SERVICES	215945.562	6.00	1270.14	10.13	9.56	3.60
12	MINING	13940.777	7.00	2037.74	981.40	815.09	1.00
	TOTAL	1258399.00	BALANCE OF PAYMENTS			-12929.641	

RESOURCES

		STOCKPILE	% USED	RECYCLE RATIO	SUBST. NUMBER	YEAR COMPLTD	STOCKPILE INCREASE
1	FIBRE & FOOD	8002.44	57.31	0.0			
2	IRON & STEEL	8432.43	15.68	0.551			
3	COPPER	9563.47	39.50	0.328			
4	NON-FERROUS	6504.09	34.96	0.140			
5	COAL	8863.89	11.36	0.0			
6	PETRO-NAT GAS	9828.62	59.91	0.0			
7	STONE & CLAY	9348.71	6.51	0.0			
8	CHEMICALS	9370.23	6.30	0.0			
9	LEAD & ZINC	4836.98	54.68	0.383			
10	ALUMINUM	6176.21	38.24	0.155			
15	URBAN LAND	2850.09	71.50	0.0			
16	ARABLE LAND	7612.07	49.25	0.0			
18	WORK UNITS	4000.69	96.27	0.0			

SYSTEM RESILIENCE

		PRESENT VALUE	THRESHOLD	RESILIENCE	ADJUSTED THRESHOLD
1	EDUCATION	2.172	1.888	0.183	1.888
2	EMPLOYMENT	1.165	1.080	0.101	1.080
3	TRANSPORTATION	0.579	0.508	0.173	0.508
4	WELFARE	79.023	73.072	0.101	73.072
5	HEALTH	62.987	51.251	0.284	51.251
6	SFTY & DEFENSE	0.578	0.505	0.179	0.505
7	MANUFACTURING	1.170	1.040	0.126	0.0
8	COMMERCIAL	0.543	0.488	0.138	0.488
9	GROTH POTENTIAL	0.555	0.483	0.185	0.483
10	AGRICULTURE	0.495	0.456	0.107	0.456
11	SERVICES	0.619	0.533	0.201	0.533
12	MINING	0.908	0.400	1.271	0.0

*****TOTAL SYSTEM EXPENDITURES*****
(MILLIONS OF DOLLARS)

RESOURCE	AMOUNT	UNIT PRICE	COST	
LAND				
URBAN LAND	7149.906	0.00011087	56755.152	
ARABLE LAND	7387.934	0.00011649	13863.539	
TOTAL				70618.687
RAW MATERIALS				
FOOD & FIBER	10017.527	0.00045000	132700.000	
IRON ORE	311.377	0.00031977	13989.922	
COPPER	231.408	0.00066349	20632.055	
OTHER NON-IRON	164.351	0.00009756	2083.260	
COAL	84.238	0.00008013	315.334	
PETRO-NAT GAS	182.601	0.00027814	1954.352	
STONE AND CLAY	70.048	0.00008969	613.387	
CHEMICALS	65.995	0.00000800	47.083	
LEAD, ZINC	386.980	0.00009552	4920.883	
ALUMINUM	262.531	0.00048784	18327.855	
TOTAL				195583.875
LABOR				
WORKERS COSTS	103266.875	0.00011415		876992.000
CAPITAL				
NEW CAPITAL GOODS				15756.070
ENVIRONMENTAL MAINTENANCE				15345.074
CAPITAL MAINTENANCE				89923.625
TOTAL				121024.750
TOTAL COSTS				1264218.00

```
*********************
*  YEAR  IS  1980   *
*********************
```

POPULATION

	PEOPLE
EDUCATION	56974.020
INSTITUTIONAL	2605.776
NON-WORKER	33777.555
UNEMPLOYED	2153.759
PAID WORKER	111083.250
UNPAID WORKER	20088.324
TOTAL	226682.937
BIRTHS	4045.573
DEATHS	2038.297
MIGRATION	448.611

PRODUCTION

		INVST.FUNDS	MAINT	OUTPUT	IMPORTS	EXPORTS	GROWTH
1	EDUCATION	21346.875	3.00	1273.37	0.0	0.0	3.20
2	TRANS & COMMUN	10910.207	6.00	1435.11	0.0	0.0	4.30
3	HEALTH&WELFARE	56291.352	4.00	1722.35	0.0	0.0	6.50
4	PUBLIC SAFETY	26137.277	3.00	1344.84	0.0	0.0	3.70
5	ADMIN & OTHER	31949.652	3.00	1923.15	288.45	428.64	4.80
6	AGRICULTURE	50793.426	7.00	1118.51	165.98	74.29	2.00
7	NON-DUR MANUF	161052.437	9.00	1202.64	169.86	8.35	-1.02
8	DURABLE MANUF	338532.687	9.00	1352.77	99.80	90.07	5.65
9	COMMUN & TRANS	138360.687	8.00	1247.60	47.65	27.00	3.20
10	WHCL-RET TRADE	230849.937	6.00	1288.32	0.22	0.0	3.30
11	SERVICES	223798.125	6.00	1311.19	10.11	6.95	3.60
12	MINING	14125.879	7.00	2109.95	983.79	843.98	1.00
	TOTAL	1304147.00	BALANCE OF PAYMENTS			-23778.879	

RESOURCES

		STOCKPILE	% USED	RECYCLE RATIO	SUBST. NUMBER	YEAR COMPLTD	STOCKPILE INCREASE
1	FIBRE & FOOD	9307.65	53.69	0.0			
2	IRON & STEEL	8217.11	17.83	0.555			
3	COPPER	9393.94	40.57	0.332			
4	NON-FERROUS	6351.91	36.48	0.145			
5	COAL	8777.78	12.22	0.0			
6	PETRO-NAT GAS	9644.91	60.66	0.0			
7	STONE & CLAY	9275.86	7.23	0.0			
8	CHEMICALS	9302.87	6.97	0.0			
9	LEAD & ZINC	5175.25	56.87	0.405			
10	ALUMINUM	5941.13	40.59	0.173			
15	URBAN LAND	2646.70	73.53	0.0			
16	ARABLE LAND	7614.45	49.24	0.0			
18	WORK UNITS	4741.94	95.73	0.0			

SYSTEM RESILIENCE

		PRESENT VALUE	THRESHOLD	RESILIENCE	ADJUSTED THRESHOLD
1	EDUCATION	2.248	1.945	0.190	1.945
2	EMPLOYMENT	1.156	1.080	0.071	0.0
3	TRANSPORTATION	0.592	0.522	0.164	0.522
4	WELFARE	79.970	73.072	0.094	0.0
5	HEALTH	66.097	53.598	0.290	53.598
6	SFTY & DEFENSE	0.593	0.520	0.175	0.520
7	MANUFACTURING	1.150	1.040	0.106	0.0
8	COMMERCIAL	0.550	0.499	0.127	0.499
9	GRCTH POTENTIAL	0.565	0.498	0.169	0.498
10	AGRICULTURE	0.493	0.456	0.083	0.0
11	SERVICES	0.632	0.550	0.186	0.550
12	MINING	0.931	0.400	1.327	0.0

*****TOTAL SYSTEM EXPENDITURES*****
(MILLIONS OF DOLLARS)

RESOURCE	AMOUNT	UNIT PRICE	COST	
LAND				
URBAN LAND	7353.305	0.00011333	59710.250	
ARABLE LAND	7385.555	0.00011664	13923.031	
TOTAL				73633.250
RAW MATERIALS				
FOOD & FIBER	10064.281	0.00045000	133568.000	
IRON ORE	334.034	0.00032121	15062.809	
COPPER	225.142	0.00068179	20629.105	
OTHER NON-IRON	173.504	0.00009928	2241.051	
COAL	86.105	0.00008662	349.417	
PETRO-NAT GAS	183.717	0.00028336	2009.074	
STONE AND CLAY	71.853	0.00008983	633.725	
CHEMICALS	67.364	0.00000800	48.464	
LEAD, ZINC	370.931	0.00009677	4792.242	
ALUMINUM	271.460	0.00048784	18960.016	
TOTAL				198293.562
LABOR				
WORKERS COSTS	106341.312	0.00011415		905430.625
CAPITAL				
NEW CAPITAL GOODS				16136.473
ENVIRONMENTAL MAINTENANCE				16441.891
CAPITAL MAINTENANCE				93143.875
TOTAL				125722.187
TOTAL COSTS				1303079.00

```
********************
*  YEAR IS  1981   *
********************
```

POPULATION

	PEOPLE
EDUCATION	56957.336
INSTITUTIONAL	2671.976
NON-WORKER	33609.961
UNEMPLOYED	2275.142
PAID WORKER	113937.375
UNPAID WORKER	19433.613
TOTAL	229085.562
BIRTHS	4088.452
DEATHS	2042.826
MIGRATION	453.366

PRODUCTION

		INVST.FUNDS	MAINT	OUTPUT	IMPORTS	EXPORTS	GROWTH
1	EDUCATION	22029.965	3.00	1313.95	0.0	0.0	3.20
2	TRANS & COMMUN	11322.605	6.00	1484.74	0.0	0.0	4.30
3	HEALTH&WELFARE	59950.266	4.00	1835.10	0.0	0.0	6.50
4	PUBLIC SAFETY	27104.348	3.00	1394.53	0.0	0.0	3.70
5	ADMIN & OTHER	33483.215	3.00	1994.95	288.37	413.70	4.80
6	AGRICULTURE	51839.922	7.00	1117.02	166.48	67.76	2.00
7	NON-DUR MANUF	159594.062	9.00	1187.08	169.72	7.53	-1.02
8	DURABLE MANUF	354072.750	9.00	1377.79	99.68	83.79	5.65
9	COMMUN & TRANS	142580.000	8.00	1272.95	47.56	25.16	3.20
10	WHOL-RET TRADE	238265.312	6.00	1328.32	0.22	0.0	3.30
11	SERVICES	231340.437	6.00	1350.08	10.09	6.53	3.60
12	MINING	14305.734	7.00	2183.43	986.67	873.37	1.00
	TOTAL	1345887.00	BALANCE OF PAYMENTS			-25898.746	

RESOURCES

		STOCKPILE	% USED	RECYCLE RATIO	SUBST. NUMBER	YEAR COMPLTD	STOCKPILE INCREASE
1	FIBRE & FOOD	10826.72	49.77	0.0			
2	IRON & STEEL	7992.89	20.07	0.559			
3	COPPER	9228.36	41.62	0.337			
4	NON-FERROUS	6195.26	38.05	0.149			
5	COAL	8690.10	13.10	0.0			
6	PETRO-NAT GAS	9462.00	61.41	0.0			
7	STONE & CLAY	9204.01	7.96	0.0			
8	CHEMICALS	9234.95	7.65	0.0			
9	LEAD & ZINC	5706.87	58.66	0.423			
10	ALUMINUM	5705.49	42.95	0.193			
15	URBAN LAND	2480.44	75.20	0.0			
16	ARABLE LAND	7680.03	48.80	0.0			
18	WORK UNITS	4925.00	95.67	0.0			

SYSTEM RESILIENCE

		PRESENT VALUE	THRESHOLD	RESILIENCE	ADJUSTED THRESHOLD
1	EDUCATION	2.319	2.006	0.192	2.006
2	EMPLOYMENT	1.149	1.080	0.065	0.0
3	TRANSPORTATION	0.602	0.536	0.152	0.536
4	WELFARE	80.659	74.452	0.104	74.452
5	HEALTH	68.679	56.096	0.281	56.098
6	SFTY & DEFENSE	0.609	0.534	0.172	0.534
7	MANUFACTURING	1.126	1.040	0.083	0.0
8	COMMERCIAL	0.556	0.510	0.113	0.510
9	GROTH POTENTIAL	0.571	0.511	0.146	0.511
10	AGRICULTURE	0.488	0.456	0.070	0.0
11	SERVICES	0.646	0.567	0.173	0.567
12	MINING	0.953	0.400	1.383	0.0

*****TOTAL SYSTEM EXPENDITURES*****
(MILLIONS OF DOLLARS)

RESOURCE	AMCUNT	UNIT PRICE	COST	
LAND				
URBAN LANC	7519.562	0.00011541	62166.719	
ARABLE LAND	7319.969	0.00011664	13860.562	
TCTAL				76027.250
RAW MATERIALS				
FCOD & FIBER	10002.988	0.00045000	133075.750	
IRCN ORE	348.573	0.00032291	15793.629	
COPPER	220.592	0.00069998	20729.250	
CTHER NON-IRON	179.298	0.00010112	2358.144	
COAL	87.680	0.00009373	386.474	
PETRO-NAT GAS	182.905	0.00028864	2045.512	
STONE ANC CLAY	72.858	0.00008999	645.869	
CHEMICALS	67.916	C.00000800	49.184	
LEAD, ZINC	355.670	0.00009782	4656.777	
ALUMINUM	275.424	0.00048784	19311.660	
TCTAL				199052.000
LABOR				
WCRKERS COSTS	109008.375	0.00011415		929659.125
CAPITAL				
NEW CAFITAL GOODS				16117.617
ENVIRCNMENTAL MAINTENANCE				17302.250
CAPITAL MAINTENANCE				95998.625
TCTAL				129418.437
TCTAL COSTS				1334156.00

* YEAR IS 1982 *

POPULATION

	PEOPLE
EDUCATION	55531.230
INSTITUTIONAL	2746.552
NON-WORKER	33757.246
UNEMPLOYED	2407.392
PAID WORKER	116756.562
UNPAID WORKER	18914.410
TOTAL	231513.625
BIRTHS	4131.785
DEATHS	2050.123
MIGRATION	458.171

PRODUCTION

		INVST.FUNDS	MAINT	OUTPUT	IMPORTS	EXPORTS	GROWTH
1	EDUCATION	22734.914	3.00	1354.36	0.0	0.0	3.20
2	TRANS & COMMUN	11769.152	6.00	1533.91	0.0	0.0	4.30
3	HEALTH&WELFARE	63847.004	4.00	1950.56	0.0	0.0	6.50
4	PUBLIC SAFETY	28107.199	3.00	1442.54	0.0	0.0	3.70
5	ADMIN & OTHER	35090.387	3.00	2065.78	288.28	407.18	4.80
6	AGRICULTURE	52895.133	7.00	1138.44	166.96	74.06	2.00
7	NON-DUR MANUF	158646.937	9.00	1177.75	169.60	8.01	-1.02
8	DURABLE MANUF	371306.187	9.00	1435.75	99.50	93.64	5.65
9	COMMUN & TRANS	147011.000	8.00	1308.54	47.47	27.74	3.20
10	WHOL-RET TRADE	245994.437	6.00	1369.89	0.22	0.0	3.30
11	SERVICES	239341.375	6.00	1393.68	10.08	7.23	3.60
12	MINING	14475.641	7.00	2220.95	988.32	888.38	1.00
	TOTAL	1391218.00	BALANCE OF PAYMENTS			-22991.512	

RESOURCES

		STOCKPILE	% USED	RECYCLE RATIO	SUBST. NUMBER	YEAR COMPLTD	STOCKPILE INCREASE
1	FIBRE & FOOD	12336.82	46.62	0.0			
2	IRON & STEEL	7757.77	22.42	0.563			
3	COPPER	9060.63	42.68	0.341			
4	NON-FERROUS	6032.26	39.68	0.155			
5	COAL	8600.76	13.99	0.0			
6	PETRO-NAT GAS	9279.05	62.15	0.0			
7	STONE & CLAY	9129.31	8.71	0.0			
8	CHEMICALS	9165.70	8.34	0.0			
9	LEAD & ZINC	6286.85	60.23	0.439			
10	ALUMINUM	5464.26	45.36	0.214			
15	URBAN LAND	2267.48	77.33	0.0			
16	ARABLE LAND	7614.51	49.24	0.0			
18	WORK UNITS	4410.94	96.22	0.0			

SYSTEM RESILIENCE

		PRESENT VALUE	THRESHOLD	RESILIENCE	ADJUSTED THRESHOLD
1	EDUCATION	2.392	2.068	0.193	2.068
2	EMPLOYMENT	1.154	1.080	0.069	0.0
3	TRANSPORTATION	0.614	0.549	0.145	0.549
4	WELFARE	81.024	74.452	0.088	0.0
5	HEALTH	71.019	58.614	0.266	58.614
6	SFTY & DEFENSE	0.623	0.549	0.166	0.549
7	MANUFACTURING	1.119	1.040	0.077	0.0
8	COMMERCIAL	0.565	0.519	0.109	0.519
9	GROTH POTENTIAL	0.581	0.523	0.137	0.523
10	AGRICULTURE	0.492	0.456	0.079	0.0
11	SERVICES	0.660	0.582	0.165	0.582
12	MINING	0.959	0.400	1.398	0.0

*****TOTAL SYSTEM EXPENDITURES*****
(MILLIONS OF DOLLARS)

RESOURCE	AMCUNT	UNIT PRICE	COST	
LAND				
URBAN LAND	7732.516	0.00011778	65453.770	
ARABLE LAND	7385.488	0.00011664	13981.184	
TCTAL				79434.937
RAW MATERIALS				
FCOD & FIBER	10048.070	0.00045000	133576.437	
IRON ORE	366.450	0.00032491	16725.855	
CCPPER	224.190	0.00071851	21667.242	
CTHER NON-IRCN	187.346	0.00010310	2519.810	
CCAL	89.344	0.00010149	427.881	
PETRO-NAT GAS	182.948	0.00029397	2091.616	
STONE ANC CLAY	74.694	0.00009016	670.204	
CHEMICALS	69.252	0.00000800	50.816	
LEAD,ZINC	359.905	0.00009870	4773.578	
ALUMINUM	287.694	0.00048784	20116.707	
TCTAL				202619.875
LABOR				
WORKERS COSTS	112345.625	C.00011415		961585.875
CAPITAL				
NEW CAPITAL GOODS				17493.777
ENVIRCNMENTAL MAINTENANCE				18074.941
CAPITAL MAINTENANCE				99130.562
TOTAL				134699.250
TCTAL COSTS				1378339.00

```
********************
*  YEAR  IS  1983  *
********************
```

POPULATION

	PEOPLE
EDUCATION	57368.719
INSTITUTIONAL	2812.591
NON-WORKER	34069.207
UNEMPLOYED	2498.718
PAID WORKER	119631.625
UNPAID WORKER	17586.469
TOTAL	233967.437
BIRTHS	4175.574
DEATHS	2058.480
MIGRATION	463.027

PRODUCTION

		INVST.FUNDS	MAINT	OUTPUT	IMPORTS	EXPORTS	GROWTH
1	EDUCATION	23462.422	3.00	1368.81	0.0	0.0	3.20
2	TRANS & COMMUN	12309.695	6.00	1567.60	0.0	0.0	4.30
3	HEALTH&WELFARE	67997.000	4.00	2035.37	0.0	0.0	6.50
4	PUBLIC SAFETY	29147.156	3.00	1466.21	0.0	0.0	3.70
5	ADMIN & OTHER	36774.703	3.00	2108.56	285.39	357.91	4.80
6	AGRICULTURE	53986.172	7.00	1165.75	166.66	74.12	2.00
7	NON-DUR MANUF	159956.625	9.00	1182.58	168.60	7.86	-1.02
8	DURABLE MANUF	393162.312	9.00	1501.11	97.70	95.69	5.65
9	COMMUN & TRANS	151964.187	8.00	1328.75	46.97	27.53	3.20
10	WHOL-RET TRADE	254367.437	6.00	1388.49	0.21	0.0	3.30
11	SERVICES	248353.750	6.00	1418.04	9.91	7.19	3.60
12	MINING	14662.324	7.00	2230.57	976.86	892.23	1.00
	TOTAL	1446142.00	BALANCE OF PAYMENTS			-22709.301	

RESOURCES

		STOCKPILE	% USED	RECYCLE RATIO	SUBST. NUMBER	YEAR COMPLTD	STOCKPILE INCREASE
1	FIBRE & FOOD	13874.93	44.01	0.0			
2	IRON & STEEL	7513.26	24.87	0.568			
3	COPPER	8886.63	43.78	0.346			
4	NON-FERROUS	5863.62	41.36	0.160			
5	COAL	8510.26	14.90	0.0			
6	PETRO-NAT GAS	9094.86	62.90	0.0			
7	STONE & CLAY	9052.55	9.47	0.0			
8	CHEMICALS	9094.74	9.05	0.0			
9	LEAD & ZINC	6026.51	61.87	0.457			
10	ALUMINUM	5216.77	47.83	0.237			
15	URBAN LAND	2114.78	78.85	0.0			
16	ARABLE LAND	7521.91	49.85	0.0			
18	WORK UNITS	4960.44	95.85	0.0			

SYSTEM RESILIENCE

		PRESENT VALUE	THRESHOLD	RESILIENCE	ADJUSTED THRESHOLD
1	EDUCATION	2.403	2.133	0.162	2.133
2	EMPLOYMENT	1.153	1.080	0.068	0.0
3	TRANSPORTATION	0.619	0.562	0.127	0.562
4	WELFARE	81.456	74.452	0.094	0.0
5	HEALTH	72.366	61.095	0.235	61.095
6	SFTY & DEFENSE	0.627	0.564	0.141	0.564
7	MANUFACTURING	1.122	1.040	0.079	0.0
8	COMMERCIAL	0.568	0.519	0.095	0.0
9	GROTH POTENTIAL	0.588	0.535	0.124	0.535
10	AGRICULTURE	0.498	0.456	0.094	0.0
11	SERVICES	0.665	0.598	0.142	0.598
12	MINING	0.953	0.400	1.383	0.0

*****TOTAL SYSTEM EXPENDITURES*****
(MILLIONS OF DOLLARS)

RESOURCE	AMCUNT	UNIT PRICE	COST
LAND			
URBAN LAND	7885.219	0.00011989	68216.187
ARABLE LAND	7478.094	0.00011700	14165.633
TCTAL			82381.812
RAW MATERIALS			
FCOD & FIBER	10172.121	0.00045000	134928.875
IRON ORE	382.193	0.00032722	17597.129
CCPPER	233.348	0.00073793	23232.078
CTHER NCN-IRCN	194.706	0.00010522	2683.099
COAL	90.495	0.00010989	469.846
PETRO-NAT GAS	184.192	0.00029940	2147.377
STONE ANC CLAY	76.763	0.00009036	697.471
CHEMICALS	70.966	0.00000800	52.700
LEAD, ZINC	374.675	0.00009950	5025.906
ALUMINUM	300.372	0.00048784	21021.910
TCTAL			207856.187
LABOR			
WORKERS COSTS	114671.187	0.00011530	995057.875
CAPITAL			
NEW CAPITAL GOODS			19279.949
ENVIRCNMENTAL MAINTENANCE			19284.312
CAPITAL MAINTENANCE			103046.312
TOTAL			141610.562
TCTAL COSTS			1426905.00

```
********************
*  YEAR  IS  1984  *
********************
```

POPULATION

	PEOPLE
EDUCATION	57539.852
INSTITUTIONAL	2861.745
NON-WORKER	34543.844
UNEMPLOYED	2562.204
PAID WORKER	122193.750
UNPAID WORKER	16745.645
TOTAL	236447.250
BIRTHS	4219.832
DEATHS	2067.873
MIGRATION	467.935

PRODUCTION

		INVST.FUNDS	MAINT	OUTPUT	IMPORTS	EXPORTS	GROWTH
1	EDUCATION	24213.207	3.00	1398.49	0.0	0.0	3.20
2	TRANS & COMMUN	12788.781	6.00	1608.83	0.0	0.0	4.30
3	HEALTH&WELFARE	72416.750	4.00	2145.83	0.0	0.0	6.50
4	PUBLIC SAFETY	30225.590	3.00	1506.14	0.0	0.0	3.70
5	ADMIN & OTHER	38539.863	3.00	2141.95	282.53	318.10	4.80
6	AGRICULTURE	55109.316	7.00	1187.60	166.46	77.28	2.00
7	NON-DUR MANUF	158839.375	9.00	1169.07	168.05	7.96	-0.59
8	DURABLE MANUF	412040.125	9.00	1557.55	96.66	101.62	5.48
9	COMMUN & TRANS	156661.000	8.00	1356.33	46.48	28.77	3.20
10	WHCL-RET TRADE	262607.250	6.00	1419.01	0.21	0.0	3.30
11	SERVICES	256832.500	6.00	1451.30	9.81	7.53	3.60
12	MINING	14861.664	7.00	2260.75	969.36	904.30	1.00
	TOTAL	1495134.00	BALANCE OF PAYMENTS		-21241.555		

RESOURCES

		STOCKPILE	% USED	RECYCLE RATIO	SUBST. NUMBER	YEAR COMPLTD	STOCKPILE INCREASE
1	FIBRE & FOOD	15643.52	41.13	0.0			
2	IRON & STEEL	7260.96	27.39	0.575			
3	COPPER	8707.21	44.91	0.351			
4	NON-FERROUS	5690.15	43.10	0.166			
5	COAL	8418.87	15.81	0.0			
6	PETRO-NAT GAS	8911.42	63.65	0.0			
7	STONE & CLAY	8974.14	10.26	0.0			
8	CHEMICALS	9022.59	9.77	0.0			
9	LEAD & ZINC	5760.97	63.55	0.475			
10	ALUMINUM	4965.00	50.35	0.261			3000.00
15	URBAN LAND	1945.73	80.54	0.0	5	1985	
16	ARABLE LAND	7459.71	50.27	0.0			
18	WORK UNITS	4874.07	96.01	0.0			

SYSTEM RESILIENCE

		PRESENT VALUE	THRESHOLD	RESILIENCE	ADJUSTED THRESHOLD
1	EDUCATION	2.448	2.187	0.148	2.187
2	EMPLOYMENT	1.154	1.060	0.069	0.0
3	TRANSPORTATION	0.627	0.574	0.115	0.574
4	WELFARE	83.749	75.853	0.125	75.853
5	HEALTH	74.983	63.349	0.227	63.349
6	SFTY & DEFENSE	0.637	0.577	0.129	0.577
7	MANUFACTURING	1.116	1.040	0.073	0.0
8	COMMERCIAL	0.574	0.529	0.106	0.529
9	GROTH POTENTIAL	0.595	0.545	0.112	0.545
10	AGRICULTURE	0.502	0.464	0.102	0.464
11	SERVICES	0.672	0.611	0.124	0.611
12	MINING	0.956	0.400	1.390	0.0

*****TOTAL SYSTEM EXPENDITURES*****
(MILLIONS OF DOLLARS)

RESOURCE	AMOUNT	UNIT PRICE	COST
LAND			
URBAN LAND	8054.270	0.00012195	71116.812
ARABLE LAND	7540.289	0.00011743	14326.637
TOTAL			85443.437
RAW MATERIALS			
FOOD & FIBER	10193.926	0.00045000	134977.812
IRON CRE	395.719	0.00032986	18394.121
COPPER	241.464	0.00075836	24751.238
CTHER NON-IRCN	201.243	0.00010748	2840.267
CCAL	91.396	0.00011893	515.001
PETRC-NAT GAS	183.443	0.00030489	2185.168
STCNE AND CLAY	78.411	0.00009059	721.217
CHEMICALS	72.144	0.00000800	54.253
LEAD,ZINC	386.863	0.00010033	5252.219
ALUMINUM	311.310	0.00048784	21804.750
TOTAL			211495.812
LABOR			
WCRKERS COSTS	117319.687	0.00011645	1032088.50
CAPITAL			
NEW CAPITAL GOODS			20693.078
ENVIRCNMENTAL MAINTENANCE			20417.000
CAPITAL MAINTENANCE			106429.625
TOTAL			147539.687
TOTAL COSTS			1476566.00

YEAR IS 1985

POPULATION

	PEOPLE
EDUCATION	57963.133
INSTITUTIONAL	2927.303
NON-WORKER	34877.398
UNEMPLOYED	2653.585
PAID WORKER	124660.562
UNPAID WORKER	15871.137
TOTAL	238953.375
BIRTHS	4264.559
DEATHS	2078.192
MIGRATION	472.894

PRODUCTION

		INVST.FUNDS	MAINT	OUTPUT	IMPORTS	EXPORTS	GROWTH
1	EDUCATION	24988.020	3.00	1400.45	0.0	0.0	3.20
2	TRANS & COMMUN	13341.801	6.00	1650.00	0.0	0.0	4.30
3	HEALTH&WELFARE	77123.750	4.00	2221.48	0.0	0.0	6.50
4	PUBLIC SAFETY	31343.926	3.00	1519.58	0.0	0.0	3.70
5	ADMIN & OTHER	40389.750	3.00	2159.45	276.98	258.33	4.80
6	AGRICULTURE	56245.781	7.00	1208.88	165.59	74.08	2.00
7	NON-DUR MANUF	159878.312	9.00	1172.51	166.90	7.52	2.25
8	DURABLE MANUF	434011.750	9.00	1608.98	94.50	98.86	4.44
9	COMMUN & TRANS	161771.250	8.00	1372.19	45.70	27.41	3.20
10	WHOL-RET TRADE	271375.937	6.00	1428.29	0.21	0.0	3.30
11	SERVICES	266168.687	6.00	1468.97	9.64	7.18	3.60
12	MINING	15054.477	7.00	2428.14	951.15	971.26	1.00
	TOTAL	1551692.00	BALANCE OF PAYMENTS			-22101.738	

RESOURCES

		STOCKPILE	% USED	RECYCLE RATIO	SUBST. NUMBER	YEAR COMPLTD	STOCKPILE INCREASE
1	FIBRE & FOOD	17462.17	38.72	0.0			
2	IRON & STEEL	7001.38	29.99	0.581			
3	COPPER	8521.88	46.09	0.356			
4	NON-FERROUS	5511.28	44.89	0.173			
5	COAL	8326.14	16.74	0.0			
6	PETRO-NAT GAS	8726.94	64.40	0.0			
7	STONE & CLAY	8893.16	11.07	0.0			
8	CHEMICALS	8948.47	10.52	0.0			
9	LEAD & ZINC	5490.82	65.26	0.495			
10	ALUMINUM	5217.42	52.62	0.284			
15	URBAN LAND	2639.54	73.60	0.0			
16	ARABLE LAND	6968.14	53.55	0.0			
18	WORK UNITS	5548.50	95.55	0.0			

SYSTEM RESILIENCE

		PRESENT VALUE	THRESHOLD	RESILIENCE	ADJUSTED THRESHOLD
1	EDUCATION	2.439	2.187	0.115	0.0
2	EMPLOYMENT	1.150	1.080	0.065	0.0
3	TRANSPORTATION	0.632	0.584	0.102	0.584
4	WELFARE	83.716	75.853	0.104	0.0
5	HEALTH	75.888	65.676	0.198	65.676
6	SFTY & DEFENSE	0.636	0.577	0.103	0.0
7	MANUFACTURING	1.116	1.040	0.073	0.0
8	COMMERCIAL	0.574	0.529	0.086	0.0
9	GROTH POTENTIAL	0.598	0.545	0.096	0.0
10	AGRICULTURE	0.505	0.464	0.090	0.0
11	SERVICES	0.673	0.611	0.100	0.0
12	MINING	1.016	0.400	1.540	0.0

*****TOTAL SYSTEM EXPENDITURES*****
(MILLIONS OF DOLLARS)

RESOURCE	AMCUNT	UNIT PRICE	COST
LAND			
URBAN LAND	7360.457	0.00012195	65106.719
ARABLE LAND	8031.859	0.00011958	18367.762
TCTAL			83474.437
RAW MATERIALS			
FOOD & FIBER	10289.875	C.00045000	136017.875
IRON ORE	408.713	0.00033282	19171.211
CCPPER	250.367	0.00077983	26326.703
OTHER NCN-IRCN	208.596	0.00010987	3003.253
COAL	92.732	0.00012865	565.560
PETRO-NAT GAS	184.481	0.00031046	2239.977
STONE AND CLAY	80.976	0.00009083	747.542
CHEMICALS	74.123	0.00000800	55.971
LEAD,ZINC	398.586	0.00010119	5468.367
ALUMINUM	321.598	0.00048784	22523.801
TOTAL			216119.937
LABOR			
WORKERS COSTS	119112.062	C.00011879	1071354.00
CAPITAL			
NEW CAPITAL GOODS			19963.594
ENVIRCNMENTAL MAINTENANCE			21660.605
CAPITAL MAINTENANCE			110422.437
TOTAL			152046.625
TCTAL COSTS			1522994.00

```
********************
*  YEAR  IS  1986  *
********************
```

POPULATION

	PEOPLE
EDUCATION	58114.336
INSTITUTIONAL	2976.434
NON-WORKER	35389.516
UNEMPLOYED	2714.927
PAID WORKER	126768.250
UNPAID WORKER	15522.336
TOTAL	241486.062
BIRTHS	4309.758
DEATHS	2089.531
MIGRATION	477.906

PRODUCTION

		INVST.FUNDS	MAINT	OUTPUT	IMPORTS	EXPORTS	GROWTH
1	EDUCATION	25787.625	3.00	1417.81	0.0	0.0	3.20
2	TRANS & COMMUN	13899.676	6.00	1699.75	0.0	0.0	4.30
3	HEALTH&WELFARE	82136.750	4.00	2323.57	0.0	0.0	6.50
4	PUBLIC SAFETY	32503.641	3.00	1549.68	0.0	0.0	3.70
5	ADMIN & OTHER	42328.430	3.00	2180.38	271.53	276.31	4.80
6	AGRICULTURE	57412.039	7.00	1218.44	163.93	77.76	2.00
7	NON-DUR MANUF	163806.750	9.00	1202.70	166.05	8.03	2.25
8	DURABLE MANUF	452393.937	9.00	1647.17	92.92	105.40	4.44
9	COMMUN & TRANS	166956.187	8.00	1393.99	44.93	29.00	3.20
10	WHCL-RET TRADE	280348.812	6.00	1449.21	0.20	0.0	3.30
11	SERVICES	275644.562	6.00	1495.97	9.47	7.62	3.60
12	MINING	15256.820	7.00	2462.47	932.09	984.99	1.00
	TOTAL	1608473.00	BALANCE OF PAYMENTS			-18970.055	

RESOURCES

		STOCKPILE	% USED	RECYCLE RATIO	SUBST. NUMBER	YEAR COMPLTD	STOCKPILE INCREASE
1	FIBRE & FOOD	19318.37	36.78	0.0			
2	IRON & STEEL	6736.84	32.63	0.589			6000.00
3	COPPER	8333.06	47.28	0.362			
4	NON-FERROUS	5329.34	46.71	0.179			
5	COAL	8231.75	17.68	0.0			
6	PETRO-NAT GAS	8538.02	65.17	0.0			
7	STONE & CLAY	8810.40	11.90	0.0			
8	CHEMICALS	8872.63	11.27	0.0			
9	LEAD & ZINC	5217.81	66.99	0.515			
10	ALUMINUM	5909.78	54.54	0.304			
15	URBAN LAND	2485.40	75.15	0.0			
16	ARABLE LAND	6976.31	53.49	0.0			
18	WORK UNITS	5353.32	95.78	0.0			

SYSTEM RESILIENCE

		PRESENT VALUE	THRESHOLD	RESILIENCE	ADJUSTED THRESHOLD
1	EDUCATION	2.466	2.237	0.127	2.237
2	EMPLOYMENT	1.153	1.080	0.068	0.0
3	TRANSPORTATION	0.641	0.584	0.096	0.0
4	WELFARE	85.585	77.425	0.128	77.425
5	HEALTH	78.065	67.718	0.189	67.718
6	SFTY & DEFENSE	0.642	0.588	0.113	0.588
7	MANUFACTURING	1.124	1.040	0.081	0.0
8	COMMERCIAL	0.577	0.529	0.092	0.0
9	GROTH POTENTIAL	0.603	0.556	0.105	0.556
10	AGRICULTURE	0.505	0.464	0.087	0.0
11	SERVICES	0.676	0.624	0.106	0.624
12	MINING	1.020	0.400	1.549	0.0

*****TOTAL SYSTEM EXPENDITURES*****
(MILLIONS OF DOLLARS)

RESOURCE	AMOUNT	UNIT PRICE	COST
LAND			
URBAN LAND	7514.598	0.00012195	66380.812
ARABLE LAND	8023.691	0.00012055	18538.430
TOTAL			84919.187
RAW MATERIALS			
FOOD & FIBER	10480.371	0.00045000	138955.250
IRON ORE	418.330	0.00033611	19818.402
COPPER	256.073	0.00080221	27717.605
OTHER NON-IRON	213.350	0.00011239	3144.415
COAL	94.389	0.00013911	622.019
PETRO-NAT GAS	188.921	0.00031619	2334.577
STONE AND CLAY	82.764	0.00009111	756.971
CHEMICALS	75.841	0.00000801	57.359
LEAD, ZINC	408.104	0.00010206	5646.445
ALUMINUM	329.189	0.00048784	23057.090
TOTAL			222119.875
LABOR			
WORKERS COSTS	121414.937	0.00012118	1115016.00
CAPITAL			
NEW CAPITAL GOODS			19853.090
ENVIRONMENTAL MAINTENANCE			22911.680
CAPITAL MAINTENANCE			114398.750
TOTAL			157163.500
TOTAL COSTS			1579218.00

```
********************
*  YEAR  IS  1987  *
********************
```

POPULATION

	PEOPLE
EDUCATION	58345.988
INSTITUTIONAL	3028.758
NON-WORKER	35870.578
UNEMPLOYED	2783.326
PAID WORKER	129158.312
UNPAID WORKER	14857.434
TOTAL	244045.562
BIRTHS	4355.437
DEATHS	2101.856
MIGRATION	482.972

PRODUCTION

		INVST.FUNDS	MAINT	OUTPUT	IMPORTS	EXPORTS	GROWTH
1	EDUCATION	26612.816	3.00	1435.71	0.0	0.0	3.20
2	TRANS & COMMUN	14453.500	6.00	1738.49	0.0	0.0	4.30
3	HEALTH&WELFARE	87475.562	4.00	2430.24	0.0	0.0	6.50
4	PUBLIC SAFETY	33706.266	3.00	1580.71	0.0	0.0	3.70
5	ADMIN & OTHER	44360.168	3.00	2280.58	266.19	270.56	4.80
6	AGRICULTURE	58601.629	7.00	1250.32	163.65	80.15	2.00
7	NON-DUR MANUF	167009.250	9.00	1223.36	165.11	8.20	2.53
8	DURABLE MANUF	470215.937	9.00	1689.68	91.29	108.61	4.34
9	COMMUN & TRANS	172168.937	8.00	1416.20	44.17	29.59	3.20
10	WHOL-RET TRADE	289478.875	6.00	1468.79	0.20	0.0	3.30
11	SERVICES	285186.125	6.00	1520.94	9.30	7.78	3.60
12	MINING	15461.820	7.00	2515.47	920.78	1006.19	1.00
	TOTAL	1664729.00	BALANCE OF PAYMENTS			-17251.570	

RESOURCES

		STOCKPILE	% USED	RECYCLE RATIO	SUBST. NUMBER	YEAR COMPLTD	STOCKPILE INCREASE
1	FIBRE & FOOD	21294.15	35.01	0.0			
2	IRON & STEEL	7829.73	34.87	0.596			
3	COPPER	8140.22	48.50	0.368			
4	NON-FERROUS	5143.82	48.56	0.187			
5	COAL	8135.02	18.65	0.0			
6	PETRO-NAT GAS	8345.87	65.96	0.0			
7	STONE & CLAY	8725.68	12.74	0.0			
8	CHEMICALS	8795.10	12.05	0.0			
9	LEAD & ZINC	4941.69	68.74	0.536			
10	ALUMINUM	6889.18	56.15	0.322			
15	URBAN LAND	2346.28	76.54	0.0			
16	ARABLE LAND	6853.44	54.31	0.0			
18	WORK UNITS	5203.69	95.97	0.0			

SYSTEM RESILIENCE

		PRESENT VALUE	THRESHOLD	RESILIENCE	ADJUSTED THRESHOLD
1	EDUCATION	2.489	2.283	0.112	2.283
2	EMPLOYMENT	1.153	1.080	0.068	0.0
3	TRANSPORTATION	0.646	0.596	0.106	0.596
4	WELFARE	87.314	79.057	0.128	79.057
5	HEALTH	80.239	69.788	0.185	69.788
6	SFTY & DEFENSE	0.648	0.599	0.101	0.599
7	MANUFACTURING	1.128	1.040	0.085	0.0
8	COMMERCIAL	0.580	0.529	0.098	0.0
9	GROTH POTENTIAL	0.608	0.556	0.093	0.0
10	AGRICULTURE	0.512	0.472	0.104	0.472
11	SERVICES	0.685	0.624	0.099	0.0
12	MINING	1.031	0.400	1.577	0.0

*****TOTAL SYSTEM EXPENDITURES*****
(MILLIONS OF DOLLARS)

RESOURCE	AMCUNT	UNIT PRICE	COST
LAND			
URBAN LAND	7653.719	0.00012195	67640.062
ARABLE LAND	8146.562	0.00012106	18875.086
TCTAL			86515.125
RAW MATERIALS			
FCOD & FIBER	10698.309	0.00045000	141662.062
IRON ORE	428.952	0.00033939	20525.043
COPPER	262.609	0.00082544	29255.145
OTHER NCN-IRCN	218.808	0.00011503	3301.541
CCAL	96.728	0.00015040	689.427
PETRC-NAT GAS	192.156	0.00032211	2418.893
STONE AND CLAY	84.724	0.00009141	788.806
CHEMICALS	77.528	0.00000804	58.963
LEAD,ZINC	418.295	0.00010294	5840.789
ALUMINUM	337.613	0.00048784	23650.254
TCTAL			228190.625
LABCR			
WCRKERS COSTS	123954.625	0.00012361	1161782.00
CAPITAL			
NEW CAPITAL GOODS			19169.094
ENVIRCNMENTAL MAINTENANCE			24170.258
CAPITAL MAINTENANCE			118294.562
TCTAL			161633.875
TCTAL COSTS			1638120.00

```
********************
*  YEAR  IS  1988  *
********************
```

POPULATION

	PEOPLE
EDUCATION	58548.379
INSTITUTIONAL	3083.341
NON-WORKER	36300.035
UNEMPLOYED	2858.508
PAID WORKER	131938.812
UNPAID WORKER	13902.902
TOTAL	246632.187
BIRTHS	4401.602
DEATHS	2117.043
MIGRATION	488.091

PRODUCTION

		INVST.FUNDS	MAINT	OUTPUT	IMPORTS	EXPORTS	GROWTH
1	EDUCATION	27464.414	3.00	1454.25	0.0	0.0	3.20
2	TRANS & COMMUN	15108.371	6.00	1794.25	0.0	0.0	4.30
3	HEALTH&WELFARE	93161.375	4.00	2542.26	0.0	0.0	6.50
4	PUBLIC SAFETY	34953.387	3.00	1612.92	0.0	0.0	3.70
5	ADMIN & OTHER	46489.426	3.00	2347.48	260.95	313.73	4.80
6	AGRICULTURE	59814.703	7.00	1274.08	163.27	84.03	2.00
7	NON-DUR MANUF	172964.687	9.00	1267.08	164.17	8.74	2.53
8	DURABLE MANUF	492210.750	9.00	1740.85	89.69	115.14	4.34
9	COMMUN & TRANS	177935.250	8.00	1440.70	43.42	30.97	3.20
10	WHOL-RET TRADE	299296.187	6.00	1490.71	0.20	0.0	3.30
11	SERVICES	295847.000	6.00	1550.49	9.14	8.16	3.60
12	MINING	15669.195	7.00	2556.77	909.00	1022.71	1.00
	TOTAL	1730914.00	BALANCE OF PAYMENTS			-13529.125	

RESOURCES

		STOCKPILE	% USED	RECYCLE RATIO	SUBST. NUMBER	YEAR COMPLTD	STOCKPILE INCREASE
1	FIBRE & FOOD	23337.18	33.58	0.0			
2	IRON & STEEL	10144.77	36.60	0.602			
3	COPPER	7942.64	49.75	0.374			
4	NON-FERROUS	4954.08	50.46	0.194			
5	COAL	8035.73	19.64	0.0			
6	PETRO-NAT GAS	8147.54	66.77	0.0			
7	STONE & CLAY	8638.50	13.62	0.0			
8	CHEMICALS	8715.22	12.85	0.0			
9	LEAD & ZINC	4660.95	70.51	0.558			2000.00
10	ALUMINUM	7948.70	57.52	0.337			
15	URBAN LAND	2163.39	78.37	0.0			
16	ARABLE LAND	6780.17	54.80	0.0			
18	WORK UNITS	5107.25	96.13	0.0			

SYSTEM RESILIENCE

		PRESENT VALUE	THRESHOLD	RESILIENCE	ADJUSTED THRESHOLD
1	EDUCATION	2.516	2.324	0.102	2.324
2	EMPLOYMENT	1.155	1.080	0.070	0.0
3	TRANSPORTATION	0.656	0.606	0.101	0.606
4	WELFARE	88.937	80.709	0.125	80.709
5	HEALTH	82.451	71.878	0.181	71.878
6	SFTY & DEFENSE	0.654	0.599	0.092	0.0
7	MANUFACTURING	1.140	1.040	0.097	0.0
8	COMMERCIAL	0.584	0.539	0.105	0.539
9	GROTH POTENTIAL	0.615	0.566	0.106	0.566
10	AGRICULTURE	0.517	0.472	0.094	0.0
11	SERVICES	0.693	0.636	0.112	0.636
12	MINING	1.037	0.400	1.592	0.0

*****TOTAL SYSTEM EXPENDITURES*****
(MILLIONS OF DOLLARS)

	RESOURCE	AMCUNT	UNIT PRICE	COST	
LAND					
	URBAN LAND	7836.609	0.00012195	69178.750	
	ARABLE LAND	8219.828	0.00012164	19140.141	
	TOTAL				88318.875
RAW MATERIALS					
	FCOD & FIBER	11002.523	0.00045000	145957.562	
	IRCN ORE	441.844	0.00034220	21319.148	
	COPPER	270.216	0.00084961	31011.324	
	CTHER NCN-IRCN	225.161	0.00011780	3482.181	
	COAL	99.287	0.00016262	764.266	
	PETRO-NAT GAS	198.325	0.00032826	2540.254	
	STONE AND CLAY	87.179	0.00009174	815.048	
	CHEMICALS	79.983	0.00000807	60.964	
	LEAD, ZINC	431.150	0.00010382	6070.168	
	ALUMINCM	347.779	0.00048784	24364.168	
	TCTAL				236384.812
LABOR					
	WCRKERS COSTS	126831.562	0.00012610		1213223.00
CAPITAL					
	NEW CAPITAL GCODS				19051.133
	ENVIRCNMENTAL MAINTENANCE				25674.289
	CAPITAL MAINTENANCE				122993.125
	TCTAL				167718.500
TCTAL COSTS					1705644.00

```
*********************
*  YEAR  IS  1989  *
*********************
```

POPULATION

	PEOPLE
EDUCATION	58657.254
INSTITUTIONAL	3131.278
NCN-WORKER	36788.715
UNEMPLOYED	2922.437
PAID WORKER	135C52.937
UNPAID WORKER	12693.312
TOTAL	249246.250
BIRTHS	4448.254
DEATHS	2133.151
MIGRATICN	493.264

PRODUCTION

		INVST.FUNDS	MAINT	OUTPUT	IMPORTS	EXPORTS	GROWTH
1	EDUCATION	28343.262	3.00	1472.46	0.0	0.0	3.20
2	TRANS & COMMUN	15776.590	6.00	1843.24	0.0	0.0	4.30
3	HEALTH&WELFARE	99216.812	4.00	2658.67	0.0	0.0	6.50
4	PUBLIC SAFETY	36246.648	3.00	1644.69	0.0	0.0	3.70
5	ADMIN & CTHER	48720.887	3.00	2466.05	255.80	319.18	4.80
6	AGRICULTURE	61070.141	7.00	1300.81	162.68	84.55	2.00
7	NON-DUR MANUF	178659.375	9.00	1303.84	163.22	8.87	2.53
8	DURABLE MANUF	514422.000	9.00	1794.41	88.11	116.96	4.34
9	COMMUN & TRANS	183824.125	8.00	1465.48	42.68	31.05	3.20
10	WHOL-RET TRADE	309385.437	6.00	1512.43	0.19	0.0	3.30
11	SERVICES	306719.562	6.00	1579.34	8.97	8.19	3.60
12	MINING	15897.395	7.00	2596.07	896.15	1038.43	1.00
	TOTAL	1798280.00	BALANCE OF PAYMENTS			-12007.434	

RESOURCES

		STOCKPILE	% USED	RECYCLE RATIO	SUBST. NUMBER	YEAR COMPLTD	STOCKPILE INCREASE
1	FIBRE & FCCD	25576.71	32.11	0.0			
2	IRON & STEEL	13297.11	37.92	0.606			
3	COPPER	774C.16	51.03	0.380			
4	NON-FERRCUS	476C.02	52.40	0.203			
5	CCAL	7933.50	20.66	0.0			
6	PETRO-NAT GAS	7943.92	67.60	0.0			
7	STONE & CLAY	8548.86	14.51	0.C			
8	CHEMICALS	8633.09	13.67	0.0			
9	LEAD & ZINC	4581.03	72.20	0.579			
10	ALUMINUM	7681.91	58.94	0.354			
15	URBAN LAND	1989.28	80.11	0.0	5	1990	
16	ARABLE LAND	5693.31	55.38	0.C			
18	WORK UNITS	524C.50	96.12	0.C			

SYSTEM RESILIENCE

		PRESENT VALUE	THRESHOLD	RESILIENCE	ADJUSTED THRESHOLD
1	EDUCATION	2.546	2.324	0.095	0.0
2	EMPLCYMENT	1.154	1.080	0.069	0.0
3	TRANSPORTATION	0.664	0.606	0.096	0.0
4	WELFARE	90.974	82.354	0.127	82.354
5	HEALTH	84.907	73.993	0.181	73.993
6	SFTY & DEFENSE	0.660	0.610	0.101	0.610
7	MANUFACTURING	1.147	1.060	0.103	1.060
8	COMMERCIAL	0.588	0.539	0.091	0.0
9	GROTH POTENTIAL	0.622	0.566	0.099	0.0
10	AGRICULTURE	0.522	0.481	0.105	0.481
11	SERVICES	0.705	0.647	0.108	0.647
12	MINING	1.042	0.400	1.604	0.0

*****TOTAL SYSTEM EXPENDITURES*****
(MILLIONS OF DOLLARS)

RESOURCE	AMOUNT	UNIT PRICE	COST	
LAND				
URBAN LAND	8010.719	0.00012195	70713.000	
ARABLE LAND	8306.691	0.00012217	19421.000	
TOTAL				90134.000
RAW MATERIALS				
FOOD & FIBER	11283.246	0.00045000	149811.312	
IRON ORE	455.227	0.00034446	22115.797	
COPPER	278.151	0.00087479	32898.641	
OTHER NON-IRON	231.785	0.00012070	3676.439	
COAL	102.230	0.00017585	850.640	
PETRO-NAT GAS	203.621	0.00033456	2656.328	
STONE AND CLAY	89.638	0.00009210	842.545	
CHEMICALS	82.135	0.00000810	63.025	
LEAD,ZINC	444.311	0.00010472	6310.262	
ALUMINUM	358.372	0.00048784	25110.375	
TOTAL				244335.187
LABOR				
WORKERS COSTS	129812.437	0.00012863	1267449.00	
CAPITAL				
NEW CAPITAL GOODS				19260.277
ENVIRONMENTAL MAINTENANCE				27385.230
CAPITAL MAINTENANCE				127751.625
TOTAL				174397.125
TOTAL COSTS				1776315.00

****
* YEAR IS 1990 *
****

POPULATION

	PEOPLE
EDUCATION	59078.441
INSTITUTIONAL	3187.312
NON-WORKER	37250.246
UNEMPLOYED	3012.617
PAID WORKER	138021.187
UNPAID WORKER	11338.043
TOTAL	251888.000
BIRTHS	4495.402
DEATHS	2147.244
MIGRATION	498.492

PRODUCTION

		INVST.FUNDS	MAINT	OUTPUT	IMPORTS	EXPORTS	GROWTH
1	EDUCATION	29250.234	3.00	1490.93	0.0	0.0	3.20
2	TRANS & COMMUN	15455.902	6.00	1906.05	0.0	0.0	4.30
3	HEALTH&WELFARE	105665.812	4.00	2780.38	0.0	0.0	6.50
4	PUBLIC SAFETY	37587.762	3.00	1677.17	0.0	0.0	3.70
5	ADMIN & OTHER	51059.457	3.00	2541.98	250.75	312.54	4.80
6	AGRICULTURE	62351.715	7.00	1324.90	162.12	87.34	2.00
7	NON-DUR MANUF	184013.250	9.00	1338.99	162.47	9.23	2.53
8	DURABLE MANUF	536731.250	9.00	1845.71	86.77	122.01	4.34
9	COMMUN & TRANS	189817.937	8.00	1495.02	41.94	32.13	3.20
10	WHOL-RET TRADE	319723.562	6.00	1536.71	0.19	0.0	3.30
11	SERVICES	317813.562	6.00	1612.56	8.81	8.48	3.60
12	MINING	16129.738	7.00	2637.05	883.59	1054.82	1.00
	TOTAL	1866598.00	BALANCE OF PAYMENTS			-9646.812	

RESOURCES

		STOCKPILE	% USED	RECYCLE RATIO	SUBST. NUMBER	YEAR COMPLTD	STOCKPILE INCREASE
1	FIBRE & FOOD	28015.46	30.65	0.0			
2	IRON & STEEL	16732.32	38.98	0.610			
3	COPPER	7533.11	52.34	0.387			
4	NON-FERROUS	4562.00	54.38	0.211			
5	COAL	7828.73	21.71	0.0			
6	PETRO-NAT GAS	7735.09	68.45	0.0			
7	STONE & CLAY	8456.88	15.43	0.0			
8	CHEMICALS	8548.78	14.51	0.0			
9	LEAD & ZINC	4667.24	73.79	0.599			
10	ALUMINUM	7409.72	60.40	0.371			
15	URBAN LAND	2616.52	73.83	0.0			
16	ARABLE LAND	6216.22	58.56	0.0			
18	WORK UNITS	5159.44	95.26	0.0			

SYSTEM RESILIENCE

		PRESENT VALUE	THRESHOLD	RESILIENCE	ADJUSTED THRESHOLD
1	EDUCATION	2.564	2.369	0.103	2.369
2	EMPLOYMENT	1.155	1.080	0.070	0.0
3	TRANSPORTATION	0.675	0.617	0.115	0.617
4	WELFARE	92.291	84.078	0.121	84.078
5	HEALTH	87.233	76.176	0.179	76.176
6	SFTY & DEFENSE	0.666	0.610	0.091	0.0
7	MANUFACTURING	1.154	1.060	0.089	0.0
8	COMMERCIAL	0.594	0.549	0.101	0.549
9	GRCTH POTENTIAL	0.629	0.577	0.111	0.577
10	AGRICULTURE	0.526	0.481	0.093	0.0
11	SERVICES	0.714	0.659	0.103	0.659
12	MINING	1.047	0.400	1.617	0.0

*****TOTAL SYSTEM EXPENDITURES*****
(MILLIONS OF DOLLARS)

RESOURCE	AMCUNT	UNIT PRICE	COST	
LAND				
URBAN LAND	7383.480	0.00012195	65111.340	
ARABLE LAND	8783.777	0.00012452	23626.008	
TOTAL				88737.312
RAW MATERIALS				
FOOD & FIBER	11548.566	0.00045000	153533.875	
IRCN ORE	468.073	0.00034629	22865.332	
CCPPER	285.774	0.00090097	34839.668	
OTHER NON-IRCN	238.135	0.00012374	3875.504	
COAL	104.768	0.00019014	942.278	
PETRO-NAT GAS	208.837	0.00034131	2776.924	
STONE ANC CLAY	91.975	0.00009250	869.441	
CHEMICALS	84.303	0.00000814	65.052	
LEAD,ZINC	456.920	0.00010556	6542.758	
ALUMINUM	368.530	0.00048784	25825.586	
TCTAL				252136.187
LABOR				
WCRKERS COSTS	132861.750	0.00013122		1323992.00
CAPITAL				
NEW CAPITAL GCCDS				19513.102
ENVIRCNMENTAL MAINTENANCE				29144.027
CAPITAL MAINTENANCE				132549.000
TCTAL				181206.125
TCTAL COSTS				1846071.00

```
********************
*  YEAR  IS  1991  *
********************
```

POPULATION

	PEOPLE
EDUCATION	59522.160
INSTITUTIONAL	3247.260
NON-WORKER	37688.773
UNEMPLOYED	3108.828
PAID WORKER	141228.937
UNPAID WORKER	9761.516
TOTAL	254557.750
BIRTHS	4543.047
DEATHS	2177.494
MIGRATION	503.776

PRODUCTION

		INVST.FUNDS	MAINT	OUTPUT	IMPORTS	EXPORTS	GROWTH
1	EDUCATION	30186.227	3.00	1509.60	0.0	0.0	3.20
2	TRANS & COMMUN	17148.465	6.00	1953.34	0.0	0.0	4.30
3	HEALTH&WELFARE	112534.000	4.00	2907.55	0.0	0.0	6.50
4	PUBLIC SAFETY	38978.496	3.00	1710.17	0.0	0.0	3.70
5	ADMIN & OTHER	53510.277	3.00	2609.51	245.79	291.56	4.80
6	AGRICULTURE	63659.625	7.00	1343.30	160.43	83.93	2.00
7	NON-DUR MANUF	189060.937	9.00	1369.61	161.48	8.95	2.73
8	DURABLE MANUF	559225.500	9.00	1894.47	85.23	118.69	4.27
9	COMMUN & TRANS	195927.500	8.00	1518.19	41.22	30.92	3.20
10	WHOL-RET TRADE	330326.187	6.00	1557.97	0.19	0.0	3.30
11	SERVICES	329153.562	6.00	1640.08	8.66	8.17	3.60
12	MINING	16365.980	7.00	2660.26	865.45	1064.10	1.00
	TOTAL	1936074.00	BALANCE OF PAYMENTS			-10311.930	

RESOURCES

		STOCKPILE	% USED	RECYCLE RATIO	SUBST. NUMBER	YEAR COMPLTD	STOCKPILE INCREASE
1	FIBRE & FOOD	30698.63	29.14	0.0			
2	IRON & STEEL	16437.56	40.05	0.614			
3	COPPER	7321.97	53.68	0.394			
4	NON-FERROUS	4360.54	56.39	0.220			
5	COAL	7721.82	22.78	0.0			
6	PETRO-NAT GAS	7521.75	69.32	0.0			
7	STONE & CLAY	8362.83	16.37	0.0			
8	CHEMICALS	8462.54	15.37	0.0			
9	LEAD & ZINC	4854.80	75.25	0.618			
10	ALUMINUM	7133.93	61.87	0.389			
15	URBAN LAND	2470.78	75.29	0.0			
16	ARABLE LAND	6180.31	58.80	0.0			
18	WORK UNITS	5699.87	95.96	0.0			

SYSTEM RESILIENCE

		PRESENT VALUE	THRESHOLD	RESILIENCE	ADJUSTED THRESHOLD
1	EDUCATION	2.579	2.369	0.089	0.0
2	EMPLOYMENT	1.151	1.080	0.067	0.0
3	TRANSPORTATION	0.682	0.629	0.105	0.629
4	WELFARE	93.526	85.721	0.112	85.721
5	HEALTH	89.539	78.387	0.175	78.387
6	SFTY & DEFENSE	0.672	0.621	0.101	0.621
7	MANUFACTURING	1.156	1.060	0.091	0.0
8	COMMERCIAL	0.596	0.549	0.087	0.0
9	GROTH POTENTIAL	0.535	0.577	0.099	0.0
10	AGRICULTURE	0.528	0.481	0.097	0.0
11	SERVICES	0.720	0.659	0.093	0.0
12	MINING	1.045	0.400	1.613	0.0

*****TOTAL SYSTEM EXPENDITURES*****
(MILLIONS OF DOLLARS)

RESOURCE	AMOUNT	UNIT PRICE	COST	
LAND				
URBAN LAND	7529.223	0.00012195	66391.625	
ARABLE LAND	8819.687	0.00012576	23981.141	
TOTAL				90372.750
RAW MATERIALS				
FOOD & FIBER	11771.523	0.00045000	156745.312	
IRON ORE	480.182	0.00034797	23578.473	
COPPER	292.848	0.00092810	36818.492	
OTHER NON-IRON	244.010	0.00012590	4077.615	
COAL	106.914	0.00020547	1038.791	
PETRO-NAT GAS	213.333	0.00034820	2892.324	
STONE AND CLAY	94.055	0.00009293	895.153	
CHEMICALS	86.240	0.00000818	66.993	
LEAD, ZINC	468.802	0.00010635	6765.133	
ALUMINUM	378.142	0.00048784	26504.539	
TOTAL				259382.500
LABOR				
WORKERS COSTS	135529.062	0.00013385		1379322.00
CAPITAL				
NEW CAPITAL GOODS				19482.809
ENVIRONMENTAL MAINTENANCE				30955.098
CAPITAL MAINTENANCE				137400.875
TOTAL				187838.750
TOTAL COSTS				1916915.00

```
********************
*  YEAR  IS  1992  *
********************
```

POPULATION

	PEOPLE
EDUCATION	60016.266
INSTITUTIONAL	3313.448
NCN-WORKER	38102.547
UNEMPLOYED	3215.862
PAID WORKER	144058.500
UNPAID WORKER	8548.941
TOTAL	257255.812
BIRTHS	4591.199
DEATHS	2210.692
MIGRATION	509.115

PRODUCTION

		INVST.FUNDS	MAINT	OUTPUT	IMPORTS	EXPORTS	GROWTH
1	EDUCATION	31152.172	3.00	1528.48	0.0	0.0	3.20
2	TRANS & CCMMUN	17851.941	6.0C	2003.34	0.0	0.0	4.30
3	HEALTH&WELFARE	119848.625	4.00	3040.44	0.0	0.0	6.50
4	PUBLIC SAFETY	40420.687	3.00	1743.74	0.0	0.0	3.70
5	ADMIN & CTHER	56078.734	3.00	2665.05	240.93	322.82	4.80
6	AGRICULTURE	64991.051	7.00	1367.12	159.97	82.06	2.00
7	NON-DUR MANUF	193983.687	9.00	1398.45	160.51	8.78	2.82
8	DURABLE MANUF	581447.062	9.00	1932.93	83.73	116.33	4.24
9	COMMUN & TRANS	202139.937	8.00	1539.52	40.51	30.12	3.20
10	WHCL-RET TRADE	341183.437	6.00	1579.29	0.18	0.0	3.30
11	SERVICES	340724.500	6.00	1667.13	8.50	7.98	3.60
12	MINING	16602.832	7.00	2707.45	853.65	1082.98	1.00
	TOTAL	2006421.00	BALANCE OF PAYMENTS			-9568.422	

RESOURCES

		STOCKPILE	% USED	RECYCLE RATIO	SUBST. NUMBER	YEAR COMPLTC	STOCKPILE INCREASE
1	FIBRE & FCOD	33582.27	27.71	0.0			
2	IRON & STEEL	16134.01	41.16	0.618			
3	CCPPER	7107.67	55.03	0.401			
4	NON-FERROUS	4156.53	58.43	0.230			
5	COAL	7612.85	23.87	0.0			
6	PETRO-NAT GAS	7304.14	70.21	0.C			5000.00
7	STONE & CLAY	8266.89	17.33	0.C			
8	CHEMICALS	8374.56	16.25	0.C			
9	LEAD & ZINC	5061.85	76.58	0.636			
10	ALUMINUM	6856.18	63.36	0.407			
15	URBAN LAND	2332.59	76.67	0.0			
16	ARABLE LAND	6112.27	59.25	0.C			
18	WORK UNITS	5968.75	95.86	0.C			

SYSTEM RESILIENCE

		PRESENT VALUE	THRESHOLD	RESILIENCE	ADJUSTED THRESHOLD
1	EDUCATION	2.592	2.369	0.094	0.0
2	EMPLOYMENT	1.149	1.080	0.064	0.0
3	TRANSPORTATION	0.689	0.629	0.095	0.0
4	WELFARE	94.545	87.282	0.103	87.282
5	HEALTH	91.761	80.617	0.171	80.617
6	SFTY & DEFENSE	0.678	0.621	0.091	0.0
7	MANUFACTURING	1.156	1.060	0.091	0.0
8	COMMERCIAL	0.598	0.549	0.091	0.0
9	GROTH POTENTIAL	0.639	0.589	0.107	C.589
10	AGRICULTURE	0.531	0.490	0.105	0.490
11	SERVICES	0.726	0.671	0.101	0.671
12	MINING	1.052	0.400	1.631	0.0

*****TOTAL SYSTEM EXPENDITURES*****
(MILLIONS OF DOLLARS)

RESOURCE	AMCUNT	UNIT PRICE	COST	
LAND				
URBAN LAND	7667.410	0.00012195	67535.625	
ARABLE LAND	8887.730	0.00012616	24238.094	
TCTAL				91773.687
RAW MATERIALS				
FOOD & FIBER	12003.578	0.00045000	159937.875	
IRON ORE	489.872	0.00034972	24176.199	
CCPPER	298.752	0.00095611	38698.852	
CTHER NON-IRON	248.974	0.00013018	4268.406	
COAL	108.973	0.00022187	1142.969	
PETRO-NAT GAS	217.619	0.00035532	3009.484	
STONE AND CLAY	95.939	0.00009340	917.768	
CHEMICALS	87.984	0.00000822	68.701	
LEAD,ZINC	478.323	0.00010708	6949.195	
ALUMINUM	385.788	0.00048784	27040.848	
TCTAL				266210.062
LABOR				
WCRKERS COSTS	138089.750	0.00013654	1434039.00	
CAPITAL				
NEW CAPITAL GOODS				19097.301
ENVIRCNMENTAL MAINTENANCE				32738.148
CAPITAL MAINTENANCE				142280.375
TOTAL				194115.812
TCTAL COSTS				1986137.00

```
********************
*  YEAR  IS  1993  *
********************
```

POPULATION

	PEOPLE
EDUCATION	60545.469
INSTITUTIONAL	3385.480
NON-WORKER	38500.918
UNEMPLOYED	3331.610
PAID WORKER	146764.125
UNPAID WORKER	7454.707
TOTAL	259982.500
BIRTHS	4635.863
DEATHS	2244.229
MIGRATION	514.511

PRODUCTION

		INVST.FUNDS	MAINT	OUTPUT	IMPORTS	EXPORTS	GROWTH
1	EDUCATION	32149.027	3.00	1547.57	0.0	0.0	3.20
2	TRANS & COMMUN	18603.273	6.00	2056.13	0.0	0.0	4.30
3	HEALTH&WELFARE	127638.687	4.00	3179.30	0.0	0.0	6.50
4	PUBLIC SAFETY	41916.238	3.00	1777.88	0.0	0.0	3.70
5	ADMIN & OTHER	58770.477	3.00	2775.36	236.15	316.88	4.80
6	AGRICULTURE	66345.125	7.00	1391.49	159.67	83.43	2.00
7	NON-DUR MANUF	199724.750	9.00	1433.49	159.52	8.99	2.82
8	DURABLE MANUF	605329.750	9.00	1974.95	82.25	118.74	4.24
9	COMMUN & TRANS	208639.500	8.00	1561.92	39.81	30.53	3.20
10	WHOL-RET TRADE	352484.000	6.00	1601.28	0.18	0.0	3.30
11	SERVICES	352900.625	6.00	1695.64	8.35	8.11	3.60
12	MINING	16838.969	7.00	2749.92	842.68	1099.97	1.00
	TOTAL	2081338.00	BALANCE OF PAYMENTS			-7899.770	

RESOURCES

		STOCKPILE	% USED	RECYCLE RATIO	SUBST. NUMBER	YEAR COMPLTD	STOCKPILE INCREASE
1	FIBRE & FOOD	36656.95	26.41	0.0			
2	IRON & STEEL	15824.66	42.29	0.622			
3	COPPER	6889.92	56.41	0.409			
4	NON-FERROUS	3949.71	60.50	0.240			5000.00
5	COAL	7501.06	24.99	0.0			
6	PETRO-NAT GAS	7587.91	71.04	0.0			
7	STONE & CLAY	8168.84	18.31	0.0			
8	CHEMICALS	8284.62	17.15	0.0			
9	LEAD & ZINC	4767.64	77.94	0.655			
10	ALUMINUM	6576.10	64.85	0.426			
15	URBAN LAND	2183.39	78.17	0.0			
16	ARABLE LAND	6043.20	59.71	0.0			
18	WORK UNITS	5801.25	96.05	0.0			

SYSTEM RESILIENCE

		PRESENT VALUE	THRESHOLD	RESILIENCE	ADJUSTED THRESHOLD
1	EDUCATION	2.603	2.369	0.099	0.0
2	EMPLOYMENT	1.149	1.080	0.064	0.0
3	TRANSPORTATION	0.696	0.641	0.106	0.641
4	WELFARE	95.428	87.282	0.093	0.0
5	HEALTH	93.910	82.846	0.165	82.846
6	SFTY & DEFENSE	0.684	0.633	0.101	0.633
7	MANUFACTURING	1.161	1.060	0.096	0.0
8	COMMERCIAL	0.601	0.549	0.095	0.0
9	GROTH POTENTIAL	0.644	0.589	0.094	0.0
10	AGRICULTURE	0.535	0.490	0.091	0.0
11	SERVICES	0.735	0.671	0.095	0.0
12	MINING	1.058	0.400	1.644	0.0

*****TOTAL SYSTEM EXPENDITURES*****
(MILLIONS OF DOLLARS)

RESOURCE	AMCUNT	UNIT PRICE	COST
LAND			
URBAN LAND	7816.513	0.00012195	68767.812
ARABLE LAND	8956.797	0.00012665	24516.039
TOTAL			93283.812
RAW MATERIALS			
FCOD & FIBER	12268.699	0.00045000	163640.500
IRON ORE	500.509	0.00035156	24831.516
COPPER	305.164	0.00098495	40733.363
CTHER NON-IRCN	254.394	0.00013357	4475.492
COAL	111.790	0.00023947	1265.141
PETRO-NAT GAS	222.699	0.00036228	3137.668
STONE AND CLAY	98.051	0.00009391	942.878
CHEMICALS	89.935	0.00000827	70.592
LEAD,ZINC	488.879	0.00010774	7145.270
ALUMINUM	394.176	0.00048784	27629.324
TOTAL			273871.500
LABOR			
WCRKERS COSTS	140962.875	0.00013929	1493197.00
CAPITAL			
NEW CAPITAL GOODS			19065.430
ENVIRCNMENTAL MAINTENANCE			34564.082
CAPITAL MAINTENANCE			147498.625
TOTAL			201128.125
TOTAL COSTS			2061480.00

```
********************
*  YEAR  IS  1994  *
********************
```

POPULATION

	PEOPLE
EDUCATION	61039.500
INSTITUTIONAL	3457.474
NON-WORKER	38927.777
UNEMPLOYED	3445.599
PAID WORKER	149793.937
UNPAID WORKER	6073.258
TOTAL	262738.062
BIRTHS	4689.039
DEATHS	2278.106
MIGRATION	519.965

PRODUCTION

		INVST.FUNDS	MAINT	OUTPUT	IMPORTS	EXPORTS	GROWTH
1	EDUCATION	33177.781	3.00	1566.88	0.0	0.0	3.20
2	TRANS & COMMUN	19415.414	6.00	2111.94	0.0	0.0	4.30
3	HEALTH&WELFARE	135935.125	4.00	3324.38	0.0	0.0	6.50
4	PUBLIC SAFETY	43467.125	3.00	1812.58	0.0	0.0	3.70
5	ADMIN & OTHER	61591.422	3.00	2847.15	231.47	360.64	4.80
6	AGRICULTURE	67734.187	7.00	1415.90	159.06	85.23	2.00
7	NON-DUR MANUF	206502.687	9.00	1476.03	158.53	9.29	2.82
8	DURABLE MANUF	631619.375	9.00	2026.22	80.79	122.31	4.24
9	COMMUN & TRANS	215495.625	8.00	1586.55	39.12	31.13	3.20
10	WHOL-RET TRADE	364309.875	6.00	1624.14	0.18	0.0	3.30
11	SERVICES	365792.375	6.00	1726.03	8.20	8.29	3.60
12	MINING	17086.344	7.00	2787.39	830.28	1114.96	1.00
	TOTAL	2162125.00	BALANCE OF PAYMENTS			-4736.262	

RESOURCES

		STOCKPILE	% USED	RECYCLE RATIO	SUBST. NUMBER	YEAR COMPLTD	STOCKPILE INCREASE
1	FIBRE & FOOD	39935.11	25.24	0.0			
2	IRON & STEEL	15508.19	43.44	0.627			
3	COPPER	6667.96	57.82	0.417			
4	NON-FERROUS	4407.73	62.28	0.249			
5	COAL	7386.68	26.13	0.0			
6	PETRO-NAT GAS	8324.04	71.80	0.0			
7	STONE & CLAY	8068.37	19.32	0.0			
8	CHEMICALS	8192.37	18.08	0.0			
9	LEAD & ZINC	4464.41	79.34	0.674			
10	ALUMINUM	6292.62	66.37	0.446			
15	URBAN LAND	2017.49	79.83	0.0			
16	ARABLE LAND	5975.32	60.16	0.0			
18	WORK UNITS	5829.19	96.11	0.0			

SYSTEM RESILIENCE

		PRESENT VALUE	THRESHOLD	RESILIENCE	ADJUSTED THRESHOLD
1	EDUCATION	2.618	2.416	0.105	2.416
2	EMPLOYMENT	1.149	1.080	0.064	0.0
3	TRANSPORTATION	0.704	0.641	0.098	0.0
4	WELFARE	96.471	88.911	0.105	88.911
5	HEALTH	96.150	85.059	0.161	85.059
6	SFTY & DEFENSE	0.690	0.633	0.091	0.0
7	MANUFACTURING	1.169	1.080	0.103	1.080
8	COMMERCIAL	0.604	0.559	0.100	0.559
9	GROTH POTENTIAL	0.650	0.600	0.104	0.600
10	AGRICULTURE	0.539	0.490	0.099	0.0
11	SERVICES	0.742	0.684	0.106	0.684
12	MINING	1.061	0.400	1.652	0.0

*****TOTAL SYSTEM EXPENDITURES*****
(MILLIONS OF DOLLARS)

RESOURCE	AMOUNT	UNIT PRICE	COST	
LAND				
URBAN LAND	7982.508	0.00012195	70166.500	
ARABLE LAND	9024.680	0.00012713	24802.824	
TCTAL				94969.312
RAW MATERIALS				
FOOD & FIBER	12570.570	0.00045000	167920.525	
IRON ORE	513.398	0.00035348	25612.441	
COPPER	312.764	0.00101472	43041.035	
OTHER NCN-IRCN	260.757	0.00013676	4700.297	
COAL	114.379	0.00025832	1395.201	
PETRO-NAT GAS	228.742	0.00036875	3276.788	
STONE ANC CLAY	100.472	0.00009445	972.355	
CHEMICALS	92.251	0.00000832	72.840	
LEAD, ZINC	501.714	0.00010842	7377.336	
ALUMINUM	404.351	0.00048784	28344.520	
TCTAL				282713.187
LABOR				
WORKERS COSTS	143964.750	0.00014209		1556550.00
CAPITAL				
NEW CAPITAL GOODS				19478.402
ENVIRCNMENTAL MAINTENANCE				36622.477
CAPITAL MAINTENANCE				153163.437
TOTAL				209264.312
TCTAL COSTS				2143496.00

```
********************
*  YEAR  IS  1995  *
********************
```

POPULATION

	PEOPLE
EDUCATION	61470.629
INSTITUTIONAL	3528.946
NCN-WORKER	39385.7C7
UNEMPLOYED	3556.804
PAID WORKER	152998.875
UNPAID WORKER	4581.574
TOTAL	265522.812
BIRTHS	4738.742
DEATHS	2312.005
MIGRATION	525.476

PRODUCTION

		INVST.FUNDS	MAINT	OUTPUT	IMPORTS	EXPCRTS	GROWTH
1	EDUCATION	34239.453	3.00	1586.34	0.0	0.0	3.20
2	TRANS & CCMMUN	20250.703	6.C0	2167.20	0.0	0.0	4.30
3	HEALTH&WELFARE	144770.812	4.00	3475.79	0.0	0.0	6.50
4	PUBLIC SAFETY	45075.395	3.00	1847.62	0.0	0.0	3.70
5	ADMIN & CTHER	64547.770	3.00	2972.79	226.87	359.07	4.80
6	AGRICULTURE	69164.125	7.00	1443.66	158.46	85.63	2.00
7	NON-DUR MANUF	213147.312	9.00	1516.35	157.53	9.41	2.82
8	DURABLE MANUF	558442.312	9.0C	2078.22	79.35	123.62	4.24
9	COMMUN & TRANS	222522.125	8.00	1611.51	38.41	31.16	3.20
10	WHOL-RET TRADE	376483.437	6.00	1647.07	0.17	0.0	3.30
11	SERVICES	379016.312	6.00	1756.31	8.05	8.31	3.60
12	MINING	17350.145	7.00	2817.18	818.08	1126.87	1.00
	TOTAL	2245008.00	BALANCE OF PAYMENTS			-3300.488	

RESOURCES

		STOCKPILE	% USED	RECYCLE RATIO	SUBST. NUMBER	YEAR COMPLTD	STOCKPILE INCREASE
1	FIBRE & FOOD	43472.71	24.10	0.0			
2	IRON & STEEL	15184.61	44.62	0.632			
3	CCPPER	6441.86	59.25	0.426			
4	NON-FERROUS	5447.55	63.68	0.256			
5	COAL	7269.21	27.31	0.0			
6	PETRO-NAT GAS	9367.92	72.47	0.0			
7	STONE & CLAY	7965.48	20.35	0.C			
8	CHEMICALS	8097.87	19.02	0.C			
9	LEAD & ZINC	4156.98	80.77	0.694			
10	ALUMINUM	6005.88	67.90	0.466			
15	URBAN LAND	1852.76	81.47	0.0	5	1996	
16	ARABLE LAND	5893.51	60.71	0.0			
18	WORK UNITS	5858.50	96.17	0.C			

SYSTEM RESILIENCE

		PRESENT VALUE	THRESHOLD	RESILIENCE	ADJUSTED THRESHOLD
1	EDUCATION	2.634	2.416	0.091	0.0
2	EMPLOYMENT	1.148	1.080	0.063	0.C
3	TRANSPORTATION	0.712	0.653	0.110	0.653
4	WELFARE	97.722	88.911	0.099	0.0
5	HEALTH	98.494	87.277	0.158	87.277
6	SFTY & DEFENSE	0.696	0.644	0.100	0.644
7	MANUFACTURING	1.175	1.080	0.088	0.0
8	COMMERCIAL	0.607	0.559	0.085	0.0
9	GROTH PCTENTIAL	0.656	0.600	0.094	0.0
10	AGRICULTURE	0.544	0.500	0.109	0.500
11	SERVICES	0.753	0.696	0.101	0.696
12	MINING	1.061	0.400	1.652	0.0

*****TOTAL SYSTEM EXPENDITURES*****
(MILLIONS OF DOLLARS)

RESOURCE	AMOUNT	UNIT PRICE	COST	
LAND				
URBAN LAND	8147.238	0.00012315	72275.125	
ARABLE LAND	9106.488	0.00012768	25121.539	
TOTAL				97396.625
RAW MATERIALS				
FOOD & FIBER	12873.395	0.00045000	172128.125	
IRON ORE	526.411	0.00035549	26415.113	
COPPER	320.414	0.00104545	45466.949	
OTHER NON-IRON	267.180	0.00013942	4913.785	
COAL	117.474	0.00027854	1544.581	
PETRO-NAT GAS	234.503	0.00037462	3409.631	
STONE AND CLAY	102.889	0.00009504	1002.812	
CHEMICALS	94.506	0.00000837	75.140	
LEAD, ZINC	514.635	0.00010911	7615.164	
ALUMINUM	414.643	0.00048784	29069.332	
TOTAL				291640.375
LABOR				
WORKERS COSTS	147140.375	0.00014494		1623321.00
CAPITAL				
NEW CAPITAL GOODS				19566.762
ENVIRONMENTAL MAINTENANCE				38889.598
CAPITAL MAINTENANCE				158952.375
TOTAL				217408.687
TOTAL COSTS				2229766.00

* YEAR IS 1996 *

POPULATION

	PEOPLE
EDUCATION	61898.547
INSTITUTIONAL	3603.708
NON-WORKER	39844.801
UNEMPLOYED	3671.234
PAID WORKER	156349.562
UNPAID WORKER	2968.583
TOTAL	268337.062
BIRTHS	4788.965
DEATHS	2346.272
MIGRATION	531.045

PRODUCTION

		INVST.FUNDS	MAINT	OUTPUT	IMPORTS	EXPORTS	GROWTH
1	EDUCATION	35335.098	3.00	1604.96	0.0	0.0	3.20
2	TRANS & COMMUN	21124.262	6.00	2228.97	0.0	0.0	4.30
3	HEALTH&WELFARE	154180.812	4.00	3632.32	0.0	0.0	6.50
4	PUBLIC SAFETY	46743.168	3.00	1881.26	0.0	0.0	3.70
5	ADMIN & OTHER	67646.000	3.00	3049.21	222.37	341.41	4.80
6	AGRICULTURE	70624.750	7.00	1470.28	157.80	86.31	2.00
7	NON-DUR MANUF	220085.937	9.00	1559.24	156.63	9.58	2.82
8	DURABLE MANUF	686519.625	9.00	2131.90	78.02	125.50	4.24
9	COMMUN & TRANS	229790.125	8.00	1639.17	37.74	31.37	3.20
10	WHOL-RET TRADE	389075.375	6.00	1671.51	0.17	0.0	3.30
11	SERVICES	392744.937	6.00	1789.50	7.90	8.38	3.60
12	MINING	17619.836	7.00	2837.25	805.80	1134.90	1.00
	TOTAL	2331487.00	BALANCE OF PAYMENTS			-2038.637	

RESOURCES

		STOCKPILE	% USED	RECYCLE RATIO	SUBST. NUMBER	YEAR COMPLTD	STOCKPILE INCREASE
1	FIBRE & FOOD	47279.81	23.02	0.0			
2	IRON & STEEL	14853.75	45.83	0.637			
3	COPPER	6211.65	60.70	0.434	1	2001	2000.00
4	NON-FERROUS	6872.90	64.78	0.262			
5	COAL	7149.10	28.51	0.0			
6	PETRO-NAT GAS	10508.88	73.08	0.0			
7	STONE & CLAY	7860.20	21.40	0.0			
8	CHEMICALS	8001.05	19.99	0.0			
9	LEAD & ZINC	3845.30	82.21	0.715			
10	ALUMINUM	5715.89	69.45	0.488			
15	URBAN LAND	2507.05	74.93	0.0			
16	ARABLE LAND	5408.45	63.94	0.0			
18	WORK UNITS	6010.32	96.16	0.0			

SYSTEM RESILIENCE

		PRESENT VALUE	THRESHOLD	RESILIENCE	ADJUSTED THRESHOLD
1	EDUCATION	2.651	2.416	0.097	0.0
2	EMPLOYMENT	1.147	1.080	0.063	0.0
3	TRANSPORTATION	0.721	0.665	0.103	0.665
4	WELFARE	98.940	90.673	0.113	90.673
5	HEALTH	100.794	89.520	0.155	89.520
6	SFTY & DEFENSE	0.701	0.644	0.089	0.0
7	MANUFACTURING	1.180	1.080	0.093	0.0
8	COMMERCIAL	0.611	0.559	0.092	0.0
9	GROTH POTENTIAL	0.663	0.611	0.105	0.611
10	AGRICULTURE	0.548	0.500	0.096	0.0
11	SERVICES	0.761	0.696	0.094	0.0
12	MINING	1.057	0.400	1.643	0.0

*****TOTAL SYSTEM EXPENDITURES*****
(MILLIONS OF DOLLARS)

RESOURCE	AMCUNT	UNIT PRICE	COST	
LAND				
URBAN LAND	7492.953	0.00012315	66409.000	
ARABLE LAND	9591.555	0.00013027	29692.258	
TCTAL				96101.250
RAW MATERIALS				
FCOD & FIBER	13185.328	0.00045000	176522.500	
IRON ORE	539.821	0.00035758	27252.910	
CCPPER	328.165	0.00107714	48031.371	
OTHER NCN-IRCN	273.654	0.00014154	5115.27C	
CCAL	120.112	0.00030018	1700.841	
PETRO-NAT GAS	240.648	0.00037991	3545.206	
STONE ANC CLAY	105.286	0.00009568	1034.383	
CHEMICALS	96.818	0.00000843	77.553	
LEAD,ZINC	528.005	0.00010981	7862.082	
ALUMINUM	425.248	0.00048784	29816.949	
TCTAL				300958.812
LABOR				
WORKERS COSTS	150339.250	0.00014786		1692862.00
CAPITAL				
NEW CAPITAL GOODS				20141.457
ENVIRCNMENTAL MAINTENANCE				41283.617
CAPITAL MAINTENANCE				164990.250
TCTAL				226415.312
TOTAL COSTS				2316337.00

```
********************
*  YEAR  IS  1997  *
********************
```

POPULATION

	PEOPLE
EDUCATION	62315.789
INSTITUTIONAL	3681.686
NON-WORKER	40315.812
UNEMPLOYED	3788.718
PAID WORKER	159737.250
UNPAID WORKER	1341.852
TOTAL	271181.187
BIRTHS	4839.723
DEATHS	2380.867
MIGRATION	536.674

PRODUCTION

		INVST.FUNDS	MAINT	OUTPUT	IMPORTS	EXPORTS	GROWTH
1	EDUCATION	36465.805	3.00	1624.41	0.0	0.0	3.20
2	TRANS & COMMUN	22017.473	6.00	2284.19	0.0	0.0	4.30
3	HEALTH&WELFARE	164202.500	4.00	3797.79	0.0	0.0	6.50
4	PUBLIC SAFETY	48472.648	3.00	1916.81	0.0	0.0	3.70
5	ADMIN & OTHER	70892.937	3.00	3115.93	217.94	380.67	4.80
6	AGRICULTURE	72120.750	7.00	1486.67	156.03	87.57	2.00
7	NON-DUR MANUF	226717.875	9.00	1598.05	155.65	9.85	2.98
8	DURABLE MANUF	714909.812	9.00	2201.55	77.33	130.05	4.19
9	COMMUN & TRANS	237208.062	8.00	1663.72	37.08	31.95	3.20
10	WHOL-RET TRADE	402002.562	6.00	1694.74	0.17	0.0	3.30
11	SERVICES	406787.187	6.00	1819.98	7.76	8.55	3.60
12	MINING	17899.582	7.00	2878.29	797.68	1151.32	1.00
	TOTAL	2419695.00	BALANCE OF PAYMENTS			1166.102	

RESOURCES

		STOCKPILE	% USED	RECYCLE RATIO	SUBST. NUMBER	YEAR COMPLTD	STOCKPILE INCREASE
1	FIBRE & FOOD	51443.98	21.89	0.0			
2	IRON & STEEL	14503.05	47.11	0.642			
3	COPPER	6274.30	61.93	0.442			
4	NON-FERROUS	8413.91	65.68	0.267			
5	COAL	7026.52	29.73	0.0			
6	PETRO-NAT GAS	10265.57	73.70	0.0			
7	STONE & CLAY	7751.99	22.48	0.0			
8	CHEMICALS	7901.54	20.98	0.0			
9	LEAD & ZINC	3527.57	83.68	0.736			
10	ALUMINUM	5420.79	71.03	0.509			3000.00
15	URBAN LAND	2349.79	76.50	0.0			
16	ARABLE LAND	5383.11	64.11	0.0			
18	WORK UNITS	6235.07	96.10	0.0			

SYSTEM RESILIENCE

		PRESENT VALUE	THRESHOLD	RESILIENCE	ADJUSTED THRESHOLD
1	EDUCATION	2.668	2.463	0.104	2.463
2	EMPLOYMENT	1.147	1.080	0.063	0.0
3	TRANSPORTATION	0.728	0.665	0.095	0.0
4	WELFARE	100.240	92.327	0.106	92.327
5	HEALTH	103.154	91.775	0.152	91.775
6	SFTY & DEFENSE	0.707	0.644	0.098	0.0
7	MANUFACTURING	1.189	1.100	0.101	1.100
8	COMMERCIAL	0.614	0.559	0.097	0.0
9	GROTH POTENTIAL	0.670	0.611	0.097	0.0
10	AGRICULTURE	0.548	0.500	0.096	0.0
11	SERVICES	0.767	0.709	0.102	0.709
12	MINING	1.061	0.400	1.653	0.0

*****TOTAL SYSTEM EXPENDITURES*****
(MILLIONS OF DOLLARS)

RESOURCE	AMCUNT	UNIT PRICE	COST
LAND			
URBAN LAND	7650.211	0.00012315	67854.875
ARABLE LAND	9616.891	0.00013160	30169.023
TOTAL			98023.875
RAW MATERIALS			
FOOD & FIBER	13443.520	0.00045000	180390.250
IRON ORE	573.371	0.00035980	29141.871
COPPER	292.721	0.00110636	44055.598
CTHER NON-IRON	282.052	0.00014326	5343.250
COAL	122.574	0.00032323	1867.995
PETRO-NAT GAS	246.239	0.00038516	3674.987
STONE AND CLAY	108.201	0.00009637	1073.705
CHEMICALS	99.507	0.00000849	80.519
LEAD, ZINC	544.825	0.00011051	8169.254
ALUMINUM	438.963	0.00048784	30785.918
TOTAL			304583.062
LABOR			
WORKERS COSTS	153502.187	0.00015083	1766986.00
CAPITAL			
NEW CAPITAL GOODS			20541.348
ENVIRCNMENTAL MAINTENANCE			43799.195
CAPITAL MAINTENANCE			171115.812
TOTAL			235456.312
TOTAL COSTS			2405048.00

```
********************
*  YEAR  IS  1998  *
********************
```

POPULATION

	PEOPLE
EDUCATION	62733.117
INSTITUTIONAL	3763.334
NON-WORKER	40789.910
UNEMPLOYED	3911.487
PAID WORKER	161516.062
UNPAID WORKER	1341.310
TOTAL	274055.437
BIRTHS	4891.020
DEATHS	2420.751
MIGRATION	542.362

PRODUCTION

		INVST.FUNDS	MAINT	OUTPUT	IMPORTS	EXPORTS	GROWTH
1	EDUCATION	37632.695	3.00	1611.42	0.0	0.0	3.20
2	TRANS & COMMUN	22966.922	6.00	2302.74	0.0	0.0	4.30
3	HEALTH&WELFARE	174875.562	4.00	3900.27	0.0	0.0	6.50
4	PUBLIC SAFETY	50266.121	3.00	1915.97	0.0	0.0	3.70
5	ADMIN & OTHER	74295.750	3.00	3182.53	211.54	292.51	4.80
6	AGRICULTURE	73655.000	7.00	1509.63	154.69	83.68	2.00
7	NON-DUR MANUF	234357.250	9.00	1634.10	153.70	9.48	2.98
8	DURABLE MANUF	745067.750	9.00	2241.46	75.48	124.60	4.19
9	COMMUN & TRANS	244959.375	8.00	1659.63	36.12	29.99	3.20
10	WHOL-RET TRADE	415455.875	5.00	1686.69	0.16	0.0	3.30
11	SERVICES	421507.250	6.00	1818.64	7.55	8.04	3.60
12	MINING	18191.609	7.00	2942.87	785.73	1177.15	1.00
	TOTAL	2513228.00	BALANCE OF PAYMENTS			-1330.148	

RESOURCES

		STOCKPILE	% USED	RECYCLE RATIO	SUBST. NUMBER	YEAR COMPLTD	STOCKPILE INCREASE
1	FIBRE & FOOD	55934.52	20.80	0.0			
2	IRON & STEEL	14137.00	48.44	0.648			
3	COPPER	6607.69	62.89	0.448			
4	NON-FERROUS	8189.05	66.60	0.272			
5	COAL	6902.15	30.98	0.0			
6	PETRO-NAT GAS	10014.89	74.34	0.0			
7	STONE & CLAY	7641.64	23.58	0.0			
8	CHEMICALS	7800.03	22.00	0.0			
9	LEAD & ZINC	3207.94	85.16	0.758			
10	ALUMINUM	5425.07	72.49	0.530			
15	URBAN LAND	2306.57	76.93	0.0			
16	ARABLE LAND	5340.12	64.40	0.0			
18	WORK UNITS	6928.07	95.71	0.0			

SYSTEM RESILIENCE

		PRESENT VALUE	THRESHOLD	RESILIENCE	ADJUSTED THRESHOLD
1	EDUCATION	2.633	2.463	0.069	0.0
2	EMPLOYMENT	1.143	1.080	0.059	0.0
3	TRANSPORTATION	0.723	0.665	0.087	0.0
4	WELFARE	99.713	92.327	0.080	0.0
5	HEALTH	103.639	94.051	0.129	94.051
6	SFTY & DEFENSE	0.699	0.644	0.086	0.0
7	MANUFACTURING	1.200	1.100	0.091	0.0
8	COMMERCIAL	0.606	0.559	0.083	0.0
9	GROTH POTENTIAL	0.667	0.611	0.092	0.0
10	AGRICULTURE	0.551	0.510	0.101	0.510
11	SERVICES	0.763	0.709	0.077	0.0
12	MINING	1.074	0.400	1.685	0.0

*****TOTAL SYSTEM EXPENDITURES*****
(MILLIONS OF DOLLARS)

RESOURCE	AMCUNT	UNIT PRICE	COST
LAND			
URBAN LAND	7693.426	0.00012315	68256.062
ARABLE LAND	9559.875	0.00013188	30302.797
TCTAL			98558.812
RAW MATERIALS			
FOOD & FIBER	13696.469	0.00045000	183678.625
IRON ORE	601.083	0.00036219	30690.016
COPPER	250.104	0.00113027	38632.414
OTHER NON-IRCN	287.365	0.00014484	5502.031
CCAL	124.375	0.00034768	2035.550
PETRO-NAT GAS	250.674	0.00039062	3786.181
STONE AND CLAY	110.354	0.00009711	1102.285
CHEMICALS	101.517	0.00000856	82.689
LEAD, ZINC	554.939	0.00011123	8371.820
ALUMINUM	446.940	0.00048784	31342.367
TOTAL			305223.687
LABOR			
WORKERS COSTS	154588.000	0.00015540	1834508.00
CAPITAL			
NEW CAPITAL GOODS			21098.285
ENVIRONMENTAL MAINTENANCE			46634.430
CAPITAL MAINTENANCE			177630.625
TOTAL			245363.312
TOTAL COSTS			2483653.00

```
********************
*  YEAR  IS  1999  *
********************
```

POPULATION

	PEOPLE
EDUCATION	62966.387
INSTITUTIONAL	3836.501
NON-WORKER	41398.871
UNEMPLOYED	4017.538
PAID WORKER	164432.500
UNPAID WORKER	308.362
TOTAL	276960.187
BIRTHS	4942.859
DEATHS	2460.873
MIGRATION	548.111

PRODUCTION

		INVST.FUNDS	MAINT	OUTPUT	IMPORTS	EXPORTS	GROWTH
1	EDUCATION	38836.926	3.00	1646.66	0.0	0.0	3.20
2	TRANS & COMMUN	23855.922	6.00	2377.83	0.0	0.0	4.30
3	HEALTH&WELFARE	186242.375	4.00	4116.40	0.0	0.0	6.50
4	PUBLIC SAFETY	52125.949	3.0C	1970.95	0.0	0.0	3.70
5	ADMIN & OTHER	77861.875	3.00	3218.55	207.33	335.41	4.80
6	AGRICULTURE	75199.750	7.00	1539.32	154.79	95.16	2.00
7	NON-DUR MANUF	239246.187	9.00	1662.62	153.14	10.75	4.12
8	DURABLE MANUF	771545.187	9.00	2309.07	75.25	143.17	3.83
9	COMMUN & TRANS	252449.000	8.00	1634.87	35.48	34.16	3.20
10	WHOL-RET TRADE	428829.687	6.00	1724.17	0.16	0.0	3.30
11	SERVICES	435791.500	6.00	1862.56	7.42	9.19	3.60
12	MINING	18467.719	7.00	3023.01	787.53	1209.20	1.00
	TOTAL	2600450.00	BALANCE OF PAYMENTS			7151.891	

RESOURCES

		STOCKPILE	% USED	RECYCLE RATIO	SUBST. NUMBER	YEAR COMPLTD	STOCKPILE INCREASE
1	FIBRE & FOOD	60763.54	19.76	0.0			
2	IRON & STEEL	13753.76	49.84	0.654			
3	COPPER	7125.35	63.67	0.453			
4	NON-FERROUS	7956.39	67.55	0.277			
5	COAL	6775.43	32.25	0.0			
6	PETRO-NAT GAS	9759.50	75.00	0.C			
7	STONE & CLAY	7528.38	24.72	0.0			
8	CHEMICALS	7695.94	23.04	0.0			
9	LEAD & ZINC	2883.16	86.66	0.781			
10	ALUMINUM	5679.42	73.84	0.550			
15	URBAN LAND	2113.17	78.87	0.0			
16	ARABLE LAND	5236.37	65.09	0.0			
18	WORK UNITS	5916.19	96.40	0.0			

SYSTEM RESILIENCE

		PRESENT VALUE	THRESHOLD	RESILIENCE	ADJUSTED THRESHOLD
1	EDUCATION	2.682	2.463	0.089	0.0
2	EMPLOYMENT	1.151	1.080	0.066	0.0
3	TRANSPORTATION	0.735	0.677	0.106	0.677
4	WELFARE	102.461	93.804	0.110	93.804
5	HEALTH	107.296	95.968	0.141	95.968
6	SFTY & DEFENSE	0.712	0.655	0.105	0.655
7	MANUFACTURING	1.208	1.100	0.098	0.0
8	COMMERCIAL	0.612	0.559	0.094	0.0
9	GROTH POTENTIAL	0.677	0.622	0.107	0.622
10	AGRICULTURE	0.556	0.510	0.09C	0.0
11	SERVICES	0.770	0.709	0.087	0.0
12	MINING	1.091	C.400	1.729	0.0

*****TOTAL SYSTEM EXPENDITURES*****
(MILLIONS OF DOLLARS)

RESOURCE	AMCUNT	UNIT PRICE	COST	
LAND				
URBAN LAND	7986.828	0.00012315	69970.687	
ARABLE LANC	9763.633	0.00013252	30835.020	
TOTAL				100805.687
RAW MATERIALS				
FOOD & FIBER	13954.863	0.00045000	187312.250	
IRON ORE	531.547	0.00036474	32462.742	
CCPPER	223.904	0.00114949	35181.539	
CTHER NON-IRCN	295.903	0.00014649	5732.492	
COAL	126.713	0.00037358	2229.062	
PETRO-NAT GAS	255.397	0.00039624	3915.501	
STONE AND CLAY	113.259	0.00009790	1143.236	
CHEMICALS	104.087	0.00000863	85.748	
LEAD,ZINC	571.006	0.00011194	8676.836	
ALUMINUM	460.317	0.00048784	32285.715	
TCTAL				309024.750
LABOR				
WORKERS COSTS	158516.312	0.00015852		1922318.00
CAPITAL				
NEW CAPITAL GCCDS				21188.207
ENVIRCNMENTAL MAINTENANCE				48767.680
CAPITAL MAINTENANCE				183546.625
TCTAL				253502.500
TOTAL COSTS				2585650.00

```
********************
*  YEAR  IS  2000  *
********************
```

POPULATION

	PEOPLE
EDUCATION	63537.133
INSTITUTIONAL	3940.458
NON-WORKER	41771.047
UNEMPLOYED	4174.422
PAID WORKER	166165.375
UNPAID WORKER	307.144
TOTAL	279895.687
BIRTHS	4995.250
DEATHS	2496.826
MIGRATION	553.920

PRODUCTION

		INVST.FUNDS	MAINT	OUTPUT	IMPORTS	EXPORTS	GROWTH
1	EDUCATION	40079.687	3.00	1633.97	0.0	0.0	3.20
2	TRANS & COMMUN	24989.539	6.00	2403.57	0.0	0.0	4.30
3	HEALTH&WELFARE	198348.000	4.00	4220.11	0.0	0.0	6.50
4	PUBLIC SAFETY	54054.594	3.00	1969.78	0.0	0.0	3.70
5	ADMIN & OTHER	81599.187	3.00	3292.15	201.24	332.44	4.80
6	AGRICULTURE	76794.687	7.00	1568.11	153.13	100.15	2.00
7	NON-DUR MANUF	252417.875	9.00	1739.56	151.15	11.62	4.12
8	DURABLE MANUF	806907.000	9.00	2357.58	73.02	151.03	-0.32
9	COMMUN & TRANS	261217.437	8.00	1696.77	34.56	35.33	3.20
10	WHOL-RET TRADE	443694.625	6.00	1717.70	0.16	0.0	10.85
11	SERVICES	452622.500	6.00	1865.73	7.22	9.51	3.60
12	MINING	18767.059	7.00	3013.16	768.83	1205.27	1.00
	TOTAL	2711490.00	BALANCE OF PAYMENTS			12161.707	

RESOURCES

		STOCKPILE	% USED	RECYCLE RATIO	SUBST. NUMBER	YEAR COMPLTD	STOCKPILE INCREASE
1	FIBRE & FOOD	65733.81	19.05	0.0			
2	IRON & STEEL	13360.84	51.27	0.661			
3	COPPER	7706.71	64.34	0.457			
4	NON-FERROUS	7720.22	68.51	0.282			
5	COAL	6646.10	33.54	0.0			
6	PETRO-NAT GAS	9494.61	75.68	0.0			
7	STONE & CLAY	7412.55	25.87	0.0			
8	CHEMICALS	7589.04	24.11	0.0			
9	LEAD & ZINC	2555.07	88.18	0.804			
10	ALUMINUM	6093.23	75.05	0.568			
15	URBAN LAND	2028.67	79.71	0.0			
16	ARABLE LAND	5175.17	65.50	0.0			
18	WORK UNITS	5993.69	96.39	0.0			

SYSTEM RESILIENCE

		PRESENT VALUE	THRESHOLD	RESILIENCE	ADJUSTED THRESHOLD
1	EDUCATION	2.642	2.463	0.073	0.0
2	EMPLOYMENT	1.153	1.080	0.068	0.0
3	TRANSPORTATION	0.732	0.677	0.083	0.0
4	WELFARE	101.094	93.804	0.078	0.0
5	HEALTH	107.097	95.968	0.116	0.0
6	SFTY & DEFENSE	0.704	0.655	0.074	0.0
7	MANUFACTURING	1.233	1.122	0.121	1.122
8	COMMERCIAL	0.606	0.559	0.084	0.0
9	GROTH POTENTIAL	0.677	0.622	0.088	0.0
10	AGRICULTURE	0.560	0.510	0.095	0.0
11	SERVICES	0.769	0.709	0.084	0.0
12	MINING	1.077	0.400	1.691	0.0

*****TOTAL SYSTEM EXPENDITURES*****
(MILLIONS OF DOLLARS)

RESOURCE	AMCUNT	UNIT PRICE	COST	
LAND				
URBAN LAND	7971.328	0.00012315	70657.875	
ARABLE LAND	9824.828	0.00013311	31048.426	
TOTAL				101706.250
RAW MATERIALS				
FOOD & FIBER	14425.844	0.00045000	193803.562	
IRCN ORE	650.008	0.00036744	33647.309	
COPPER	214.260	0.00116571	34187.691	
CTHER NON-IRCN	301.603	0.00014818	5916.781	
COAL	129.333	0.00040108	2434.633	
PETRO-NAT GAS	264.889	0.00040210	4104.441	
STONE AND CLAY	115.834	0.00009875	1177.533	
CHEMICALS	106.905	0.00000870	88.487	
LEAD, ZINC	584.289	0.00011265	8920.648	
ALUMINUM	469.968	0.00048784	32960.230	
TCTAL				317241.062
LABOR				
WORKERS COSTS	160171.687	0.00016332		2000951.00
CAPITAL				
NEW CAPITAL GCODS				21948.355
ENVIRONMENTAL MAINTENANCE				52225.328
CAPITAL MAINTENANCE				191410.062
TCTAL				265583.687
TOTAL COSTS				2685481.00

CAPITAL CREDITS TO SECTOR FOR PLANT EXPANSION, ENVIRONMENTAL TREATMENT COSTS,

YEAR					<SECTORS>							
1971	0.0	638.884	0.0	0.0	0.0	45.000	19130.531	31367.336	3195.622	3196.422	6386.137	45.000
1972	0.0	764.085	0.0	0.0	0.0	525.055	22493.484	37171.109	4010.146	4297.578	6773.840	525.055
1973	0.0	1015.452	0.0	0.0	0.0	511.232	29952.336	49450.437	5281.754	5588.496	9234.305	511.232
1974	0.0	975.564	0.0	0.0	0.0	566.028	28700.883	47463.012	5104.230	5443.848	8736.785	566.028
1975	0.0	1032.393	0.0	0.0	0.0	595.409	30376.379	50230.016	5400.129	5757.375	9252.191	595.409
1976	0.0	1044.687	0.0	0.0	0.0	634.008	30706.621	50809.297	5477.043	5857.449	9305.660	634.008
1977	0.0	1065.745	0.0	0.0	0.0	664.164	31308.184	51823.000	5594.391	5992.887	9461.949	664.164
1978	0.0	1103.440	0.0	0.0	0.0	698.480	32404.727	53649.496	5796.594	6215.684	9777.137	698.480
1979	0.0	1164.769	0.0	0.0	0.0	742.317	34200.734	56628.281	6120.766	6566.160	10311.516	742.317
1980	0.0	1219.337	0.0	0.0	0.0	795.451	35784.645	59270.246	6414.859	6892.133	10761.555	795.451
1981	0.0	1215.042	0.0	0.0	0.0	842.019	35609.254	59031.879	6412.016	6917.227	10634.789	842.019
1982	0.0	1226.976	0.0	0.0	0.0	877.303	35931.977	59595.445	6485.801	7012.180	10690.609	877.303
1983	0.0	1314.219	0.0	0.0	0.0	928.017	38498.543	63839.922	6942.301	7499.109	11471.754	928.017
1984	0.0	1320.510	0.0	0.0	0.0	990.031	38625.262	64110.965	6998.559	7592.578	11423.035	990.031
1985	0.0	1380.408	0.0	0.0	0.0	1044.142	40368.113	67013.500	7319.695	7946.184	11924.625	1044.142
1986	0.0	1423.957	0.0	0.0	0.0	1106.402	41612.324	69110.062	7562.344	8226.187	12248.051	1106.402
1987	0.0	1441.341	0.0	0.0	0.0	1169.913	42070.324	69923.750	7674.672	8376.617	12307.566	1169.913
1988	0.0	1536.704	0.0	0.0	0.0	1234.384	44866.738	74557.875	8177.273	8917.906	13145.148	1234.384
1989	0.0	1621.355	0.0	0.0	0.0	1318.251	47322.437	78655.500	8634.082	9425.035	13840.711	1318.251
1990	0.0	1692.009	0.0	0.0	0.0	1404.821	49355.453	82065.562	9021.973	9864.867	14391.414	1404.821
1991	0.0	1749.740	0.0	0.0	0.0	1493.829	50998.363	84840.937	9346.230	10242.527	14808.504	1493.829
1992	0.0	1791.088	0.0	0.0	0.0	1581.979	52150.656	86814.125	9588.227	10537.414	15063.312	1581.979
1993	0.0	1851.821	0.0	0.0	0.0	1667.923	53886.691	89738.437	9926.270	10927.023	15515.937	1667.923
1994	0.0	1943.669	0.0	0.0	0.0	1763.605	56546.480	94181.625	10423.789	11481.949	16262.203	1763.605
1995	0.0	2027.695	0.0	0.0	0.0	1874.193	58956.672	98232.500	10888.152	12012.668	16903.402	1874.193
1996	0.0	2117.680	0.0	0.0	0.0	1989.143	61541.277	102572.812	11384.059	12577.539	17596.344	1989.143
1997	0.0	2193.629	0.0	0.0	0.0	2112.598	63696.281	106220.250	11313.184	13080.738	18133.613	2112.598
1998	0.0	2290.668	0.0	0.0	0.0	2246.774	66473.250	110894.687	12352.051	13700.105	18862.488	2246.774
1999	0.0	2290.610	0.0	0.0	0.0	2363.449	66354.812	110821.750	12398.426	13816.492	18651.887	2363.449
2000	0.0	2496.944	0.0	0.0	0.0	2501.769	72406.500	120849.187	13485.426	14986.480	20466.250	2501.769

SUMMARY TABLE - STATE OF THE SYSTEM
(SCALED TO ORIGINAL VALUE)

YEAR	POPULATION (NP)	PUBLIC FUNDS (G)	PRIVATE FUNDS (I)	QUALITY LEVEL (Q)	NATURAL ORE USAGE (N)	ENERGY USAGE (E)	FARM AND LAND USAGE (F)	EMPLOYED WORKERS (W)	TREATED ECO-MEDIA (M)
1.	1.0000	1.0000	1.0000	1.0000	1.0000	1.0000	1.0000	1.0000	1.0000
2.	1.0106	1.0835	1.0400	0.9180	1.0381	1.0681	1.0183	1.0188	1.0766
3.	1.0213	1.1570	1.0514	0.9325	1.0675	1.0462	1.0407	1.0499	1.1221
4.	1.0321	1.2341	1.1265	0.9568	1.1070	0.9945	1.0723	1.0890	1.1602
5.	1.0431	1.3029	1.1530	0.9773	1.1220	0.9739	1.0925	1.1324	1.2041
6.	1.0541	1.3736	1.1656	0.9926	1.1666	0.9660	1.1075	1.1688	1.2412
7.	1.0653	1.4427	1.2197	1.0088	1.2161	0.9849	1.1222	1.2055	1.2813
8.	1.0766	1.5097	1.2618	1.0282	1.2819	1.0039	1.1436	1.2467	1.3286
9.	1.0880	1.5787	1.3098	1.0492	1.3702	1.0250	1.1665	1.2910	1.3813
10.	1.0995	1.6523	1.3464	1.0658	1.4297	1.0448	1.1803	1.3295	1.4240
11.	1.1112	1.7302	1.3736	1.0789	1.4670	1.0597	1.1846	1.3628	1.4576
12.	1.1230	1.8085	1.4149	1.0969	1.5281	1.0754	1.2021	1.4045	1.4983
13.	1.1349	1.8940	1.4726	1.1050	1.5908	1.0891	1.2204	1.4336	1.5314
14.	1.1469	1.9786	1.5205	1.1202	1.6458	1.0974	1.2342	1.4667	1.5659
15.	1.1591	2.0740	1.5796	1.1230	1.7036	1.1118	1.2203	1.4891	1.6129
16.	1.1713	2.1728	1.6353	1.1343	1.7429	1.1328	1.2365	1.5179	1.6485
17.	1.1838	2.2933	1.6938	1.1469	1.7873	1.1594	1.2591	1.5497	1.6836
18.	1.1963	2.4145	1.7614	1.1607	1.8399	1.1912	1.2853	1.5956	1.7273
19.	1.2090	2.5523	1.8307	1.1753	1.8947	1.2259	1.3107	1.6229	1.7691
20.	1.2218	2.6873	1.8986	1.1889	1.9472	1.2565	1.3066	1.6610	1.8141
21.	1.2347	2.8270	1.9687	1.1994	1.9962	1.2825	1.3256	1.6944	1.8511
22.	1.2478	2.9712	2.0358	1.2090	2.0366	1.3073	1.3461	1.7264	1.8881
23.	1.2611	3.1364	2.1076	1.2199	2.0808	1.3406	1.3686	1.7623	1.9274
24.	1.2744	3.3007	2.1871	1.2315	2.1334	1.3725	1.3934	1.7998	1.9708
25.	1.2879	3.4871	2.2688	1.2440	2.1865	1.4092	1.4189	1.8395	2.0130
26.	1.3016	3.6684	2.3525	1.2562	2.2405	1.4418	1.4154	1.8795	2.0570
27.	1.3154	3.8574	2.4373	1.2675	2.2776	1.4720	1.4360	1.9191	2.1053
28.	1.3293	4.0705	2.5279	1.2628	2.2832	1.4944	1.4505	1.9326	2.1318
29.	1.3434	4.2653	2.6069	1.2833	2.3270	1.5225	1.4770	1.9818	2.1902
30.	1.3576	4.5053	2.7217	1.2797	2.3636	1.5582	1.5033	2.0024	2.2185

STATE OF THE SYSTEM

YEARS

4.505
4.055
3.604
3.154
2.703
2.253
1.802
1.352
0.901
0.451
0.0

YEARS

1.0 4.3 7.7 11.0 14.3 17.7 21.0 24.3 27.7 31.0 34.3

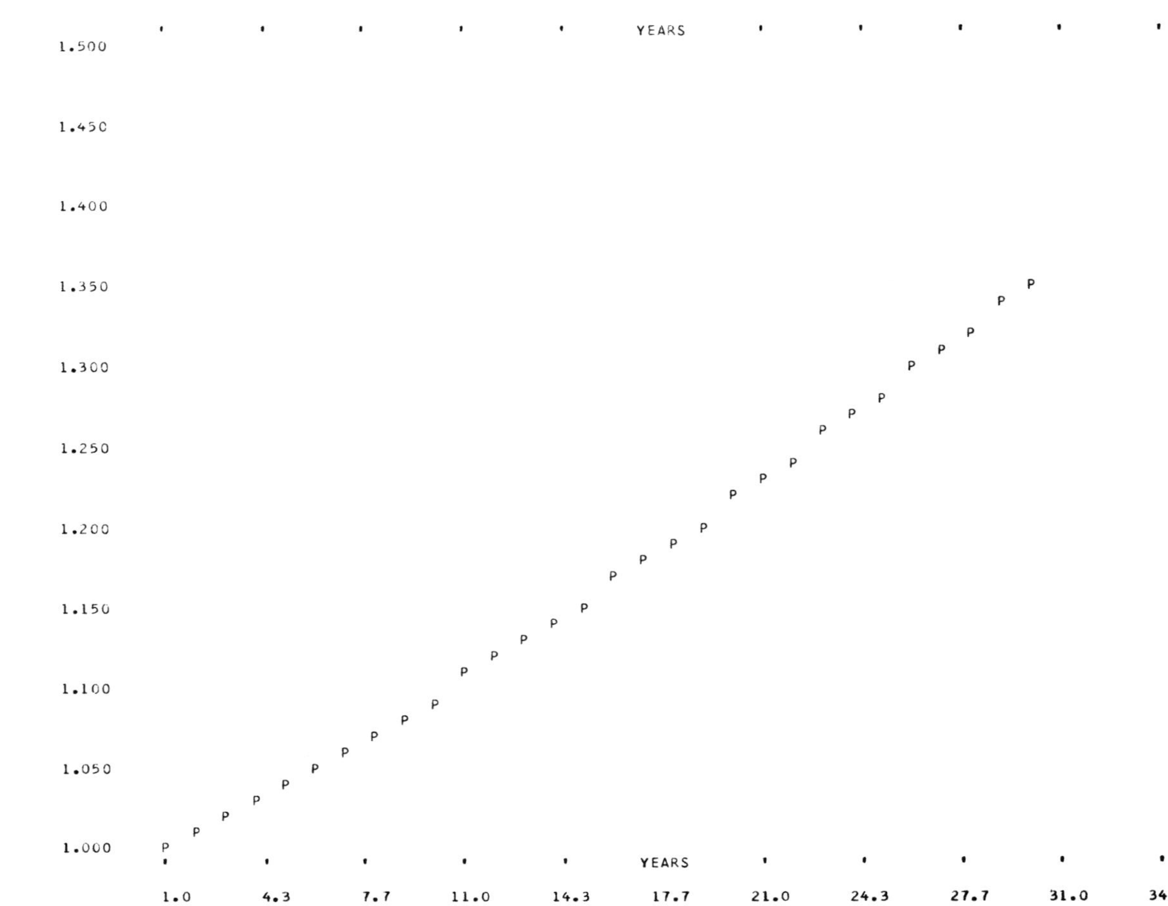
DETAIL GRAPH ------ POPULATION
YEARS
1.500
1.450
1.400
1.350
1.300
1.250
1.200
1.150
1.100
1.050
1.000
YEARS
1.0
4.3
7.7
11.0
14.3
17.7
21.0
24.3
27.7
31.0
34.3

DETAIL GRAPH ------ PUBLIC FUNDS

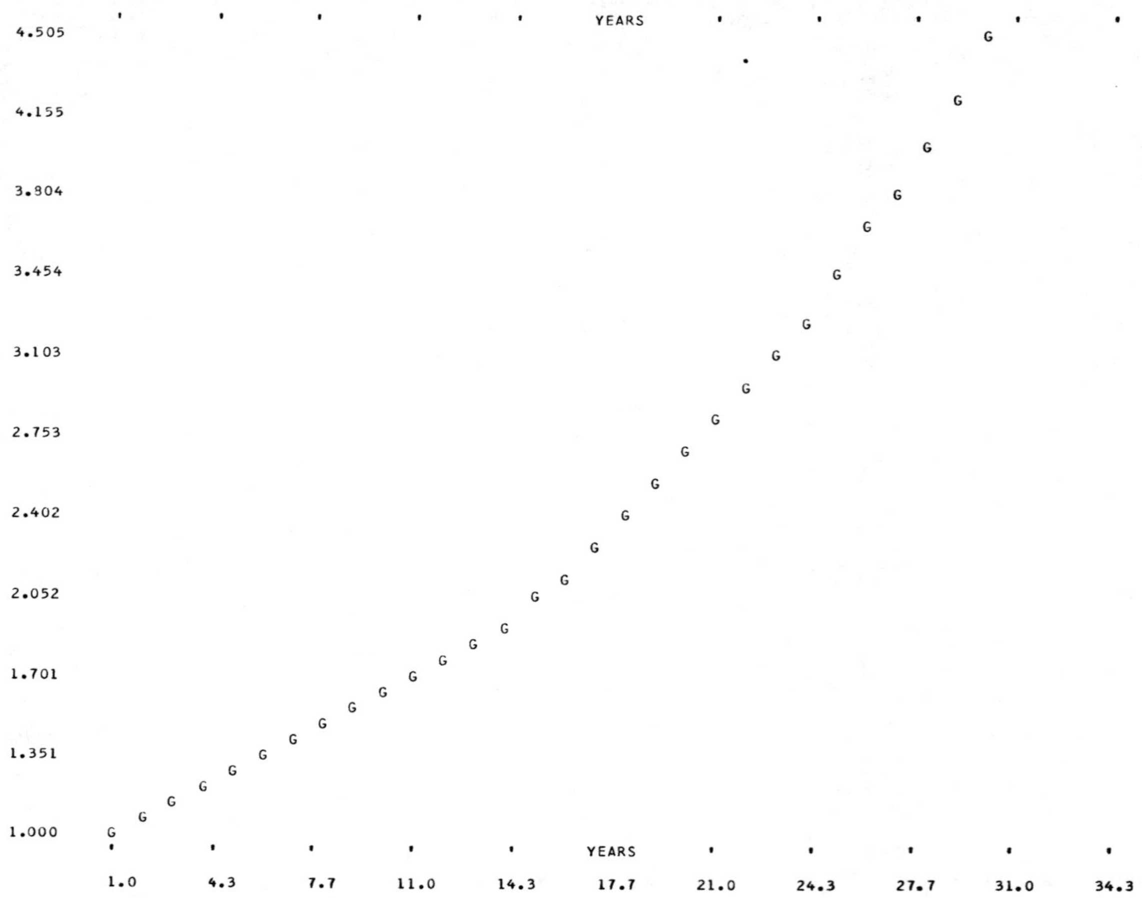

YEARS

4.505

4.155

3.804

3.454

3.103

2.753

2.402

2.052

1.701

1.351

1.000

YEARS

1.0 4.3 7.7 11.0 14.3 17.7 21.0 24.3 27.7 31.0 34.3

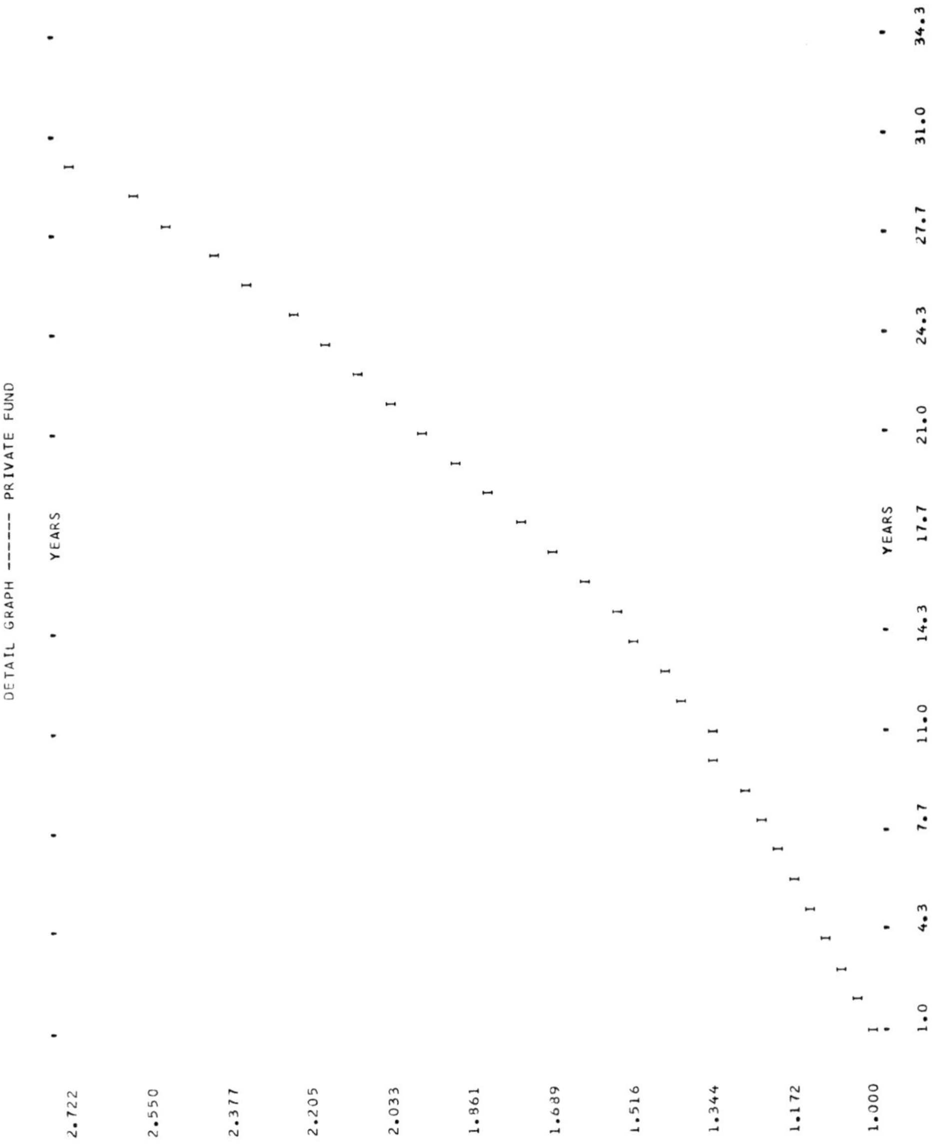

DETAIL GRAPH ------ PRIVATE FUND

YEARS

2.722
2.550
2.377
2.205
2.033
1.861
1.689
1.516
1.344
1.172
1.000

YEARS

1.0 4.3 7.7 11.0 14.3 17.7 21.0 24.3 27.7 31.0 34.3

DETAIL GRAPH ------ NATURAL ORES

YEARS

2.364
2.227
2.091
1.955
1.818
1.682
1.545
1.409
1.273
1.136
1.000

YEARS

1.0 4.3 7.7 11.0 14.3 17.7 21.0 24.3 27.7 31.0 34.3

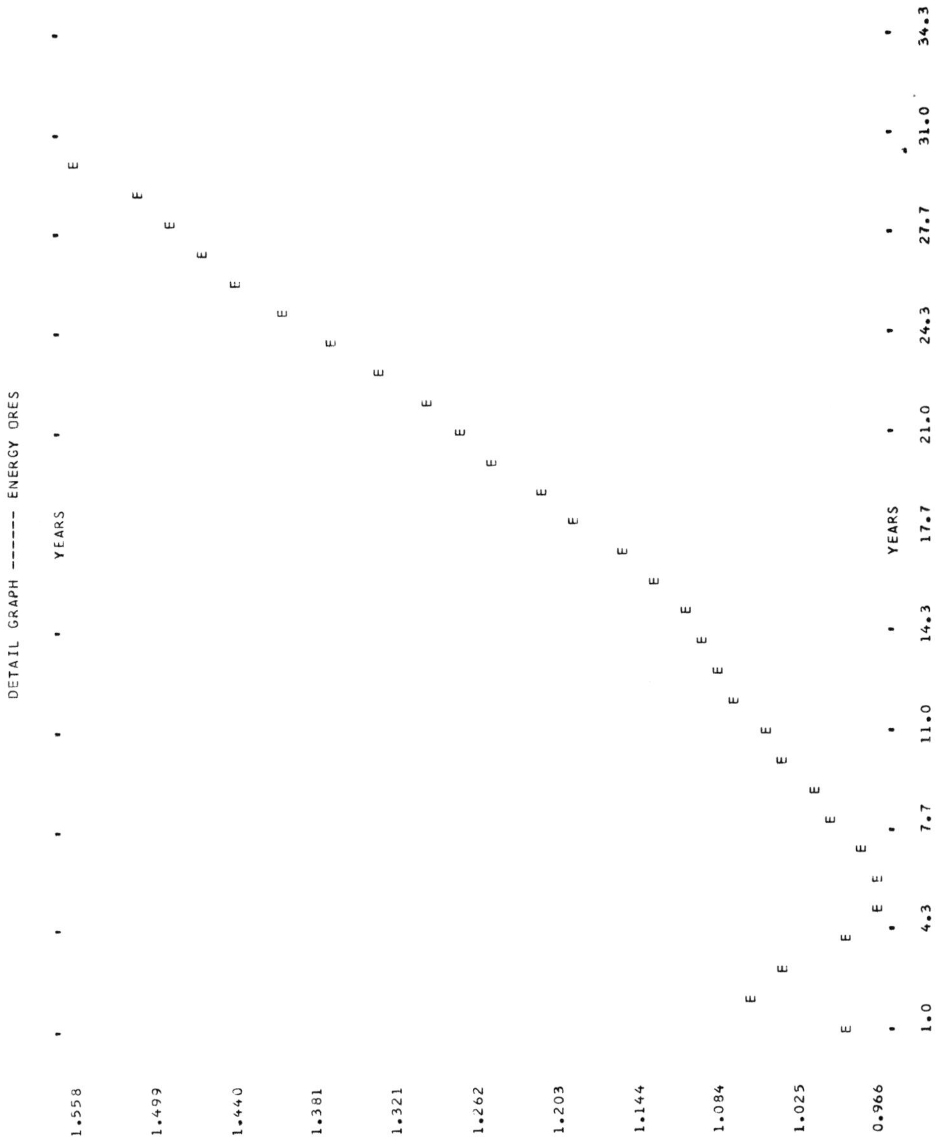

DETAIL GRAPH ------ ENERGY ORES

YEARS

1.558
1.499
1.440
1.381
1.321
1.262
1.203
1.144
1.084
1.025
0.966

YEARS

1.0 4.3 7.7 11.0 14.3 17.7 21.0 24.3 27.7 31.0 34.3

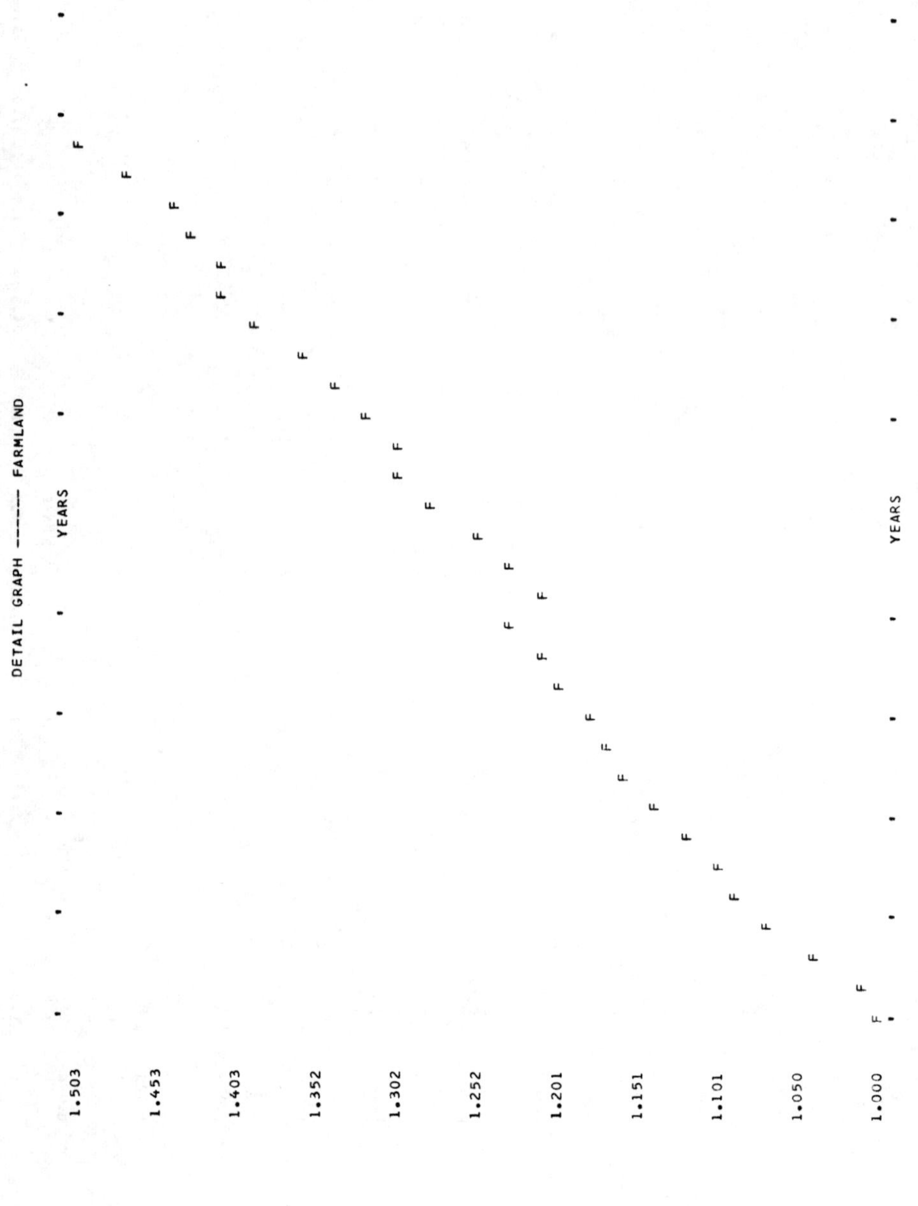

DETAIL GRAPH ------ FARMLAND

YEARS

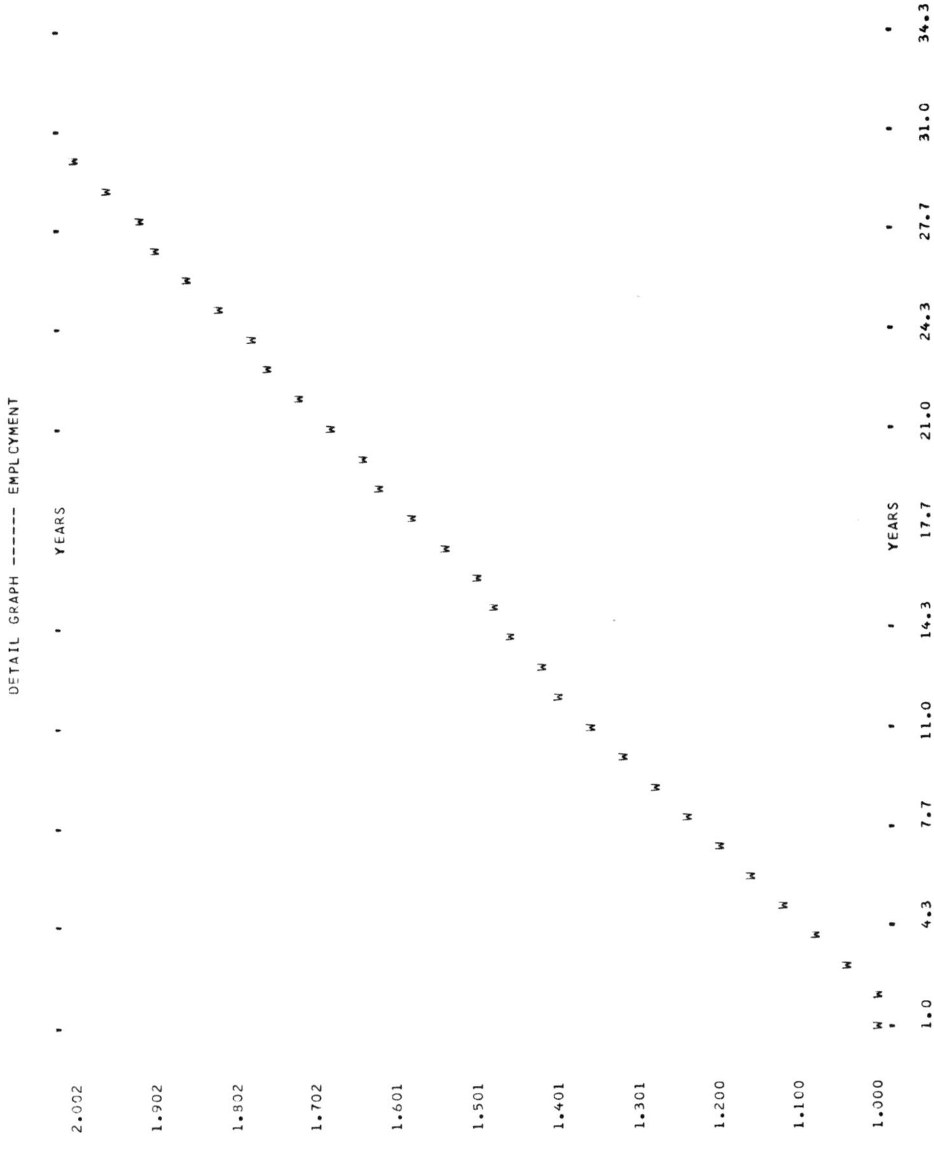

DETAIL GRAPH ------ EMPLCYMENT

YEARS

2.002
1.902
1.802
1.702
1.601
1.501
1.401
1.301
1.200
1.100
1.000

YEARS

1.0 4.3 7.7 11.0 14.3 17.7 21.0 24.3 27.7 31.0 34.3

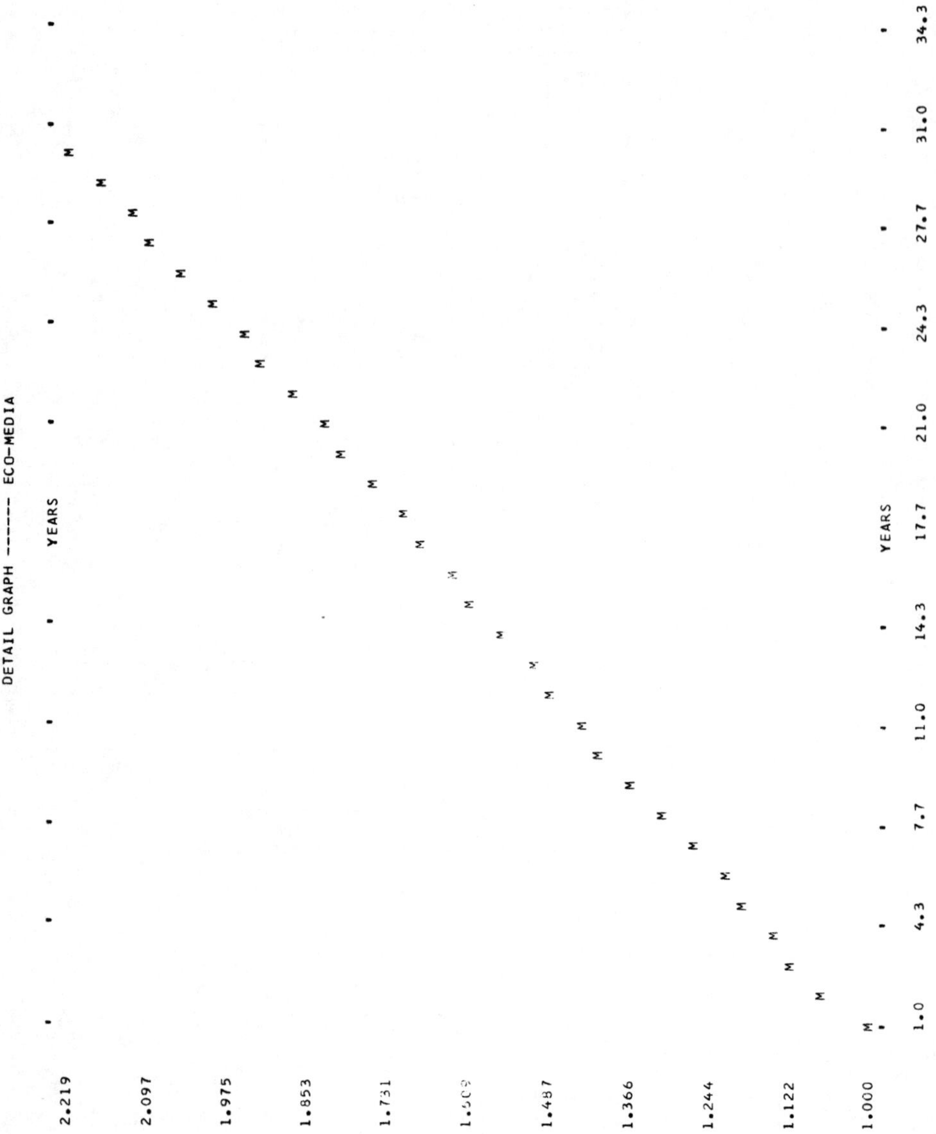

DETAIL GRAPH ------ ECO-MEDIA

YEARS

2.219
2.097
1.975
1.853
1.731
1.609
1.487
1.366
1.244
1.122
1.000

YEARS

1.0 4.3 7.7 11.0 14.3 17.7 21.0 24.3 27.7 31.0 34.3

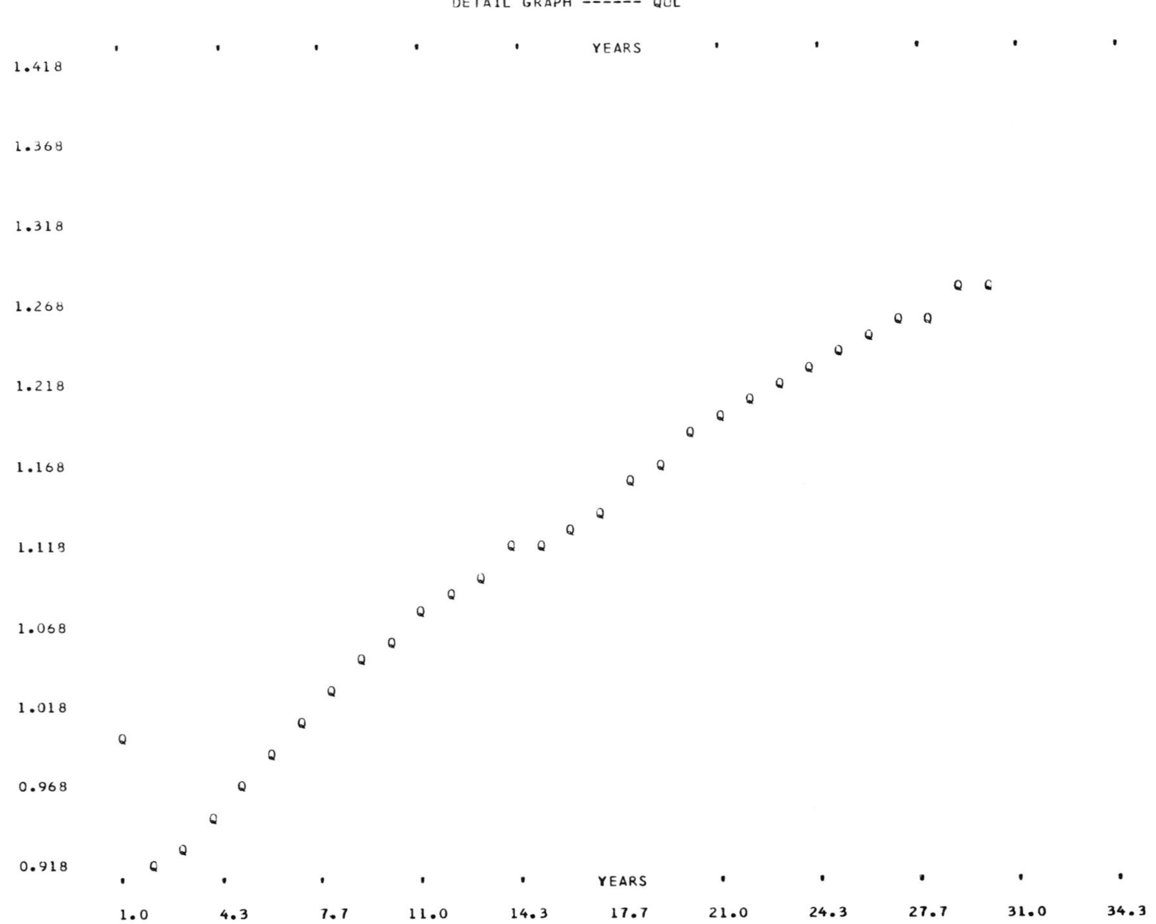
DETAIL GRAPH ------ QOL
YEARS
1.418
1.368
1.318
1.268
1.218
1.168
1.118
1.068
1.018
0.968
0.918
YEARS
1.0
4.3
7.7
11.0
14.3
17.7
21.0
24.3
27.7
31.0
34.3

TABLE NUMBER ONE - POPULATION
(SCALED TO ORIGINAL VALUE)

YEAR	TOTAL POPULATION (NP)	UNDER 18 YEARS (1)	18-24 YEARS (2)	25-64 YEARS (3)	OVER 64 YEARS (4)
1.	0.9912	0.3438	0.1250	0.4459	0.0998
2.	1.0017	0.3438	0.1278	0.4535	0.1002
3.	1.0123	0.3439	0.1305	0.4614	0.1004
4.	1.0230	0.3441	0.1330	0.4695	0.1004
5.	1.0339	0.3413	0.1389	0.4777	0.1003
6.	1.0448	0.3387	0.1448	0.4860	0.1000
7.	1.0559	0.3361	0.1507	0.4944	0.0995
8.	1.0671	0.3336	0.1544	0.5053	0.0989
9.	1.0784	0.3313	0.1581	0.5162	0.0982
10.	1.0898	0.3291	0.1618	0.5273	0.0974
11.	1.1014	0.3270	0.1655	0.5366	0.0982
12.	1.1130	0.3251	0.1660	0.5492	0.0989
13.	1.1248	0.3293	0.1607	0.5619	0.0995
14.	1.1368	0.3336	0.1553	0.5747	0.0999
15.	1.1488	0.3381	0.1499	0.5876	0.1002
16.	1.1610	0.3429	0.1445	0.6005	0.1004
17.	1.1733	0.3478	0.1390	0.6135	0.1006
18.	1.1857	0.3522	0.1343	0.6266	0.1006
19.	1.1983	0.3566	0.1297	0.6397	0.1006
20.	1.2110	0.3610	0.1311	0.6470	0.1005
21.	1.2238	0.3654	0.1327	0.6543	0.1003
22.	1.2368	0.3699	0.1345	0.6615	0.1001
23.	1.2499	0.3744	0.1365	0.6687	0.0999
24.	1.2632	0.3788	0.1387	0.6758	0.0997
25.	1.2766	0.3834	0.1403	0.6835	0.0995
26.	1.2901	0.3879	0.1420	0.6914	0.0993
27.	1.3038	0.3924	0.1436	0.6994	0.0990
28.	1.3176	0.3970	0.1453	0.7075	0.0988
29.	1.3315	0.4016	0.1470	0.7157	0.0986
30.	1.3457	0.4062	0.1487	0.7240	0.0984

TABLE NUMBER TWO - PUBLIC SECTOR OUTPUT UNITS
(SCALED TO ORIGINAL VALUE)

YEAR	EDUCATION (E)	TRANSPORTATION (T)	HEALTH (H)	PUBLIC SAFETY (S)	ADMINISTRATION 2A)
1.	1.0000	1.0000	1.0000	1.0000	1.0000
2.	1.0010	1.0366	1.0396	1.0117	1.1675
3.	1.0110	1.0908	1.0873	1.0304	1.2743
4.	1.0443	1.1232	1.1614	1.0710	1.4334
5.	1.0885	1.1943	1.2508	1.1210	1.5531
6.	1.1228	1.2252	1.3335	1.1621	1.6631
7.	1.1588	1.2740	1.4221	1.2055	1.7469
8.	1.1958	1.3256	1.5162	1.2504	1.8065
9.	1.2340	1.3806	1.6162	1.2968	1.8607
10.	1.2734	1.4351	1.7224	1.3448	1.9231
11.	1.3140	1.4847	1.8351	1.3945	1.9949
12.	1.3544	1.5339	1.9506	1.4425	2.0658
13.	1.3688	1.5676	2.0354	1.4662	2.1086
14.	1.3985	1.6088	2.1458	1.5061	2.1419
15.	1.4004	1.6500	2.2215	1.5196	2.1594
16.	1.4178	1.6997	2.3236	1.5497	2.1804
17.	1.4357	1.7385	2.4302	1.5807	2.2806
18.	1.4542	1.7942	2.5423	1.6129	2.3475
19.	1.4725	1.8432	2.6587	1.6447	2.4660
20.	1.4909	1.9061	2.7804	1.6772	2.5420
21.	1.5096	1.9533	2.9076	1.7102	2.6095
22.	1.5285	2.0033	3.0404	1.7437	2.6650
23.	1.5476	2.0561	3.1793	1.7779	2.7754
24.	1.5669	2.1119	3.3244	1.8126	2.8471
25.	1.5863	2.1672	3.4758	1.8476	2.9728
26.	1.6050	2.2290	3.6323	1.8813	3.0492
27.	1.6244	2.2842	3.7978	1.9168	3.1159
28.	1.6114	2.3027	3.9003	1.9160	3.1825
29.	1.6467	2.3778	4.1164	1.9709	3.2186
30.	1.6340	2.4036	4.2201	1.9698	3.2922

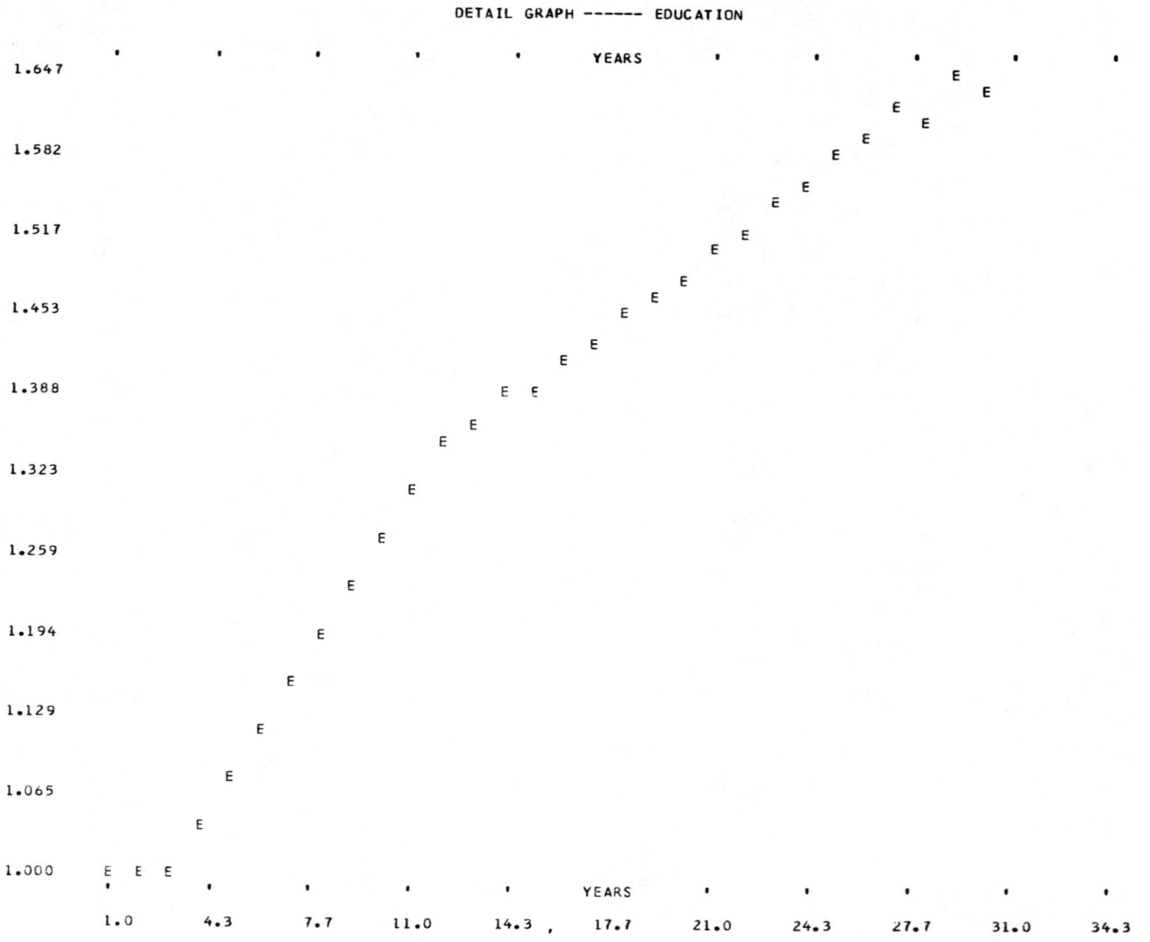
DETAIL GRAPH ------ EDUCATION
YEARS
1.647
1.582
1.517
1.453
1.388
1.323
1.259
1.194
1.129
1.065
1.000
YEARS
1.0
4.3
7.7
11.0
14.3 ,
17.7
21.0
24.3
27.7
31.0
34.3

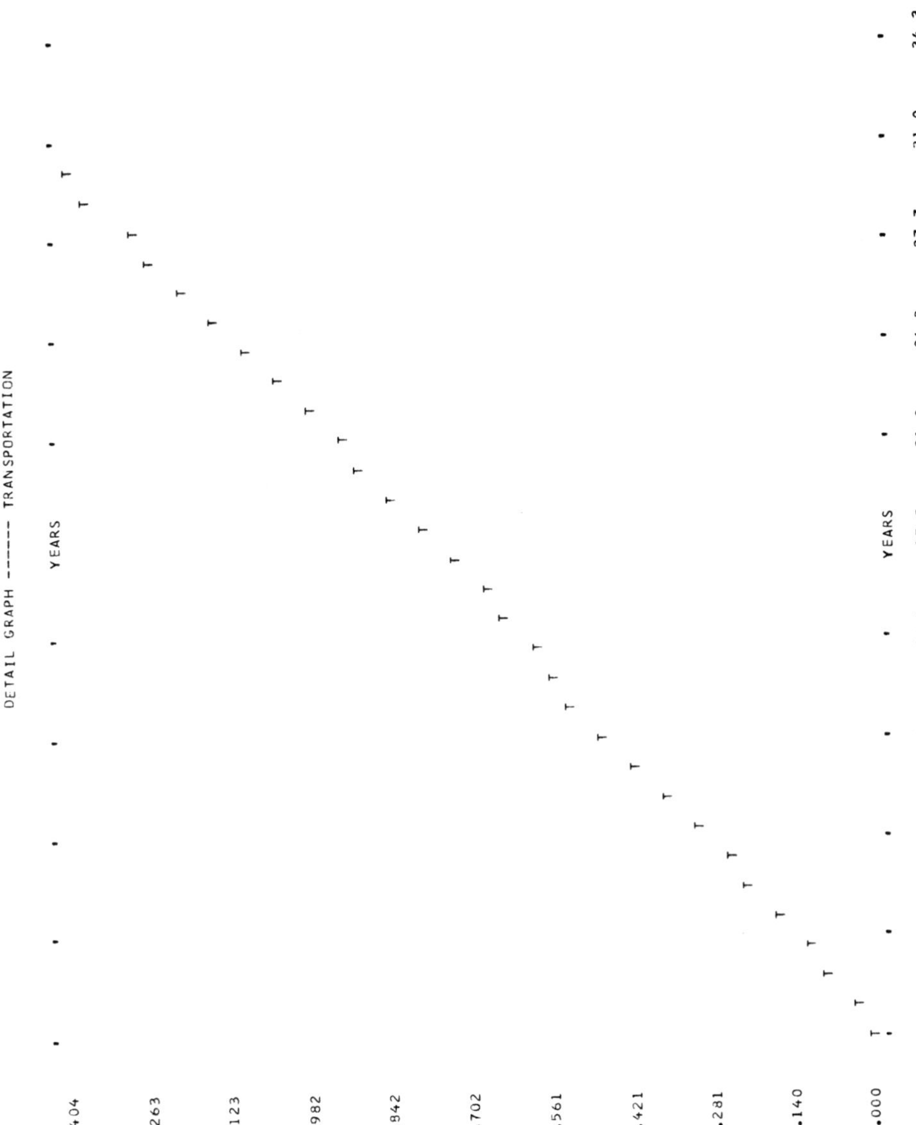

DETAIL GRAPH ------ TRANSPORTATION

YEARS

2.404
2.263
2.123
1.982
1.842
1.702
1.561
1.421
1.281
1.140
1.000

YEARS

1.0 4.3 7.7 11.0 14.3 17.7 21.0 24.3 27.7 31.0 34.3

DETAIL GRAPH ------ HEALTH & WELFARE

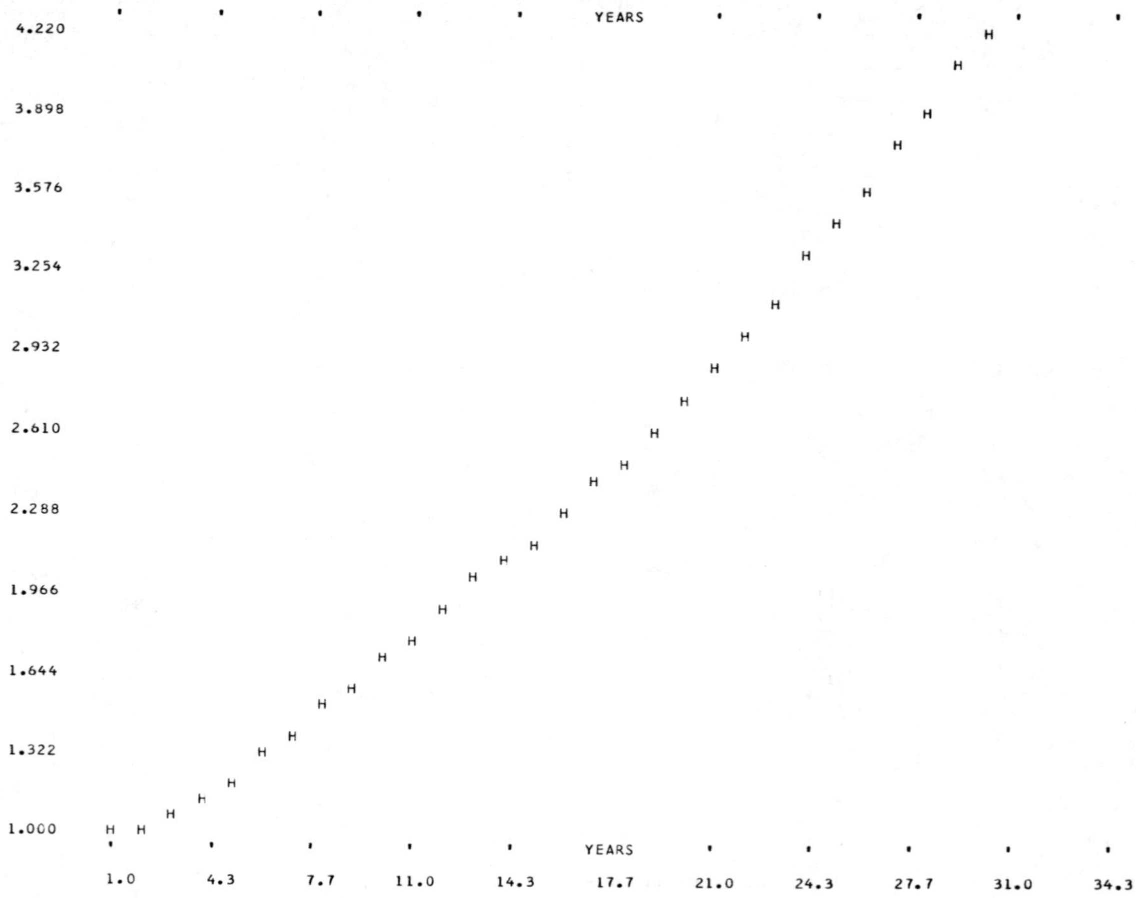

YEARS

4.220
3.898
3.576
3.254
2.932
2.610
2.288
1.966
1.644
1.322
1.000

YEARS

1.0 4.3 7.7 11.0 14.3 17.7 21.0 24.3 27.7 31.0 34.3

DETAIL GRAPH ------ PUBLIC SAFETY

YEARS

1.971
1.874
1.777
1.680
1.583
1.485
1.388
1.291
1.194
1.097
1.000

YEARS

1.0 4.3 7.7 11.0 14.3 17.7 21.0 24.3 27.7 31.0 34.3

DETAIL GRAPH ------ ADMINISTRATION & OTHER

YEARS

3.292
3.063
2.834
2.605
2.375
2.146
1.917
1.688
1.458
1.229
1.000

YEARS

1.0 4.3 7.7 11.0 14.3 17.7 21.0 24.3 27.7 31.0 34.3

TABLE NUMBER THREE – PRIVATE SECTOR OUTPUT UNITS
(SCALED TO ORIGINAL VALUE)

YEAR	AGRICULTURE (A)	NON-DURABLE MANUFACTURE (N)	DURABLE MANUFACTURE (D)	COMMERCIAL (C)	WHOLE & RET. TRADE (W)	SERVICES (S)	MINING (M)
1.	1.0000	1.0000	1.0000	1.0000	1.0000	1.0000	1.0000
2.	1.0025	1.0510	1.0088	1.0052	1.0077	0.9948	1.5282
3.	0.9927	1.1396	1.0332	1.0188	1.0242	1.0233	1.6028
4.	1.0336	1.1637	1.0688	1.0532	1.0555	1.0568	1.6843
5.	1.0276	1.2159	1.0768	1.0843	1.1003	1.1093	1.7573
6.	1.0466	1.2065	1.1191	1.1140	1.1347	1.1484	1.8259
7.	1.0623	1.1996	1.1662	1.1446	1.1710	1.1862	1.8957
8.	1.0872	1.1981	1.2310	1.1804	1.2088	1.2270	1.9664
9.	1.1097	1.2029	1.3075	1.2188	1.2481	1.2701	2.0377
10.	1.1185	1.2026	1.3528	1.2476	1.2883	1.3112	2.1100
11.	1.1170	1.1871	1.3778	1.2729	1.3283	1.3501	2.1834
12.	1.1384	1.1777	1.4357	1.3085	1.3699	1.3937	2.2209
13.	1.1658	1.1826	1.5011	1.3288	1.3885	1.4180	2.2306
14.	1.1876	1.1691	1.5575	1.3563	1.4190	1.4513	2.2608
15.	1.2089	1.1725	1.6090	1.3722	1.4283	1.4690	2.4281
16.	1.2184	1.2027	1.6472	1.3940	1.4492	1.4960	2.4625
17.	1.2503	1.2234	1.6897	1.4162	1.4688	1.5209	2.5155
18.	1.2741	1.2671	1.7409	1.4407	1.4907	1.5505	2.5568
19.	1.3008	1.3038	1.7944	1.4655	1.5124	1.5793	2.5961
20.	1.3249	1.3390	1.8457	1.4950	1.5367	1.6126	2.6370
21.	1.3433	1.3696	1.8945	1.5182	1.5580	1.6401	2.6603
22.	1.3671	1.3985	1.9328	1.5395	1.5793	1.6671	2.7074
23.	1.3915	1.4335	1.9749	1.5619	1.6013	1.6956	2.7499
24.	1.4159	1.4760	2.0262	1.5865	1.6241	1.7260	2.7874
25.	1.4437	1.5163	2.0782	1.6115	1.6471	1.7563	2.8172
26.	1.4703	1.5592	2.1319	1.6392	1.6715	1.7895	2.8373
27.	1.4867	1.5980	2.2015	1.6637	1.6947	1.8200	2.8783
28.	1.5096	1.6341	2.2415	1.6596	1.6867	1.8186	2.9429
29.	1.5393	1.6626	2.3091	1.6949	1.7242	1.8626	3.0230
30.	1.5681	1.7396	2.3576	1.6968	1.7177	1.8657	3.0132

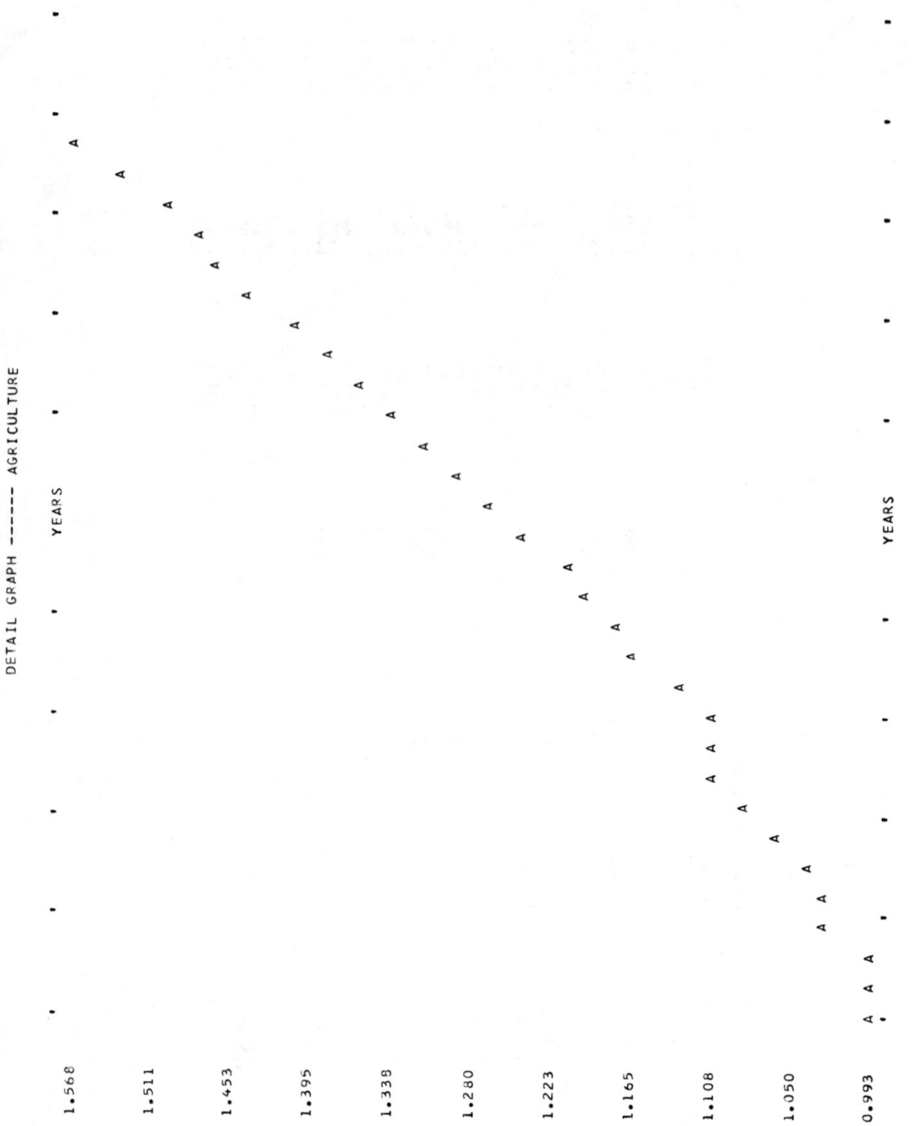

```
                              DETAIL GRAPH ------ AGRICULTURE

        .    .    .    .    .   YEARS   .    .    .    .    .
1.568                                                     A
                                                        A
1.511
                                                      A
                                                    A
1.453                                              A
                                                  A
1.395                                           A
                                               A
1.338                                        A
                                           A
1.280                                    A
                                       A
1.223                                A
                                   A
                                 A
1.165                          A
                             A
                           A
1.108              A  A  A
                 A
1.050          A
             A
         A A
0.993 A A A
      .    .    .    .    .   YEARS   .    .    .    .    .

     1.0  4.3  7.7  11.0 14.3  17.7  21.0 24.3 27.7 31.0 34.3
```

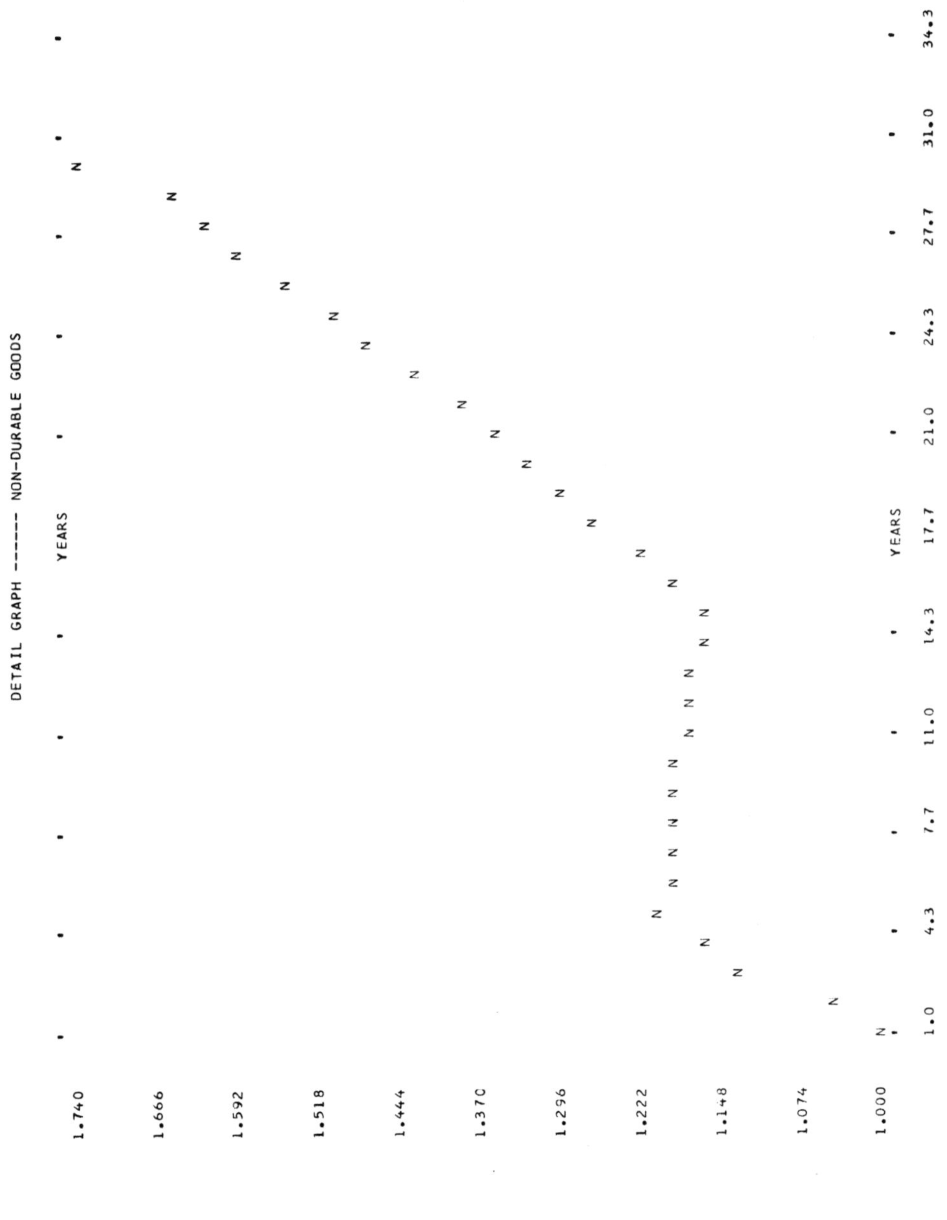

DETAIL GRAPH ------ NON-DURABLE GOODS

YEARS

1.740
1.666
1.592
1.518
1.444
1.370
1.296
1.222
1.148
1.074
1.000

YEARS

1.0 4.3 7.7 11.0 14.3 17.7 21.0 24.3 27.7 31.0 34.3

DETAIL GRAPH ------ DURABLE GOODS

YEARS

2.358
2.222
2.086
1.950
1.815
1.679
1.543
1.407
1.272
1.136
1.000

YEARS

1.0 4.3 7.7 11.0 14.3 17.7 21.0 24.3 27.7 31.0 34.3

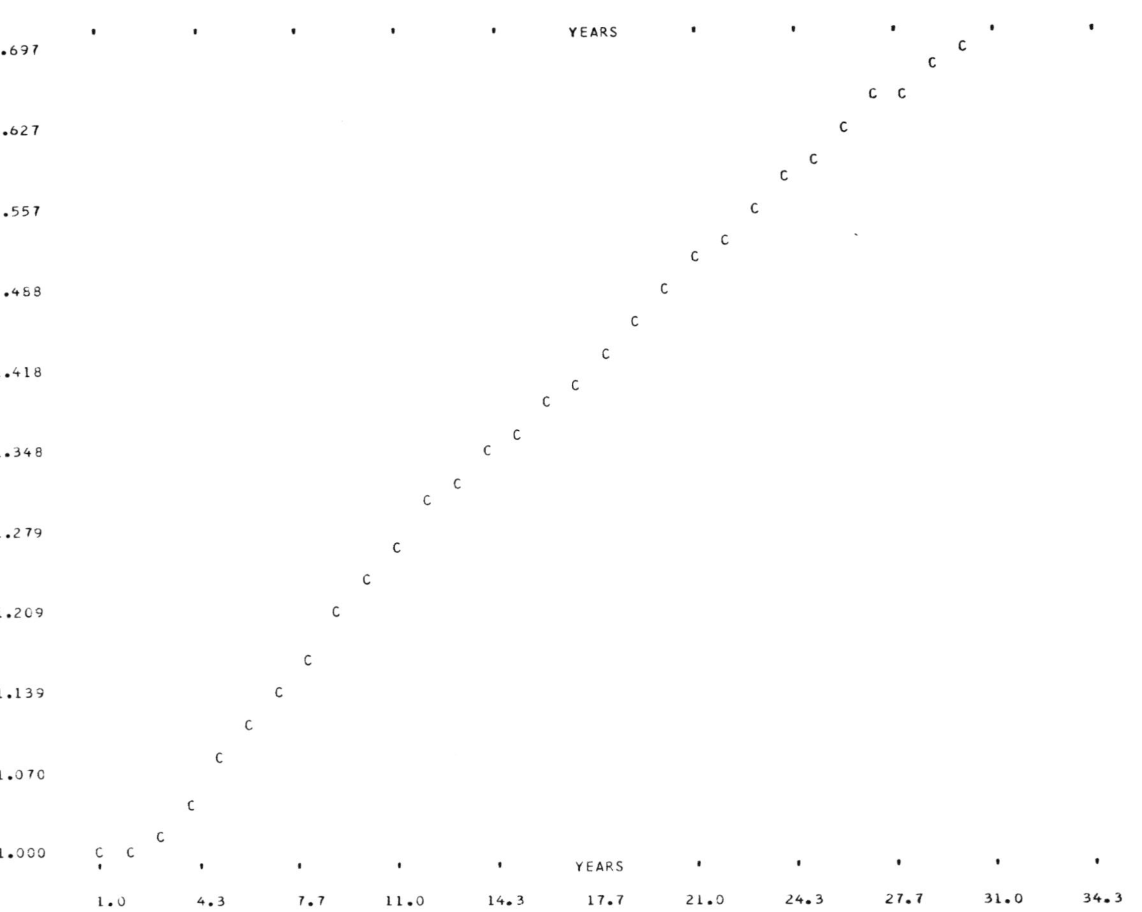
DETAIL GRAPH ------ COMMUN. & TRANS.
YEARS
1.697
1.627
1.557
1.488
1.418
1.348
1.279
1.209
1.139
1.070
1.000
YEARS
1.0
4.3
7.7
11.0
14.3
17.7
21.0
24.3
27.7
31.0
34.3

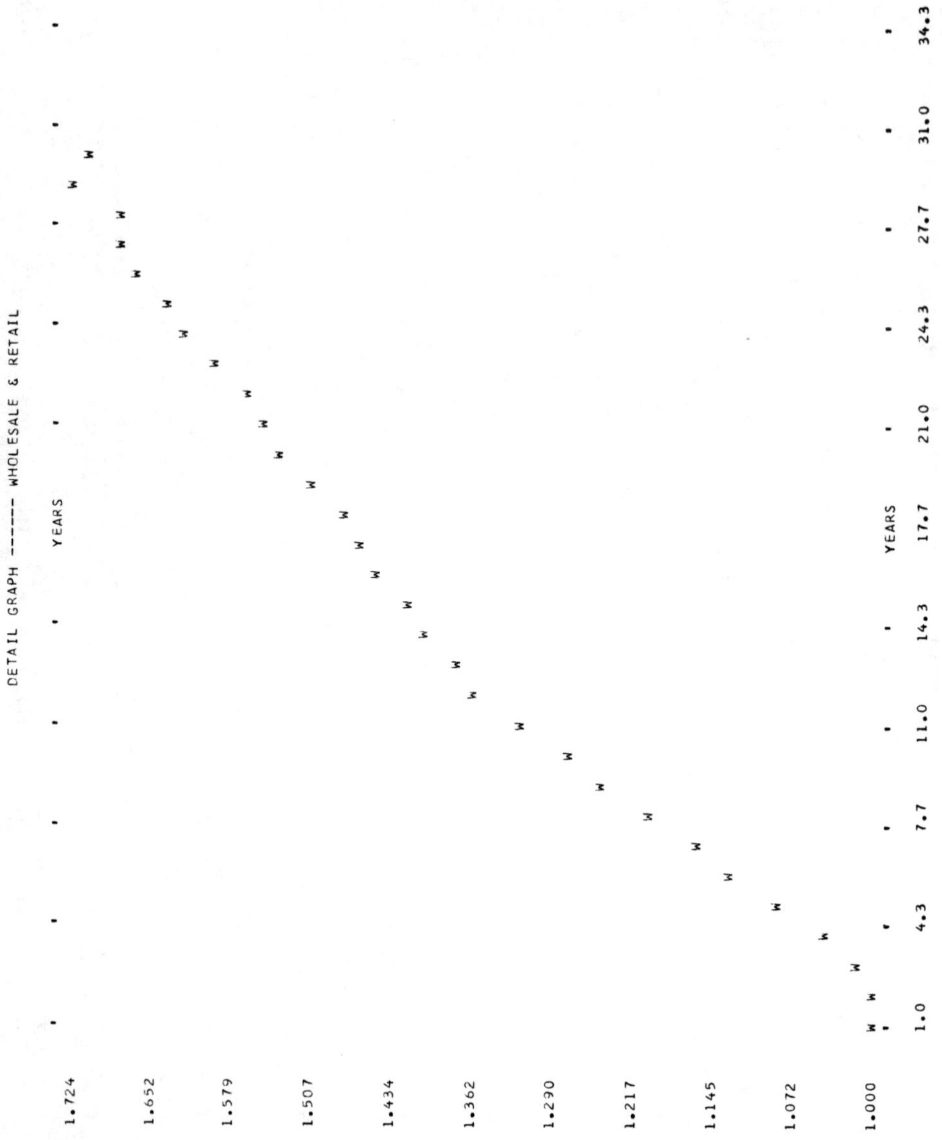

DETAIL GRAPH ------ WHOLESALE & RETAIL

YEARS

1.724
1.652
1.579
1.507
1.434
1.362
1.290
1.217
1.145
1.072
1.000

YEARS

1.0 4.3 7.7 11.0 14.3 17.7 21.0 24.3 27.7 31.0 34.3

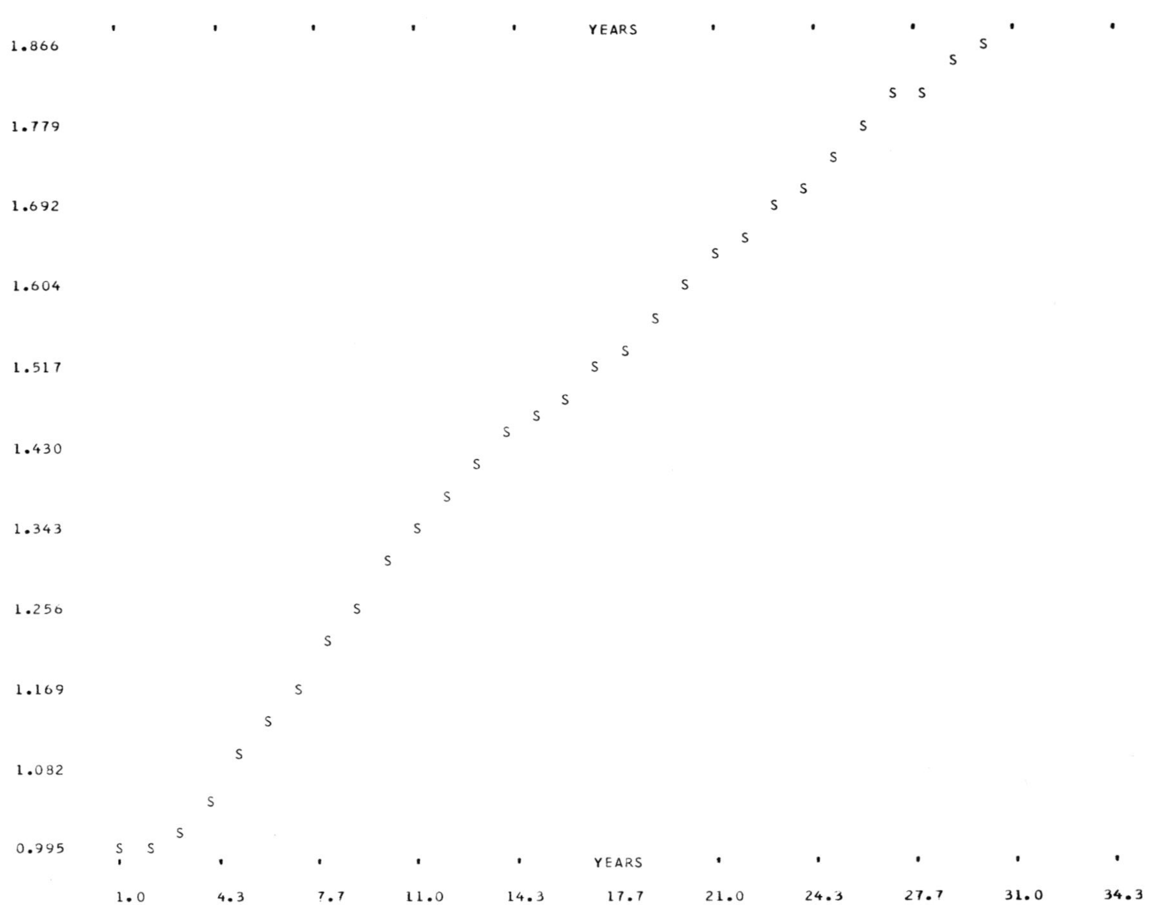

DETAIL GRAPH ------ SERVICES
YEARS
1.866
1.779
1.692
1.604
1.517
1.430
1.343
1.256
1.169
1.082
0.995
YEARS
1.0
4.3
7.7
11.0
14.3
17.7
21.0
24.3
27.7
31.0
34.3

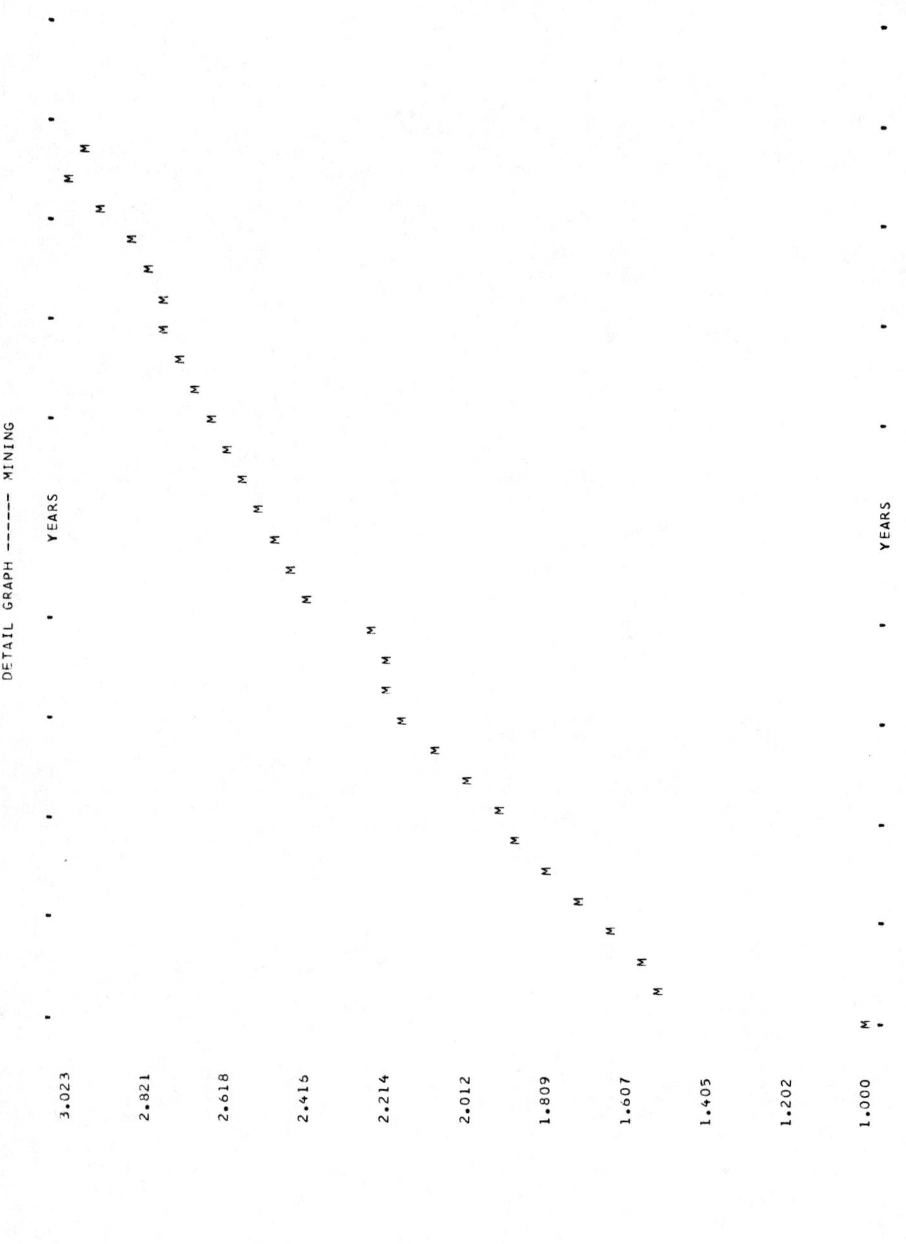

DETAIL GRAPH ------ MINING

YEARS

3.023
2.821
2.618
2.416
2.214
2.012
1.809
1.607
1.405
1.202
1.000

YEARS

1.0 4.3 7.7 11.0 14.3 17.7 21.0 24.3 27.7 31.0 34.3

TABLE NUMBER FOUR - NATURAL RESOURCES USAGE
(SCALED TO ORIGINAL VALUE)

YEAR	FOOD (F)	IRON (I)	COPPER (K)	OTHER NON-FERROUS (O)
1.	1.0000	1.0000	1.0000	1.0000
2.	1.0309	1.0130	1.0473	1.0539
3.	1.0789	1.0401	1.0763	1.0860
4.	1.1102	1.0953	1.0724	1.1534
5.	1.1402	1.1269	1.0400	1.1993
6.	1.1443	1.1986	1.0155	1.2856
7.	1.1484	1.2832	0.9779	1.3871
8.	1.1594	1.3896	0.9457	1.5104
9.	1.1730	1.5415	0.9256	1.6435
10.	1.1785	1.6536	0.9006	1.7350
11.	1.1713	1.7256	0.8824	1.7930
12.	1.1766	1.8141	0.8968	1.8735
13.	1.1911	1.8920	0.9334	1.9471
14.	1.1937	1.9590	0.9659	2.0124
15.	1.2049	2.0233	1.0015	2.0860
16.	1.2272	2.0709	1.0243	2.1335
17.	1.2527	2.1235	1.0504	2.1881
18.	1.2884	2.1873	1.0809	2.2516
19.	1.3212	2.2536	1.1126	2.3179
20.	1.3523	2.3172	1.1431	2.3814
21.	1.3784	2.3771	1.1714	2.4401
22.	1.4056	2.4251	1.1950	2.4897
23.	1.4366	2.4778	1.2207	2.5439
24.	1.4720	2.5416	1.2511	2.6076
25.	1.5074	2.6060	1.2817	2.6718
26.	1.5440	2.6724	1.3127	2.7365
27.	1.5742	2.8414	1.1709	2.8205
28.	1.6038	2.9757	1.0004	2.8737
29.	1.6341	3.1265	0.8956	2.9590
30.	1.6892	3.2179	0.8570	3.0160

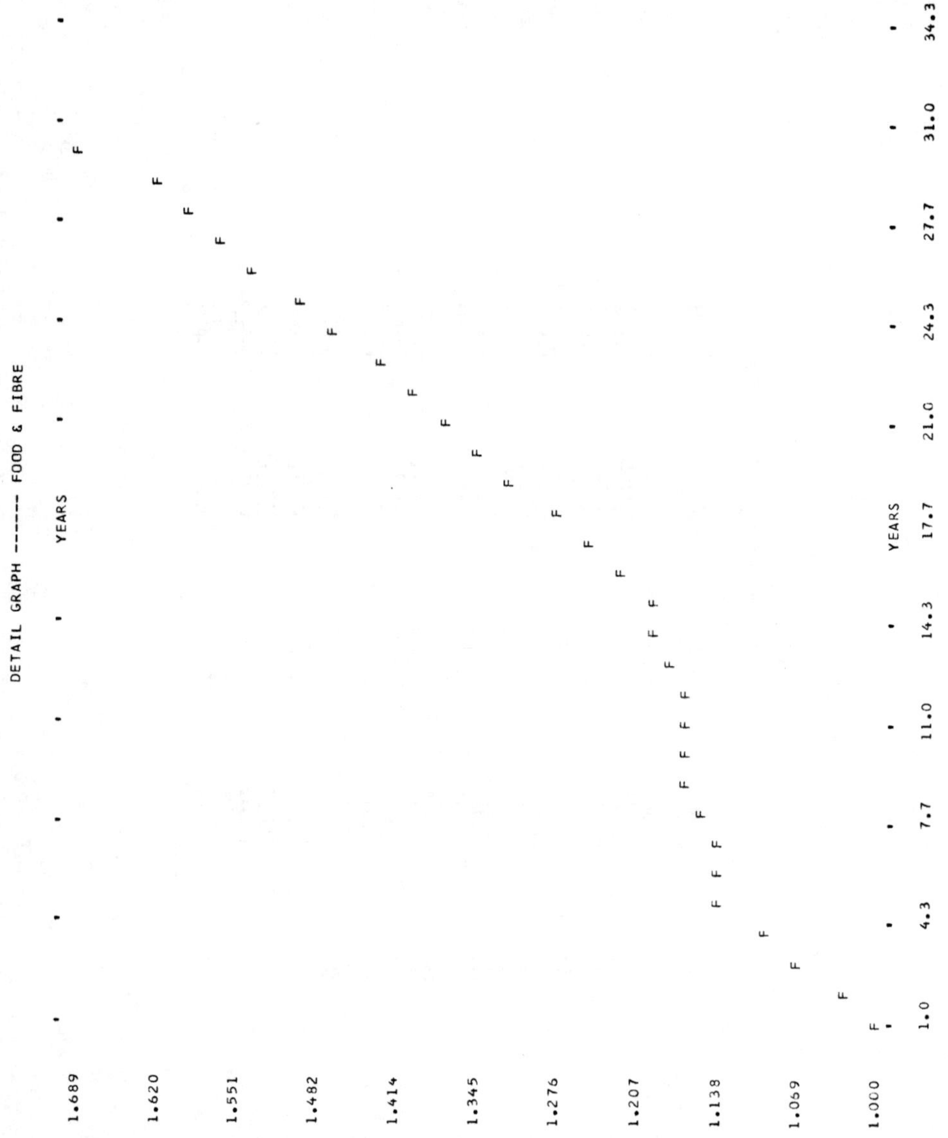

DETAIL GRAPH ------ FOOD & FIBRE

YEARS

1.689
1.620
1.551
1.482
1.414
1.345
1.276
1.207
1.138
1.069
1.000

YEARS

1.0 4.3 7.7 11.0 14.3 17.7 21.0 24.3 27.7 31.0 34.3

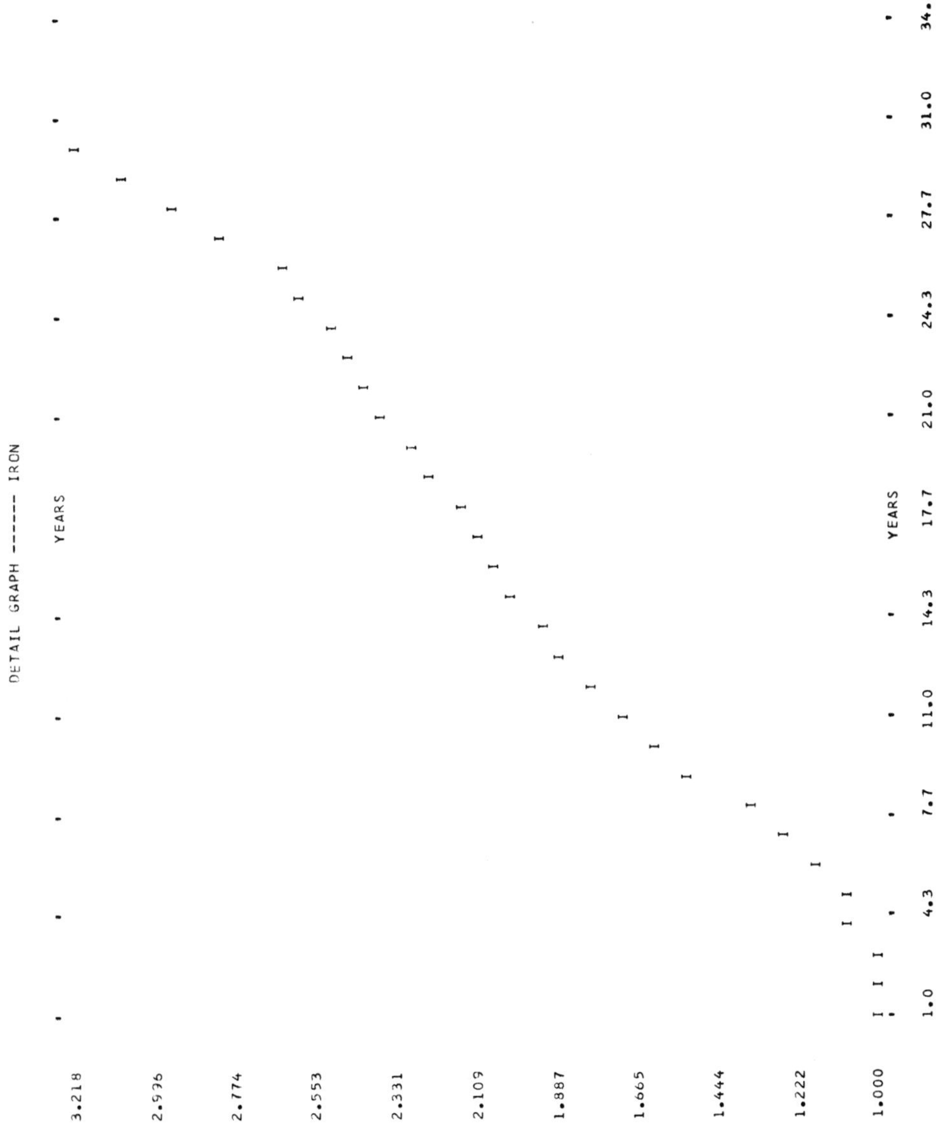

DETAIL GRAPH ------ IRON

YEARS

3.218
2.996
2.774
2.553
2.331
2.109
1.887
1.665
1.444
1.222
1.000

YEARS

1.0 4.3 7.7 11.0 14.3 17.7 21.0 24.3 27.7 31.0 34.3

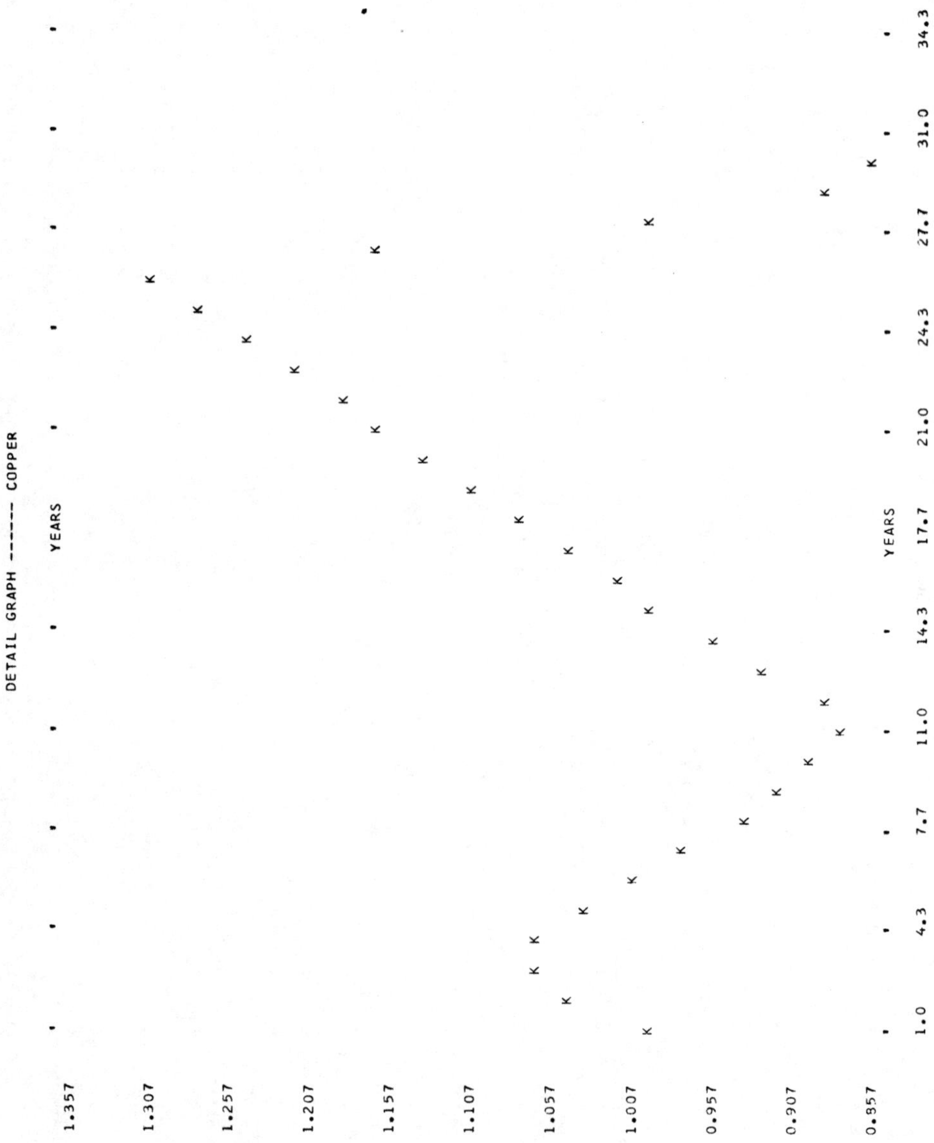

DETAIL GRAPH ------ COPPER

YEARS

1.357
1.307
1.257
1.207
1.157
1.107
1.057
1.007
0.957
0.907
0.857

YEARS

1.0 4.3 7.7 11.0 14.3 17.7 21.0 24.3 27.7 31.0 34.3

TABLE NUMBER FIVE - RAW MATERIAL USAGE; CONT.,
(SCALED TO ORIGINAL VALUE)

YEAR	COAL (K)	OIL (T)	STONE & CLAY (S)	CHEMICALS (C)	LEAD (L)	ALUMINUM (A)
1.	1.0000	1.0000	1.0000	1.0000	1.0000	1.0000
2.	1.0923	1.0439	1.0854	1.0689	1.0157	1.0148
3.	1.2352	0.8571	1.1363	1.1256	1.0483	1.0410
4.	1.3738	0.6151	1.1762	1.1598	1.0825	1.0768
5.	1.5071	0.4406	1.2071	1.1924	1.0963	1.0866
6.	1.5728	0.3591	1.2386	1.2141	1.1322	1.1281
7.	1.6101	0.3597	1.2733	1.2393	1.1727	1.1744
8.	1.6461	0.3616	1.3191	1.2754	1.2292	1.2378
9.	1.6848	0.3652	1.3735	1.3199	1.2093	1.3127
10.	1.7221	0.3674	1.4089	1.3473	1.1592	1.3573
11.	1.7536	0.3658	1.4286	1.3583	1.1115	1.3821
12.	1.7869	0.3659	1.4646	1.3850	1.1247	1.4385
13.	1.8099	0.3684	1.5052	1.4193	1.1709	1.5019
14.	1.8279	0.3669	1.5375	1.4429	1.2089	1.5566
15.	1.8546	0.3690	1.5878	1.4825	1.2456	1.6080
16.	1.8878	0.3778	1.6228	1.5168	1.2753	1.6459
17.	1.9346	0.3843	1.6613	1.5506	1.3072	1.6881
18.	1.9857	0.3966	1.7094	1.5977	1.3473	1.7389
19.	2.0446	0.4072	1.7576	1.6427	1.3885	1.7919
20.	2.0954	0.4177	1.8034	1.6861	1.4279	1.8426
21.	2.1383	0.4267	1.8442	1.7248	1.4650	1.8907
22.	2.1795	0.4352	1.8811	1.7597	1.4948	1.9289
23.	2.2358	0.4454	1.9226	1.7987	1.5277	1.9709
24.	2.2876	0.4575	1.9700	1.8450	1.5679	2.0218
25.	2.3495	0.4690	2.0174	1.8901	1.6082	2.0732
26.	2.4022	0.4813	2.0644	1.9364	1.6500	2.1262
27.	2.4515	0.4925	2.1216	1.9901	1.7026	2.1948
28.	2.4875	0.5013	2.1638	2.0303	1.7342	2.2347
29.	2.5343	0.5108	2.2208	2.0817	1.7844	2.3016
30.	2.5867	0.5298	2.2713	2.1381	1.8259	2.3498

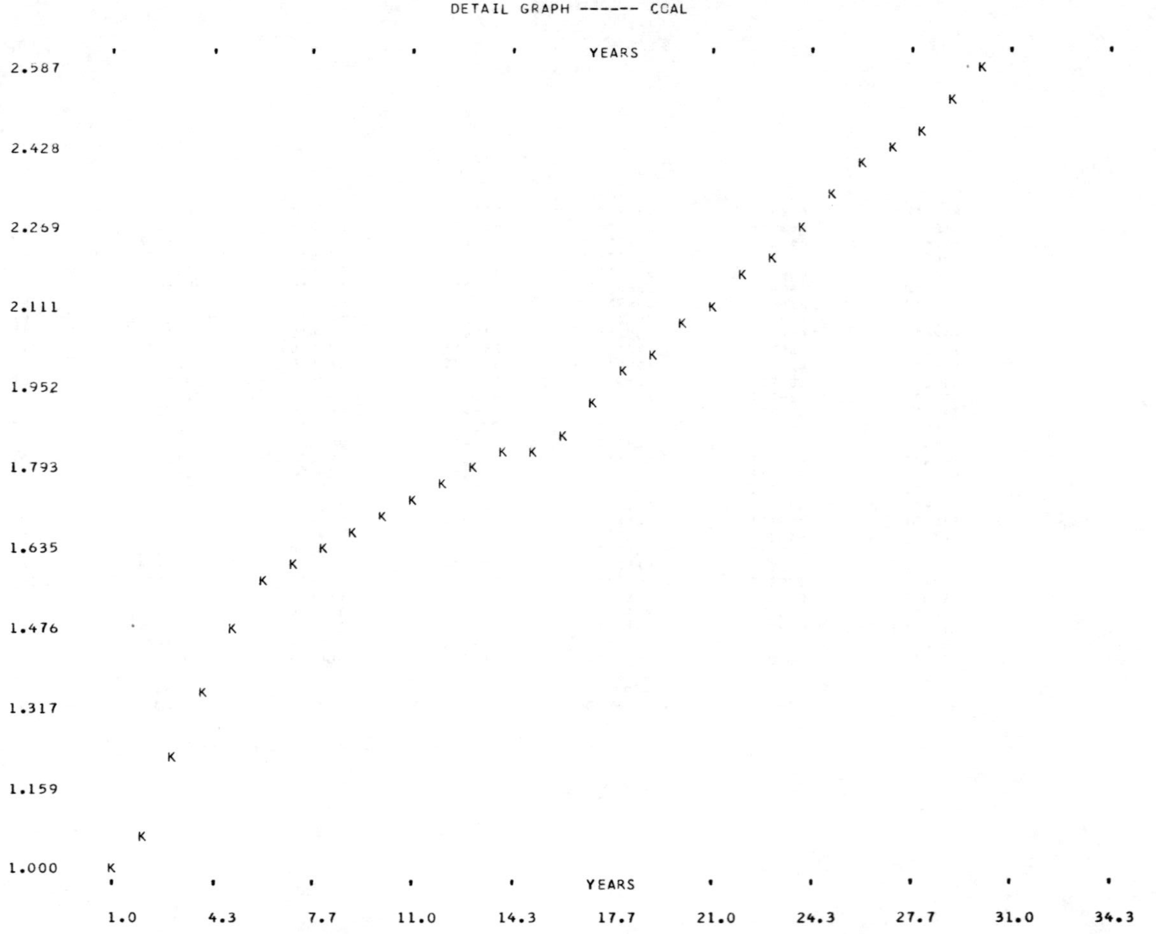
DETAIL GRAPH ------ COAL
YEARS
2.587
2.428
2.269
2.111
1.952
1.793
1.635
1.476
1.317
1.159
1.000
YEARS
1.0
4.3
7.7
11.0
14.3
17.7
21.0
24.3
27.7
31.0
34.3

DETAIL GRAPH ------ OIL

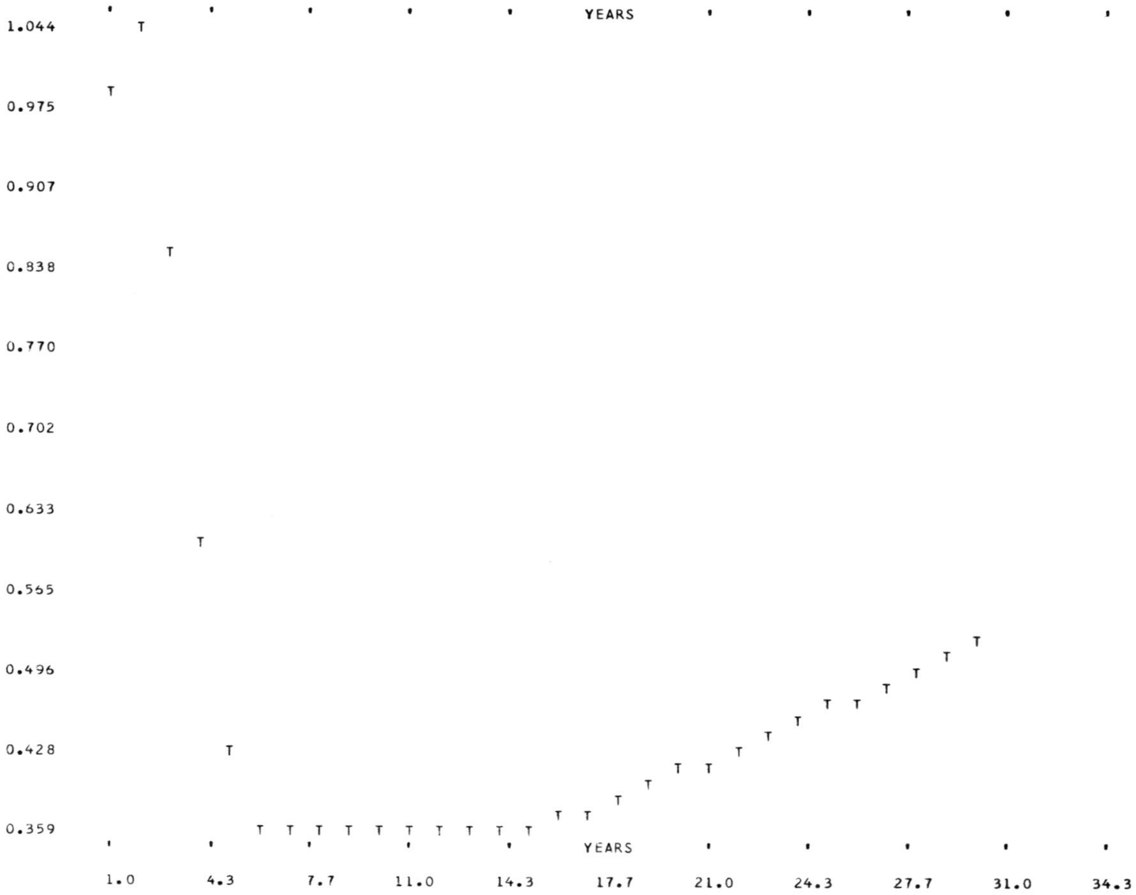

YEARS

1.044
0.975
0.907
0.838
0.770
0.702
0.633
0.565
0.496
0.428
0.359

YEARS

1.0 4.3 7.7 11.0 14.3 17.7 21.0 24.3 27.7 31.0 34.3

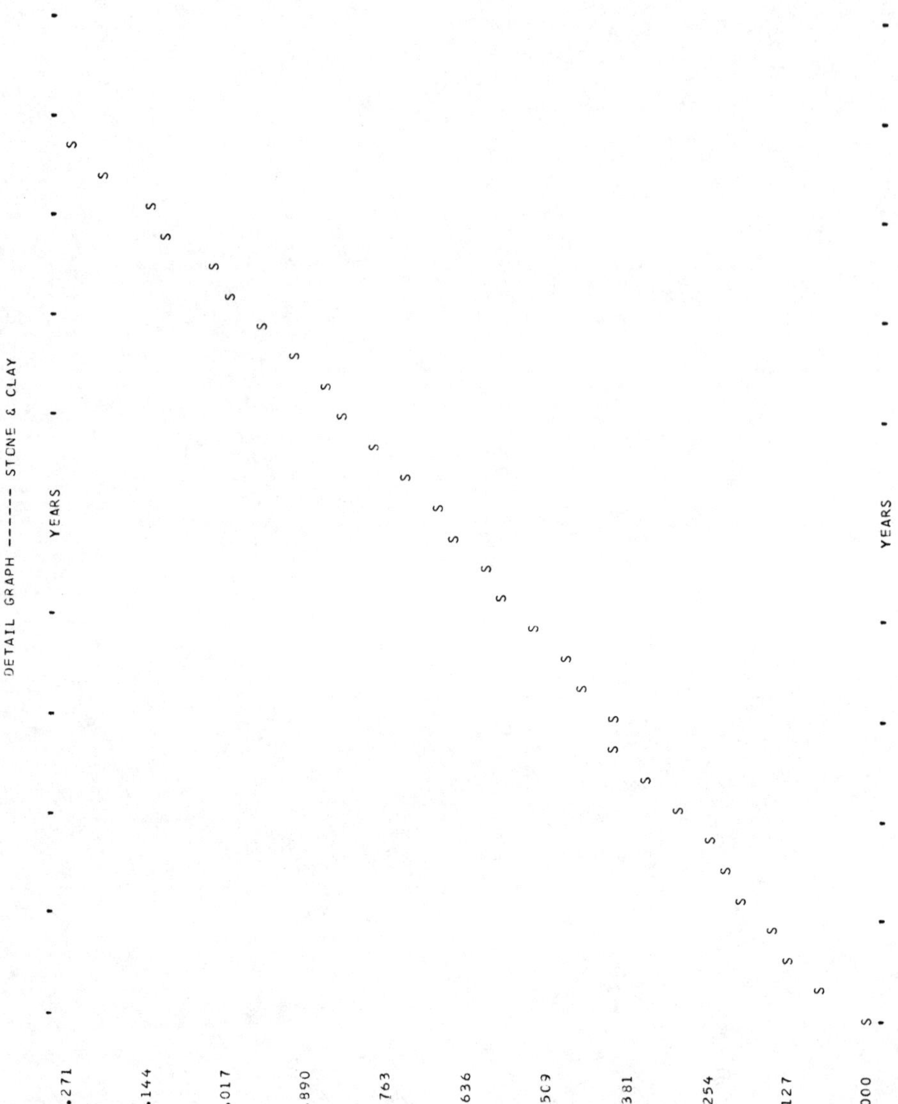

DETAIL GRAPH ------ STONE & CLAY

YEARS

2.271
2.144
2.017
1.890
1.763
1.636
1.509
1.381
1.254
1.127
1.000

1.0 4.3 7.7 11.0 14.3 17.7 21.0 24.3 27.7 31.0 34.3

YEARS

DETAIL GRAPH ------ CHEMICALS & FERTILIZERS

YEARS

2.138
2.024
1.910
1.797
1.683
1.569
1.455
1.341
1.228
1.114
1.000

YEARS

1.0 4.3 7.7 11.0 14.3 17.7 21.0 24.3 27.7 31.0 34.3

DETAIL GRAPH ------ LEAD & ZINC

YEARS

1.826

1.743

1.661

1.578

1.496

1.413

1.330

1.248

1.165

1.083

1.000

YEARS

1.0 4.3 7.7 11.0 14.3 17.7 21.0 24.3 27.7 31.0 34.3

TABLE NUMBER SIX
UNEMPLOYMENT AND QOL VALUES

YEAR	UNEMPLOYMENT (U)	QUALITY (Q)
1.	0.0369	1.0000
2.	0.0524	0.9180
3.	0.0405	0.9325
4.	0.0356	0.9568
5.	0.0354	0.9773
6.	0.0418	0.9926
7.	0.0403	1.0088
8.	0.0383	1.0282
9.	0.0373	1.0492
10.	0.0427	1.0658
11.	0.0433	1.0789
12.	0.0378	1.0969
13.	0.0415	1.1050
14.	0.0399	1.1202
15.	0.0445	1.1230
16.	0.0422	1.1343
17.	0.0403	1.1469
18.	0.0387	1.1607
19.	0.0388	1.1753
20.	0.0374	1.1889
21.	0.0404	1.1994
22.	0.0414	1.2090
23.	0.0395	1.2199
24.	0.0389	1.2315
25.	0.0383	1.2440
26.	0.0384	1.2562
27.	0.0390	1.2675
28.	0.0429	1.2628
29.	0.0360	1.2833
30.	0.0361	1.2797

TABLE NUMBER SEVEN - LAND, AIR AND WATER USAGE
(SCALED TO ORIGINAL VALUE)

YEAR	URBAN (U)	ARABLE (F)	TREATED UNITS OF MEDIA (A)	(W)
1.	1.0000	1.0000	1.0000	1.0000
2.	1.0128	1.0112	1.0206	1.1862
3.	1.0487	0.9945	1.0655	1.2607
4.	1.0808	1.0258	1.1075	1.3187
5.	1.1246	1.0126	1.1544	1.3866
6.	1.1561	1.0223	1.2047	1.4324
7.	1.1894	1.0288	1.2608	1.4800
8.	1.2282	1.0433	1.3277	1.5352
9.	1.2711	1.0554	1.4024	1.5966
10.	1.3073	1.0551	1.4611	1.6485
11.	1.3368	1.0457	1.5071	1.6896
12.	1.3747	1.0551	1.5702	1.7311
13.	1.4018	1.0683	1.6241	1.7618
14.	1.4319	1.0772	1.6798	1.7945
15.	1.3085	1.1474	1.7289	1.8687
16.	1.3359	1.1462	1.7782	1.9116
17.	1.3607	1.1638	1.8239	1.9569
18.	1.3932	1.1743	1.8831	2.0111
19.	1.4241	1.1867	1.9399	2.0622
20.	1.3126	1.2548	2.0036	2.1148
21.	1.3385	1.2600	2.0570	2.1569
22.	1.3631	1.2697	2.1065	2.2034
23.	1.3896	1.2795	2.1596	2.2522
24.	1.4191	1.2892	2.2190	2.3051
25.	1.4484	1.3009	2.2784	2.3548
26.	1.3321	1.3702	2.3426	2.4041
27.	1.3600	1.3738	2.4105	2.4609
28.	1.3677	1.3800	2.4379	2.5030
29.	1.4021	1.3948	2.5179	2.5742
30.	1.4171	1.4035	2.5541	2.6115

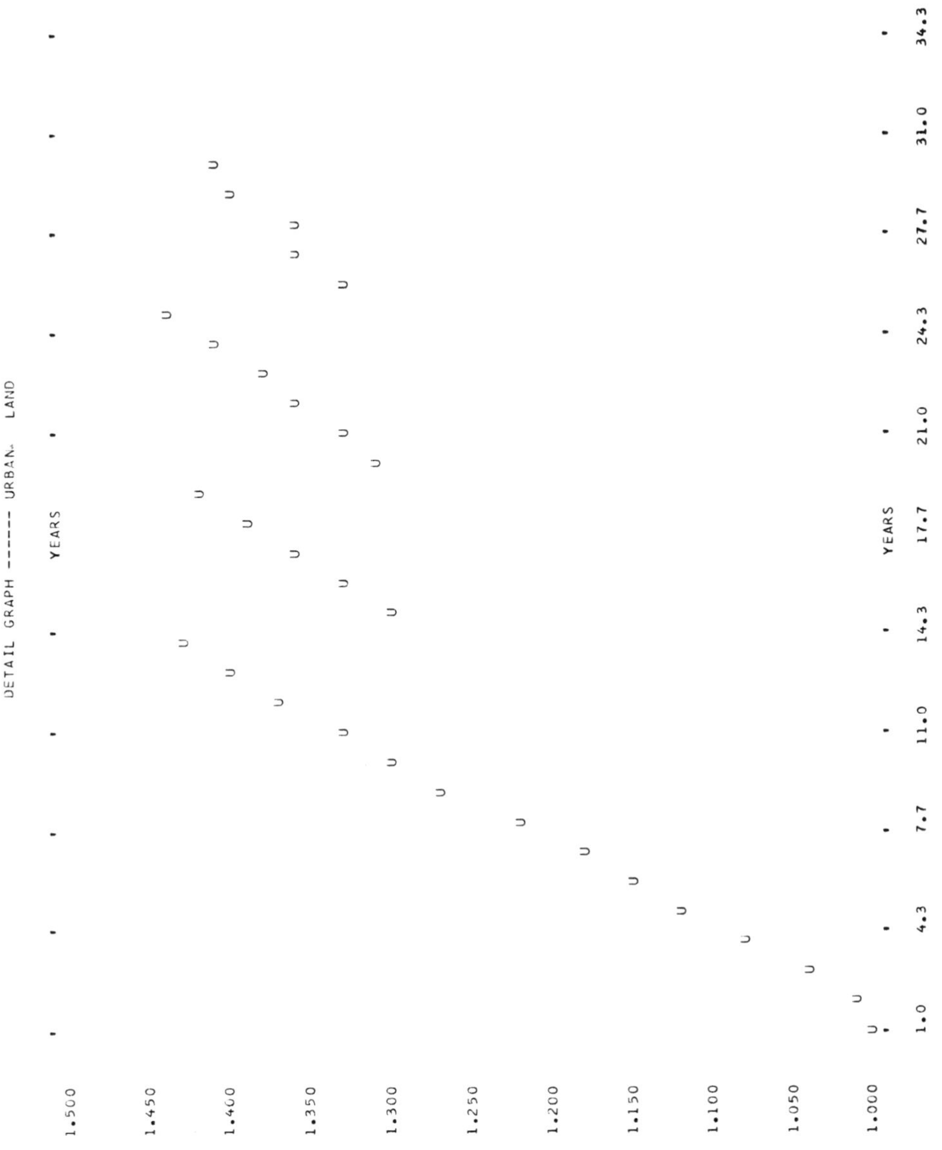

DETAIL GRAPH ------ URBAN. LAND

YEARS

1.500
1.450
1.400
1.350
1.300
1.250
1.200
1.150
1.100
1.050
1.000

YEARS

1.0 4.3 7.7 11.0 14.3 17.7 21.0 24.3 27.7 31.0 34.3

DETAIL GRAPH ------ ARABLE LAND

```
                               DETAIL GRAPH ------ ARABLE LAND
          .    .    .    .    .   YEARS   .    .    .    .    .
1.494

1.444

1.394                                                      F F
                                                         F
                                                      F F
1.344

1.294                                               F
                                                  F
                                                F
                                              F
1.244                                      F F

1.194
                                      F
                                    F
                                  F
1.144                          F F

1.094
                             F
                           F
                   F F   F
1.044                  F
                     F
        F          F
         F       F
0.994 F    F
      .    .    .    .    .   YEARS   .    .    .    .    .
     1.0  4.3  7.7 11.0 14.3  17.7  21.0 24.3 27.7 31.0 34.3
```

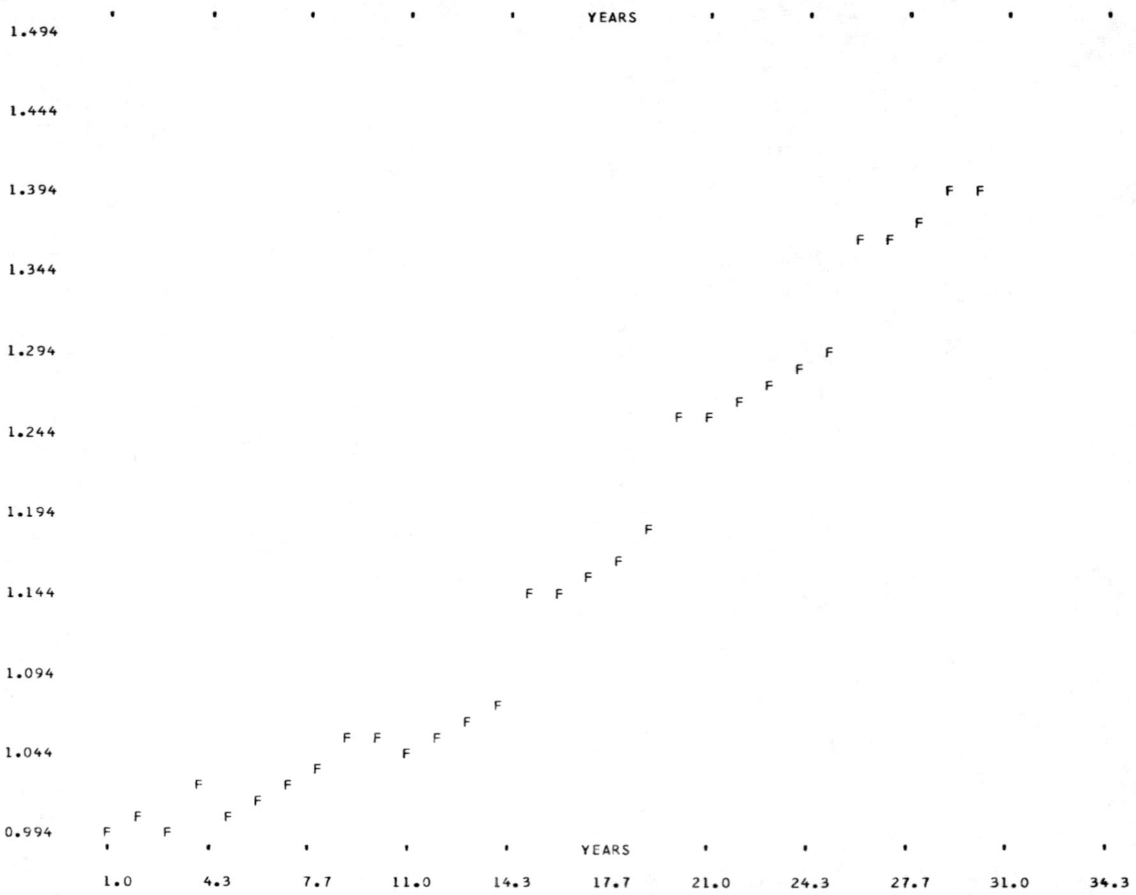

DETAIL GRAPH ------ TREATED UNITS OF AIR

YEARS

2.554
2.399
2.243
2.088
1.932
1.777
1.622
1.466
1.311
1.155
1.000

YEARS

1.0 4.3 7.7 11.0 14.3 17.7 21.0 24.3 27.7 31.0 34.3

DETAIL GRAPH ------ TREATED UNITS OF WATER

YEARS

2.612
2.450
2.289
2.128
1.967
1.806
1.645
1.483
1.322
1.161
1.000

YEARS

1.0 4.3 7.7 11.0 14.3 17.7 21.0 24.3 27.7 31.0 34.3

Appendix C
Program Flowcharts

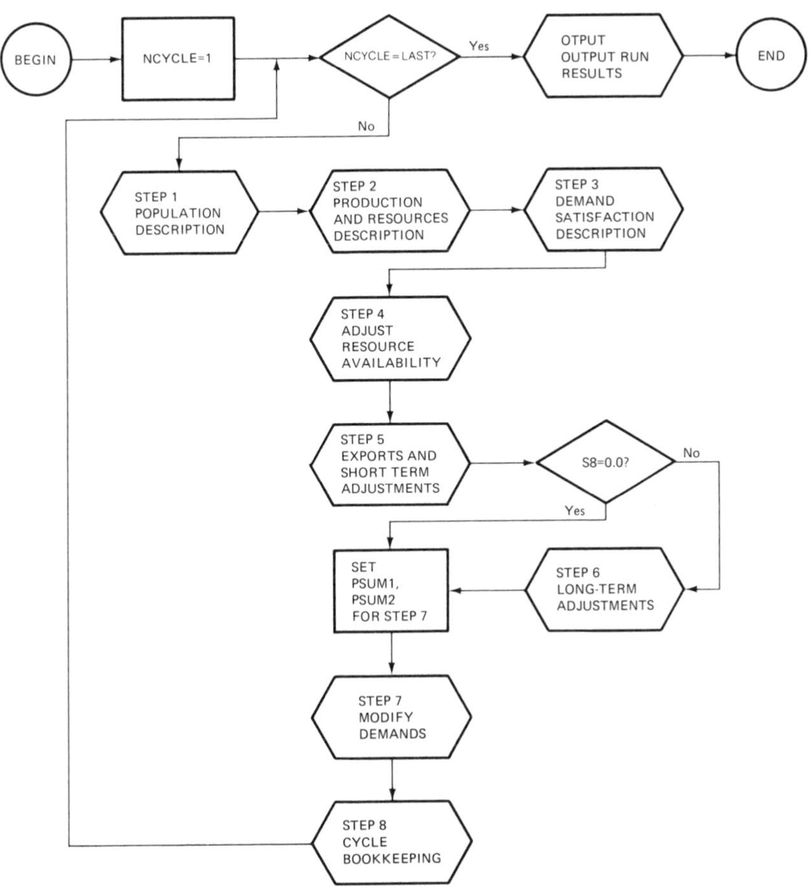

Figure C-1. Flowchart for the SOS-2 Executive Program, Main.

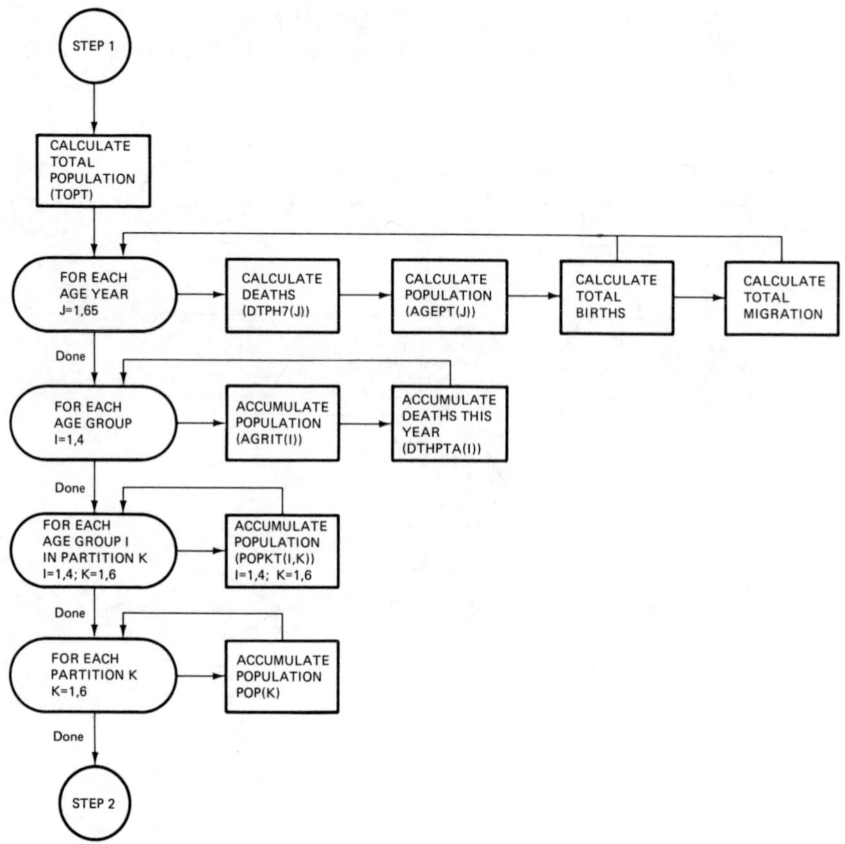

Figure C-2. Flowchart for Step 1: Describe the Population.

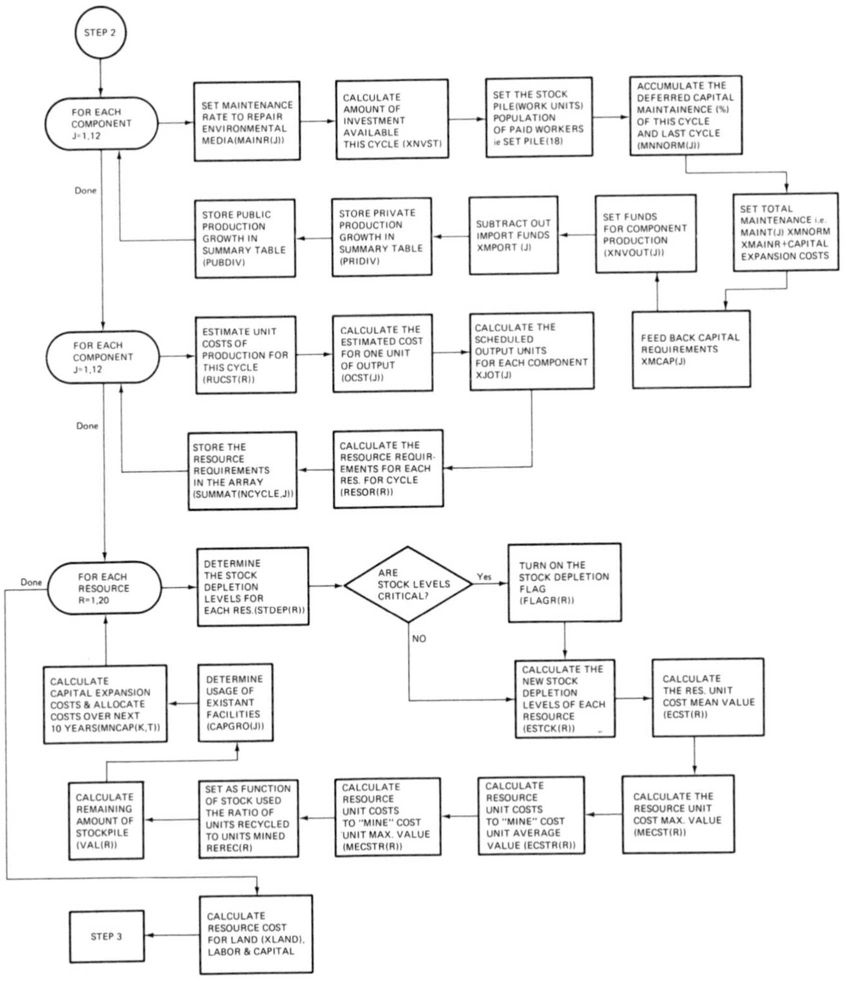

Figure C-3. Flowchart for Step 2: Describe the Production Components.

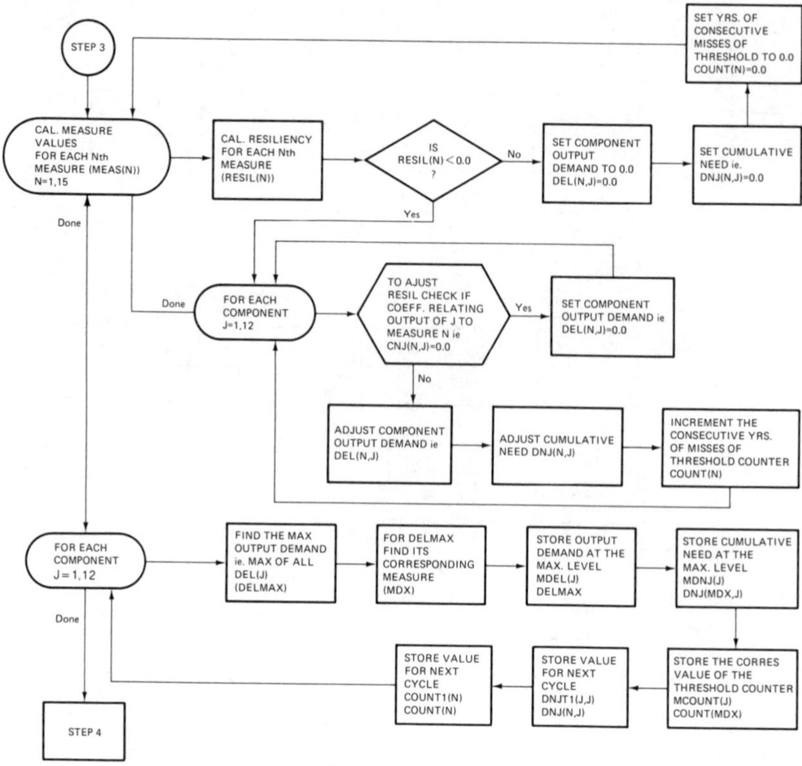

Figure C-4. Flowchart for Step 3: Describe the State of the System.

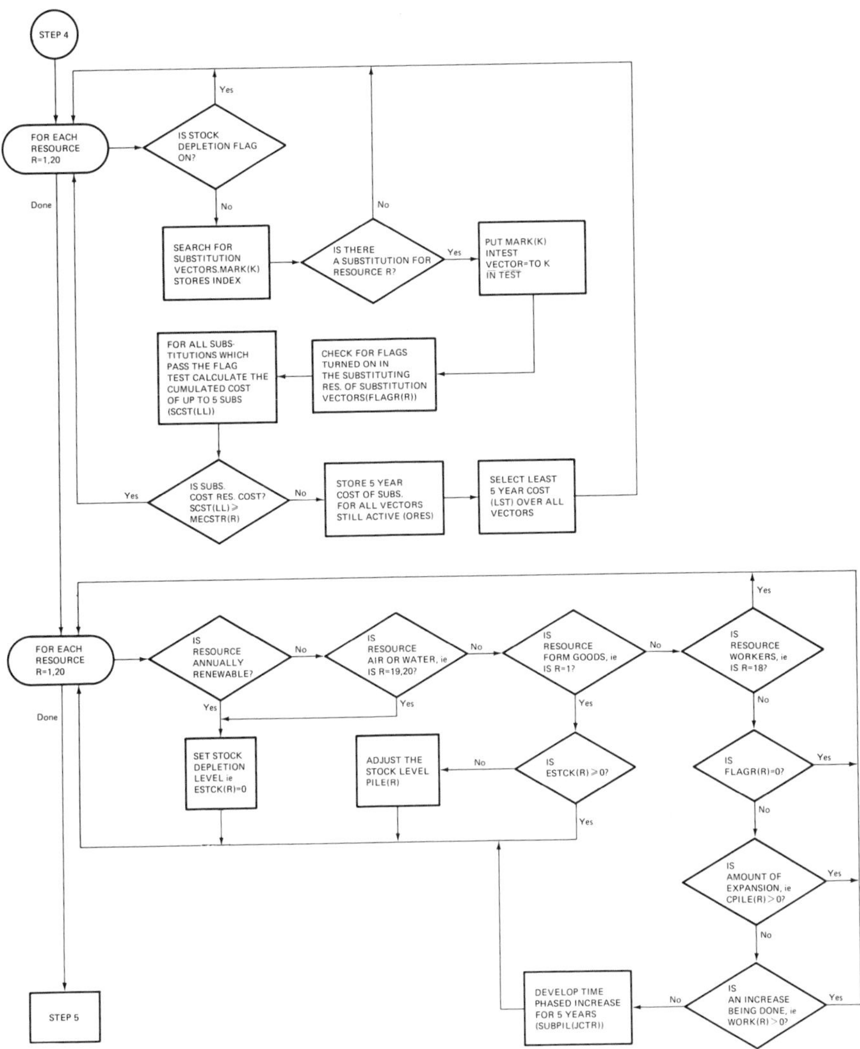

Figure C-5. Flowchart for Step 4: Adjust Resource Reserves and Utilization Factors.

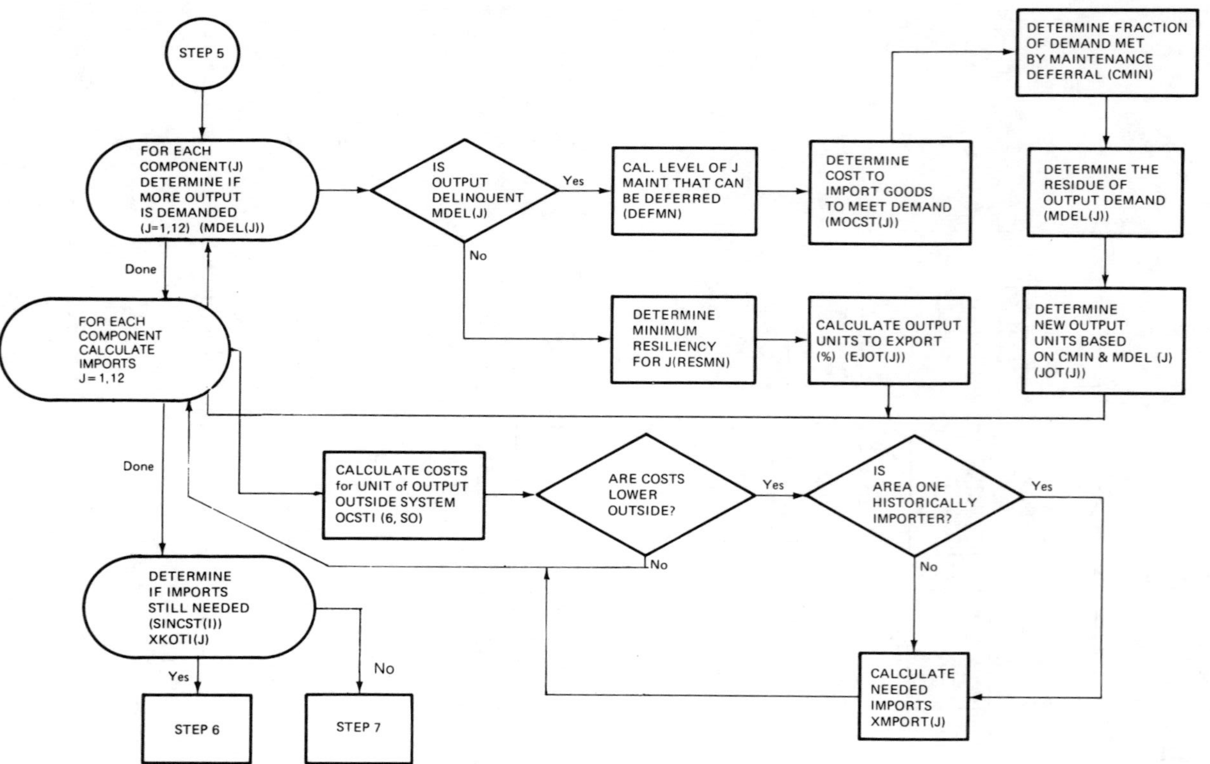

Figure C-6. Flowchart for Step 5: Perform Short Term Output Adjustments.

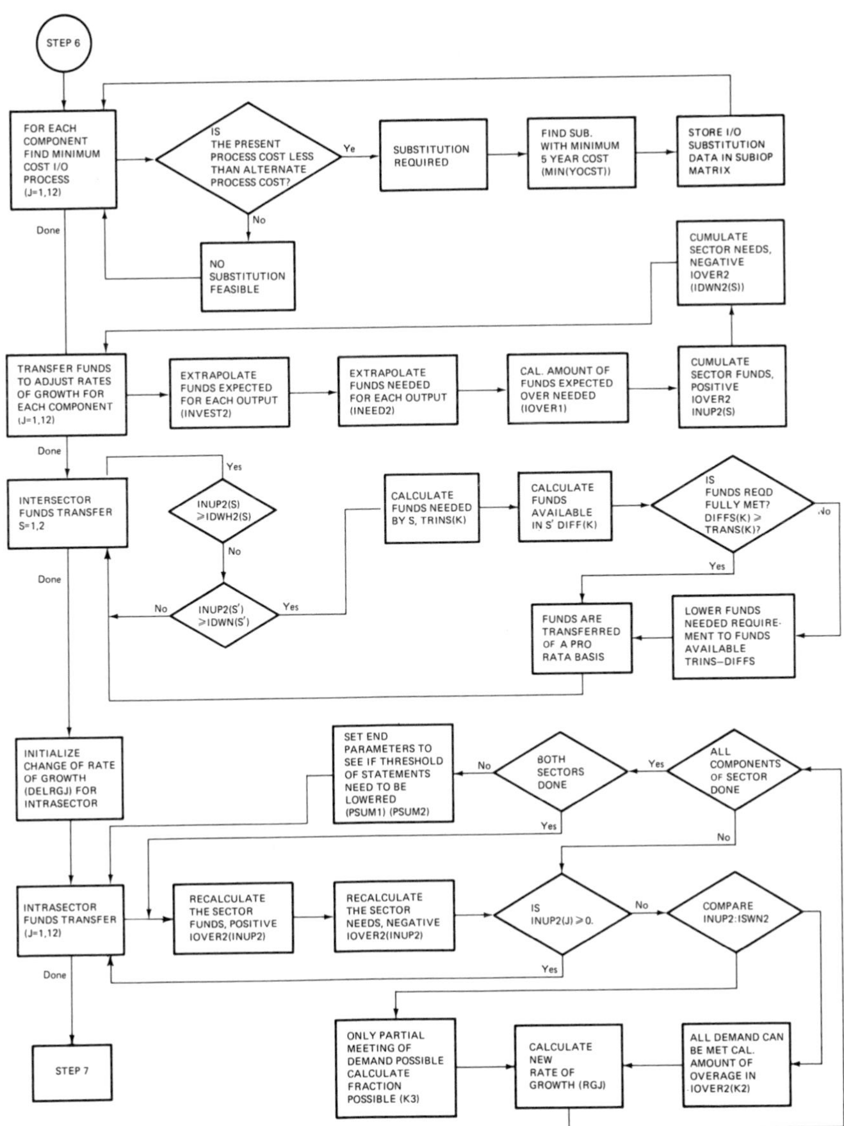

Figure C-7. Flowchart for Step 6: Perform Long Term Component Output Adjustments.

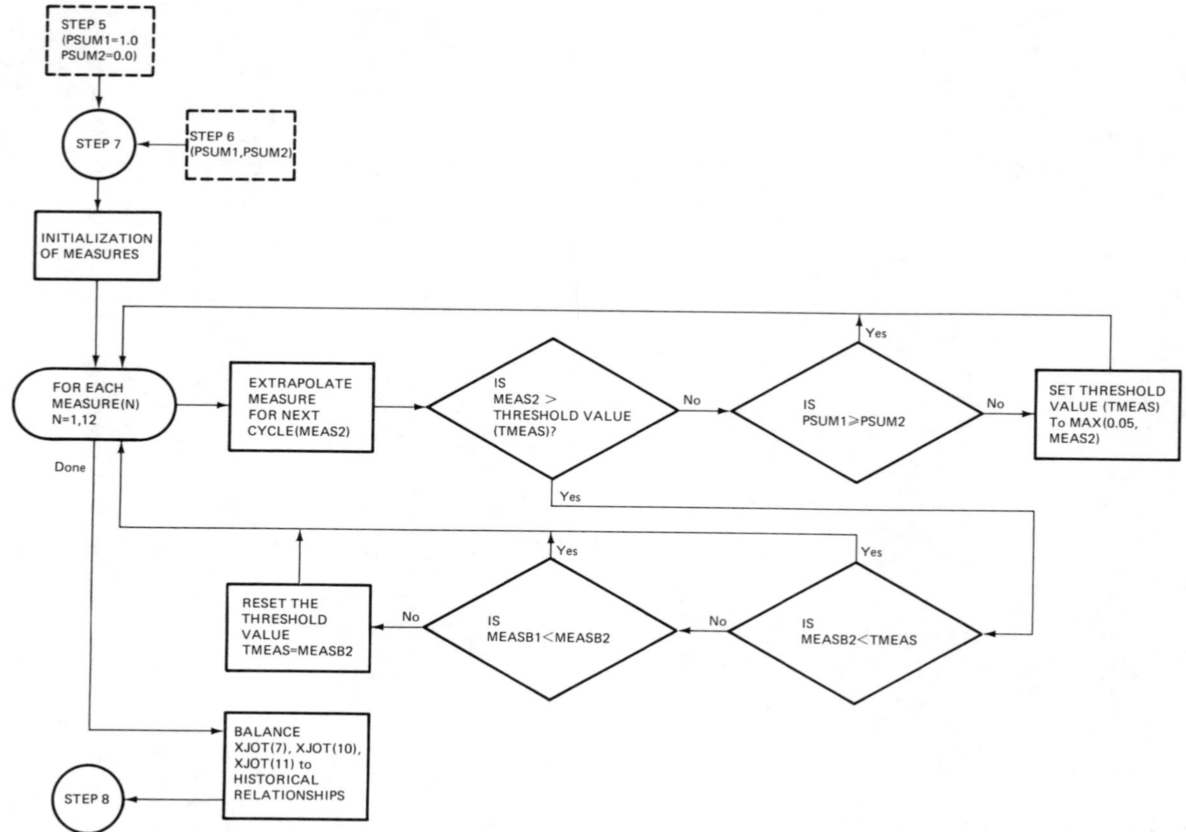

Figure C-8. Flowchart for Step 7: Adjust Long Term Population Demands.

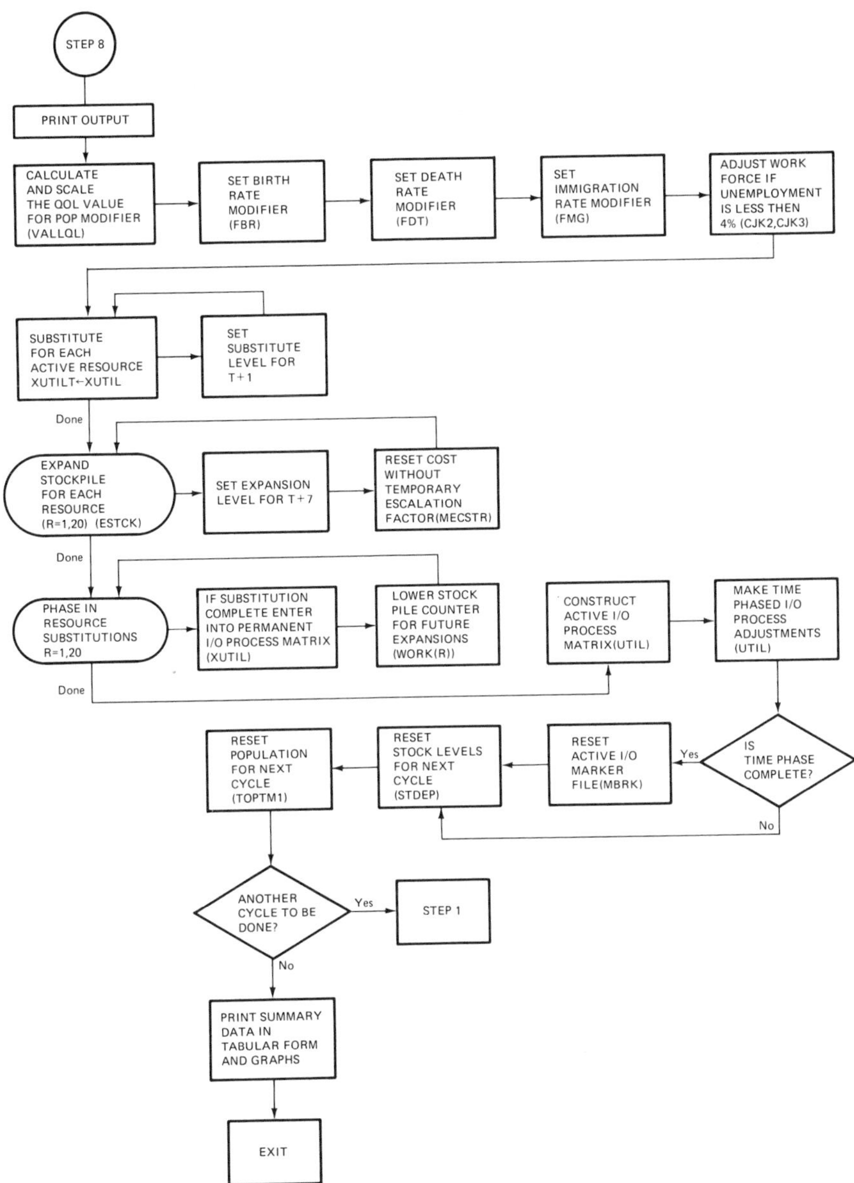

Figure C-9. Flowchart for Step 8: Reset Data Base for Next Cycle.

Notes

Chapter 1
Introduction

1. Peterson, E.K., "Limitations in Classical Planning," in *Alternate Futures and Environmental Quality,* page 101, Environmental Studies Division, Washington Environmental Research Center, U.S. Environmental Protection Agency, Washington, D.C., 1973.

2. U.S. House of Representatives, Committee on Public Works, "A National Public Works Investment Policy," U.S. Government Printing Office, Washington, D.C., November 1974.

3. Martino, Joseph, *Technological Forecasting for Decision Making*, Policy Science Book Series, American Elsevier Publishing Co., New York, 1972.

4. International Research and Technology, Incorporated, *Forecasting, Planning, Resource Allocation Source Book*, Washington, D.C., undated (circa 1974).

5. U.S. House of Representatives, Committee on Public Works, op. cit.

6. Malthus, T.R., "An Essay on the Principle of Population," 1798, reprinted in G. Hardin, ed., *Population, Evolution and Birth Control*, W.H. Freeman and Co., San Francisco, 1969.

7. von Neumann, John, "Can We Survive Technology?" *Fortune Magazine*, June 1955, pp. 106-108, 151-152.

8. Landberg, Hans H., *The U.S. Resource Outlook: Quantity and Quality*, The Johns Hopkins University Press, Baltimore, Md., 1972.

9. Bishop, A.B., H.H. Fullerton, A.B. Crawford, M.D. Chambers and M. McKee. *Carrying Capacity in Regional Environmental Management*, Washington Environmental Research Center, U.S. Environmental Protection Agency, Washington, D.C., February 1974 (GPO # EPA-60015-74-021).

Chapter 2
Scenario Analysis

1. Malthus, T.R., "An Essay on the Principle of Population," 1798, reprinted in G. Hardin, ed., *Population, Evolution and Birth Control*, W.H. Freeman and Co., San Francisco, 1969.

2. von Neumann, John, "Can We Survive Technology?" *Fortune Magazine*, June 1955, pp. 106-108, 151-152.

3. Malthus, op. cit.

4. Ibid.

5. Landberg, Hans H., *The U.S. Resource Outlook: Quantity and Quality*, The Johns Hopkins University Press, Baltimore, Md., 1972.

Chapter 3
Carrying Capacity: A Perspective for Environmental Management

1. Bishop, A.B., H.H. Fullerton, A.B. Crawford, M.D. Chambers and M. McKee. *Carrying Capacity in Regional Environmental Management*, Washington Environmental Research Center, U.S. Environmental Protection Agency, Washington, D.C., February 1974 (GPO # EPA-60015-74-021).

2. Deitchman, S.J., "Modelling Comprehensive Pollution Control," at Operations Research/Systems Analysis Association (ORSA) National Meeting—1972, New Orleans, La.

3. Lotka, A.J., *Elements of Physical Biology*, Williams and Wilkins, Baltimore, Md., 1925; and Vito Volterra, "Variations and Fluctuations of Numbers of Individuals in Animal Species Living Together," in *Animal Ecology*, McGraw-Hill Book Co., New York, 1926, pp. 409-448.

Chapter 4
Resources of the Human Ecosystem

1. Landberg, Hans H., *The U.S. Resource Outlook: Quantity and Quality*, The Johns Hopkins University Press, Baltimore, Md., 1972.

2. von Neumann, John, "Can We Survive Technology?" *Fortune Magazine*, June 1955, pp. 106-108, 151-152.

3. Lovejoy, W.F., and P.T. Homan, *Methods of Estimating Reserves of Crude Oil, Natural Gas, and Natural Gas Liquids*, The John Hopkins University Press, Baltimore, Md., 1965.

Chapter 5
Model Overview

1. Quinn, J.A., *Human Ecology*, Anchor Books, Hamden, Conn., 1971.

Bibliography

Council on Environmental Quality, *The Annual Report of the Council on Environmental Quality*, Nos. 1-5, Washington, D.C., (1970-1974).

Dansereau, P., *Biography, An Ecological Perspective*, The Ronald Press, New York, 1957.

Dasmann, R.F., *Wildlife Biology*, John Wiley & Sons, London, 1964.

Holling, C.S., and Goldberg, M.A., "The Nature and Behavior of Ecological Systems," in *An Anthology of Selected Readings for the National Conference on Managing the Environment,* page 1-21, International City Management Association, Washington, D.C., May 1973.

House, P.W., et al., *The Quality of Life Concept—A Potential New Tool for Decision-Makers*, "Washington Environmental Research Center," Environmental Protection Agency, March 1973.

Kormondy, Edward, *Concepts of Ecology,* Prentice Hall, Englewood Cliffs, N.J., 1969.

McLeod, J., "Simulation in the Service of Society," La Jolla, Cal., Vol. 4, No. 8, August 1974.

Meadows, D.H., D.L. Meadows, Randers, Jr., and W.W. Behrens, III, *The Limits to Growth*, Potomac Associates, Signet Book, New York, 1972.

Meadows, D.L., and D.H. Meadows, *Toward Global Equilibrium: Collected Papers*, Wright-Allen Press, Cambridge, Mass., 1973.

National Academy of Sciences, *Mineral Resources and the Environment*, Washington, D.C., 1975, National Academy of Sciences.

National Commission on Materials Policy, *Material Needs and the Environment Today and Tomorrow*, Washington, D.C., 1973, Government Printing Office.

Odum, Eugene, "Ecosystem Theory in Relation to Man," in *Ecosystem Structure and Function, Proceedings of the Thirty-First Annual Biology Colloquium*, edited by John Wiens, pages 15-16, Oregon State University Press, Corvallis, Ore., 1972.

Stanford Research Institute, *Draft Outline—Quality of Life Indicators Based on Intolerability Thresholds*. Menlo Park California (circa 1975).

Toffler, A., *Future Shock*, Random House, New York, 1970.

Turk, Turk, and Wittes, *Ecology, Pollution, Environment*, W.B. Saunders Co., Philadelphia, 1972.

U.S. Department of Commerce, *Survey of Current Business,* No. 1-12, 1970-1971, Washington, D.C., Government Printing Office.

U.S. Department of Commerce, *Statistical Abstract of the United States, 1971*, (92nd Edition) Washington, D.C. 1971, Government Printing Office.

About the Authors

Peter W. House received the B.A. from American International College, the M.A. from Clark University, and the Ph.D. in Public Administration from Cornell University. Dr. House has served with the U.S. Environmental Protection Agency, where he was Director of the Environmental Studies Division and Deputy Director of the Washington Environmental Research Center in the Office of Research and Development. Among others, this Division worked on the Strategic Environmental Assessment System (SEAS). During his research at the Washington Center for Metropolitan Studies and at Environmetrics, Inc., Dr. House directed the development of gaming simulation models that have been used as teaching and research tools for the study of urban and regional problems including the well-known CITY I model. As a research economist for the U.S. Department of Agriculture, Dr. House performed a number of significant studies in the area of suburban/farmland and preferential tax assessment. He is a member of the American Society for Public Administration, Director of the National Gaming Council and a member of the Board of Trustees for the World Simulation Councils, Inc. Dr. House is currently on leave from the Environmental Protection Agency and a visiting scholar at the Institute of Transportation Studies, University of California, Berkeley.

Edward R. Williams is Deputy Director, Quantitative Analysis Division, Office of Business and Legislative Issues, Bureau of Domestic Commerce. He received the B.A. in Physics from Bowdoin College, and the M.S. from Michigan State University. Prior to 1973 Mr. Williams spent fifteen years in general operations research/systems analysis, centering on development and application of large scale models. This work was applied to Tactical and Strategic analysis in support of the Department of Army, and also involved experience in large domestic/environmental models and urban spatial models. This included responsibility for development and application of the Strategic Environmental Assessment Systems (SEAS) and Spatial Pollution Analysis and Comparative Evaluation (SPACE) System.